Governing Urban Indonesia

The **Australian National University (ANU) Indonesia Project** is a leading international centre of research and graduate training on the economy and society of Indonesia. Since its inception in 1965 by Professor H.W. Arndt, the Project has been at the forefront of Indonesian studies in Australia and internationally. The ANU Indonesia Project is part of the Arndt-Corden Department of Economics in the Crawford School of Public Policy, College of Asia and the Pacific, ANU.

Through producing and disseminating high-quality research, including publishing the respected *Bulletin of Indonesian Economic Studies*, and hosting public dialogues, institutional capacity building and institutional networking, the ANU Indonesia Project aims to support the establishment of critical research-based public policies in Indonesia, particularly in the areas of (i) trade and development; (ii) agriculture, resources and the environment; (iii) politics, media and governance and (iv) social policy, gender equality, social inclusion and human capital. Furthermore, our activities aim to ensure the next generation of Indonesian researchers are nurtured and fostered.

The Indonesia Update has been conducted annually since 1983. It is organised by the ANU Indonesia Project, and receives support from the Australian Government Department of Foreign Affairs and Trade, the ANU Department of Political and Social Change, and the ANU Indonesia Institute.

The **ISEAS – Yusof Ishak Institute** (formerly Institute of Southeast Asian Studies) is an autonomous organisation established in 1968. It is a regional centre dedicated to the study of sociopolitical, security, and economic trends and developments in Southeast Asia and its wider geostrategic and economic environment. The Institute's research programs are grouped under Regional Economic Studies (RES), Regional Strategic and Political Studies (RSPS), and Regional Social and Cultural Studies (RSCS). The Institute is also home to the ASEAN Studies Centre (ASC), the Singapore APEC Study Centre, and the Temasek History Research Centre (THRC).

ISEAS Publishing, an established academic press, has issued more than 2,000 books and journals. It is the largest scholarly publisher of research about Southeast Asia from within the region. ISEAS Publishing works with many other academic and trade publishers and distributors to disseminate important research and analyses from and about Southeast Asia to the rest of the world.

Indonesia Update Series

Governing Urban Indonesia

EDITED BY
EDWARD ASPINALL · AMALINDA SAVIRANI

YUSOF ISHAK INSTITUTE

First published in Singapore in 2024 by
ISEAS Publishing
30 Heng Mui Keng Terrace
Singapore 119614

E-mail: publish@iseas.edu.sg
Website: http://bookshop.iseas.edu.sg

All rights reserved. No part of this publication may be reproduced, translated, stored in a retrieval system, or transmitted in any form or by any means, electronic, mechanical, photocopying, recording or otherwise, without the prior permission of the ISEAS – Yusof Ishak Institute.

© 2024 ISEAS – Yusof Ishak Institute, Singapore

The responsibility for facts and opinions in this publication rests exclusively with the authors and their interpretations do not necessarily reflect the views or the policy of the Institute or its supporters.

ISEAS Library Cataloguing-in-Publication Data

Names: Aspinall, Edward, editor. | Savirani, Amalinda, editor. | Indonesia Update Conference (40th : 2023 : Australian National University).
Title: Governing urban Indonesia / edited by Edward Aspinall and Amalinda Savirani.
Description: Singapore : ISEAS – Yusof Ishak Institute, 2024. | Series: Indonesia Update ; 2023 | Includes bibliographical references and index.
Identifiers: ISBN 9789815203714 (softcover) | ISBN 9789815203721 (hardcover) | ISBN 9789815203738 (ebook PDF) | ISBN 9789815203745 (epub)
Subjects: LCSH: Urban policy—Indonesia. | Indonesia—Social conditions.
Classification: DS644.4 I41 2023

Cover image: Online motorcycle taxi drivers waiting for commuters, Jalan Sudirman, Jakarta, 2019.
Photo by Ray Yen

Edited and typeset by Tracy Harwood, Canberra
Indexed by Angela Grant, Sydney
Printed in Singapore by Markono Print Media Pte Ltd

Contents

Tables	vii
Figures	ix
Contributors	x
Acknowledgements	xii
Glossary	xiv

1	Governing urban Indonesia: Trends and challenges *Edward Aspinall and Amalinda Savirani*	1
2	Shifting modalities of urban governance: Indonesian cities over the long term *Abidin Kusno*	24
3	Urbanisation in Indonesia: Demographic changes and spatial patterns, 2000–2020 *Meirina Ayumi Malamassam and Luh Kitty Katherina*	46
4	Urban planning in Indonesia and its contribution to Southern Planning *Sonia Roitman*	75
5	Local budgets in urban Indonesia: Different characteristics need different policies *Erman Rahman, Ihsan Haerudin and Ronaldo Octaviano*	98
6	Patterns of urban government in Indonesia: The role of civil society coalitions and mobilisation *Mochamad Mustafa*	129
7	Citizens into consumers: The impact of gated communities on Jakarta's periphery *Corry Elyda*	150

8	Housing at an impasse: Living in a state of protracted transit in rental social housing in Jakarta *Clara Siagian*	174
9	Drainage politics: The political economy of flood management in Indonesian cities *Yogi Setya Permana*	197
10	Governing garbage: Solid waste management reform in Surabaya *Nur Azizah*	218
11	Traffic congestion in urban Indonesia: What can we learn from the Jakarta metropolitan area? *Muhammad Halley Yudhistira and Andhika Putra Pratama*	244
12	Contested public spaces in urban Indonesia *Rita Padawangi*	267
13	Urban security governance in contemporary Jakarta *Ian Wilson*	286
14	Leading the way: A mayor's perspective on urban leadership in Indonesia *Bima Arya Sugiarto*	306
Index		321

Tables

3.1	Urbanisation trends across regions in Indonesia, 2000–2020	50
3.2	Cities and districts in Indonesia with urban populations over one million, 2000–2020	52
3.3	Indicators for rural-urban classification in Indonesia, 2020	56
3.4	Urban localities (*desa* and *kelurahan*) in Indonesia by region, 2000–2020	57
3.5	Urban localities (*desa* and *kelurahan*) in Indonesia in 2020 and their origin	58
3.6	Agricultural households across regions in Indonesia, 2003–2013	63
5.1	Seven district types	102
5.2	Seven district types, general characteristics	104
5.3	Average human development index (HDI) based on district category, 2016–2022	105
5.4	Average poverty rate based on district category, 2016–2022 (%)	106
5.5	Average per capita regional gross domestic product (RGDP) based on district category, 2016–2022	107
5.6	School enrolment rate for students aged 13–15 years (13-15 SER) based on district category, 2016–2022 (%)	108
5.7	Proportion of births attended by professional health workers (attended births) based on district category, 2016–2022 (%)	109
5.8	Access to clean drinking water based on district category, 2016–2022 (%)	110
5.9	Access to proper sanitation based on district category, 2016–2022 (%)	110

5.10	Composition of local taxes and levies (PDRD) and contributions to total budget revenue and regional gross domestic product (2017–2021 average)	113
5.11	District compliance with mandatory personnel spending, 2017–2021	118
5.12	Proportion of non-personnel health spending to total spending, and non-compliant districts, 2018–2021	122
5.13	Public service infrastructure spending by district category, 2019 and 2021	124
7.1	Voting in South Tangerang mayoral election, 2020	167
8.1	Housing career scheme as envisioned by the Jakarta Department of Public Housing and Settlement Areas	183
11.1	Metropolitan rail services: Major world cities	251

Figures

3.1	Proportion of urban population in 2020 across world regions	47
3.2	Population pyramids of urban and rural Indonesia, 2000–2020 (millions)	53
3.3	Urban localities in Indonesia, 2010	59
3.4	Urban localities in Indonesia, 2020	60
5.1	Categorisation of districts by population density and per cent of urbanised villages/wards	103
5.2	Per capita budget revenues, 2017–2021	112
5.3	Local budget spending (%) by economic classification and district category, 2017–2021	115
5.4	Local budget spending (%) by economic classification and district category, adjusted (without transfers), 2017–2021	117
5.5	Local budget spending (%) by government function and district category, 2017–2021	119
5.6	Per capita spending based on functions and district categories, 2021 (Rp million per person)	120
8.1	Distribution of *rusunawa* (social housing) in Jakarta	181
9.1	Flood cases: Surabaya, Semarang and Bandung district, 2010–2021	202
10.1	Sorting activities at Jambangan material recovery facility	230
11.1	Time spent commuting one way per work day (% of commuters)	246
11.2	Modal shift of Jakarta metropolitan area commuters, 2002–2018 (%)	248
11.3	Jakarta toll road networks	253

Contributors

Edward Aspinall, Professor, Department of Political and Social Change, Coral Bell School of Asia Pacific Affairs, Australian National University, Canberra

Nur Azizah, PhD candidate, Department of Political and Social Change, Australian National University; and Lecturer, Department of Politics and Government, Universitas Gadjah Mada, Yogyakarta

Corry Elyda, Freelance writer and researcher for various institutions, South Tangerang, Indonesia

Ihsan Haerudin, Senior Technical Component Lead, USAID ERAT, The Asia Foundation, Jakarta

Luh Kitty Katherina, Researcher, Research Center for Population, National Research and Innovation Agency (BRIN), Jakarta

Abidin Kusno, Professor, Faculty of Environmental and Urban Change, York University, Toronto, Canada

Meirina Ayumi Malamassam, Researcher, Research Center for Population, National Research and Innovation Agency (BRIN), Jakarta

Mochamad Mustafa, Program Director, Governance and Democracy, The Asia Foundation, Jakarta

Ronaldo Octaviano, Program Officer, USAID ERAT, The Asia Foundation, Jakarta

Rita Padawangi, Associate Professor, College of Interdisciplinary and Experiential Learning, Singapore University of Social Sciences

Yogi Setya Permana, PhD candidate, KITLV – Universiteit Leiden, the Netherlands; and National Research and Innovation Agency (BRIN), Jakarta

Andhika Putra Pratama, Research Associate, Faculty of Economics and Business, Universitas Indonesia

Erman A. Rahman, Activity Director, USAID ERAT, The Asia Foundation, Jakarta

Sonia Roitman, Associate Professor, Development Planning, University of Queensland, Brisbane

Amalinda Savirani, Associate Professor, Department of Politics and Government, Universitas Gadjah Mada, Yogyakarta

Clara Siagian, PhD candidate, Australian National University; and Senior Researcher, Center for Child Protection and Wellbeing (PUSKAPA), Universitas Indonesia

Bima Arya Sugiarto, Mayor of Bogor City, 2014–2024

Ian Douglas Wilson, Principal Fellow, Indo-Pacific Research Centre, Murdoch University, Perth, Western Australia

Muhammad Halley Yudhistira, Research Fellow, Faculty of Economics and Business, Universitas Indonesia; and Visiting Fellow, Indonesia Project, Crawford School of Public Policy, Australian National University, Canberra

Acknowledgements

The chapters in this volume were presented as papers at the fortieth annual Indonesia Update conference held at the Australian National University (ANU), 15–16 September 2023. This book is the thirtieth in the series of Indonesia Update volumes to be published by ISEAS – Yusof Ishak Institute. The Indonesia Update conferences and books are activities of the ANU Indonesia Project, and we thank the Project and its directors, Professors Blane D. Lewis and Budy Resosudarmo, for entrusting us with convening and editing this volume, and to the participants who shared their expertise on Indonesian urban governance by contributing papers and chapters.

The Indonesia Update is made possible by the contributions of many people. In particular, we are grateful for the tireless work of Indonesia Project staff, Kathryn Whitney, Lydia Napitupulu, Nesita Anggraini, Alex Gotts and Lolita Morena, without whom the conference would not have been such a great success. We also appreciate the large team of volunteers who helped run the conference, and the numerous colleagues and guests who chaired sessions. We also extend our thanks to HE Siswo Pramono, Ambassador of the Republic of Indonesia to Australia, and the Dean of the ANU College of Asia and the Pacific, Professor Helen Sullivan, for opening the conference, and for their support for Indonesia-related research at ANU.

We acknowledge the Australian Government Department of Foreign Affairs and Trade for its support for the conference and publication, and for its ongoing support of the Indonesia Project. The conference also received support from the Department of Political and Social Change at the ANU Coral Bell School of Asia Pacific Affairs, the ANU Indonesia Institute and the College of Asia and the Pacific, and the Asia Foundation. Research work that led to the conceptualisation of this volume was conducted with the support of the Australian Research Council (DP180101148, 'Local Politics, Governance and Public Goods in Southeast Asia').

Finally, we thank Tracy Harwood for her expert copyediting, Karina Pelling for preparing the maps, Angela Grant for preparing the index, Maxine McArthur for proofreading the book and the team at ISEAS for producing this volume.

Edward Aspinall and Amalinda Savirani
July 2024

Glossary

3Rs	reduce, reuse, recycle
Abujapi	Asosiasi Badan Usaha Jasa Pengamanan Indonesia (Indonesian Security Industry Association)
AI	artificial intelligence
AMAK	Aliansi Masyarakat Anti Korupsi (Surabaya Anti-Corruption Community Alliance)
APBD	*anggaran pendapatan dan belanja daerah* (local or subnational government budget)
APBN	*anggaran pendapatan dan belanja negara* (Indonesian central government budget)
Apeksi	Asosiasi Pemerintah Kota Seluruh Indonesia (Association of Indonesian Municipal Governments)
banjar (*adat*)	a local community that implements traditional law in Bali
Banser	paramilitary affiliate of the mass Islamic organisation Nahdlatul Ulama
Bappenas	Badan Perencanaan Pembangunan Nasional (National Development Planning Agency)
becak	three-wheel pedicab
BKKBN	Badan Kependudukan dan Keluarga Berencana Nasional (National Population and Family Planning Agency)
BNI	Bank Negara Indonesia
BNN	Badan Narkotika Nasional (National Narcotics Agency)
BNPB	Badan Nasional Penanggulangan Bencana (National Agency for Disaster Management)
BPBD-K	Badan Penanggulangan Bencana Daerah-Kota/Kabupaten (Regional Disaster Management Agency)

BPN	Badan Pertanahan Nasional (National Land Agency)
BPS	Badan Pusat Statistik (Statistic Indonesia, the Central Statistics Agency)
BSD city	Bumi Serpong Damai city
BtW	Bike to Work
BUMN	*badan usaha milik negara* (state-owned enterprise)
bupati	district head, regent
CCTV	closed circuit television (video surveillance)
DAU	Dana Alokasi Umum (General Allocation Grant)
desa	rural village
DIBI	Data Informasi Bencana Indonesia (Indonesian Disaster Information Database)
DKI Jakarta	Daerah Khusus Ibukota Jakarta (Special Capital Region Jakarta)
DPRD	Dewan Perwakilan Rakyat Daerah (regional assembly, regional parliament)
DPRKP	Dinas Perumahan Rakyat dan Kawasan Pemukiman (Jakarta Department of Public Housing and Settlement Areas)
ERAT	Tata Kelola Pemerintahan yang Efektif, Efisien dan Kuat (Efficient, Effective and Strong Governance)
ERP	electronic road pricing
FBR	Forum Betawi Rempug (Betawi Brotherhood Forum)
GDP	gross domestic product
Golkar	Golongan Karya (the state political party under the New Order, and a major post–New Order party)
gotong royong	working together, mutual cooperation
GRS	Gerakan Rakyat Surabaya (Surabaya Citizens' Movement)
gusti	elite
hansip	*pertahanan sipil* (civil security guard)
HDI	human development index
HMI	Himpunan Mahasiswa Islam (Islamic Student Association)
IDP	internally displaced person
IPAL	*instalasi pengolahan air limbah* (wastewater treatment plant)
ITS	Institut Teknologi Surabaya (Surabaya Institute of Technology)

IUIDP	Integrated Urban Infrastructure Development Program
Jabodebek	Jakarta and the surrounding metropolitan area, including Bogor, Depok and Bekasi
Jabodetabek	Jakarta and the surrounding metropolitan area, including Bogor, Depok, Tangerang and Bekasi
Jabotabek	Jakarta and the surrounding metropolitan area, including Bogor, Tangerang and Bekasi
jago	'fighting cock' or champion
JICA	Japan International Cooperation Agency
Jokowi	(President) Joko Widodo (2014–2024)
JPPR	Jaringan Pendidikan Pemilih untuk Rakyat (Voter Education Network for the People)
JRMK	Jaringan Rakyat Miskin Kota (Urban Poor People's Network)
kabupaten	rural district, regency
Kadin	Kamar Dagang dan Industri Indonesia (Chamber of Business and Commerce)
KAI	Kereta Api Indonesia (Indonesian Railways, the state railway company)
kampung	self-built urban settlement
kawula	'common people'
keamanan	security
kecamatan	subdistrict
kelurahan	ward (urban village administrative unit)
ketertiban	order
KIP	Kampung Improvement Program
KMS	Kota Madya Surabaya (Surabaya City Region)
Kopkamtib	Operational Command for the Restoration of Security and Order
kota	city, municipality
Kotaku program	Kota Tanpa Kumuh (City without Slums)
KPK	Komisi Pemberantasan Korupsi (Corruption Eradication Commission)
KTP	Kartu Tanda Penduduk (identity card)
LBH Jakarta	Lembaga Bantuan Hukum Jakarta (Legal Aid Institute, Jakarta)
LRT	light rail transit
MPWH	Ministry of Public Works and Housing (Kementerian Pekerjaan Umum dan Perumahan Rakyat)

MRF	material recovery facility (*pusat daur ulang*)
MRT	mass rapid transit
musrenbang	*musyawarah perencanaan pembangunan* (development planning deliberations)
musyawarah	community meeting and discussion, usually to take a collective decision
Nahdlatul Ulama	traditionalist Islamic organisation founded in 1926
NAHP	National Affordable Housing Program (Program Nasional Perumahan Terjangkau)
New Order	political regime under President Suharto, 1966–1998
NGO	non-government organisation
OECD	Organisation for Economic Cooperation and Development
ormas	*organisasi masyarakat* (social organisation)
OSR	own-source revenue
PAN	Partai Amanat Nasional (National Mandate Party)
Pancasila	the five guiding principles of the Indonesian state (belief in God, humanitarianism, nationalism, democracy and social justice; or, in another formulation: belief in one supreme God, just and civilised humanity, national unity, democracy led by wisdom and prudence through consultation and representation, and social justice)
PDI-P	Partai Demokrasi Indonesia-Perjuangan (Indonesian Democratic Party of Struggle)
PDRD	*pajak daerah dan retribusi daerah* (local taxes and levies)
pembangunan	development
pemekaran	proliferation or expansion of subdistricts or districts
Pemuda Pancasila	nationalist paramilitary organisation (Pancasila Youth)
perda	*peraturan daerah* (regional government by-law)
perkotaan	urban area
peroemahan rakjat	people's housing
Perpres	*peraturan presiden* (presidential regulation)
PKH	Program Keluarga Harapan (Family Hope Program)
PKK	Pembinaan Kesejahteraan Keluarga (Family Welfare and Empowerment Program)
PLN	Perusahaan Listrik Negara (state electricity company)

PMII	Persatuan Mahasiswa Islam Indonesia (Indonesian Islamic Students' Association)
PNPM	Program Nasional Pemberdayaan Masyarakat (National Program for Community Empowerment)
Podes	Potensi Desa (Village Potential)
posyandu	*pos pelayanan terpadu* (community-based integrated healthcare post)
PP	*peraturan pemerintah* (government regulation)
PPP	public-private partnership
preman	gangster, thug
PSEL	*pengolahan sampah menjadi energi listrik* (processing waste into electrical energy)
PT SO	PT Sumber Organik (private waste management company)
Pusdakota	Pusat Pemberdayaan Komunitas Perkotaan (Centre for Urban Community Empowerment)
rakyat	'common people'
reformasi	reform; name for the post-Suharto period (since 1998)
RGDP	regional gross domestic product
Rp	Indonesian rupiah
RPJMN	Rencana Pembangunan Jangka Menengah Nasional (National Medium Term Development Plan)
RT	*rukun tetangga* (neighbourhood association)
RTRW	*rencana tata ruang wilayah* (spatial plan)
rusunawa	*rumah susun sederhana sewa* (rental social housing)
RW	*rukun warga* (citizens' association)
satpam	*satuan pengamanan* (security guard)
Satpol PP	civil ordinance police
Siskamling	Sistem Keamanan Lingkungan (Environment Security System)
TNI	Tentara Nasional Indonesia (Indonesian National Army)
UPF	Unilever Peduli Foundation
US$	United States dollar
USAID	United States Agency for International Development
Walhi Surabaya	Wahana Lingkungan Hidup Indonesia Surabaya (Indonesian Forum for the Environment, Surabaya Chapter)

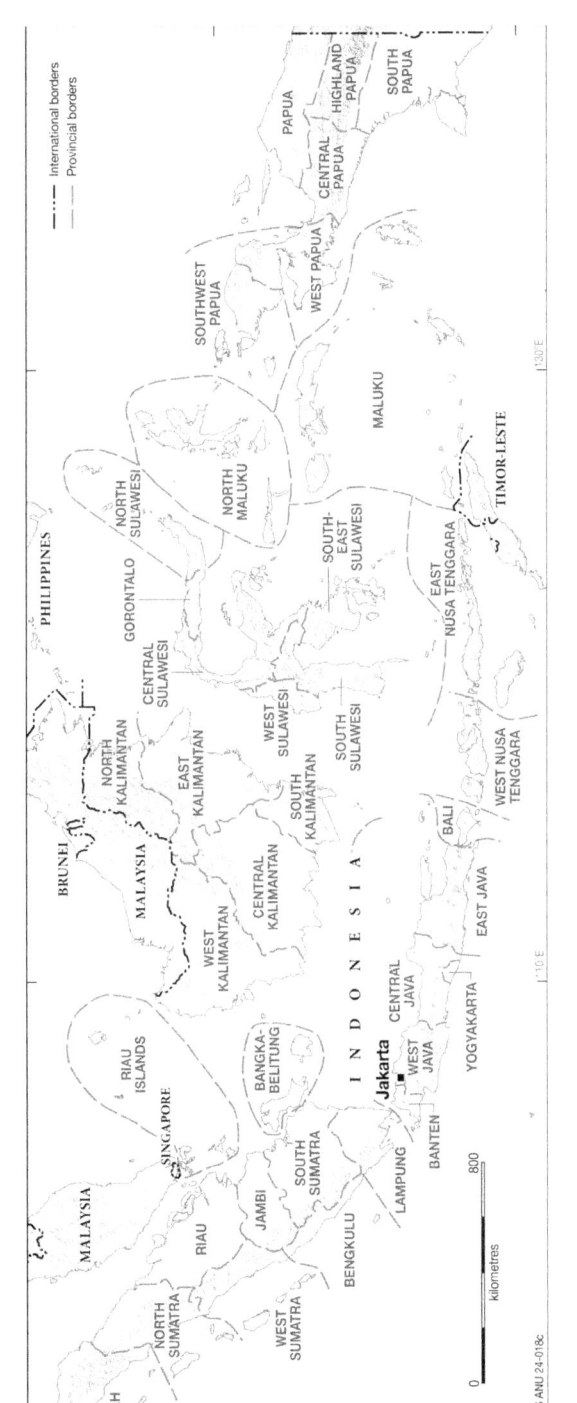

1 Governing urban Indonesia: Trends and challenges

Edward Aspinall and Amalinda Savirani

Indonesia is an increasingly urban society. In 2011, for the first time, the number of people living in Indonesia's towns and cities exceeded those living in rural areas. That number is steadily increasing. By 2020, 56 per cent of Indonesians were urban dwellers (Malamassam and Katherina, this volume). In 2045, when Indonesia will celebrate 100 years of independence, it is estimated that 220 million people, or 70 per cent of the population, will live in towns and cities (Roberts et al. 2019: 2).

Recognising this reality requires a shift in perception. For much of the past century, Indonesians have viewed their national identity as reflecting the overwhelmingly rural composition of Indonesian society. The country's political movements have mostly competed for support in the villages. National governments have focused on servicing and securing the country's vast rural population. Back in the 1920s, when the young nationalist leader Sukarno imagined an archetypal Indonesian, he thought of 'Marhaen', a small farmer living in West Java (Soekarno 1960). Two decades later, when Sukarno proclaimed independence in 1945, only 12.5 per cent of the population lived in urban areas (Roberts et al. 2019: 1), more than 70 per cent were peasant farmers and 75 per cent of GDP (gross domestic product) was derived from agriculture (Metcalf 1952: 7). Indonesia's national revolution played out mostly in the countryside and, over the subsequent two decades, the political parties that fought for control of Indonesia's government did so mostly by mobilising rural supporters. When Suharto assumed power in 1966, initiating his 32-year authoritarian New Order regime, still only 16 per cent of the population lived in towns and cities, a figure that had risen to 40 per cent by the time he resigned in 1998.[1] Even so, Suharto's regime focused single-mindedly on securing its rural base, promoting agricultural and infrastructure development in the villages while celebrating achievements such as self-sufficiency in rice production. Even during the post-Suharto *reformasi* era, as Indonesia has become an increasingly urban society, its presidents have practised forms of 'agro nationalism' that emphasise 'Indonesia's agrarian identity in policy and propaganda' (Graham 2020).

While Indonesia's rural identity retains significant purchase over the imagination of both ordinary Indonesian citizens and national leaders, that orientation is no longer grounded in the sociological reality it once was. Not only is Indonesia already a majority urban society, and is set to become more so, but the urban population increasingly sets the pace for the country's economy, culture and politics. In 2012, for example, the consultancy firm McKinsey estimated that the urban economy contributed 74 per cent of Indonesian GDP, and projected that figure would rise to 86 per cent by 2030 (Oberman et al. 2012: 3). Meanwhile, Indonesian national culture, while always having been shaped by urban dwellers, increasingly has an urban middle-class tone, with everything from new religious movements to new popular music, artistic, linguistic and lifestyle trends emanating primarily from the country's urban centres.

This volume zeroes in on the political and governance consequences of Indonesia's urban transformation. These consequences are profound. To consider how urban Indonesia is changing Indonesian politics, we need look no further than the career of its most recent president: Joko Widodo (Jokowi). Jokowi had a path to the presidency that would have been hard to imagine in any earlier era of Indonesian politics. He came to the presidency not as a member of Indonesia's traditional political elite, nor as a military officer, bureaucrat or party-machine man, but as mayor of the town of Surakarta (Solo), in Central Java (2005–2012) and as governor of Jakarta (2012–2014). In both places, Jokowi built a can-do reputation as a problem-solver who could improve the everyday lives of the residents of his city (Mas'udi 2016); in this regard he was widely viewed as a representative of a new generation of reforming local government leaders (see, for example, the cover story of *Tempo* magazine, 22–28 December 2008). As mayor of Solo, Jokowi took various popular initiatives to improve the town's amenities, including negotiating the relocation of unauthorised vendors from its streets and parks, removing informal riverside settlements to reduce flooding, and renovating traditional

---

1   https://data.worldbank.org/indicator/SP.URB.TOTL.IN.ZS?locations=ID, viewed 30 March 2024.

markets (Bunnell et al. 2013: 863–67). He then used this reputation to run successfully for election as governor of Jakarta in 2012, promising in his campaign to deal with many of the longstanding and chronic problems that afflicted the city. During Jokowi's brief term in office as governor, he took steps to improve service delivery and infrastructure, including by accelerating the development of a modern transportation system (complete with a subway) and cleaning up the city's waterways in order to reduce flooding. Some of these initiatives were tougher in Jakarta than in Solo; notably, removing informal settlements along rivers encountered greater resistance and ultimately led to widespread social conflict and forced relocations (see Siagian, this volume).

As is well known, Jokowi went on to leverage his record of achievement as Jakarta governor to win the presidency in 2014. From there, he turned his attention to national development, including a major focus on rural areas (Warburton 2016). But he also threw his weight behind various infrastructure projects in the capital and other major cities, and inaugurated a new high-speed train between Jakarta and Bandung. Most famously, he developed a new signature project: planning and initiating construction of a new national capital (Ibu Kota Nusantara) in North Kalimantan. Jokowi described this new capital as a means of reducing the compounding 'burdens' associated with the almost 30-million population of the Greater Jakarta region: 'Those burdens are very, very heavy, causing problems that keep coming up and are hard to solve, problems to do with traffic congestion, problems to do with floods, and now, on top of all that, problems to do with air pollution' (Erwanti 2023). By moving central government offices to a new capital, Jokowi said he hoped to lessen such burdens on the Jakarta megalopolis and provide Indonesia's bureaucrats with a city that was environmentally sustainable and had world-class amenities. It would be, in other words, a city that avoided the shortcomings that afflict other Indonesian cities. When critics said the government's money would be better spent fixing Jakarta, and would give rise to new forms of inequality (e.g. Wiryono and Rastika 2023), the government responded that fixing Jakarta would be more expensive than building a new capital (Intan 2022; on the new capital plans, see Lau et al. 2023).

In this brief survey of the career of Jokowi and its entanglement with urban life, urban planning and urban politics, we already see many of the main themes that animate this book: the old and new problems of urban Indonesia that increasingly occupy the energies and attention of Indonesian politicians and planners, the emergence of a new generation of Indonesian politicians trying to come up with new solutions to these problems, and how structural challenges such as inequality and informality can both impede these efforts and shape the nature of the solutions ultimately arrived at. Our volume, in short, uses an urban lens to reflect upon the question of Indonesian democracy. Discussing how urban Indonesia is governed, and will be governed in the future, means discussing the future of Indonesia itself.

The remainder of this introductory chapter comprises four main sections, each corresponding to a major theme addressed in this volume. First, we briefly discuss the governance challenges—both old and new—that arise as more and more Indonesians pack into urban areas: these include classic problems of urban life such as traffic congestion, air pollution, inadequate waste disposal, poor water supply and emerging ecological problems such as flooding, land subsidence and inundation linked to sea level rise, as well as all the normal problems of service delivery in fields such as housing, health care, education and social welfare. Second, we highlight that city governments confront not only technical, planning and financial obstacles when trying to overcome these problems: many of the key underlying challenges they face are *political*, and are associated with corruption, policy capture and collusion between government officials and powerful business interests. In a third section, we sketch how Indonesian cities are responding. We note that a new pattern of political reform has emerged, with city mayors in many locations developing a new governance style that emphasises responsiveness, technocratic planning and a more livable urban environment. We consider what factors may be driving this new trend, and why it is not emerging uniformly across all urban areas. In a fourth section, we zero in on a key social feature of Indonesia's urban areas—their persistent and growing inequality—and discuss the ways in which this inequality shapes urban governance, and complicates the picture of urban democratisation discussed in the preceding section. Finally, we conclude by pointing to some of the major lessons to be drawn from the volume.

Urban governance challenges

In mid-2023, during the weeks and months leading to the conference upon which this book is based, Jakarta was in the grip of an air pollution crisis. For weeks, smog levels in the capital were among the worst in the world—sometimes the very worst in the world. President Joko Widodo—himself with a month-long hacking cough observers speculated was caused by the pollution—called in ministers and told them to take action, without offering much in the way of guidance on how to do so (Haizan 2023). Environmental experts say that the pollution, which has been worsening year by year, is mostly caused by road transportation and industrial combustion in and around the city (Lestari et al. 2022). It is more than a mere inconvenience: it has recently been estimated that air pollution causes over 10,000 deaths a year in Jakarta alone (Syuhada et al. 2023: 1). While forest fires have previously been, and remain, a major contributor to air pollution in Indonesia, the increasing severity of urban-sourced pollution is a sign of Indonesia's urbanisation, and a symptom of the kind of problems it will increasingly encounter as it becomes a more urban society.

Air pollution is only one of the problems urban Indonesians face. Daily life can be a real chore for residents of Indonesia's towns and cities, especially those who live in the biggest urban centres such as Jakarta, Surabaya, Medan and Bandung. In Jakarta especially, traffic gridlock is never far away. As Muhammad Halley Yudhistira and Andhika Putra Pratama show in their contribution to this volume, Jakarta consistently ranks as one of the worst cities for traffic congestion in the world, with almost a quarter of commuters spending at least 90 minutes commuting (one-way) to their workplace every day; cities like Surabaya, Bandung and Medan, they warn, are less congested but are only a few years behind (see also van Mead 2016). Walking through Indonesia's major urban centres is often equally challenging, with absent or poor-quality pavements meaning that pedestrians have to dodge motorbikes, cars and other vehicles.

Another massive challenge, the focus of Nur Azizah's chapter in this volume, is management of solid waste. Much of the huge amount of garbage produced daily by urban residents (8 million tonnes per day in major urban areas alone: Aprilia 2021: 5) is burned, dumped in rivers or accumulates in mountainous open dumpsites. Jakarta alone sends around 7,000 tonnes per day to the massive Bantargebang waste site located in Bekasi to the east of the city (Dean and Paddock 2020). Providing clean potable water and effective sewerage systems is equally challenging— it has recently been estimated that only 2 per cent of the households of Jakarta proper are connected to the public sewerage system (Prevost et al. 2020), while overall 'only 1 percent of wastewater in urban areas [is] collected and treated properly' (Eng et al. 2020: 269). Meanwhile, in 2017 it was estimated that only 37 per cent of urbanites had access to a piped water supply, but with that piped water itself generally considered not drinkable without boiling (USAID 2017). Most urban people, if they do not buy bottled water, get most of their water from groundwater wells, though this is itself a health hazard given pollution of the watertable (though much of the refillable bottled water on the market is also poor quality: Komarulzaman et al. 2017).

Urban Indonesia also faces mounting ecological problems, made worse by climate change. Periodic flooding, much of it caused by deforestation and construction in water catchments, is a serious hazard in many urban areas, as Yogi Setya Permana explains in his chapter in this volume. Large tracts of many towns, especially those that line the north coast of Java such as Jakarta, Cirebon, Pekalongan and Semarang, already experience periodic inundation during king tides and/or heavy rain, and are predicted to sink into the sea over coming years and decades (Kimmelman 2017; Ley 2021). Jakarta itself has been called the 'fastest-sinking city in the world' and is experiencing land subsidence at a rate of 1–15 centimetres per year, with about half the city already below sea level (Lin and Hidayat 2018). One major cause is excessive groundwater use: as noted above, inadequate supply of piped water means that many households draw their water from wells, with significant inequality of clean water access (Kooy 2014). But Jakarta is not alone. For example, Semarang, the capital of Central Java, is sinking at a rate of 10–12 centimetres annually (Aditiya and Ito 2023). The government plans a massive, and controversial, sea wall in Jakarta to prevent inundation, and similar plans are either being prepared or implemented for other vulnerable cities, including Semarang (see, for example, Mufti 2019). Seawater encroachment, meanwhile, is one of the reasons President Widodo and other government leaders cite for moving the Indonesian capital city to an inland site in Kalimantan.

In addition to dealing with these problems regarding the urban environment, leaders of city governments have to deal with all the normal challenges that local governments throughout Indonesia face: delivering high-quality services to citizens in fields like education and health as Indonesia tries to make the transition to a knowledge-based economy and ensure that government bureaucracies work well and deliver effectively for residents.

Urban Indonesians thus experience problems of daily life—traffic jams, pollution and all the rest of it—that would be familiar to urbanites in other parts of the world, especially in the Global South. Many of these problems have accumulated over a long period during which Indonesia's urban population growth outstripped the capacity of city governments to provide the physical and governmental infrastructure to service the swelling urban population. For decades, especially during the New Order years, rapid urbanisation was largely driven by rural-urban migration, as poor Indonesians moved away from the countryside to find work in the cities, either in the informal sector or, especially during the New Order's final decade, in the industrial and service sectors that were rapidly expanding in and around them.

In this period, cities thus expanded largely as a result of informal, organic and unplanned processes of growth, with newly arrived migrants moving into the crowded self-built settlements known as *kampung* that housed most urban dwellers (see Abidin Kusno's chapter in this volume for a review of the historical development of these *kampung*). Depictions of life in these *kampung* in Jakarta and other major cities during the New Order years (e.g. Guinness 2009; Jellinek 1991; Murray 1991) not only portray the remarkable resilience and ingenuity of *kampung* dwellers, they also paint a picture of the very poor living conditions typically experienced in them, conditions not dissimilar to those found in the slums or shanty towns that swelled around many cities in the Global South (Davis 2005) (even if scholars of urban life in Indonesia have generally been reluctant to use these pejorative terms).

Decades of efforts by *kampung* dwellers to improve their homes and living environments (Reerink and van Gelder 2010), as well as government efforts through measures such as the famous Kampung Improvement Program (e.g. Silas 1992), have transformed most of these urban *kampung*, replacing flimsy shacks with solid brick or cement homes, covering open drains and transforming muddy paths into neatly cemented alleyways (for a recent account of the centrality of *kampung* to Indonesian urbanism, see Kusno 2019). Thus, according to UN-Habitat data, the proportion of Indonesia's urban residents living in dwellings classified as slums dropped from 35 per cent in 2000 to 19 per cent in 2020.[2] Even so, while many *kampung* dwellers have tried to formalise their possession of land (e.g. Lund 2020: 126–50), the unplanned nature of these settlements and the fact that *kampung* residents still lack formal legal title continues to contribute to governance problems and social conflicts. These can arise when governments carry out urban improvement programs (e.g. clearing riverbanks in order to alleviate flooding, or opening up green spaces) by forcibly clearing *kampung* without providing adequate compensation, or by moving residents to social housing in ways that destroy their livelihoods and sense of community (as detailed in Clara Siagian's chapter in this volume).

More recently, however, as demographers Meirina Ayumi Malamassam and Luh Kitty Katherina observe in their chapter in this volume, the pattern of urbanisation has changed. Their wide-ranging overview of urbanisation trends shows that migration is no longer the main driver of urban growth. That is now a seemingly technical process of reclassification of rural areas as urban, something that occurs as population density increases in areas formerly considered rural and as these regions build more modern amenities and infrastructure. Many of Indonesia's *kabupaten*, officially considered to be rural districts, thus now have fully

---

2   https://data.worldbank.org/indicator/EN.POP.SLUM.UR.ZS?locations=ID, viewed 12 April 2024.

urban characteristics (see chapter by Erman Rahman, Ihsan Haerudin and Ronaldo Octaviano, this volume). These *kabupaten* are often 'ill-prepared to manage urban development processes' (Mardiansjah et al. 2021: 24). This shift is thus associated with a pattern of urban growth that includes greatly expanding urban sprawl around major centres, expansion in the number of small and medium-sized towns, and urbanisation of many formerly rural regions. These processes are visible throughout Indonesia but especially so in Java, which is well on the way to becoming an 'island of mega-urban regions' (Firman 2017).

The result is that new sorts of problems of urban growth have been added to the old ones, such as how to build transport infrastructure to connect massively sprawling urban agglomerations, including those that cross municipal, district and even provincial boundaries, and how to restrict building in areas ringing cities in order to preserve water supplies and prevent flooding. The scale of such problems can be daunting. The province of Jakarta, for instance, was estimated to have a night-time population of 11 million in 2019, with that number climbing to 14.2 million people during the day as commuters stream into the city from surrounding districts (Martinez and Masron 2020: 6). Similarly, Medan, the largest city in Sumatra, has a population of 5 million during the day but only 2.7 million at night (Syahputra 2023).

The political sources of Indonesia's urban governance challenges

Why do Indonesian governments, national and local, struggle to deal with the problems of urban living, amenities and environment summarised above?

One explanation is obvious: governments are simply overwhelmed by the sheer magnitude of the challenge. Problems such as traffic congestion and flooding have accumulated over many years and require massive investment in physical infrastructure and new governmental systems to address them. Muhammad Halley Yudhistira and Andhika Putra Pratama, in their chapter on traffic congestion in Greater Jakarta, show that one of the major impediments to development of the capital's railway systems has simply been the massive investment required (though they also point to the need for more integrated planning and management across the Greater Jakarta metropolitan area). Likewise, Nur Azizah explains in her chapter that Surabaya's relatively successful management of solid waste in recent years has been built in part on large-scale investment, including the construction of a waste-to-energy plant that would be beyond the capacity of most Indonesian urban areas. At the same time, as the chapter by Erman Rahman, Ihsan Haerudin and Ronaldo Octaviano makes clear, despite

Indonesia's decentralised system of government, the local governments in charge of Indonesia's urban areas have limited fiscal resources; indeed, their chapter shows that per capita government revenues are generally lower in urban districts than in rural districts, despite urban areas having greater ability to raise their own revenues.

The financial burden of fixing the problems that afflict Indonesia's towns and cities is undeniably important, but it is a core contention of this volume that the chief barriers to resolving Indonesia's urban problems are fundamentally political. Understanding the political sources of Indonesia's urban challenges is thus a second major theme of this volume.

Indonesia's urban problems are fundamentally political problems because resolving them requires city governments to develop the independence, and to muster the political will, to challenge the powerful vested interests that undermine urban planning and effective implementation of regulations designed to enhance city life. Governments are often unable to do so. Studies of Indonesian political economy and of local politics in the post-Suharto period (e.g. Aspinall and van Klinken 2010; Hadiz 2010) provide us with guidance for why this is so: such studies point to the close informal relations that link powerful business and political actors at all levels of Indonesian government. Sometimes, these ties take the form of longstanding clientelist relationships between politicians and businesspeople, but they also manifest in the form of payments of kickbacks, bribes and informal fees of various kinds. Indonesia's high-cost elections, in which political candidates regularly have to reach out to business backers in order to fund their clientelist election campaigns, help drive these dynamics (Aspinall and Berenschot 2019). However, it is not only civilian politicians who participate in these exchanges: so too do bureaucrats, as well as security and law enforcement officials, such as police, military and prosecutors (see the chapters by Yogi Setya Permana and Bima Arya Sugiarto in this volume for examples).

Such patterns of connections between business and politics regularly give rise to lax enforcement of planning and other regulations, as well as to policy capture, which occurs when business actors are able to influence the design of policies in ways that favour them. When people discuss these phenomena in Indonesia they regularly use terms such as 'corruption', 'collusion' and 'money politics' to describe the dynamics at play. While these terms are not inaccurate, they should not lead us to think of these problems as being aberrations within Indonesia's system of government. Rather, informal ties between business and political actors and the undermining or manipulation of regulations are so widespread that they constitute structural features of Indonesian politics in the post-Suharto period (despite all the efforts at reform).

How is all this relevant to urban governance? Yogi Setya Permana's chapter on urban flooding provides an excellent primer. He shows that the flooding that regularly afflicts Indonesian towns and cities is not merely a symptom of environmental mismanagement resulting from factors such as poor training, knowledge or capacity among relevant government officials, and it is not even primarily caused by inadequate or poorly designed investment in flood protection infrastructure. Instead, he argues, flooding is, at root, a political problem. Specifically, he argues, flooding arises as a result of 'collusion between state and business actors'. Business actors regularly violate flood prevention and other environmental regulations. For example, property developers build on watershed areas or fail to provide proper drainage facilities in their housing estates, and polluting factory owners dump waste into rivers. They can do such things because they pay informal fees to, or otherwise maintain informal connections with, local government officials in the relevant planning or environmental agencies, local politicians, or other state actors (collusion between factory and military officers is a particular problem in one of Permana's case study sites). In short, problems such as urban flooding are intimately connected to the nature of the local political economy, especially to the webs of informal ties and resource flows that connect political and economic actors.

Such problems involve high-level corruption in which well-resourced property developers, for example, use their economic power and political influence to secure spatial plans that advantage them, while lower down in the system, officials in charge of enforcing municipal ordinances (such as to move informal vendors off pavements, or to ensure that private waste disposal companies dispose of their waste hygienically) might themselves be taking informal fees in exchange for turning a blind eye to violations. It is also important to note that such patterns are deeply entrenched historically. As Abidin Kusno's historical overview chapter in this volume makes clear, urbanisation during the Suharto years, while building on colonial legacies, was driven by a 'growth coalition' that linked the president and his political allies to property developers and other business actors who had little interest in paying attention to the needs of ordinary urban residents, especially the urban poor.

The final chapter in our volume involves a significant change in perspective, but one that also draws attention to the political sources of Indonesia's urban governance challenges. It is authored by one of the more prominent of the recent generation of city leaders: the former mayor of Bogor, Bima Arya Sugiarto. As well as serving as mayor of Bogor from 2014 to 2024, Sugiarto has also held the position of chairperson of Apeksi (Asosiasi Pemerintah Kota Seluruh Indonesia, Association of Indonesian

Municipal Governments), and is thus well placed to understand the challenges that Indonesia's city leaders experience both from a personal perspective and through intensive interactions with his counterparts from across the country. Importantly, his chapter, which draws primarily on his own experiences as mayor, reinforces the political nature of many of the challenges facing city governments in Indonesia, including the tendency towards corruption exerted by Indonesia's high-cost election campaigns and the difficulty of accommodating the wide range of actors interested in attaining contracts, projects and other rewards from the city budget.

Understanding this context helps us understand why dealing with the problems of Indonesian cities requires not only better quality urban planning and massive investment, but also significant political and governance reform. This topic is a third major theme of our volume, which we turn to now.

Urban governance and political reform

Given this rather gloomy background, it is striking that many Indonesian cities have in fact shown themselves as being capable of reform over recent decades. In fact, some cities have become virtual laboratories of political change for the country as a whole, pioneering new methods of delivering services to residents, improving amenities, tackling longstanding urban problems, and, in at least some cases, taking action to reduce entrenched corruption and increase citizen participation.

To a large extent, in the public imagination, this wave of urban political change has been associated with the emergence of prominent individual urban politicians, especially mayors. President Widodo is the best-known example, but he is only one of a new type of city leader who has risen to national prominence in the post-Suharto period, especially during the past decade or so. While the first generation included Jokowi and his contemporaries, a second generation includes figures such as Tri Rismaharini, popularly known as Bu Risma (mayor of Surabaya, 2010–2020, and later Jokowi's Minister of Social Affairs) and Ridwan Kamil (mayor of Bandung, 2013–2018, later governor of West Java), as well as Jokowi's deputy and successor as governor of Jakarta (2014–2017), Basuki Tjahaja Purnama (Ahok).

These individuals have achieved national fame from their efforts to make their cities more livable for residents, more efficient at delivering services and more attractive to visitors. They have produced what we can think of as a 'standard model' of urban political reform that has involved paying attention to basic infrastructure, such as road paving and city parks, increasing the efficiency of the city bureaucracy and services, making them more responsive to citizens, and opening up feedback and complaint mechanisms by which citizens can notify the government of problems that need fixing. City leaders have also tended to be at the forefront of broader public welfare reform. For example, when Joko Widodo was still mayor of Solo, he was one of the first local leaders to introduce a free healthcare program, a policy that was later rolled out nationally.

Some cities have become especially well known for being at the forefront of reform. Perhaps the best-known example is Surabaya, the capital of East Java province, which is something of a star exhibit in this volume. Surabaya occupies a central position in Mochamad Mustafa's analysis of urban reform and is held up as an exemplar of successful flood management in the chapter by Yogi Setya Permana and as a leader in solid waste management in the chapter by Nur Azizah. This city, with a population of around 3 million (10 million if we include the surrounding urban sprawl) was once a byword for urban grime. Over the past 25 years, a series of reforming mayors—most famously Risma, at the time of writing the Minister of Social Affairs—has rebranded the city as 'clean and green', and residents and visitors alike praise the city's new sense of cleanliness, and its parks and open spaces. As Nur Azizah explains in her chapter, the city has built a massive waste-to-energy incinerator, developed a system of neighbourhood-level waste banks and introduced environmental 'cadres'. Crucially, the Surabaya model also involved governance reform, including new online reporting and complaints systems for citizens, and the introduction of e-budgeting and e-procurement systems that have since been used as models around the country.

Generally speaking, the new generation of reforming leaders such as Risma and Jokowi must be viewed as a product of the post-Suharto democratisation. In pursuing policies of local governance reform and striving to deliver better services to citizens, they have largely been motivated by the desire to respond to voter aspirations and thus secure victories in competitive electoral contests (Aspinall 2014).

However, it should be stressed that democratisation has not had this effect everywhere. Not every city or town in Indonesia has become a model of governance reform. In many Indonesian urban centres, old patterns of patronage politics and corruption continue to stand in the way of urban reform, with political elites and their business backers dining out on infrastructure, reclamation and similar projects, but doing little to improve the lives of ordinary residents. Many of the most clientelist local governments found in Indonesia are in relatively small towns in less-developed regions, especially provincial capitals and other towns that are highly dependent on the government bureaucracy or extractive industry for their economic life (Aspinall and Berenschot 2019: 240, 245).

Some much more populous and developed urban centres are also sites of predatory elite capture. Mochamad Mustafa shows in his chapter that the city of South Tangerang, one of the country's wealthiest urban districts, located on the periphery of Jakarta, has long been ruled by members of one of Indonesia's most notorious political dynasties, and has experienced major corruption scandals, with the city's leaders effectively combining predatory behaviour with improved delivery of health care, education and other services.

How do we explain this variation? In the existing literature, and much popular discourse, a favoured explanation is that individual leadership is key to governance reform at the local level in Indonesia (see especially von Luebke 2009). Prominent mayors, such as Jokowi, Risma and Ridwan Kamil have garnered significant attention for the role they have played in pursuing processes of urban reform. There is no denying that such individuals have played an important part in changing city government. They have done so in part by modelling new patterns of behaviour (such as Jokowi's famous spot inspections of government offices to ensure bureaucrats were at their posts and working hard, or Risma's well-publicised participation in public street sweeping and other clean-up events), and in part by developing new methods to monitor budgets and bureaucrats in ways that allow them to detect abuses and thus produce more efficient and effective government. (See, for example, Governor Ahok's use of a new e-budgeting mechanism to expose collusion between local politicians, bureaucrats and contractors in public procurement in Jakarta: Aspinall and Berenschot 2019: 172–73.) In this light, it is possible to see the processes of urban reform that these leaders have pioneered as being primarily technocratic and top-down; in her chapter on public space in cities, Rita Padawangi accordingly refers to such leaders as practising a form of 'managerial leadership'.

The chapter by Mochamad Mustafa makes an important intervention into this debate. He argues that, beyond the influence of individual leadership and technocratic reform, a key factor determining how effectively city governments deliver services to their citizens is the nature of the political coalitions that underpin them. In urban centres with an active and diverse civil society able to put pressure on city governments to deliver, and to support reforming leaders when they confront entrenched vested interests, it is easier for mayors to initiate reform. He illustrates this argument by way of an analysis of the recent history of Surabaya, which, as already noted, is lauded in several chapters in this volume as a good governance standout. Mustafa ascribes Surabaya's success to the relatively active and varied character of civil society in that city which, he suggests, has provided a 'conducive environment' for urban reform.

In his account, relatively early in the post-Suharto *reformasi* period, civil society protest led to the removal of one mayor who was seen as unable to improve the city, and his replacement by a reformer, Bambang DH (Risma's predecessor), who, with civil society support, faced down corrupt elements in the bureaucracy and local parliament. Yogi Setya Permana's and Nur Azizah's analyses of, respectively, flood management and solid waste disposal largely confirm this analysis. Mustafa contrasts the Surabaya story with that of the city of Bogor, where a reform-oriented leader, Bima Arya Sugiarto (who contributes a chapter to this volume), had to operate in a much less rich and diverse civil society context, and thus, lacking allies for his reform efforts, ended up making more compromises over his good governance agenda.

This emphasis on the role of civil society accords with our own observations, and helps to explain why cities have been at the forefront of governance reform in post-Suharto Indonesia. Generally speaking, civil society activity is more buoyant in cities than in rural areas, due to the relative prosperity and more diverse nature of urban economies and, hence, societies (which also helps explain why cities with economies built around bureaucratic employment and government expenditure are relatively rarely sites of reform; such places tend to have much less space for expression of diverse social and political interests: Aspinall and Berenschot 2019: 245). Certainly, many initiatives to improve city life have begun with civil society groups. For example, recent moves to introduce bicycle lanes in cities started when community members, organised in 'Bike to Work' (BtW) groups, lobbied local governments to provide such lanes. BtW now has chapters in many cities in Indonesia and, at the time of writing, more than 114,000 followers on Instagram. In other cases, civil society organisations have pushed city governments on issues such as decent housing rights for the poor, introducing air quality measurements and taking circular economy initiatives to promote garbage recycling. And it is not only middle-class city residents who have taken such initiatives; members of the urban poor have done so as well. For example, in the 2017 Jakarta gubernatorial election, various urban poor communities, organised with the help of a group known as the Urban Poor Consortium, made political deals with governor candidate Anies Baswedan, convincing him to sign 'political contracts', in which he promised not to evict them from their homes in exchange for their votes (Savirani and Aspinall 2017; Savirani and Guntoro 2020).

In some ways, of course, we should not be surprised that Indonesia's cities have been at the forefront of post-Suharto political and governance reform. The word 'city' itself derives from the Latin *civitas*, referring to the citizenry, and urban scholars sometimes suggest that cities have historically been closely linked to the concept of democracy, as well as being places where novel methods of claim-making and organising politics have been forged (e.g. Barnett 2014; Isin 2002). Comparative scholars have long posited various explanations for why urbanisation and democratisation might be linked, including that the relative density of urban life facilitates collective political action and enhances 'civic capital' of the population (Glaeser and Steinberg 2016).

Of course, recent processes of democratic decline in Indonesia should make us hesitate to adopt an overly optimistic analysis of the democratic potential of the processes of urban reform discussed above—not least given that this decline was overseen by President Widodo (Power 2018), who was so lauded previously as being one of Indonesia's leading 'progressive' mayors. While members of the new generation of urban reformers have undoubtably been motivated by open electoral competition, delivering improved services and amenities in order to win votes, there is considerable variation in the way they mix technocratic reform (including new techniques for top-down monitoring and control by the mayor) with measures to increase popular participation and input (for example, many cities have been pioneering various apps and online measures by which citizens can convey complaints and report problems to the government). As already noted, while some mayors have been backed by active civil society, others have found ways to combine improved service delivery with continued pursuit of clientelist strategies. More broadly still, there are also questions about *which* urban residents get to participate in and guide these new political experiments, and who gets to benefit from them. This is because, as well as being locations of political experimentation, Indonesia's urban areas are also sites of major social inequality.

Urban governance and social inequality

Urban inequality is a fourth major theme that threads its way through most of the chapters in this volume. Various reports have shown that inequality has increased sharply in the post-Suharto period (Gibson 2017; World Bank 2016). According to the World Bank (2016: 2) most of the benefits of economic growth during this period benefited about 20 per cent of the population, creating a considerably larger middle class, but leaving much of the population behind. To be sure, generally speaking, residents of urban areas are more prosperous than their rural counterparts. Of the top twenty districts with the highest human development index scores in 2023, for example, eighteen were cities and the other two were highly urbanised *kabupaten* (BPS 2023). Yet while Indonesia's urban areas house most of the country's middle class, and almost all of its wealthiest citizens, they also retain large numbers of poor people: in 2019 it was estimated that nearly 7 per cent of the urban population lived below the poverty line, with a similar proportion classified as 'near poor' (ADB 2022: 3). As a result, while inequality has increased everywhere, it is highest in 'the most prosperous areas—that is, in multidistrict metro cores and their urban peripheries' (Roberts et al. 2019: 7).

In this regard, Indonesia fits the global norm whereby 'larger and more prosperous cities tend to be more unequal than smaller, less prosperous, cities' (Roberts et al. 2019: 8). High levels of social inequality are also, as Sonia Roitman emphasises in her chapter in this volume, a characteristic of the urban social landscape that Indonesia shares with many countries in the Global South. And, just like in many global cities, urban inequality manifests itself visibly in Indonesia: in the most expensive areas of Jakarta, for instance, one can easily pay for a meal costing the Jakarta monthly minimum wage in a fancy restaurant and find, just across the street, a family living under a bridge and struggling to survive.

But inequality also produces social segregation into separate urban spaces. Space is not only in short supply in urban areas, it is typically deeply contested. Across Indonesia's urban areas, as already alluded to, private developers—some of whom are among the very wealthiest Indonesians—have played a dominant role in steering, even capturing, urban planning and land use policy since the New Order period. As part of what Abidin Kusno calls the New Order regime's urban 'growth coalition', major developers such as Ciputra built gated communities and new towns for wealthy and middle-class residents around the outskirts of Jakarta, benefiting from their close links with the Suharto government (see also Firman 2019; Arai 2001; Winarso and Firman 2002). Consistent with the pattern described above, this expansion of privatised residential space was accompanied by widespread violations of city planning documents, or their amendment to suit developers, in a context in which 'developers … often bribed the authorities and the local governments' (Rukmana 2015: 358). Indeed, in such locations land acquisition often takes place via a 'land mafia' (Bachriadi and Aspinall 2023) involving developers, public officials and politicians. Such relationships continue to the present day (Savirani 2017), as the expansion of private housing estates for middle-class consumers continues apace. In the meantime, the housing backlog for the poor reached 12.7 million in 2023 (Simanungkalit 2023).

In her chapter in this volume, Corry Elyda provides a telling discussion of the resulting housing inequality. She focuses not on the story of collusion between wealthy developers and local governments, but on the social and political consequences of gated communities. She describes life in such communities of South Tangerang, where many wealthy urbanites live, commuting to Jakarta every work day. In doing so she identifies a pattern of extreme and growing social segregation, with the middle class and wealthy residents of these communities having few interactions with the poor residents who live in the *kampung* that surround their gated communities, and largely relying on private provision of basic infrastructure and amenities. In analysing this situation, she identifies another obstacle to political reform in urban Indonesia: because many of the wealthiest urban residents are protected from the hard scrabble that plays out beyond the walls of their communities, they have little incentive to care about public facilities or support politicians who provide them. As one resident of a gated community told Elyda: 'I am not a citizen. I am a consumer'. As a result, there is a kind of withdrawal from city politics by middle-class residents—many of them, who might otherwise be expected to demand better services and performance from politicians at election times (rather than being satisfied with the gifts of money or other forms of patronage provided to poorer voters), do not bother to vote. This dynamic helps explain why South Tangerang municipality, despite being one of the wealthiest districts of Indonesia, has continued to be dominated by a notorious political dynasty.

Of course, this pattern of social segregation and exclusion does not arise naturally: it is produced, and policed. Ian Wilson explores how this happens in his chapter on the changing nature of security provision in Jakarta, where he traces the rise of new professionally run private security companies, challenging and partly displacing older forms of security provided by so-called 'social organisations' in Jakarta's *kampung*. In a context in which, he says, wealthy Jakartans increasingly demand 'physical and moral security and detachment/autonomy from the city's infrastructural and social woes', it is the growing private security industry that acts as gatekeeper in both business and residential spaces 'via screening, monitoring and regulation of entitlement of entry into private spaces'.

If social inequality shapes the nature of both political participation and segregation in urban Indonesia, it also affects the political transformations currently underway in the country's cities and towns. We have already noted that, historically and to the present day, most of the poor and near-poor live in informal *kampung*. While informality—another defining feature of urban Indonesia that, as stressed in Sonia Roitman's chapter, is shared with other Global South cities—can manifest in terms of various forms of self-help and self-management that help the urban poor to survive (Suhartini and Jones 2023), it also makes *kampung* dwellers vulnerable, insofar as they lack formal legal title to their residences and often also lack official permission for their petty trade or other livelihood activities.

Accordingly, forced relocations (*penggusuran*) of *kampung* dwellers to make way for private developments and public infrastructure projects have long been a part of the urban development story in Indonesia, as have periodic clean-ups of informal traders of various kinds. Critically, such actions have not disappeared along with the rise of the new model of urban political reform discussed above; on the contrary they have often been a feature of it. Members of the urban poor frequently pay the price for the city infrastructure and beautification projects by which the new generation of reforming city mayors and other leaders burnish their political reputations. Their visions of neat, clean and physically attractive 'global cities' are fundamentally middle-class visions.

Two chapters in this volume zero in on this issue. In her discussion of the management of public space in urban Indonesia, Rita Padawangi highlights that many of the new green spaces that have come to symbolise urban renewal in cities such as Bandung and Jakarta have been created through processes of forced relocation. Among other examples, she discusses the case of Teras Cikapundung, an aesthetically pleasing riverbank park in Bandung that Ridwan Kamil presented as one of his signature achievements, which was built on the site of a *kampung* whose residents were forced to move aside. In pointing to the community-led management of public space that often occurs at the *kampung* level, she sees signs of a more hopeful model of inclusive management of public space—but one that may be difficult to apply at scale.

Clara Siagian focuses on the aftermath of evictions in Jakarta, this time caused by various infrastructure projects, primarily for flood prevention. She identifies one area where the new city politics differs from that of the past: in the New Order period, victims of *penggusuran* were often left to fend for themselves, or even expelled from the city; in the post-Suharto period city leaders such as Jokowi and Ahok have at least expressed concern about the fate of evictees, and often used dialogue in order to persuade them to be willing to move (certainly, this was characteristic of Jokowi's approach in Solo, though less so in Jakarta). While this new more conciliatory approach often does not work out in practice (in the case of Jakarta, the tenure of Ahok as governor was characterised by a large number of forced evictions), those pushed aside are now often provided alternative housing in the form of apartments in social housing complexes. As Siagian shows, however, the social consequences can still be devastating, as poor residents are ripped away from the *kampung* environments that provided them with social support and livelihoods, resulting in feelings of social isolation and alienation.

Conclusion

Indonesia confronts many challenges as it becomes increasingly urbanised: challenges of flooding, waste management, traffic congestion and more. This volume does not provide a single, uniform perspective on the nature of those challenges, nor on what can be done about them. Instead, the chapter authors draw on different disciplinary perspectives to examine urban governance from a variety of angles. What sets this volume apart from others that have tackled the challenges of Indonesia's urbanisation in recent times (e.g. Roitman and Rukmana 2023) is the overarching political framework it adopts. Taken together, the volume shows how Indonesia's urbanisation is transforming the nature of politics and governance in Indonesia. It also shows that the successes or failures of governments at various levels as they respond to the growing challenges of urban governance are shaped, to a large degree, by underlying political (and political economy) dynamics. To understand how Indonesia is going about managing its urban transition, we need, in other words, to understand city politics: that field which 'defines and regulates how the city should be organised, how it should allocate its resources and how—and by whom—it should be governed' (Pierre 2011: 1).

As readers will discover, adopting this perspective does not hold out the prospect of easy solutions to Indonesia's urban problems. It is not simply that the magnitude of the problems is so daunting. More fundamentally, resolving them requires doing more than finding the right policy prescriptions and technical solutions. Because the problems are so embedded in political processes and practices that have deep historical roots and are part of the basic structure—especially the informal structure—of Indonesia's political life, fixing them also requires broader processes of political change and reform.

Even so, it is hoped that readers will not find this to be a pessimistic volume—at least not unrelentingly so. The story of post-Suharto democratisation has produced numerous positive as well as negative results. In recent times, the story at the national level has been generally gloomy, as a slow but seemingly inexorable slide in the quality of Indonesia's democracy has occurred. But this volume shows that, when we look at the city level, there are many stories of success and positive change, including examples of city governments taking seriously the challenges of structural reform, marshalling their resources to tackle the various environmental, infrastructure and service challenges they face, and engaging in novel partnerships and coalitions when doing so. Together, they indicate that there are positive models of reform and considerable capacity within Indonesia's varied urban communities to produce better urban governance and more livable Indonesian cities into the future.

References

ADB (Asian Development Bank). 2022. *Building Resilience of the Urban Poor in Indonesia*. ADB. https://dx.doi.org/10.22617/TCS210404-2

Aditiya, Arif and Takeo Ito. 2023. 'Present-day land subsidence over Semarang revealed by time series InSAR new small baseline subset technique'. *International Journal of Applied Earth Observation and Geoinformation* 125: 103579. doi.org/10.1016/j.jag.2023.103579

Aprilia, Aretha. 2021. 'Waste management in Indonesia and Jakarta: Challenges and way forward'. Background paper, 23rd ASEF Summer University, Education Department, Asia-Europe Foundation. https://asef.org/wp-content/uploads/2022/01/ASEFSU23_Background-Paper_Waste-Management-in-Indonesia-and-Jakarta.pdf

Arai, Kenichiro. 2001. 'Only yesterday in Jakarta: Property boom and consumptive trends in the late New Order metropolitan city'. *Japanese Journal of Southeast Asian Studies* 38(4): 481–511. http://hdl.handle.net/2433/56763

Aspinall, Edward. 2014. 'Health care and democratization in Indonesia'. *Democratization* 21(5): 803–23. doi.org/10.1080/13510347.2013.873791

Aspinall, Edward and Gerry van Klinken, eds. 2010. *The State and Illegality in Indonesia*. KITLV Press.

Aspinall, Edward and Ward Berenschot. 2019. *Democracy for Sale: Elections, Clientelism, and the State in Indonesia*. Cornell University Press. doi.org/10.7591/9781501732997

Bachriadi, Dianto and Edward Aspinall. 2023. 'Land mafias in Indonesia'. *Critical Asian Studies* 55(3): 331–53. doi.org/10.1080/14672715.2023.2215261

Barnett, Clive. 2014. 'What do cities have to do with democracy?' *International Journal of Urban and Regional Research* 38(5): 1625–43. doi.org/10.1111/1468-2427.12148

BPS (Badan Pusat Statistik, Statistics Indonesia). 2023. 'Metode baru Indeks Pembangunan Manusia, 2022–2023 [New method, Human Development Index, 2022–2023]'. BPS. www.bps.go.id/id/statistics-table/2/NDEzIzI=/-metode-baru--indeks-pembangunan-manusia.html

Bunnell, Tim, Michelle Ann Miller, Nicholas A. Phelps and John Taylor. 2013. 'Urban development in a decentralized Indonesia: Two success stories?' *Pacific Affairs* 86(4): 857–76. doi.org/10.5509/2013864857

Davis, Mike. 2005. *Planet of Slums*. Verso.

Dean, Adam and Richard C. Paddock. 2020. 'Jakarta's trash mountain: "When people are desperate for jobs, they come here"'. *New York Times*, 27 April. www.nytimes.com/2020/04/27/world/asia/indonesia-jakarta-trash-mountain.html

Eng, Fook Chuan, Irma Magdalena Setiono and Risyana Sukarma. 2020. 'Water supply & sanitation'. In *Indonesia Public Expenditure Review*, 268–85. World Bank.

Erwanti, Marlinda Oktavia. 2023. 'Jokowi di IKN sebut beban Jakarta sangat berat: Macet, banjir, dan polusi [Jokowi in new capital says Jakarta has very heavy burdens: Traffic, floods, and pollution]'. *DetikNews*, 21 September. https://news.detik.com/berita/d-6943534/jokowi-di-ikn-sebut-beban-jakarta-sangat-berat-macet-banjir-dan-polusi

Firman, Tommy. 2017. 'The urbanisation of Java, 2000–2010: Towards "the island of mega-urban regions"'. *Asian Population Studies* 13(1): 50–66. doi.org/10.1080/17441730.2016.1247587

Firman, Tommy. 2019. 'The continuity and change in mega-urbanization in Indonesia: A survey of Jakarta–Bandung Region (JBR) development'. *Habitat International* 33(4): 327–39. doi.org/10.1016/j.habitatint.2008.08.005

Gibson, Luke. 2017. 'Towards a more equal Indonesia'. Oxfam Briefing Paper.

Glaeser, Edward L. and Bryce Millett Steinberg. 2016. *Transforming Cities: Does Urbanization Promote Democratic Change?* NBER Working Paper No. 22860. National Bureau of Economic Research. www.nber.org/papers/w22860

Graham, Colum. 2020. 'Indonesia's agro nationalism in the pandemic'. *New Mandala*, 4 June. www.newmandala.org/indonesias-agro-nationalism-in-the-pandemic

Guinness, Patrick. 2009. *Kampung, Islam and State in Urban Java*. NUS Press.

Hadiz, Vedi R. 2010. *Localising Power in Post-Authoritarian Indonesia: A Southeast Asia Perspective*. Stanford University Press.

Haizan, Rhea Yasmine Alis. 2023. 'Nursing a persistent cough, Jokowi calls for air pollution measures in Jakarta as locals complain of respiratory issues'. Channel News Asia, 15 August. www.channelnewsasia.com/asia/indonesia-joko-widodo-jokowi-greater-jakarta-air-pollution-health-acute-respiratory-infection-3700291

Intan, Ghita. 2022. 'Pemerintah: Benahi Jakarta lebih mahal ketimbang bangun ibu kota baru [Government: Fixing Jakarta is more expensive than building a new capital city]'. *VOA Indonesia*, 14 July. www.voaindonesia.com/a/pemerintah-benahi-jakarta-lebih-mahal-ketimbang-bangun-ibu-kota-baru/6658769.html

Isin, Engin F. 2002. 'City, democracy and citizenship: Historical images, contemporary practices'. In *Handbook of Citizenship Studies*, edited by Engin F. Isin and Bryan S. Turner, 305–16. Sage.

Jellinek, Lea. 1991. *The Wheel of Fortune: The History of a Poor Community in Jakarta*. Allen & Unwin.

Kimmelman, Michael. 2017. 'Jakarta is sinking so fast, it could end up underwater'. *New York Times*, 21 December. www.nytimes.com/interactive/2017/12/21/world/asia/jakarta-sinking-climate.html

Komarulzaman, Ahmad, Eelke de Jong and Jeroen Smits. 2017. 'The switch to refillable bottled water in Indonesia: A serious health risk'. *Journal of Water and Health* 15(6): 1004–14. doi.org/10.2166/wh.2017.319

Kooy, Michelle. 2014. 'Developing informality: The production of Jakarta's urban waterscape'. *Water Alternatives* 7(1): 35–53.

Kusno, Abidin. 2019. 'Middling urbanism: The megacity and the kampung'. *Urban Geography* 41(7): 954–70. doi.org/10.1080/02723638.2019.1688535

Lau, Julia M., Athiqah Nur Alami, Siwage Dharma Negara and Yanuar Nugroho, eds. 2023. *The Road to Nusantara: Process, Challenges and Opportunities*. ISEAS Publishing.

Lestari, Puji, Maulana Khafid Arrohman, Seny Damayanti and Zbigniew Klimont. 2022. 'Emissions and spatial distribution of air pollutants from anthropogenic sources in Jakarta'. *Atmospheric Pollution Research* 13(9): 101521. doi.org/10.1016/j.apr.2022.101521

Ley, Lukas. 2021. *Building on Borrowed Time: Rising Seas and Failing Infrastructure in Semarang*. University of Minnesota Press.

Lin, Mayuri Mei and Rafki Hidayat. 2018. 'Jakarta, the fastest-sinking city in the world'. BBC News, 13 August. www.bbc.com/news/world-asia-44636934

Lund, Christian. 2020. *Nine-Tenths of the Law: Enduring Dispossession in Indonesia*. Yale University Press.
Mardiansjah, Fadjar Hari, Paramita Rahayu and Deden Rukmana. 2021. 'New patterns of urbanization in Indonesia: Emergence of non-statutory towns and new extended urban regions'. *Environment and Urbanization ASIA* 12(1): 11–26. doi.org/10.1177/0975425321990384
Martinez, Rafael and Irna Nurlina Masron. 2020. 'Jakarta: A city of cities'. *Cities* 106: 102868. doi.org/10.1016/j.cities.2020.102868
Mas'udi, Wawan. 2016. 'Creating legitimacy in decentralized Indonesia: Joko "Jokowi" Widodo's path to legitimacy in Solo, 2005–2012'. PhD thesis. University of Melbourne. http://hdl.handle.net/11343/127411
Metcalf, John E. 1952. *The Agricultural Economy of Indonesia*. U.S. Department of Agriculture.
Mufti, Riza Roidila. 2019. 'Semarang–Demak toll road to connect more Java cities'. *Jakarta Post*, 26 September. www.thejakartapost.com/news/2019/09/26/semarang-demak-toll-road-connect-more-java-cities.html
Murray, Alison J. 1991. *No Money, No Honey: A Study of Street Traders and Prostitutes in Jakarta*. Oxford University Press.
Oberman, Raoul, Richard Dobbs, Arief Budiman, Fraser Thompson and Morten Rossé. 2012. *The Archipelago Economy: Unleashing Indonesia's Potential*. McKinsey Global Institute. www.mckinsey.com/featured-insights/asia-pacific/the-archipelago-economy
Pierre, Jon. 2011. *The Politics of Urban Governance*. Palgrave Macmillan.
Power, Thomas P. 2018. 'Jokowi's authoritarian turn and Indonesia's democratic decline'. *Bulletin of Indonesian Economic Studies* 54(3): 307–38. doi.org/10.1080/00074918.2018.1549918
Prevost, Christophe, Dikshya Thapa and Mark Roberts. 2020. 'Cities without sewers: Solving Indonesia's wastewater crisis to realize its urbanization potential'. *World Bank Blogs*, 17 February. https://blogs.worldbank.org/en/eastasiapacific/cities-without-sewers-solving-indonesias-wastewater-crisis-realize-its-urbanization
Reerink, Gustaaf and Jean-Louis van Gelder. 2010. 'Land titling, perceived tenure security, and housing consolidation in the kampongs of Bandung, Indonesia'. *Habitat International* 34(1): 78–85. doi.org/10.1016/j.habitatint.2009.07.002
Roberts, Mark, Frederico Gil Sander and Sailesh Tiwari, eds. 2019. *Time to ACT: Realizing Indonesia's Urban Potential*. World Bank. doi.org/10.1596/978-1-4648-1389-4
Roitman, Sonia and Deden Rukmana, eds. 2023. *Routledge Handbook of Urban Indonesia*. Routledge.
Rukmana, Deden. 2015. 'The change and transformation of Indonesian spatial planning after Suharto's New Order regime: The case of the Jakarta metropolitan area'. *International Planning Studies* 20(4): 350–70. doi.org/10.1080/13563475.2015.1008723
Savirani, Amalinda. 2017. 'Jakarta is still the oligarchs' turf'. *New Mandala*, 12 June. www.newmandala.org/jakarta-still-oligarchs-turf
Savirani, Amalinda and Edward Aspinall. 2017. 'Adversarial linkages: The urban poor and electoral politics in Jakarta'. *Journal of Current Southeast Asian Affairs* 36(3): 3–34. doi.org/10.1177/186810341703600301

Savirani, Amalinda and Guntoro. 2020. 'Between street demonstrations and ballot box: Tenure rights, elections, and social movements among the urban poor in Jakarta'. *PCD Journal* 8(1): 13–27. doi.org/10.22146/pcd.v8i1.414

Silas, Johan. 1992. 'Government-community partnerships in kampung improvement programmes in Surabaya'. *Environment and Urbanization* 4(2): 33–41. doi.org/10.1177/095624789200400204

Simanungkalit, Panangian. 2023. 'Mengatasi 12,7 juta "backlog" perumahan [Overcoming the 12.7 milllion housing backlog]'. *Kompas*, 25 August. www.kompas.id/baca/english/2023/08/24/mengatasi-127-juta-backlog-perumahan

Soekarno. 1960. *Marhaen and Proletarian*. Modern Indonesia Translation Series. Cornell University.

Suhartini, Ninik and Paul Jones. 2023. *Beyond the Informal: Understanding Self-Organized Kampungs in Indonesia*. Springer.

Syahputra, Andika. 2023. 'Transportasi massal bus listrik kota Medan dan dukungan PLN [Mass electric bus transport in Medan city and support from the state electricity company]'. *Detik*, 15 December. www.detik.com/sumut/berita/d-7089220/transportasi-massal-bus-listrik-kota-medan-dan-dukungan-pln

Syuhada, Ginanjar, Adhadian Akbar, Donny Hardiawan, Vivian Pun, Adi Darmawan, et al. 2023. 'Impacts of air pollution on health and cost of illness in Jakarta, Indonesia'. *International Journal of Environmental Research and Public Health* 20(4): 1–14. doi.org/10.3390/ijerph20042916

USAID. 2017. 'Real impact: Indonesia. Indonesia urban water, sanitation, and hygiene project'. USAID. https://2012-2017.usaid.gov/sites/default/files/documents/1865/IUWASH_Real_Impact_Case_Example_051713_508.pdf

van Mead, Nick. 2016. 'The world's worst traffic: Can Jakarta find an alternative to the car?' *The Guardian*, 23 November. www.theguardian.com/cities/2016/nov/23/world-worst-traffic-jakarta-alternative

von Luebke, Christian. 2009. 'The political economy of local governance: Findings from an Indonesian field study'. *Bulletin of Indonesian Economic Studies* 45(2): 201–30. doi.org/10.1080/00074910903040310

Warburton, Eve. 2016. 'Jokowi and the new developmentalism'. *Bulletin of Indonesian Economic Studies* 52(3): 297–320. doi.org/10.1080/00074918.2016.1249262

Winarso, Haryo and Tommy Firman. 2002. 'Residential land development in Jabotabek, Indonesia: Triggering economic crisis?' *Habitat International* 26(4): 487–506. doi.org/10.1016/S0197-3975(02)00023-1

Wiryono, Singgih and Icha Rastika. 2023. 'Soal IKN, Anies: Bangun kota di tengah hutan timbulkan ketimpangan baru [Regarding the new capital, Anies: Building a city in the middle of the forest creates new inequalities]'. *Kompas*, 22 November. https://nasional.kompas.com/read/2023/11/22/12245121/soal-ikn-anies-bangun-kota-di-tengah-hutan-timbulkan-ketimpangan-baru

World Bank. 2016. *Indonesia's Rising Divide: Why Inequality Is Rising, Why it Matters and What Can Be Done*. World Bank. http://documents.worldbank.org/curated/en/267671467991932516/Indonesias-rising-divide

2 Shifting modalities of urban governance: Indonesian cities over the long term

Abidin Kusno[1]

If there is an assumption in urban historiography that every epoch will produce a governing regime appropriate to its time, Indonesia is perhaps a fine case in point. In 1950, soon after the transfer of sovereignty from the Dutch to the new republic, the Indonesian government convened the Congress of Healthy Housing for the People (Kongres Peroemahan Rakjat Sehat) in Bandung. The political leaders of the newly independent Indonesia were aware of the housing gap in colonial rule and regarded *peroemahan rakjat* (people's housing) as one of the major goals of the Indonesian revolution. In 1952, during the second congress in Jakarta, Vice-President Mohammad Hatta indicated that this goal 'won't be realised in two years. It won't be completed in ten or twenty years. However, in forty years or in half a century we will be able to fulfil our wish, if we are committed and make effort with confidence' (Hatta 1954: 254).

Yet, by the 1970s, with the violent death of Sukarnoist socialism and the rise of Suharto's New Order, the notion of *peroemahan rakjat* (with its association of the state's mass housing program supported by community self-help, which Hatta (1954: 257) called '*auto-aktivitet*' and '*gotong-royong*') had eroded into a failed utopia of the past. The new political regime, encouraged by international development agencies such as the World Bank, preferred to enable the private capital market to determine the prices of land and housing. This shift at once ensured urban development would be, above all, an arena for business interests. For the next several decades, the Indonesian city was governed by an urban growth coalition

---

1 I thank Robert Cribb, Edward Aspinall and Amalinda Savirani for their helpful comments on an earlier version of this chapter.

that consisted of the president and other government elites, the military and business groups. By the mid-1980s, fuelled by neoliberal ideas of deregulation and privatisation, it was clear the government's urban development program was being driven by the short-term interests of capitalist modernisation, not by any long-term vision of social planning for the public, as was perhaps envisioned by Hatta.

The episodes above indicate the historical characteristics of two different eras—the early postcolonial period with its emphasis on social programs and people's housing, and the authoritarian New Order with its emphasis on capitalist growth. But they also point to another important phenomenon: the evolution of Indonesian national politics is often tied to changes in urban politics, but shifts in policy often involve not only a break with the past, but also a continuity (often in hybrid form) with what came before. Today, in the time of *reformasi* and its afterlife, there is still something from the past that seems to persist, and this chapter seeks to explore this persistence in order to understand the modalities of governing urban Indonesia over time. It points to key continuities in patterns of urban governance over the long term, especially in the application of governing styles that developed out of colonial rule and its spatial politics.

To begin my exploration, I first sketch the initial reception to decentralisation ideas and policies in Indonesia in the 1980s, and how this reception strengthened the Indonesian urban growth coalition during the second half of Suharto's New Order. I then historicise the character of this coalition by identifying some practices from the colonial era, with a focus on the ways in which the relatively autonomous domain of *kampung*—self-built settlements in urban neighbourhoods—were governed. The chapter then moves forward to our time to reflect on how urban governance and urban politics in the post-*reformasi* era have been shaped by the habitus of the earlier times. This chapter therefore does not seek to present a comprehensive picture of the history of urban governance in Indonesia, or to chronologically cover every era. I skip the 1940s–1960s period to focus on some practices of the past that continue to shape or haunt the culture of urban governance in Indonesia today. I discuss mainly Jakarta and its surrounding areas, but I hope some of the lessons and questions raised by my analysis could serve as a material for discussing issues in other Indonesian cities.

The 1980s turning point

The 1970s and the 1980s are generally considered to be a very challenging period for central governments worldwide. In the advanced capitalist countries, global recessions in the mid-1970s and early 1980s, deindustrialisation and the growing global reach of multinational companies provided grounds for a reduction in the role of central governments, making way for a broader space for market rationality and privatisation. This shift quickly became a global trend. From the mid-1980s, powerful international organisations, such as the World Bank, began promoting 'decentralisation' to developing countries, often as part of so-called structural adjustment programs. These organisations recommended the 'devolution of governmental responsibilities from strong central governments to localities' (Miraftab et al. 2008: 1). Local and/or city governments were now expected to engage with market principles or business models by partnering with what were presumed to be more efficient non-state actors such as private companies and civil society organisations. This shift, in turn, would create more inclusive and democratic governance—so went the aspiration.

In Indonesia, a similar but also different set of challenges came to the fore. In the mid-1980s, leaders of the Indonesian state had become aware of the serious impacts of the recent world recession and falls in oil prices. Meanwhile, public demands for more equitable distribution of benefits from development were on the rise. One analyst of the time described the difficulties facing the central government as 'probably the greatest since the establishment of the New Order' (Hadad 1983: 3). With few financial resources to rely on, President Suharto called for a 'tightening of our belts' and 'assistance and participation of the whole Indonesian people' (ibid.: 4). The government reached a consensus that the state alone could no longer bear the cost of development, and that the concept of development itself had to be broadened to incorporate increased participation of private sector actors and 'community self-help'. But such an expanded concept of development did not involve a distribution of power. Instead, it simply meant a 'delegation of authority', such as to 'the district head as an official of the central government at the district level' (Hendrata 1983: 29). Be that as it may, under this new approach large cities would come to serve as a coordinator of various stakeholders: government institutions, the private sector and the wider community. They would become 'national centers, provincial (subnational) centers, centers in remote (transmigration) areas' (Firman 1991: 20).

But Indonesian cities were not so prepared to play such a role. Part of the problem, as Schiller (1991: 25) points out, lay in the government's institutional culture:

> There are a wide range of government agencies with overlapping responsibilities in urban plan preparation and in local plan enforcement ... those responsible for plan preparation and those responsible for plan enforcement are often in different institutions, and the quality of communications between those preparing plans and those who manage

urban development is often poor. Those charged with preparing plans often do not take full account of the urban manager's need to respond quickly to changing urban development needs, and those charged with enforcing plans often do not take the time to find out what considerations and priorities were behind land use and urban service plans.

Meanwhile, by the mid-1980s rapid urban expansion had been taking place in major cities and their outlying areas (Firman 1991). This process had de-ruralised the hinterland, pushing more and more farmers into the city where many found themselves working in the informal sector. Haphazard development in cities and their outskirts had exerted tremendous pressure on the social and natural environments surrounding the urban centres.

This combination of bureaucratic inefficiency and haphazard urban development benefited the private sector, including President Suharto's family and cronies. From the 1980s, it was increasingly clear that Jakarta was being subjected to the interests of an elite growth coalition consisting of the central government (ruled by the president and his *keluarga besar*, or extended family), the city government (led by a governor with a military background) and a consortium of business partners. They formed what Malo and Nas (1996) called a 'strategic group' that was central to the functioning of a state-led corporatist structure (MacIntyre 1991). This structure was a system that incorporated various elements of Indonesian society through state-controlled associations, organised around the head of the central government, who stood at the apex, and a tight control of citizen participation. Around the president were the military, business groups and other submissive members of the coalition who, in turn, were surrounded by a series of subsidiary groups, institutions and other intermediaries. At the periphery were the common people (*rakyat*). The *rakyat* were the most important inhabitants of the city, but they were not part of the strategic group and, according to Malo and Nas (1996: 130), 'they are not organized and do not promote common plans'.

I discuss the various intermediaries and the governing of the *rakyat* below; it is sufficient for now to indicate that this corporatist structure enabled top-down government by ruling elites whose coalition was capable also of harnessing international development agencies to serve their interests. In the 1980s and the 1990s, the interests of the regime's core strategic group largely drove development of Jakarta and its surroundings, as the centre of capital investment. Rio Tambunan, a former head of the Jakarta Dinas Tata Kota (Urban Planning Bureau) recalled that 'land use could be easily changed following the wishes of property developers' (Tambunan 2002). An illustrative example is in order, but first we consider a prior approach from the 1970s.

Jabotabek: Domestic politics, global power and urban form

In the early 1970s, the United Nations commissioned a group of international experts to help the Indonesian government in formulating a spatial plan to help guide Jakarta's growth (Cowherd 2005; Giebels 1986).[2] A team of Dutch planners proposed a spatial plan that covered Jakarta, Bogor, Tangerang and Bekasi, known then as Jabotabek. The Dutch team basically tried to transplant the concept of Dutch national planning (known as the Randstad-bundled deconcentration) onto Jakarta and the surrounding province of West Java where Jakarta is located.[3] The idea, therefore, was to deconcentrate Jakarta by encouraging high density growth in the region's subcentres.

The first team proposed in 1973 a masterplan of a linear T shape in which the subcentres would be organised around a railway line that connected Tangerang in the west, Bekasi in the east and Bogor in the south. There were good reasons for such a configuration. The team was aware that informal practices of bribery and corruption, rather than any formal rules, governed Indonesian cities. Regulations were often unenforceable, so land use restrictions would likely be useless. Thus, the only way to avoid such practices setting the direction of Jakarta's development was to use infrastructure, such as the proposed T-line railway, to stimulate both formal and informal development. Specifically, by building the proposed railway line, they hoped to concentrate development along an east-west corridor, leaving intact watershed protection areas in the south-east and the south-west—the Serpong-Depok Aquifer Zones. Furthermore, it was hoped the railway's domination would reduce reliance on roads and cars. In 1981, a second team went further, encouraging urban development along the east-west corridor by crossing the north-south railway line with more east-west corridors (Cowherd 2005).

However, by the late 1980s, the government had abandoned this linear masterplan. Why? The growth coalition of the Suharto regime had come up with a different plan. They preferred roadways over a railway network, as automobiles seemed to promise a speedier drive towards market liberalisation and privatisation of everyday life. The flow of automobiles and toll road businesses would bring an American-style suburban lifestyle to Jakarta (Cowherd 2005), and it would also handsomely reward

---

2 This section is drawn from the account of Lambert J. Giebels (1986), a planner from the Dutch National Physical Planning Agency, who assisted Cipta Karya, a bureau for planning and human settlements of the Ministry of Public Works, and from a fine analysis of Robert Cowherd (2005). See also Stolte (1995).
3 West Java and the Netherlands have almost the same land area.

the toll road developers and operators—who included the president's own children.

Accordingly, in 1993, a new Jabotabek team endorsed a plan to build a Jakarta Outer Ring Road as the central supporting scaffolding for urban development (Cowherd 2005: 179). This configuration effectively countered the earlier masterplan. We do not know the details of how the new Jabotabek plan managed to displace the earlier version, but the new Ring-Radial (Concentric) Model plan would increase land values along the ring of development, and such spatial configuration around Jakarta would allow the city to be accessed by cars from all sides. The new model thus favours real estate development, toll road developers and automobile industries. We also do not know what deals were made between the government and business leading to the change, but the new concentric plan soon developed into a 'finger model' that encouraged low-density sprawling urbanisation in the form of New Towns in the ecologically sensitive regions south-east and south-west of Jakarta. As if to speed up the expansion, between 1985 and 1999, the National Land Agency issued land permits for developers to develop 80,000 hectares around the outskirts of Jakarta (Silver 2008: 164). Clusters of new developer-built towns mushroomed around the ring road and its offshoots. This pattern of development sacrificed the aquifer recharge zone and agricultural lands around Jakarta and added to traffic pressure both in Jakarta and in the surrounding suburbia (Douglass 2010).

The role of global urban governance

While more research is needed to consider the extent of the involvement of the World Bank, Asian Development Bank, International Monetary Fund, USAID, and the United Nations Centre for Human Settlements (now known as UN-Habitat) in this change of urban form, the Integrated Urban Infrastructure Development Program (IUIDP) that these groups sponsored included the development of an urban road system for Jakarta and surrounding areas, among other components (Schiller 1991; Schulte Nordholt 1995; Steinberg 1991).

The IUIDP, which was introduced in 1985, was founded on the principles of 'speed and simplicity' in its approach to urban planning (Zaris et al. 1988: 16). It introduced various innovations to urban planning in Indonesia, the most important of which was a new emphasis on public-private partnerships (PPPs). According to Mitchell-Weaver and Manning (1991–92: 55), PPPs are a form of 'corporatism' where 'several parties have combined forces—established an institutional relationship—in order to define and/or accomplish various developmental objectives'. Initially an industrialised-country public policy prescription, its presence in Indonesia in the 1980s reflected not only the global spread of new policy ideas but also the dependence of the Indonesian government on first world donors to finance infrastructure projects. As part of structural adjustment programs, PPPs came to Indonesia to promote privatisation, deregulation and decentralisation. The question, however, is to what extent PPPs have been adapted to the tradition of Indonesian corporatism and private rule over Indonesian urban development, leading to the proliferation of privately run new town and suburban development projects around Jakarta referred to above.

While the PPP model in theory requires collaboration between government and the private sector on an equal footing, in practice it was shaped by the structure and logic of New Order corporatism. All of the agencies and groups that took part in PPPs—the Department of Home Affairs, various regional and local planning agencies, the National Land Agency, Ministry of (Population and) Environment, Department of Industry, regional investment boards, developers and entrepreneurs, and urban residents and community groups—were themselves never free of state control (Schulte Nordholt 1995). Their bargaining power was tied to the positions they occupied in the New Order's corporatist structure and in the informal system of rent-seeking and capital accumulation that operated through it. As a result, the new PPP approach was itself wide open to practices of collusion and favouritism, with illegal fees (*pungutan liar*, or *pungli*) being widespread and the private actors participating in these projects becoming more dependent on government, not less.

The consultants for the IUIDP claimed that the program would accommodate 'the needs, capabilities and potential' of the Indonesian situation (Zaris et al. 1988: 18–19). They also said the IUIDP was an example of 'action planning' in contrast to the 'conventional planning mechanism', which they criticised as 'clumsy' and unsuitable for the accelerated development of developing countries (ibid.: 13). The IUIDP organised urban planning around an action-oriented approach based on a strategic assessment of 'speed' and 'practicality'. As time was of the essence, according to this approach, those in charge of the new plan were not interested in visions that would require long-term planning. Instead, they indicated that the IUIDP:

> is focussed on action ... it aims to facilitate those [short to medium-term development] decisions and promote development. It does not seek to place some mystical significance on what the town will be like in 20 years; instead it recognises that the long-term pattern results from the aggregation of a whole series of [short-term] development decisions,

some taken by government agencies, but most taken by private agencies or individuals over which government has relatively little control. (Zaris et al. 1988: 18–19)

The consultants did not make clear what had made the government lag behind; what they suggested was that private sector actors were very much prepared to embrace the new emphasis on short-term projects, and act on them right away. Yet, while government had relatively little direct control over the new urban projects being pioneered by private agencies, it was still crucial to the informal deals that facilitated them.[4]

The upshot of the episode was that the neoliberal ideas and interests promoted by the World Bank and other international development agencies, notably their advocacy of privatisation and of short-term and quick implementation of fast-track projects (Peck and Theodore 2015), proved to be quite compatible with the existing cultural setting and political structure of New Order Indonesia. The new approach was easily incorporated into the logic of Suharto's growth coalition. In other words, it posed no challenge to the habitus of rule in an Indonesian context that had developed out of colonial relations.

Roots

The Dutch colonial state governed Indonesia through a system of rule that gave space for traditional rulers to govern the colony, albeit in subordinate positions. This hierarchically organised partnership produced a tradition of rule that influenced the governing style of Suharto's New Order. In this section, instead of focusing on the inter-elite coalition that united Dutch colonialists and Javanese traditional rulers (for this system, see for example Sutherland 1979), I focus on how, during the colonial period, the elite (*gusti*) governed the common people (*rakyat/kawula*) through intermediaries who reigned at the level of the *kampung* in both urban (*kota*) and rural (*desa*) areas.

A starting point for this analysis is to recognise that from the early formation of the colonial state, administrative elites installed a system of binary rule that differentiated Europeans from Inlanders (natives), with a separate category of 'Foreign Orientals' for Arabs and ethnic Chinese outside the binary. The colonists divided administrative power between a Europeesch Bestuur (European administration) and Inlandsch Bestuur (Indigenous administration or *pangreh praja*). In urban areas, the

---

4 Schulte Nordholt (1995: 200) indicates he heard a report that the PPP in West Java suggested that the 'public actor must carry the burdens of land dispossession, after which the private actor can rake in his benefits'.

non-Europeans lived in distinct compounds under their own leaders. Thus, there were Kampung Cina, Kampung Arab, Kampung Melayu, Kampung Bali, and so on, in the major towns and cities of colonial Indonesia. Each *kampung* was governed by a chief from the respective community. These chiefs were known variously (depending on time and space) as *lurah/bekel/petinggi/jaro/kuwu*, and they governed the *rakyat* using the local political traditions of their groups. Hanif Nurcholis, a scholar of public administration, referred to them as *pemerintahan semu/palsu* (pseudo government) (Nurcholis n.d.). The leaders were first nominated by either *bupati* (district head) or other formal officials before they were elected by members of *kampung* communities. Other than this, most of the time, the colonial state refrained from intervening in the local affairs of these *kampung*. Members of the various ethnic groups built their own houses, with their own methods, on the spaces the colonial authorities allocated to them. The authorities referred to these *kampung* as *inlandse gemeenten* (indigenous districts) but they were not governmental units. Instead, they were considered a 'community' space and, relatively autonomous, they received no public services.

How did the relatively autonomous urban *kampung* fit with the centralised structure of the Netherlands Indies government? And how might the colonial past enable us to understand the way *kampung* are governed today? Peter Nas (1990: 102) indicates that it was not until 1925 that the government abolished the *inlandse gemeenten* as separate entities and incorporated *kampung* into city-wide government. European council members (who represented European citizens) pushed for this change because they were concerned about the potential spread of disease caused by unsanitary conditions in the *inlandse gemeenten*. Be that as it may, the *kampung* occupied a huge urban area and, even after incorporation, the municipalities lacked the financial capacity and knowledge to administer them. Thus, as far as issues of governance were concerned, for most of the colonial period, the Indonesian *kampung* remained outside municipal jurisdiction even thought they were situated within the territory of the municipality.

If we spatialise the indirect rule of the Dutch colonial era, we see that the colonial system of governance divided Indonesian cities into planned or built areas (*bebouwde kom*) reserved for private companies and individuals, in which property ownership was recognised, and unplanned areas (*niet bebouwde kom*) where *kampung* with their local systems of land tenure were located (Santoso 2009). This created a dualism within the Dutch administration of colonial space. The *Atlas van Tropisch Nederland* provides a good sense of spatial administration (KNAG 1938). Published in 1938, the atlas demarcated Dutch administrative boundaries (which represented the *bebouwde kom*) but showed very little evidence of the boundaries of native areas (which we could understand as under *niet bebouwde kom*). Throughout the Dutch colonial era, *kampung* remained an area of neglect, if not a blind spot, for the colonial administration.

The colonial government's officials realised how little they knew about *kampung* and their inhabitants. In Jakarta and elsewhere, when urban officials sought to improve the living conditions of the urban masses, their programs were often insensitive to *kampung* life (Frederick 1989: 9). The budgets allocated to such programs were very low. Accordingly, they barely served even as preventive measures against further deterioration of living conditions in the *kampung*. The colony being the colony, there was no Housing Act (like the one in the Netherlands) that produced social housing for the working class. As Freek Colombijn (2011: 438) indicates: 'public housing was to some extent an alien concept in colonial Indonesia. The economy of the Dutch East Indies was essentially a liberal one and most construction was undertaken by the private sector. Why should the government bother to provide public housing at all?'.

Throughout the colonial era the private sector was at the forefront of urban development. It produced privately built housing for private individuals who owned or rented. It also built housing for companies and government employees. This production of space contributed to the expansion of *bebouwde kom*. Meanwhile the common people continued their practices of 'self-help housing' in the *niet bebouwde kom* of *kampung*. In Johan Silas's words (2005: 10), they '*me-rumah-kan sendiri* (housed themselves)'. Today, we understand the latter as housing in the 'informal' domain. This colonial housing policy prefigures a participatory strategy of rule which involves the business sector and the common people through their own efforts (*usaha masyarakat*).

Perhaps because of this long neglect, *kampung* dwellers often saw initiatives to improve *kampung* settlements, which began in major cities in the 1920s, as hostile interventions. In Surabaya, according to Frederick (1989: 7), Indonesians saw the establishment of the municipality in the early twentieth century as a form of aggression directed against *kampung* folk. The introduction of a drinking water system which required payment by *kampung* dwellers led to misunderstandings, so did municipal taxes on bicycles and markets. The *kampung* folk of Surabaya viewed such innovations as 'unjust impositions made by a foreign, incomprehensible administrative system to which *kampung* people were subject but did not belong' (ibid.: 9). They also viewed with suspicion the Indonesian elites who served in the municipal councils. While some Indonesian elites did work on behalf of *kampung* folk (but generally without meaningful results due to the limits set by the colonial government), they generally understood their struggles to be associated with national politics instead of municipal politics. They were after all not *kampung* people themselves. They were interested in, but had little in common with, the *rakyat* who inhabited the *kampung*. In Jakarta, Abeyasekere (1987: 124) points out, the rift or antagonism in urban society was less between the coloniser and the colonised, but between the municipality and *kampung* folk.

In short, in the colonial city, there was a profound gap between the government and the world of the urban masses. Even today, *kampung* people often view the city government (and its backers, such as the bureaucracy, the military, business groups and international development agencies) with distrust and even fear. Out of this historical rift, too, the anti-*kampung* attitudes of urban elites and city planners have developed in tandem with urban development policy (see chapter by Siagian, this volume).

The key point is that the gap that exists between government and *kampung* is in part a legacy of the system of indirect rule through which the Dutch governed their colony. For most of the colonial period, the *desa* and the urban *kampung* were outside the colonial government's responsibility, even though the Dutch could always break through the autonomy of *kampung* when it served their interests to do so. The attitude of non-interference was always politically and economically motivated. Leaving the *rakyat* alone as much as possible was a way for colonial rulers to diminish the risk of rebellion; promoting 'self-help' obscured their unwillingness to distribute resources to promote 'native welfare' or to build infrastructure that could integrate urban *kampung* settlements into the city.

Yet, while colonial authorities boasted that they were preserving the integrity of *desa* and *kampung*, they never left them alone. On the contrary, the worlds of *desa* and *kampung* were filled with stories of exploitation and taxation imposed by governing elites. The Inlandsch Bestuur, and its informal apparatus of thugs, was responsible for this side of colonial rule. Below the formal structure of government thus lay a locally run shadowy world of operators who served as intermediaries between the ruling elites and the subalterns—a system that has lingering legacies to the present.

The local intermediaries

These intermediaries were essentially a manifestation of indirect rule, because they often worked informally for both the elites above them and for the *rakyat* who relied on them for connection with the world of power outside the *kampung*. Today, Indonesians know such intermediaries with terms such as *jawara, preman, oknum* and *ketua* (headmen) of certain *ormas* (social organisations) that rule the streets, markets, parking lots, sidewalks and some neighbourhoods of major cities in Indonesia, running protection rackets and other forms of thuggery (Barker 2009; Ryter 1998; Wilson 2015). Such groups developed out of the colonial system of indirect rule which gave autonomy to local headmen to rule, often by way of thuggery.

To understand the local practice of indirect rule, we need to briefly discuss politics in rural Java. It may seem out of context to set a rural scene for an understanding of urban politics, especially in the rapidly growing areas such as Batavia/Jakarta. However, as far as *kampung* were concerned, rural traditions have often been transplanted into the urban environment either by the authorities or by the *kampung* people themselves. Moreover, one of the popular sayings about the capital city has been that 'Jakarta is not a city, but a conglomeration of villages' (Malo and Nas 1996: 100).

Onghokham (2003) was one of the first scholars to notice the political importance of local-level coercion and intimidation in colonial Java. In his study of lord and peasant relations in the Madiun region of East Java in the nineteenth century, he noticed the crucial role of thugs who served as intermediaries between the local *bupati* and the peasants. Onghokham argued that in the late nineteenth century, the colonial state was trying to govern the villages, but because it lacked a tool with which it could control villagers directly, it resorted to a system of rule that gave opportunities to local intermediaries, powerbrokers and thugs of various styles to reign in the villages. These actors were known categorically as *jago* (literally fighting cocks or champions).

The figure of the *jago* took various forms, and was known by various names, across time and space (van Till 2011). Often, their power lay in their ability to serve as informants and agents of both higher-level authorities and the villagers. Needed both by the ruler and the ruled, such figures became the organisers of a 'partnership of expectation' between the two divided worlds (Onghokham 2003: 140), even though they were often unreliable and their information was largely untrustworthy. Still, for the colonial state, they constituted an important non-official apparatus for keeping colonial *rust en orde* (peace and order) (ibid.: 143). The Dutch knew that their policies had little sway in the world of *desa* and *kampung*. The local political bosses eased their task of maintaining control. It therefore was in Dutch interests that the Inlandsch Bestuur worked with *jago* to rule in the *desa* and the *kampung*. Such a deal worked in both rural and urban settings, especially before the modernisation of the police force in the 1920s.

This system of informal rule might have declined after the modernisation of the police force, but it never disappeared. Margreet van Till (2011: 176) argues that in the early twentieth century the people living in *kampung* in Batavia's suburbs relied on 'self-appointed "protectors"', which included 'the *preman, jago*, tax collectors and religious leaders'. To be sure, the local-level strongmen have changed a great deal in postcolonial times, alongside the changing sociopolitical environment (Ryter 1998). The earlier types, which were mostly rooted in rural life, have evolved into new urban types ranging from the well-known *preman* groups which dominate informal security arrangements in most cities, through many other categories that shade into various forms of religious and state authority such as *jawara, oknum, kyai, pak haji, dukun* and *pak lurah*. Individually or collectively, they constitute a shadowy area of power that is not always easy for the state to govern, and which defies easy analysis and categorisation by outside observers. Collectively, such actors constitute a security apparatus that combines formal and informal practices (and which in today's urban centres is increasingly being supplemented by professional and technologically driven security actors: see Wilson, this volume). Government officials and private actors alike can mobilise such forces to evict *kampung* dwellers and clear land for private urban development, but such actors themselves still constitute an important force occupying the space between local communities and the state, a space that (local) government agencies have never been able to fully control (Barker 2009; Wilson 2015).

The past in the present

Skipping the era of the Japanese occupation, the Revolution and the early post-independence Sukarno–Hatta period allows us to feel that we have come full circle.[5] If we move forward to the early 1970s—about the same time as Dutch experts proposed a linear public transport system for Jakarta, as discussed earlier—the Indonesian government implemented a housing strategy that seemed to follow the colonial pattern mentioned earlier (Leaf 1993; Silas 2005): housing for the upper middle class was privately built by property developers (represented by Real Estate Indonesia, the peak organisation of property companies, established in 1972). A few years later, in 1975, a national housing company called Perumnas (Perumahan Nasional) was created to build houses for the formal workers, with priority given to civil servants. Meanwhile, the relatively poor population and workers in the informal sector were accommodated in the 'self-help'

---

5 For Jakarta's urban history from 1942 to 1966, see Abeyasekere (1987).

kampung housing, most of which was built on the informal land market, with or without the support of the Kampung Improvement Program.[6]

This arrangement has profoundly shaped the contemporary urban form of Jakarta. It has divided the Indonesian city further into different classes and managed to keep *kampung* as non-government units on lands that resemble the colonial status of *niet bebouwde kom*. Throughout the New Order period and into the present, *kampung* are either left alone and unattended or are opened to development and land speculation. Under the pretext of *pembangunan* (development), *kampung* were subjected to evictions throughout the New Order. These evictions used various methods from gentle to harsh: *bujukan, ganti rugi, kebakaran, buldoser, intimidasi* (persuasion, compensation, arson, bulldozer, intimidation) (Dorleans 1994: 56–61). Using these methods were various intermediaries (continuing the role of such liminal actors from the colonial period) in the form of the contemporary *jago*, such as *preman*, as well as the police and the army. Media of the time typically characterised the methods of evictions as *'brutal, sembrawut, kacau, kaku dan selalu memilukan'* ('brutal, confusing, chaotic, inflexible and always agonising') (ibid.: 57).

With the army's support, the old *rust en orde* was perfected with a series of new measures characteristic of Suharto's New Order. First was the exercise of biopower: the control of *desa* and *kota* through the discourse of a 'clean environment' to erase any remnants or traces of communist threats, supplemented by the building of an apparatus of social control through the extension of mechanisms (created under Japanese occupation) such as the *rukun warga* (citizens' association) and *rukun tetangga* (neighbourhood association) system of neighbourhood governance. Second was the militarisation of the built environment through the establishment of supplementary security forces known as *satpam* (private security), *hansip* (civil defence) and *gardu/posko* (security posts) (see Wilson, this volume). Third was the interiorisation of public spaces through the building of shopping malls, and the elimination of sidewalks to prevent crowds from gathering on the streets. Army control was further sustained by the appointment of military men as *kepala daerah* (regional heads, that is, governors or mayors), especially in important

---

6   Some *kampung* received support through the Kampung Improvement Program (KIP), which was inspired by Dutch *kampongs verbetering* in the 1920s. The KIP was launched by Governor Ali Sadikin in 1968 and supported by the World Bank from 1974 to 1982 to provide basic urban services such as footpaths, water drainage and sanitation. Since the 1980s the KIP has evolved into various schemes and has changed from a physical approach to community-based development. See Silas (2005).

provinces and major cities. Despite the top-down repressive political system, the *kampung* continued to be governed by its sociocultural beliefs, some of which were drawn from the rural imaginary of the supernatural and the ghosts that took the form of the urban criminals—a belief that perfected the state of criminality (Siegel 1998).

In some ways one could argue that the political control structure of the New Order was a hybrid production interweaving colonial, precolonial and postcolonial models of governance. Comparing Law 5/1974 on Local Government with the organisation of the Dutch colonial state in the early twentieth century, Heather Sutherland (1979: 159) comments:

> even the legal basis of the two regimes was much the same. Indeed, given the great changes of the last few decades in Java, it is surprising how many similarities remain between Pangreh Praja [colonial 'native' administration] traits and contemporary administrative characteristics. Officials again served to maintain popular political obedience; councils were again subordinate to men appointed by the center—a uniformed Beamtenstaat [civil service state] in the making.

For Indonesian scholars, the principles of regional administration as outlined in Law 5/1974 laid out the governing function of heads of various levels of regional government (governor, *bupati* or district head, mayor, and *camat* or subdistrict head), in terms drawn from 'the traditional civil service (*pamong praja*) since precolonial times' (Hendrata 1983: 30). The *pamong praja's* primary function, according to Ismid Hadad (1983: 6), 'has been to collect tribute and taxes from the people in the interests of the rulers. They were not accustomed to serving the needs of the poor'. Malo and Nas (1996: 100) conclude that:

> post-independence Jakarta has basically retained the centralist metropolitan government traits so characteristic of most of its colonial history ... despite frequent administrative reorganization, Jakarta has always been a highly penetrated system with limited local autonomy and restricted citizen participation.

As far as the urban form is concerned, throughout much of the New Order, the 'strategic group' introduced at the start of this chapter transformed the city of Jakarta through a series of presidential decrees that exempted well-connected business partners of Suharto from planning controls. Some of these decrees created path-dependency for subsequent urban development, some of which continue to this day, such as reclamation in Jakarta Bay. Under the New Order, regulation was flexible; environmental controls were weak; planning was a joke. The period of the 1980s and 1990s, according to Tambunan (2002) was marked by the violation of many urban regulations, which were meant to control urban growth but instead became a tool for speculation. For example, the Location Permits (Izin Lokasi) issued to developers, which were meant to guide land use, became tickets for the National Land Agency and developers to sell and resell land which they had no intention of building on in accordance with the provisions of their permits. Similarly, administrators could readily adjust the city's spatial planning by-laws for the benefit of developers: for instance, reducing the target for green space from 37.2 per cent of the city's land area in the 1965–1985 by-laws to just 13.94 per cent in the 2005–2010 by-laws (*Jakarta Post* 2009).

We have thus inherited a mess from the Suharto era. In Jakarta, a damaged urban form has degraded the natural environment, and it cannot be easily fixed. Residents of Jakarta are forced to live at a point of no return … except perhaps imagining an 'escape from Jakarta'.

Back to (speculating on) the future

While post-Suharto governors and mayors have inherited a mess, including the exploitative hierarchical tradition of corporatism, they are perhaps in a better position to deal with it than their New Order predecessors. Political decentralisation in 1999 devolved resources and responsibilities from the central government to the districts and municipalities at the subprovincial level. Local leaders now possess a larger share of state resources, and local legislative councils (DPRD) can also shape the fate and fortune of mayors and governors, and of the districts and municipalities they control.

Under these conditions, what has happened to the New Order–era growth coalition of the strategic group? I would suggest that political decentralisation has given local governments the opportunity to organise their own corporatist growth coalitions. The business groups that survived the financial crisis that accompanied the collapse of the New Order can see in today's political landscape multiple ways of adapting their investment strategies to fit with the political culture of the regions, especially in areas where the local governments aspire to upgrade the property values of their cities. Decentralisation has also made it easier for city governments to directly engage some sectors of urban development with the global world—for better or worse. Direct access to deals with international donor groups and multinational corporations offers city governments more opportunities to market their assets. They can also brand their locality in the image of a global city, with a huge impact on the urban form. The old model of public-private partnership has adapted to the new circumstances, though it continues to rely on both formal and informal security actors. Thanks to the deepening of democratic consciousness, meanwhile, there are more attempts to invite participation from civil society groups, such as non-government organisations and universities, who work with or on behalf of the common people, in urban planning and decision-making.

Overall, the value of post-Suharto decentralisation remains uncertain. There are recorded cases with varying degrees of success (such as Semarang, Solo and Surabaya), there are cases that raise only questions (such as South Tangerang).[7] For sure, mayors today behave more like political entrepreneurs, and they tend to consider their long-term career advancement, often by pursuing popular short-term welfare and beautification projects. Quite a few simply reproduce the traditions of the Suharto era in their own locales.

During his successful campaign for the presidency in 2014, Joko Widodo (Jokowi)—after serving as governor of Jakarta from 2012 to 2014—stated that the pressure to change the oppressive political culture of Suharto would take, in his words a (national) 'mental revolution'. He claimed that, after the fall of Suharto, reforms had merely aimed at institutional revamp:

> None has yet focused on the mindset or the culture of politics in Indonesia ... there is still a large number of *tradisi* [traditions] or *budaya* [cultures] that are evolving and growing rapidly, creating repression as in the New Order. These range from corruption, intolerance of differences, greed, selfishness, a tendency to use violence in problem solving, legal harassment, and opportunism. These are still going on, with some going more rampant ... It is time to take corrective action ... by imposing a mental revolution. (Widodo 2014)

Setting aside the observation that at least several of these conditions have worsened since he became president (see Power and Warburton 2020), Jokowi claimed that he started this movement when leading Surakarta (Solo), where he served as mayor (2005–2012), and continued it in Jakarta. It was not until the 2014–2017 term of his successor, Governor Basuki Tjahaja Purnama (Ahok), that the tensions or conflicts between different corporatist entities (which formed the traditional web of relations underpinning government in Jakarta) became more visible. We heard about the shaking of City Hall's bureaucratic culture; the mistrust between the governor and the city council; the battle with *preman*; the tough negotiation between business groups and the governor; radical Islamic groups' campaign against Ahok; internal divisions among community organisations; tensions within civil society; and continuous

---

7 For these cases and more, see other chapters in this volume, especially by Azizah, Elyda, Mustafa and Permana.

clashes between City Hall and *kampung* dwellers (Kusno 2023). It is not clear if these conflicts were an expression of 'mental revolution', but they certainly strained the old tradition of 'harmony from above' and 'consensus from below'.[8]

The discarding of the centralised system of governance and the transfer of various mandates to local governments may have shaken the repressive *tradisi* or *budaya* bequeathed from the Suharto era. The democratic principles of transparency, accountability and participation as well as direct elections of governors and mayors (which can produce a new type of elected leadership) have perhaps changed the power relations game in the city (and the nation). But change in the structure of (urban) governance does not mean an end to old patterns of informal relations. Beneath the official bureaucracy, one can imagine a restructuring of old relations is taking place in and through local political cultures. The social groups that constituted the building blocks of traditional corporatism are now relatively independent or free. They may continue to find a place for themselves simply by reconstituting old relations within the new circumstances (van Klinken and Aspinall 2010). Predatory practices can survive within a participatory framework as spaces are still available for collusion and corruption among local interest groups. Only case-by-case studies will be able to consider if the local government of today is less corrupt and more efficient in its delivery of public goods and services than those of the past, and if the marginalised *rakyat* are better served and more empowered to assert their interests in urban planning and development outcomes.

For the urban poor, post-*reformasi* decentralisation has offered opportunities to participate in urban politics (typically with the assistance of non-government organisations and community groups). They can form alliances and make deals with politicians and the city government to safeguard their communities (Savirani and Aspinall 2017). On the economic side, they are more exposed to the costs and benefits of engaging in speculative enterprises, especially by financialising their *kampung* land. They, too, can become investors by making their *kampung* land bankable. The recent financialisation of the *kampung* land market (promoted by the World Bank following the call of Hernando de Soto) has increasingly compromised the *kampung's* traditional sociality (Astuti et al. in prep.; Kusno 2013). What we have seen in the past few years (especially in Jakarta) is an increasing number of 'self-evictions' among

---

8 For a discussion on how 'harmony is strongly determined from the top, while real consensus should emanate from the bottom' in the local politics of the Suharto era, see Malo and Nas (1996: 121–23).

kampung dwellers as they sell off their land (after certification) to interested developers. With the dissolution of the informal land market, the urban *kampung* have entered the web of financial capitalism, breaking down the longstanding division between *kampung* and private property zones in the city. They have become more marketable—and more unaffordable—for the urban poor.

Decentralisation offers Indonesian cities a chance to change, to compete and to speculate. Arguably, what has changed most over recent decades, however, is the extent of environmental degradation. The perennial issues of housing, *macet* (traffic congestion), *banjir* (flooding), as well as the relatively new issue of poor air quality, are being worsened in Jakarta by the impending threat of climate change, which evidently is beyond the city's governing capacity to control. In this context, it perhaps makes sense that President Widodo revived the idea of building a new capital, in faraway Kalimantan, with the idea of decentralisation for the nation-state coming to mean something like a withdrawal from Jakarta, an escape from its dystopic present. Perhaps it is not so disastrous for Jakarta to sink after all, so long as the nation-state can be saved by moving the capital city to a more 'natural' setting in a place presumably without a colonial history, where a smart city can be planned.

It remains to be seen whether in such a space a new form of governance and urban democracy could emerge. This chapter serves as a reminder that old political cultures continue to evolve with new urban forms. It shows how the shifting modalities of governing urban Indonesia from the colonial era to our time are shaped by enduring power relations that evolve in and through the transformation of urban forms.

References

Abeyasekere, Susan. 1987. *Jakarta: A History*. Oxford University Press.

Astuti, Wahyu K., Abidin Kusno and Regina Suryadjaja. in prep. 'Kostplatform and the financialization of Jakarta's kampung'. Paper under revision for *Indonesia*.

Barker, Joshua. 2009. 'Negara Beling: Street-level authority in an Indonesian slum'. In *State of Authority: The State in Society in Indonesia*, edited by Joshua Barker and Gerry van Klinken, 17–46. Cornell University Press. www.jstor.org/stable/10.7591/j.ctv1nhm5g

Colombijn, Freek. 2011. 'Public housing in post-colonial Indonesia: The revolution of rising expectations'. *Bijdragen tot de Taal-, Land-en Volkenkunde* 167(4): 437–58. doi.org/10.1163/22134379-90003579

Cowherd, Robert. 2005. 'Does planning culture matter? Dutch and American models in Indonesian urban transformations'. In *Comparative Planning Cultures*, edited by Bishwapriya Sanyal, 165–92. Routledge.

Dorleans, Bernard. 1994. 'Perencanaan kota dan spekulasi tanah di Jabotabek [Urban planning and land speculation in Jabotabek]'. *Prisma: The Indonesian Indicator* 2(XIII): 41–61.
Douglass, Michael. 2010. 'Globalization, mega-projects and the environment: Urban form and water in Jakarta'. *Environment and Urbanization ASIA* 1(1): 45–65. doi.org/10.1177/097542530900100105
Firman, Tommy. 1991. 'Some thoughts on urban development policy'. *Prisma: The Indonesian Indicator* 51: 17–22.
Frederick, William H. 1989. *Visions and Heat: The Making of the Indonesian Revolution.* Ohio University Press.
Giebels, Lambert J. 1986. 'JABOTABEK: An Indonesian-Dutch concept on metropolitan planning of the Jakarta-region'. In *The Indonesian City: Studies in Urban Development and Planning*, edited by Peter J.M. Nas, 101–15. Foris Publications.
Hadad, Ismid. 1983. 'Development and community self-help in Indonesia'. *Prisma: The Indonesian Indicator* 28: 3–20.
Hatta, Mohammad. 1954. *Kumpulan Karangan Mohammad Hatta* [Collection of essays by Mohammad Hatta]. Vol. 3. Penerbit Balai Buku Indonesia.
Hendrata, Lukas. 1983. 'Bureaucracy, participation and distribution in Indonesian development'. *Prisma: The Indonesian Indicator* 28: 21–32.
Jakarta Post. 2009. 'More green space!' *Jakarta Post* editorial, 7 November.
KNAG (Koninklijk Nederlandsch Aardrijkskundig Genootschap). 1938. *Atlas van Tropisch Nederland.* KNAG.
Kusno, Abidin. 2013. *After the New Order: Space, Politics, and Jakarta.* University of Hawai'i Press. doi.org/10.21313/hawaii/9780824837457.001.0001
Kusno, Abidin. 2023. *Jakarta: The City of a Thousand Dimensions.* NUS Press. doi.org/10.2307/jj.6338490
Leaf, Michael. 1993. 'Land rights for residential development in Jakarta, Indonesia: The colonial roots of contemporary urban dualism'. *International Journal of Urban and Regional Research* 17: 477–91. doi.org/10.1111/j.1468-2427.1993.tb00236.x
MacIntyre, Andrew. 1991. *Business and Politics in Indonesia.* Allen and Unwin.
Malo, Manasse and Peter J.M. Nas. 1996. 'Queen city of the East and symbol of the nation: The administration and management of Jakarta'. In *The Dynamics of Metropolitan Management in Southeast Asia*, edited by Jürgen Rüland, 99–131. ISEAS Publishing.
Miraftab, Faranak, Christopher Silver and Victoria A. Beard. 2008. 'Situating contested notions of decentralized planning in the Global South'. In *Planning and Decentralization: Contested Spaces for Public Action in the Global South*, edited by Victoria A. Beard, Faranak Miraftab and Christopher Silver, 1–18. Routledge.
Mitchell-Weaver, Clyde and Brenda Manning. 1991–92. 'Public-private partnerships in third world development: A conceptual overview'. *Studies in Comparative International Development* 26(4): 45–67. doi.org/10.1007/BF02743762
Nas, Peter J.M. 1990. 'The origin and development of the urban municipality in Indonesia'. *Sojourn* 5(1): 86–112. www.jstor.org/stable/41056790

Nurcholis, Hanif. n.d. 'Sejarah pemerintahan lokal/daerah di Indonesia [History of local/regional government in Indonesia]'. Modul 1, MAPU5204. https://pustaka.ut.ac.id/lib/wp-content/uploads/pdfmk/MAPU5204-M1.pdf

Onghokham. 2003. *The Thugs, the Curtain Thief, and the Sugar Lord: Power, Politics, and Culture in Colonial Java*. Metafor Publishing.

Peck, Jamie and Nik Theodore. 2015. *Fast Policy: Experimental Statecraft at the Thresholds of Neoliberalism*. University of Minnesota Press. doi.org/10.5749/minnesota/9780816677306.001.0001

Power, Thomas and Eve Warburton, eds. 2020. *Democracy in Indonesia: From Stagnation to Regression?* ISEAS Publishing. doi.org/10.1355/9789814881524

Ryter, Loren. 1998. 'Pemuda Pancasila: The last loyalist free men of Suharto's order?' *Indonesia* 66: 44–73. doi.org/10.2307/3351447

Santoso, Jo. 2009. *The Fifth Layer of Jakarta*. Graduate Program of Urban Planning—Centropolis, Tarumanagara.

Savirani, Amalinda and Edward Aspinall. 2017. 'Adversarial linkages: The urban poor and electoral politics in Jakarta'. *Journal of Current Southeast Asian Affairs* 36(3): 3–34. doi.org/10.1177/186810341703600301

Schiller, Jim. 1991. 'Public and private participation in urban planning: A political economy perspective'. *Prisma: The Indonesian Indicator* 51: 23–33.

Schulte Nordholt, Nico. 1995. 'New forms of urban infrastructural development policy in Indonesia'. In *Issues in Urban Development: Case Studies from Indonesia*, edited by Peter J.M. Nas, 193–208. Research School CNWS.

Siegel, James. 1998. *A New Criminal Type in Jakarta: Counter-Revolution Today*. Duke University Press. doi.org/10.1515/9780822382515

Silas, Johan. 2005. 'Perjalanan panjang perumahan Indonesia dalam dan sekitar abad XX [The long journey of Indonesian housing in and around the twentieth century]'. In *Kota Lama Kota Baru: Sejarah Kota-kota di Indonesia*, edited by Freek Colombijn et al. Ombak Press.

Silver, Christopher. 2008. *Planning the Megacity: Jakarta in the Twentieth Century*. Routledge.

Steinberg, Florian. 1991. 'Urban infrastructure development in Indonesia'. *Habitat International* 15(4): 3–26. doi.org/10.1016/0197-3975(91)90043-K

Stolte, Wim. 1995. 'From Jabotabek to Pantura'. In *Issues in Urban Development: Case Studies from Indonesia*, edited by Peter J.M. Nas, 228–45. Research School CNWS.

Sutherland, Heather. 1979. *The Making of a Bureaucratic Elite*. Heinemann Educational Books.

Tambunan, Rio. 2002. 'Tata ruang Jakarta diubah atas pesan sponsor [Jakarta's spatial layout was changed based on a sponsor's message]'. *Suara Pembaharuan*, 3 March.

van Klinken, Gerry and Edward Aspinall. 2010. 'Building relations: Corruption, competition and cooperation in the construction industry'. In *The State and Illegality in Indonesia*, edited by Edward Aspinall and Gerry van Klinken, 139–64. KITLV Press. doi.org/10.1163/9789004253681_009 van Till, Margreet. 2011. *Banditry in West Java, 1869–1942*. NUS Press. doi.org/10.2307/j.ctv1qv167

Widodo, Joko. 2014. 'Revolusi mental'. *Kompas*, 10 May.

Wilson, Ian Douglas. 2015. *The Politics of Protection Rackets in Post–New Order Indonesia: Coercive Capital, Authority and Street Politics*. Routledge. doi.org/10.4324/9780203799192

Zaris, Roslan, Tom Carter and Ian Green. 1988. 'An action plan approach to strategic urban development planning: A case study from Indonesia'. *Habitat International* 12(4): 13–19. doi.org/10.1016/0197-3975(88)90004-5

3 Urbanisation in Indonesia: Demographic changes and spatial patterns, 2000–2020

Meirina Ayumi Malamassam and Luh Kitty Katherina

More than half of the world's population currently lives in urban areas. As reported by the World Bank (2023), the global urban population share has increased markedly from only about one-third in 1960 to 57 per cent in 2022, pointing to the occurrence of urbanisation—the process by which a growing proportion of a country's population lives in urban areas—in many parts of the world (Firman 2018; Jones and Mulyana 2015). However, an absolute increase in the size of the urban population does not necessarily indicate urbanisation. As pointed out by Crankshaw and Borel-Saladin (2019), an increasing number of urban inhabitants over a particular period is not always accompanied by a significant growth in the urban population share. The growth of the urban population can only be considered urbanisation when its rate exceeds that of national and/or rural population growth.

Observers often consider migration from rural to urban areas to be the main cause of urbanisation (examples in the Indonesian mass media include Nugraheni 2022 and Utami 2023). However, urbanisation can also result from other reasons, such as natural population increase and reclassification of rural areas as urban areas (Dyson 2011; Zelinsky 1971). Natural population increase can be the major contributor to urbanisation when urban areas experience lower mortality rates and higher fertility rates than rural areas (Crankshaw and Borel-Saladin 2019). Further, in several countries, such as the United States and India—and, as we shall see, Indonesia—the reclassification of a rural locality as urban can also play an important role in increasing urbanisation rates (Firman 2018; Jain and Korzhenevych 2020; Jiang et al. 2022). Indeed, compared to other causes of urbanisation, reclassification can have a more direct effect on changing the size and structure of urban populations (Jiang et al. 2022).

Scholars generally agree that urbanisation is a crucial factor in accelerating economic development (Zhang 2016). Higher urban population shares can lead to higher national incomes and productivity rates. Certainly, high-income countries have higher urban population shares, at around 81 per cent, than middle- and low-income countries, respectively at 53 per cent and 34 per cent (World Bank 2023). Variations in the share of urban population can also be observed across regions of the world. As illustrated in Figure 3.1, more than 80 per cent of the populations in North America, and Latin America and the Caribbean, reside in urban areas. Meanwhile, less than half of South Asians and sub-Saharan Africans do so. The United Nations Department of Economic and Social Affairs has pointed out that the urbanisation rates of countries with a high share of urban populations are generally slower since they have reached saturation in urban growth (UNDESA 2018). In contrast, those with a low share of the urban population, such as less-developed countries, have greater potential to experience accelerated urbanisation along with economic development. More than half of the population of East Asia and the Pacific—a region with enormous variation in economic development between countries—live in urban areas.

Figure 3.1 Proportion of urban population in 2020 across world regions

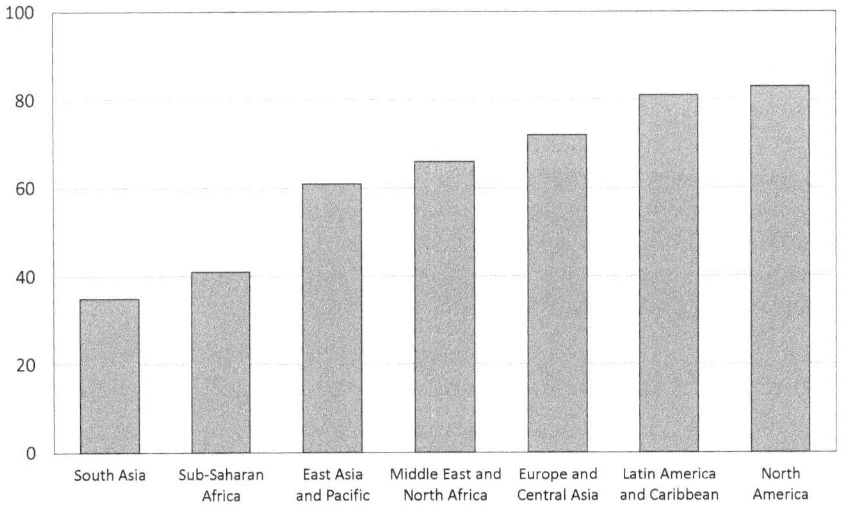

Source: World Bank (2023).

Turning to the topic of this chapter, urbanisation has been a major feature in Indonesia's population dynamics for the past 20 years. From 2000 to 2010, the annual average rate of urban population growth in the country was 3.3 per cent, nearly twice the average growth rate of the total population in the period. From 2010 to 2020, urban population growth slowed to 2.8 per cent annually. However, this decrease was in line with slower overall population growth of about 1.5 per cent per year during the same period. Statistics Indonesia projects the population growth rate will decrease further in the next 30 years (BPS 2023b). This might mean that the urban population growth rate will also drop. Nonetheless, it will continue to exceed the total population growth rate. Thus, urbanisation is expected to continue in the future. Given this situation, exploring urban population dynamics is essential for understanding future trends in regional development in Indonesia and for planning the country's development path.

Accordingly, this chapter examines the relatively rapid process of urbanisation that has occurred in Indonesia over the past two decades. In doing so, it analyses data on population profiles and rural-urban classification to identify the key demographic changes and spatial patterns driving urbanisation in Indonesia. We find that reclassification of rural areas as urban areas has been a major driver of urbanisation. Our study also sheds light on the potential implications of urbanisation patterns across regions in the country. The chapter is divided into five sections. In the first section we sketch out in broad terms the trends in urban and rural population growth. The next section considers whether demographic drivers, such as different rates of growth of the urban and rural populations, and rural-to-urban migration, can explain Indonesia's rapid urbanisation. We then explore the reclassification of rural localities as urban and the formation of new urban localities, concluding that the former process has been a major driver of the increase in Indonesia's urban population. Next we discuss spatial patterns of urbanisation, especially the startlingly high degree of urbanisation in the Java-Bali region, and finally we conclude by pointing to some implications of Indonesia's rapid urbanisation, and raising the question of whether the country's system of classifying urban areas needs modification.

Changes in Indonesia's urban population, 2000–2020

The proportion of Indonesia's population classified as urban has increased significantly in the past 60 years. In 1960, Indonesians who lived in urban areas comprised about 15 per cent of the total population (World Bank 2023). It took about 30 years to double this proportion. In 2011, the urban proportion of the population passed 50 per cent. In 2020, it was reported that about 56 per cent of Indonesian residents lived in urban areas (BPS 2023a). However, there are wide variations in urbanisation trends across regions in the country, as indicated in Table 3.1.

Among all regions, only the Java-Bali region has the majority of its population living in urban areas. In 2020, two out of three Java-Bali residents lived in urban areas. In contrast, only about a third of people in Eastern Indonesia lived in urban areas. However, all regions have experienced a significant increase in the proportion of their populations living in urban areas. In addition, in terms of absolute numbers, the total urban population in regions beyond Java-Bali has doubled in the past 20 years.

Despite a slowdown over the years, the growth rate of the urban population in all regions has exceeded their total population growth rates. Further, regions beyond Java have shown a higher rate of urbanisation than the national rate over the past ten years. Among Indonesia's major regions, Eastern Indonesia (which includes West Nusa Tenggara, East Nusa Tenggara, Maluku, North Maluku, West Papua and Papua) has had the highest urban population growth. In the past two decades, its urban population growth rate was above 4 per cent annually. Meanwhile, Sulawesi was the region with the lowest urban population growth rate between 1990 and 2000. In recent years, the Java-Bali region—which has by far the largest urban population—has shown the lowest urban population growth rate—fitting the general pattern, mentioned above, that urban growth rates tend to decline as the urban share of the population increases.

Table 3.1 also demonstrates uneven distribution of the urban population in Indonesia. In 2020, approximately two-thirds of the urban population of the country lived in the Java-Bali region. Although this region's share of the urban population has slightly decreased, the concentration of the urban population in this region—which comprises only about 7 per cent of the total land area of Indonesia—has persisted over time. The slow decline of this region's share of Indonesia's total urban population is in line with its slowing population growth rate, which is mainly attributed to lower fertility rates. As reported by Statistics Indonesia (BPS 2023a), all provinces in the Java-Bali region have fertility rates below the replacement level of 2.1. The region with the second-highest share of urban population is Sumatra. One in six urban residents in Indonesia live in this region. Unlike the Java-Bali region, the share of urban population in Sumatra has remained relatively steady over time.

Table 3.1 further reveals that very low shares of the urban population live in Kalimantan, Sulawesi and Eastern Indonesia. The urban populations in Eastern Indonesia and Kalimantan, which combined comprise almost

Table 3.1 Urbanisation trends across regions in Indonesia, 2000–2020

Region and year	Total population (millions)	Urban population (millions)	Urban population (%)	Annual rate, total population growth (%)	Annual rate, urban population growth (%)	Share of Indonesia's urban population (%)
Indonesia						
2000	201.1	85.4	42.4	1.2	4.4	–
2010	237.6	118.3	49.8	1.7	3.3	–
2020	275.7	155.5	56.4	1.5	2.8	–
Sumatra						
2000	40.5	14.0	34.5	1.1	4.2	16.4
2010	50.6	19.8	39.1	2.3	3.6	16.7
2020	60.0	26.6	44.3	1.7	3.0	17.1
Java-Bali						
2000	124.1	60.5	48.8	1.2	4.5	70.9
2010	140.5	82.3	58.6	1.3	3.1	69.6
2020	158.7	105.3	66.3	1.2	2.5	67.7
Kalimantan						
2000	10.9	4.0	36.3	1.9	4.7	4.7
2010	13.8	5.8	42.1	2.3	3.8	4.9
2020	17.1	8.3	48.7	2.2	3.7	5.3
Sulawesi						
2000	14.4	4.0	27.9	1.4	3.8	4.7
2010	17.4	5.8	33.6	1.9	3.8	4.9
2020	20.3	8.4	41.1	1.6	3.6	5.4
Eastern Indonesia						
2000	11.2	2.9	25.6	0.3	4.9	3.3
2010	15.3	4.6	30.0	3.2	4.9	3.9
2020	19.7	7.0	35.6	2.6	4.3	4.5

Source: Authors' calculations based on data from BPS (2001, 2012, 2023a).

two-thirds of the country's total land area, are less than 10 per cent of the total urban population. However, their shares have gradually increased over time. This increase was also in line with the considerable increase in the share of the total population in these regions, a change which can mainly be attributed to high birth rates, particularly in Eastern Indonesia provinces. Also, a significant shift in out-migration patterns in recent years has contributed to the increase in the population share in these regions.

While provinces in Java Island are still prominent destinations for internal migration in Indonesia, the share of out-migrants moving to Kalimantan and Eastern Indonesia has increased significantly (Malamassam 2022; Sukamdi and Mujahid 2015).

The growth of the urban population can also be observed by the increasing number of cities and districts (*kota* and *kabupaten*) with high urban populations (Table 3.2). In 2020, Indonesia had 39 districts with urban populations over one million, a significant increase from only 19 such districts in 2000 (BPS 2000, 2023a). In addition, in 2020 there were 40 districts with an urban population of 500,000–1,000,000 and 47 districts with urban populations of 300,000–500,000, up from 27 and 25 districts in 2000, respectively. As indicated in Table 3.2, districts with an urban population of more than one million are not only those with the status of autonomous city (*kota*), but they can also be found among *kabupaten*—an administrative unit generally thought of as being a rural district. Most of these districts are situated in the areas surrounding major autonomous cities. For example, Bogor, Tangerang and Bekasi districts surround the periphery of Jakarta province; Bandung district is located just next to Bandung city; Sidoarjo district is adjacent to Surabaya city; and Deli Serdang district surrounds Medan city.

In addition to their spatial distribution, a critical aspect to consider when examining urban population profiles in Indonesia is their age composition. Figure 3.2 illustrates the changing structure of the age composition of urban and rural Indonesians in 2000, 2010 and 2020. It can be seen that there have been considerable changes in age structures over time.

In 2000, the proportion of young adults in urban areas was noticeably higher than in rural areas. In addition, the broader base of the rural pyramid in 2000 represented the demographically young population in this area. In 2010, a difference in the proportion of young working age groups living in urban and rural areas can still be easily observed. However, by 2020 the urban and rural population pyramids look remarkably similar. Both areas displayed relatively equal proportions across population subgroups below 40 years. This pattern reflects a gradual shift towards higher age groups within the age structures of both urban and rural areas. Also, the relatively similar share of different age groups, particularly in the children and young adult age groups, in both pyramids reflects a low fertility rate and high life expectancy in both areas.

Table 3.2 Cities and districts in Indonesia with urban populations over one million, 2000–2020

2000	2010	2020	
Bandung (2.7)	Bogor (3.8)	Bogor (5.2)	South Tangerang (1.4)
Surabaya (2.6)	Surabaya (2.8)	Bandung (3.7)	Jember (1.3)
East Jakarta (2.3)	East Jakarta (2.7)	East Jakarta (3.1)	Cianjur (1.2)
Bandung (2.1)	Bandung (2.7)	Tangerang (3.1)	Bandar Lampung (1.2)
Bogor (2.0)	Bandung (2.4)	Bekasi (3.1)	Batam (1.2)
Tangerang (1.9)	Bekasi (2.3)	Surabaya (2.9)	Sleman (1.1)
Medan (1.9)	Tangerang (2.3)	Bekasi (2.6)	Central Jakarta (1.1)
West Jakarta (1.9)	West Jakarta (2.3)	Medan (2.5)	Banyuwangi (1.1)
South Jakarta (1.8)	Bekasi (2.1)	Bandung (2.5)	Bogor (1.1)
Bekasi (1.6)	Medan (2.1)	West Jakarta (2.4)	Banyumas (1.1)
North Jakarta (1.4)	South Jakarta (2.1)	South Jakarta (2.2)	Indramayu (1.1)
Palembang (1.4)	Tangerang (1.8)	Depok (2.1)	Tegal (1.1)
Sidoarjo (1.3)	Sidoarjo (1.8)	Cirebon (2.1)	Brebes (1.0)
Tangerang (1.3)	Depok (1.7)	Sidoarjo (2.1)	Pekanbaru (1.0)
Semarang (1.3)	North Jakarta (1.6)	Tangerang (1.9)	
Depok (1.1)	Cirebon (1.6)	Karawang (1.9)	
Cirebon (1.1)	Semarang (1.5)	North Jakarta (1.8)	
Makassar (1.1)	Palembang (1.4)	Palembang (1.7)	
Deli Serdang (1.0)	Deli Serdang (1.4)	Semarang (1.7)	
	Makassar (1.3)	Deli Serdang (1.6)	
	South Tangerang (1.3)	Sukabumi (1.6)	
	Karawang (1.3)	Garut (1.5)	
	Malang (1.2)	Malang (1.5)	
	Garut (1.0)	Makassar (1.4)	
	Jember (1.0)	West Bandung (1.4)	

Note: The number in parentheses is the urban population in millions. Shaded cells are districts (*kabupaten*); unshaded cells are autonomous cities (*kota*).

Source: Authors' calculations based on data from BPS (2000, 2010b, 2023a).

Drivers of urbanisation: Population growth and migration

When it comes to explaining the growth of Indonesia's urban population, it is useful to start with two explanations that have traditionally had much sway in the Indonesian literature: population increase, and rural-urban migration.

With respect to the former explanation, it is obvious that variations in the population structure across urban and rural areas can be influenced by differences in demographic indicators, notably fertility and mortality. If fertility rates are higher, and mortality rates lower, in one part of the population than another, then the population share of that part of

Chapter 3 Demographic changes and spatial patterns, 2000–2020   53

Figure 3.2   Population pyramids of urban and rural Indonesia, 2000–2020 (millions)

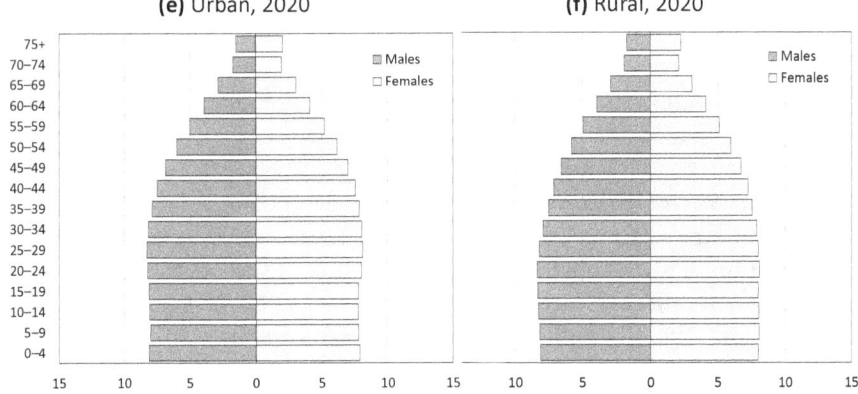

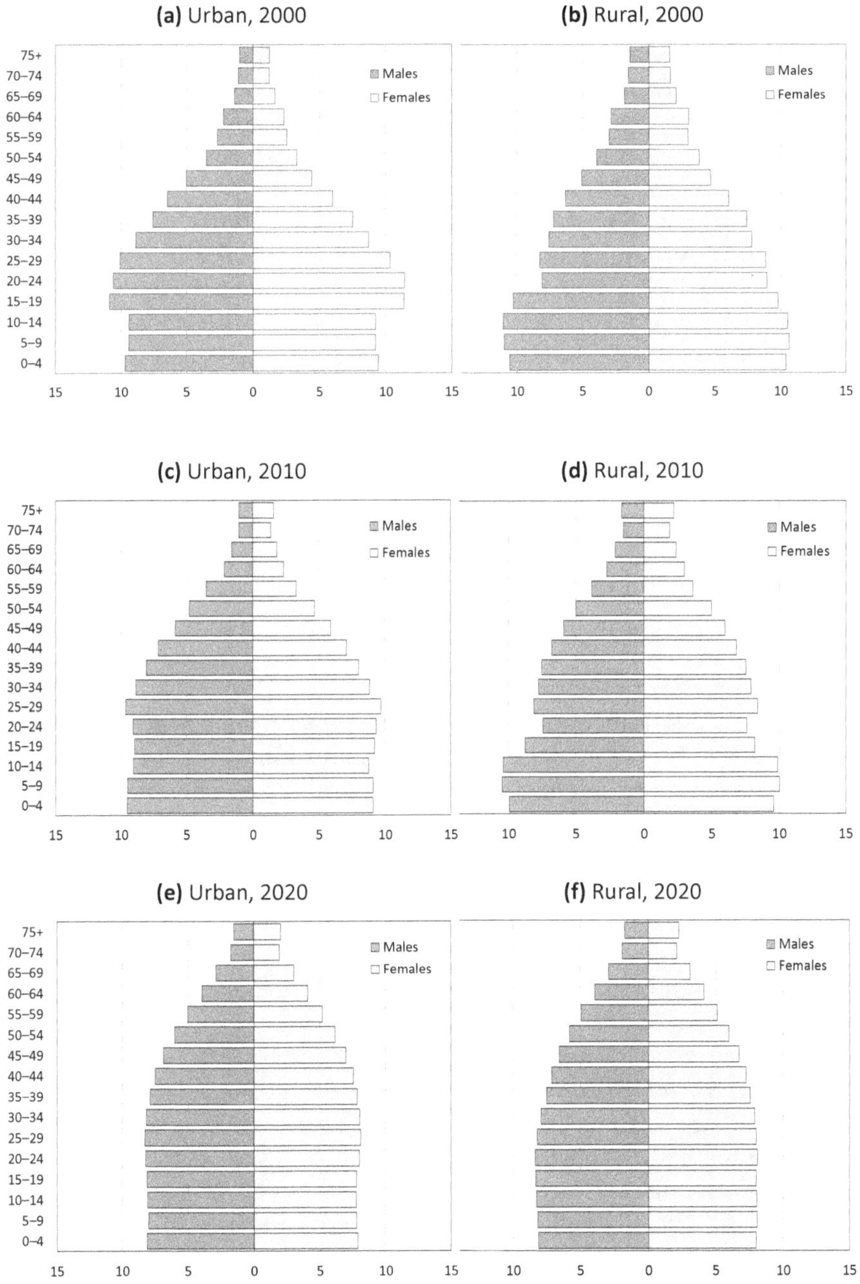

Source: Authors' calculations based on data from BPS (2001, 2012, 2023a).

the population will increase over time. In the 1960s and 1970s, it was commonly argued that such natural increase was making a greater contribution to urbanisation in the country than other drivers such as rural-urban migration and reclassification of localities' status (UNESCAP 1981, cited in Firman 2004). More recently, however, the National Population and Family Planning Agency (Badan Kependudukan dan Keluarga Berencana Nasional, BKKBN) indicated that fertility rates in urban Indonesia (2.4 births per woman) were slightly lower than those in rural areas (2.5 births per woman) (BKKBN 2019), while the number of deaths in urban areas in the past five years was higher than in rural areas. Since 2017, about 4.4 million urban households have experienced at least one death, compared to only 3.3 million rural households (BPS 2023a). With this situation, one would expect population growth in urban areas to be slower than in rural areas. Additionally, we would expect the ageing of the population to be more apparent in urban areas (Jones and Mulyana 2015). However, the trend in Indonesia's urban population size and structure suggests the opposite: the population is growing more rapidly in urban than in rural areas, and the urban population is also ageing less rapidly. Therefore, urbanisation today cannot be attributed solely (or even mainly) to natural population increase.

Scholars often point to rural-to-urban migration as an alternative explanation for urbanisation. Fox (2012), in an analysis of African trends, for example, argued that migration from rural to urban districts in response to working opportunities in manufacturing and service sectors in cities has been the major cause of urbanisation in that continent. In Indonesia, rural-to-urban migration has been a prominent pattern within the spatial structure of internal migration, particularly in the form of intra-province and intra-island migration (Malamassam 2022). Given the situation of low birth rates in urban areas, Jones and Mulyana (2015) have argued that the young age structure in urban areas has mainly been attributable to rural-urban migration. Urban regions offer a wide range of working opportunities, both in formal and non-agricultural informal sectors. These opportunities can work as a strong pull for in-migration to urban areas, particularly among young adults.

In fact, in the 1990s, as the natural increase rate of urban areas slowed, there was a general consensus that internal migration was a very important contributor to urban population growth in Indonesia (UNESCAP 1993). At this time, about two-thirds of urban growth was attributed to migration from rural areas (Douglass 1997). Jones and Mulyana (2015) found that urban areas had over three times the proportion of recent migrants compared to rural areas. However, the rate of recent internal migration in Indonesia has slowed from about 3 per cent in 1990 to 1.8 per cent in

2020 (BPS 2016, 2023a). This suggests that rural-urban migration, while still significant, is less important than it once was in the growth of the urban population. Instead, we should look to other factors, such as the transformation of rural into urban areas.

Reclassification and proliferation of urban areas

Urbanisation is fundamentally a matter of whether the population share is increasing in areas that are classified as being urban in a particular country. Different governments, as well as different international organisations, can and do apply different classification systems to distinguish between urban and rural locales.

In Indonesia, rural-to-urban reclassification occurs at the level of *desa* (village) and *kelurahan* (ward). *Desa* and *kelurahan* are the lowest-level government or administrative units in Indonesia, and are located directly below the *kecamatan* (subdistrict). Generally speaking, people think of *desa* as being rural and *kelurahan* as urban (the two units are also governed differently: for example, *desa* have elected village heads, while *kelurahan* are headed by appointed civil servants). However, the rural and urban status discussed in this chapter refers not to this administrative status, that is, whether a location is classified as a *desa* or *kelurahan*, but to the classification made by Statistics Indonesia based on localities' development levels. It is important to note that the classification of some localities might differ from their governance status: thus there are *desa* that Statistics Indonesia classifies as being urban and *kelurahan* that it classifies as rural (see also the discussion by Rahman, Haerudin and Octaviano, this volume).

Statistics Indonesia releases a list of urban and rural localities every ten years, shortly before the population census begins. The organisation bases its classification of localities on scoring of three main criteria: population density (scores range from 1 to 8), proportion of agricultural households (scores range from 1 to 8) and access to urban facilities (scores range from 0 to 9). The indicators for each criterion are presented in Table 3.3. With a maximum possible score of 25, a locality is classified as urban if its score is equal to 9 or higher.[1]

---

1 This classification method has been used since the 2000 Population Census. However, there was a slight change in the indicators used prior to the 2020 census. The possible maximum score in 2000 and 2010 was 26 and a locality was classified as urban if its cumulative score was equal to or higher than 10. In these periods, Statistics Indonesia listed ten indicators for the access to urban facilities criterion. However, it removed access to a movie theatre from the list in the 2020 census.

Table 3.3 Indicators for rural-urban classification in Indonesia, 2020

Criteria	Indicator	Score
(1) Population density per km^2	<500	1
	500–1,249	2
	1,250–2,499	3
	2,500–3,999	4
	4,000–5,999	5
	6,000–7,499	6
	7,500–8,499	7
	≥8,500	8
(2) Proportion of agricultural households (%)	≥70.00	1
	50.00–69.99	2
	30.00–49.99	3
	20.00–29.99	4
	15.00–19.99	5
	10.00–14.99	6
	5.00–9.99	7
	<5.00	8
(3) Access to urban facilities	Kindergarten (TK) available within 2.5 km radius	1
	Lower secondary school (SMP) within 2.5 km radius	1
	Upper secondary school (SMA) within 2.5 km radius	1
	Public market within 2 km radius	1
	Shopping centre within 2 km radius	1
	General or maternity hospital within 5 km radius	1
	Hotel/billiard centre/pub/discotheque/karaoke place/beauty shop present	1
	Proportion of households using cable telephones ≥2%	1
	Proportion of households using state-owned electricity (PLN) ≥95%	1

Note: For criteria (1) and (2), scores are derived from a single indicator, ranging from 1 to 8. For criterion (3), the score is accumulated from nine indicators (with total scores ranging from 0 to 9). Thus, the possible cumulative score from the three criteria ranges from 2 to 25. A locality is classified as an urban area if its cumulative score is equal to or greater than 9.

Source: BPS (2020).

With this background in mind, it is apparent that there will be two types of rural-to-urban reclassification that might be influential in Indonesia: changes in the classification of existing localities from rural to urban, and the formation of new urban localities due to the proliferation of subdistricts or districts (a process known in Indonesian as *pemekaran*).

The results of the rural-to-urban reclassification in the census have a crucial impact on determining the spatial coverage of urban areas in Indonesia and, in turn, affect the growth of the urban population—or, in other words, the growth of the population classified as urban. We find that reclassification has a significant impact on urbanisation in Indonesia. As presented in Table 3.4, the proportion of all localities (i.e. *desa* and *kelurahan*) classified as being urban in Indonesia has increased from 19 per cent in 2000 to 21 per cent in 2010 and 35 per cent in 2020. A particularly significant increase in the number of urban localities can be observed between 2010 and 2020, rising from 15,786 to 29,640 urban localities—an increase of approximately 90 per cent.

Table 3.4 indicates there was not a significant increase in the share of urban localities in all regions in Indonesia between 2000 and 2010. The increase in urban localities was much more pronounced between 2010 and 2020. However, during this time frame, the increase in the proportion of urban localities in the Java-Bali region noticeably exceeded that in other regions. The share of urban localities in this region had already reached more than a third in 2010, while the proportion of urban localities in other regions was still far below this mark. Between 2000 and 2010, the provinces with the highest increase in urban localities in the Java-Bali region were West Java and Banten. During this period, development in

Table 3.4 Urban localities (*desa* and *kelurahan*) in Indonesia by region, 2000–2020

Region	Number of urban localities			% of urban localities		
	2000*	2010	2020	2000*	2010	2020
Sumatra	2,450	3,495	7,131	13.2	14.6	27.8
Java-Bali	7,701	9,508	16,868	30.1	36.7	64.9
Kalimantan	501	688	1,464	8.3	10.1	20.2
Sulawesi	856	1,300	2,517	11.3	13.4	23.7
Eastern Indonesia	523	795	1,660	7.4	7.4	11.5
Indonesia	12,031	15,786	29,640	18.5	20.5	35.3

Note: * Estimated from Population Census 2000 datasets. Not all villages were covered by the 2000 census, so there may be undercounts/overcounts in the estimations.

Source: Authors' calculations based on data from BPS (2000, 2010a, 2020).

these provinces was closely linked to the expansion of industrial activities in the peri-urban areas of Jakarta. Urban growth during that time was significantly influenced by global investment flows (Firman et al. 2007) that fostered industrial activities, leading to the formation and expansion of urban agglomerations, especially around Jakarta.

The increase in the number of urban localities over time might not only occur as a result of the change of localities' status from rural to urban due to their increasing levels of development. It can also result from the creation of new localities through *pemekaran*. Table 3.5 shows the distribution of urban localities across regions in 2020 by origin. It indicates that most of the new urban localities have resulted from rural-to-urban reclassification, with a relatively small number originating from the splitting of existing urban areas. Among all regions, the emergence of new urban areas due to this process is most common in Eastern Indonesia. Overall, we conclude the creation of new urban localities through *pemekaran* has not been a major driver of urbanisation in Indonesia.

Table 3.5 Urban localities (*desa* and *kelurahan*) in Indonesia in 2020 and their origin

Region	Number of urban localities	Existing urban localities from 2010		Urban localities resulting from reclassification		Urban localities resulting from proliferation (*pemekaran*)	
		N	%	N	%	N	%
Sumatra	7,131	3,207	45.0	3,527	49.5	397	5.6
Java-Bali	16,868	9,293	55.1	7,511	44.5	64	0.4
Kalimantan	1,464	663	45.3	722	49.3	79	5.4
Sulawesi	2,517	1,255	49.9	1,106	43.9	156	6.2
Eastern Indonesia	1,660	778	46.9	604	36.4	278	16.7
Indonesia	29,640	15,196	51.3	13,470	45.4	974	3.3

Source: Authors' calculations based on data from BPS (2010a, 2020).

Spatial patterns of urban areas in Indonesia

Distribution of urban localities across regions in Indonesia in 2010 and 2020 can be seen in the maps of the country in Figures 3.3 and 3.4, respectively. More detailed depictions of the spatial patterns of urban and rural areas in each major region are presented in the maps in the Appendix. Significant changes in the spatial patterns of urban localities in Indonesia in 2020 can be easily observed from these maps.

Figure 3.3 Urban localities in Indonesia, 2010

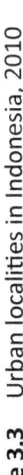

Source: Authors' drawing based on data from BPS (2010a); map boundaries are extracted from geospatial data from Indonesia's Geospatial Information Agency (BIG).

Figure 3.4 Urban localities in Indonesia, 2020

Source: Authors' drawing based on data from BPS (2020); map boundaries are extracted from geospatial data from Indonesia's Geospatial Information Agency (BIG).

Currently, most areas in the Java-Bali region are urban. Looking at the historical trends in this region, Sumitro (1977, cited in Jones 1988: 141) had suggested that Java would eventually become an island city. It appears that this prediction is coming true, with Figure 3.4 showing that Java has evolved into an urbanised island. In the Java-Bali region, the increase in urban localities was concentrated in East Java and West Java during 2010–2020, driven by the expansion of existing urban agglomerations and the formation of urban corridors that extend from East Java to Banten (Firman 2017). In particular, the urban agglomeration of Surabaya is expanding, integrating with Malang, and extending through intermediate urban centres to major cities such as Yogyakarta, Semarang, Bandung, Jakarta and Serang.

When we look at regions outside Java-Bali on the map, it is obvious that there are huge disparities in the country's urban development. As seen in Figure 3.4, urban localities in the Java-Bali region are spread over the island, but in Kalimantan, Sulawesi and Eastern Indonesia they tend to be concentrated in particular districts—which are mostly autonomous cities (*kota*). This pattern reflects persistent problems of development inequality in Indonesia. Even so, many new urban area agglomerations can also be observed in other regions. Sumatra, Kalimantan and Sulawesi have all begun to experience notable increases in urban localities, with more than a fifth of their localities being classified as urban in 2020.

One of the critical aspects of urbanisation in Indonesia is that the process is marked by the transition of urban areas from being concentrated on a single focal point to having multiple centres of activity (Firman 2017). Therefore, many urban agglomerated areas have extended their boundaries in all directions, surpassing their official administrative boundaries (the expansion of Surabaya noted above being just one of the most obvious examples). These expanded areas often also encompass diverse economic entities, often characterised by the coexistence of agricultural and non-agricultural activities near the urban hubs (Champion and Hugo 2004). Figure 3.4 depicts the expansion of urban centres around existing autonomous cities. They are progressively expanding to their surrounding districts or peri-urban areas. This pattern is not exclusive to the Java-Bali region, as cities in other regions are also experiencing substantial urban expansion.

The significant increase in urban localities between 2010 and 2020 is also closely related to intensive infrastructure development efforts. For example, the construction of toll roads throughout the island of Java has connected almost the entire island. Travel time between Jakarta and Surabaya by toll roads now takes only 10 hours, compared to the 20 hours it previously took on the Jakarta-Surabaya national highway. Similarly, toll road construction in Sumatra has recorded significant progress. Since 2020, toll roads have been built in two provinces in the southern part of the island (Lampung and South Sumatra). It is expected that they will reach the northernmost province (Aceh) in 2024. This situation matches the high increase in the number of urban localities in other provinces. In Kalimantan, Sulawesi and Eastern Indonesia, the emergence of several new urban agglomerated areas can be associated with increasing intensity of mining and other extractive industries. Such activities often attract in-migrant workers and encourage the development of urban facilities in areas that previously had rural status. In these and many other areas that experienced rapid development of rural localities, the emergence of urban areas often gives rise to a blurring of the distinction between urban and rural areas (Firman 2004; Mardiansjah et al. 2021; McGee 1991).

As well as toll roads, other government development programs have also played an important role in driving rural-urban reclassification between 2010 and 2020. Under Presidential Regulation 3/2016 on Acceleration of the Implementation of National Strategic Projects, the national government has launched a multitude of infrastructure development schemes to foster regional economic growth. One of the schemes is the development of National Tourism Strategic Areas (Kawasan Strategis Pariwisata Nasional). The government has designated five tourism areas as 'superpriority' destinations under this project scheme: Lake Toba in North Sumatra, Borobudur in Central Java, Mandalika in West Nusa Tenggara, Labuan Bajo in East Nusa Tenggara and Likupang in North Sulawesi. Under the scheme, these areas have been targeted with substantial investments and infrastructure development in the tourism sector. Mandalika, one of the project locations, has undergone landscape changes since the intensive construction of an international street circuit (a motorcycle racetrack) began in 2020. Land use transformation can also be observed in Praya, Central Lombok, since operation of the Lombok International Airport began in late 2011. These construction projects have led to a significant increase in urban localities in the surrounding areas. In the Pujut subdistrict, for instance, where the circuit and airport are located, there were no urban localities in 2010, but six in 2020. A similar trend was observed in Samosir district—part of which is in the middle of Lake Toba. Urban localities in this district expanded from five in 2010 to seventeen in 2020.

One factor that influences the extension of urban areas in Indonesia is the spillover of the urban population into the areas that surround large cities and metropolitan areas. Cities and metropolitan areas have experienced a decrease in their population growth rate in recent years.

However, this decline has been accompanied by simultaneous increases in the population growth rate in their surrounding areas or peripheral regions (Firman et al. 2007; Katherina 2014). In Jakarta, this phenomenon has been evident since the 1980s, and similar trends have been observed in several other major cities across the country since the 1990s, and points to the swelling of expansive peri-urban areas around the major cities, as discussed above.

However, it should also be noted that the expansion of new urban areas can arise from factors not directly linked to urban spillover, one of which is rural industrialisation (Shi and Cao 2020). Katherina (2023) highlighted several case studies of this trend in West Java province. Some new urban agglomerations that were non-existent in 2010 have emerged in 2020 as a result of rural industrialisation and/or the development of other modern sectors. This phenomenon is particularly evident in the southern part of the province, for example, in the Garut and Tasikmalaya districts. The extension and emergence of urban areas in these districts are heavily affected by the development of tourism-related activities.

A final important observation is that urban population growth caused by widescale reclassification of rural localities as urban will likely be linked to significant changes in land carrying capacity and land use. By definition (given the criteria used to determine urban status), such urban areas will tend to be associated with high population densities and decreasing numbers of agricultural households. Indeed, as indicated in Table 3.6, the proportion of agricultural households has decreased remarkably in all regions in the country. In Java-Bali region, in particular, by 2013 only about one out of every three households had at least one member working in the agricultural sector.

Table 3.6 Agricultural households across regions in Indonesia, 2003–2013

Regions	Number of agricultural households		% of agricultural households	
	2003	2013	2003	2013
Sumatra	6,615,985	6,287,602	60.0	48.4
Java-Bali	18,448,237	13,836,731	51.8	35.3
Kalimantan	1,631,251	1,556,229	52.5	42.3
Sulawesi	2,417,439	2,260,964	63.0	53.2
Eastern Indonesia	2,119,272	2,193,943	69.7	57.2
Indonesia	31,232,184	26,135,469	55.2	40.8

Source: BPS (2013).

Accordingly, it is likely that the growth of the urban population is resulting in associated changes in land use, notably the loss of agricultural land. This situation, in turn, can have a great impact on the transformation of agricultural activities and food security in the country. As argued by Rondhi et al. (2019), agricultural land conversion poses a significant threat to Indonesia's food security, particularly its ability to sustain its dependence on rice as a primary staple food. Moreover, Katherina (2023) has pointed out that as regions become more urbanised, agricultural activities tend to decrease, and their contribution to the agricultural sector drops. Several urbanising districts in West Java have experienced a substantial decrease in the productivity of their agricultural sector. By the same token, the contributions of trades and services, as well as transportation and warehousing sectors, have become more prominent in regional incomes.

Conclusion

Our analysis shows that Indonesia has become an urbanised country, with more than half of the population living in urban areas. However, this urbanised pattern is prominent mostly in the Java-Bali region, where the urban share is about two-thirds of the total population. The high level of urbanisation in this core region suggests it is likely to continue to serve as Indonesia's economic powerhouse, although its urban population growth rate has started to decelerate. Kalimantan, which has been designated as the home of Indonesia's new capital city, has experienced a considerable increase in its urban population, with the urban share currently at almost half of its total population. The development of the new capital city and its supporting infrastructure will likely further drive this urbanisation in coming years. By contrast, Eastern Indonesia is the region with the lowest share of urban population. Only about a third of its population is located in urban areas. However, a relatively steady urban population growth rate of about 4 per cent per year in the past 20 years could signal an accelerating pace of urbanisation in this region, too.

We have seen that, over the long term, urbanisation in Indonesia has been influenced by three main causes: natural population increase, rural-urban migration, and the urbanisation of rural areas and resulting reclassification of localities as urban in character (Firman 2017). While our analysis shows that natural population increase and rural-urban migration were important drivers of urbanisation in earlier decades, review of locality classification data from Statistics Indonesia between 2010 and 2020 has shown considerable expansion in the coverage of urban areas. Thus, it can be said that reclassification has played a major role in recent urbanisation in the country.

While this process of urbanisation via reclassification is clearly linked to the development of previously rural areas, our analysis also raises the question of whether the classification method used to judge the rural-urban status of localities in Indonesia should be updated. We believe it should. For the past 20 years, the criteria and scoring system used to ascertain whether a particular locale is urban or rural has remained essentially the same. However, it is possible that the long-used indicators of population density and numbers of agricultural households no longer accurately represent whether a locality is best characterised as urban. The United States, in its 2020 census, changed the minimum threshold for qualification as an urban area from having a minimum of 2,500 persons to at least 5,000 persons or 2,000 housing units, resulting in the reclassification of about 1,000 areas from urban to rural (Ratcliffe 2022:12). The United States also replaced population density with housing unit density as the basis for the delineation of rural and urban areas. The new indicator is considered to be a more direct measure of a developed landscape (ibid.).

There is also a question as to whether the classification of areas into two distinct categories—rural and urban—is sufficient to provide a precise description of the development status of a locality. For example, an urban locality in South Jakarta must have distinctive urban features compared to an urban locality in Eastern Indonesia. There will almost certainly be a wide gap in the quality of urban facilities, for example, higher education facilities or shopping centres, separating these two localities. Thus, people who live in 'urban' areas in less-developed regions may not enjoy similar levels of social services as their counterparts in more-developed regions. When, as analysts, we use the rural-urban dichotomy we tend to assume there is a clear distinction between these two categories. However, the trends in Indonesia, and the huge variation of urban localities, suggest that the distinction between urban and rural regions in the country is blurred. For such reasons, we believe it is necessary to devise an updated threshold that takes into account current trends in regional development and that would assist scholars and policymakers to better understand the delineation of urban and rural areas in Indonesia. The addition of a new category 'semi-urban'[2] should also be considered to cover areas that share both rural and urban characteristics.

---

2   The term 'semi-urban' covers areas with a mix of rural and urban features, and can include peri-urban areas and areas that exist independently outside urban clusters. 'Peri-urban' specifically refers to rural-urban transitional zones located in the city outskirts.

Despite these reservations, we certainly expect that urbanisation in Indonesia will continue, along with the government's efforts to accelerate national development. While the pace of urbanisation in the Java-Bali region is predicted to slow in coming years, other regions are projected to experience rapid urban growth. This urbanisation of Indonesia's population will result in economic transformations and affect regional planning throughout the country. Social change will occur, as communities across the country transform from being agricultural rural societies to modernised industrial urban societies. Whatever the extent and pace of these changes, Indonesians—policymakers, scholars and ordinary citizens alike—need to anticipate the impact of the changes that rapid urbanisation will bring.

References

BKKBN (Badan Kependudukan dan Keluarga Berencana Nasional). 2019. *Laporan Hasil Survey Kinerja dan Akuntabilitas Program KKBPK (SKAP) Keluarga Tahun 2019* [Report on the results of the 2019 survey of performance and accountability of KKBPK program (SKAP)]. BKKBN and BPS.

BPS (Badan Pusat Statistik, Statistics Indonesia). 2000. '2000 Population Census'. Complete data files provided by the Australian Data Archive, Australian National University.

BPS (Badan Pusat Statistik, Statistics Indonesia). 2001. *Population of Indonesia: Results of the 2000 Population Census Series L2.2*. BPS.

BPS (Badan Pusat Statistik, Statistics Indonesia). 2010a. 'Klasifikasi perkotaan dan perdesaan di Indonesia [Classification of rural and urban in Indonesia]'. BPS.

BPS (Badan Pusat Statistik, Statistics Indonesia). 2010b. 'Penduduk menurut wilayah, daerah perkotaan/perdesaan, dan jenis kelamin, Indonesia, tahun 2010 [Population by region, urban/rural area, and sex, Indonesia, 2010]'. BPS. https://sensus.bps.go.id/topik/tabular/sp2010/10/91622/0

BPS (Badan Pusat Statistik, Statistics Indonesia). 2012. *Population of Indonesia: Results of Indonesia Population Census 2010*. BPS.

BPS (Badan Pusat Statistik, Statistics Indonesia). 2013. *Laporan Hasil Sensus Pertanian 2013 (Pencacahan Lengkap)* [Report of 2013 Census of Agriculture Data (full enumeration)]. BPS.

BPS (Badan Pusat Statistik, Statistics Indonesia). 2016. 'Migrasi risen tahun 1980–2015 [Recent migration 1980–2015]'. BPS. www.bps.go.id/staticktable/2011/01/07/1273/migrasi-risen-recent-migrationtahun-1980-1985-1990-1995-2000-2005-2010-dan-2015.html

BPS (Badan Pusat Statistik, Statistics Indonesia). 2020. 'Klasifikasi desa perkotaan dan perdesaan di Indonesia 2020 [Classification of urban and rural villages in Indonesia 2020]'. BPS.

BPS (Badan Pusat Statistik, Statistics Indonesia). 2023a. *Penduduk Indonesia Hasil Long Form Sensus Penduduk 2020* [Population of Indonesia results from 2020 Long Form Population Census]. BPS.

BPS (Badan Pusat Statistik, Statistics Indonesia). 2023b. 'Proyeksi penduduk Indonesia 2020–2050: Hasil Sensus Penduduk 2020 [The 2020–2050 Indonesian population projection: Results of Population Census 2020]'. BPS.

Champion, Tony and Graeme Hugo. 2004. 'Introduction: Moving beyond the urban-rural dichotomy'. In *New Forms of Urbanization*, edited by Tony Champion and Graeme Hugo, 3–24. Ashgate Publishing Company.

Crankshaw, Owen and Jacqueline Borel-Saladin. 2019. 'Causes of urbanisation and counter-urbanisation in Zambia: Natural population increase or migration?' *Urban Studies* 56(10): 2005–20. doi.org/10.1177/0042098018787964

Douglass, Mike. 1997. 'Structural change and urbanization in Indonesia: From the "old" to the "new" international division of labour'. In *Urbanization in Large Developing Countries: China, Indonesia, Brazil, and India*, edited by Gavin W. Jones and Pravin Visaria, 111–41. Oxford University Press.

Dyson, Tim. 2011. 'The role of the demographic transition in the process of urbanization'. *Population and Development Review* 37(S1): 34–54. doi.org/10.1111/j.1728-4457.2011.00377.x

Firman, Tommy. 2004. 'Demographic and spatial patterns of Indonesia's recent urbanisation'. *Population, Space and Place* 10(6): 421–34. doi.org/10.1002/psp.339

Firman, Tommy. 2017. 'The urbanisation of Java, 2000–2010: Towards "the island of mega-urban regions"'. *Asian Population Studies* 13(1): 50–66. doi.org/10.1080/17441730.2016.1247587

Firman, Tommy. 2018. 'Demographic patterns of Indonesia's urbanization, 2000–2010: Continuity and change at the macro level'. In *Contemporary Demographic Transformations in China, India, and Indonesia*, edited by Christophe Z. Guilmoto and Gavin W. Jones, 255–69. Springer International Publishing.

Firman, Tommy, Benedictus Kombaitan and Pradono. 2007. 'The dynamics of Indonesia's urbanisation, 1980–2006'. *Urban Policy and Research* 25(4): 433–54. doi.org/10.1080/08111140701540752

Fox, Sean. 2012. 'Urbanization as a global historical process: Theory and evidence from sub-Saharan Africa'. *Population and Development Review* 38(2): 285–310. doi.org/10.1111/j.1728-4457.2012.00493.x

Jain, Manisha and Artem Korzhenevych. 2020. 'Urbanisation as the rise of census towns in India: An outcome of traditional master planning?' *Cities* 99: 102627. doi.org/10.1016/j.cities.2020.102627

Jiang, Leiwen, Bryan Jones, Deborah Balk and Brian C. O'Neill. 2022. 'The importance of reclassification to understanding urban growth: A demographic decomposition of the United States, 1990–2010'. *Population, Space and Place* 28(6): e2562. doi.org/10.1002/psp.2562

Jones, Gavin W. 1988. 'Urbanization trends in Southeast Asia: Some issues for policy'. *Journal of Southeast Asian Studies* 19(1): 137–54. www.jstor.org/stable/20070996

Jones, Gavin W. and Wahyu Mulyana. 2015. *Urbanization in Indonesia*. UNFPA Indonesia. https://indonesia.unfpa.org/en/publications/monograph-series-no-4-urbanization-indonesia

Katherina, Luh Kitty. 2014. 'Tren urbanisasi pada secondary cities di Indonesia periode tahun 1990–2010 [Urbanization trend in Indonesia's secondary cities, 1990–2010]'. *Jurnal Kependudukan Indonesia* 9(2): 73–82. doi.org/10.14203/jki.v9i2.12

Katherina, Luh Kitty. 2023. 'Rural-to-urban reclassification and its impact on urbanization in Indonesia: A case study of West Java province'. *IOP Conference Series: Earth and Environmental Science* 1263: 012015. doi.org/10.1088/1755-1315/1263/1/012015

Malamassam, Meirina Ayumi. 2022. 'Spatial structure of youth migration in Indonesia: Does education matter?' *Applied Spatial Analysis and Policy* 15(4): 1045–74. doi.org/10.1007/s12061-022-09434-6

Mardiansjah, Fadjar Hari, Paramita Rahayu and Deden Rukmana. 2021. 'New patterns of urbanization in Indonesia: Emergence of non-statutory towns and new extended urban regions'. *Environment and Urbanization ASIA* 12(1): 11–26. doi.org/10.1177/0975425321990384

McGee, T.G. 1991. 'The emergence of desakota regions in Asia: Expanding a hypothesis'. In *The Extended Metropolis: Settlement Transition in Asia*, edited by Norton Ginsburg, Bruce Koppel and T.G. McGee, 3–26. University of Hawai'i Press.

Nugraheni, Siwi. 2022. 'Urbanisasi dari perspektif desa [Urbanisation from a rural perspective]'. *Kompas*, 26 April. www.kompas.id/baca/analisis-ekonomi/2022/04/25/urbanisasi-dari-perspektif-desa?utm_source=kompasid&utm_medium=link_shared&utm_content=copy_link&utm_campaign=sharinglink

Ratcliffe, Michael. 2022. 'Census Bureau's urban and rural classification and overview of 2020 urban area criteria'. Paper presented to the New York State Data Center Affiliates Meeting, 6 October. https://dol.ny.gov/system/files/documents/2022/11/urban-rural-classification-and-2020-urban-area-criteria-slides.pdf

Rondhi, Mohammad, Pravitasari Anjar Pratiwi, Vivi Trisna Handini, Aryo Fajar Sunartomo and Subhan Arif Budiman. 2019. 'Agricultural land conversion and food policy in Indonesia: Historical linkages, current challenges, and future directions'. In *Current Trends in Landscape Research*, edited by Lothar Mueller and Frank Eulenstein, 631–64. Springer International Publishing. doi.org/10.1007/978-3-030-30069-2_29

Shi, Qiujie and Guangzhong Cao. 2020. 'Urban spillover or rural industrialisation: Which drives the growth of Beijing Metropolitan Area'. *Cities* 105: 102354. doi.org/10.1016/j.cities.2019.05.023

Sukamdi and Ghazy Mujahid. 2015. *Internal Migration in Indonesia*. UNFPA Indonesia. https://indonesia.unfpa.org/sites/default/files/pub-pdf/FA_Isi_BUKU_Monograph_Internal_Migration_ENG.pdf

UNDESA (United Nations Department of Economic and Social Affairs). 2018. 'The speed of urbanization around the world'. UNDESA. www.un.org/development/desa/pd/content/speed-urbanization-around-world

UNESCAP (United Nations Economic and Social Commission for Asia and the Pacific). 1993. *Annual Report 24 April 1992 – 29 April 1993*. Official Records Economic and Social Council, UNESCAP.

Utami, Larasati Dyah. 2023. 'Mendagri ingin pemerintah desa maksimal tekan laju urbanisasi [Minister of Home Affairs wants village governments to maximally reduce the rate of urbanisation]'. *Tribunnews*, 29 August. www.tribunnews.com/nasional/2023/08/29/mendagri-ingin-pemerintah-desa-maksimal-tekan-laju-urbanisasi

World Bank. 2023. 'Urban population (% of total population)'. World Bank. Accessed 25 January 2024, https://data.worldbank.org/indicator/SP.URB.TOTL?view=chart

Zelinsky, Wilbur. 1971. 'The hypothesis of the mobility transition'. *Geographical Review* 61(2): 219–49. doi.org/10.2307/213996

Zhang, Xing Quan. 2016. 'The trends, promises and challenges of urbanisation in the world'. *Habitat International* 54(3): 241–52. doi.org/10.1016/j.habitatint.2015.11.018

Appendix 3.1 Distribution of urban localities in Sumatra region, 2010 and 2020

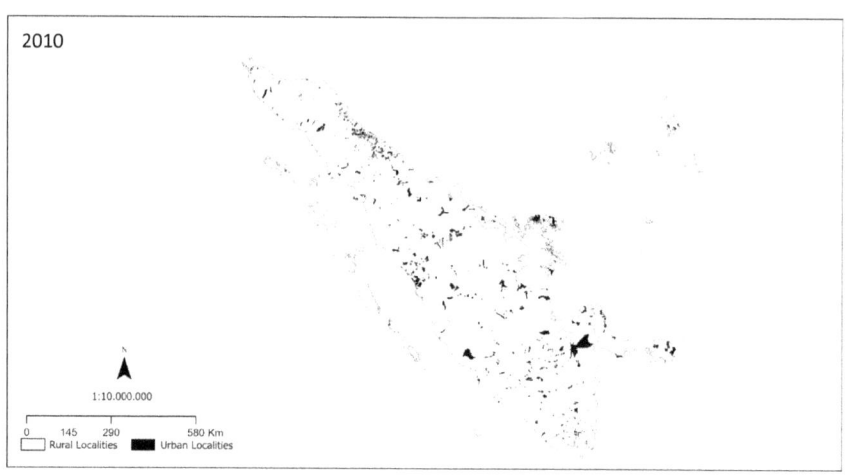

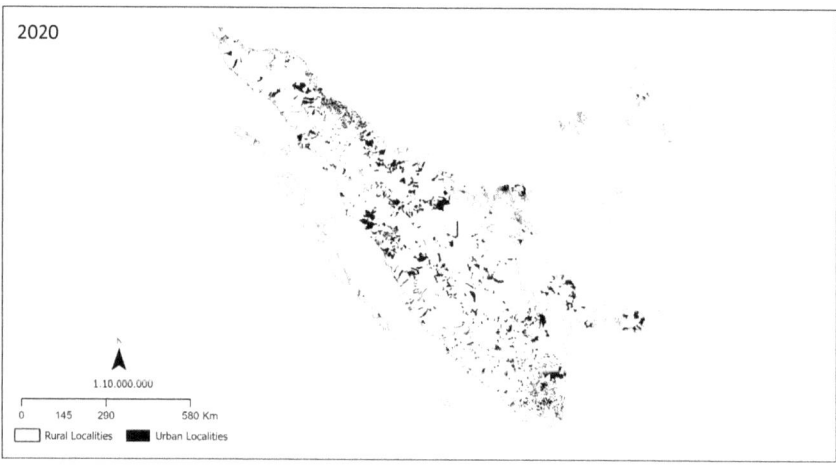

Source: Authors' drawing based on data from BPS (2010a, 2020); map boundaries are extracted from geospatial data from Indonesia's Geospatial Information Agency (BIG).

Appendix 3.2 Distribution of urban localities in Java-Bali region, 2010 and 2020

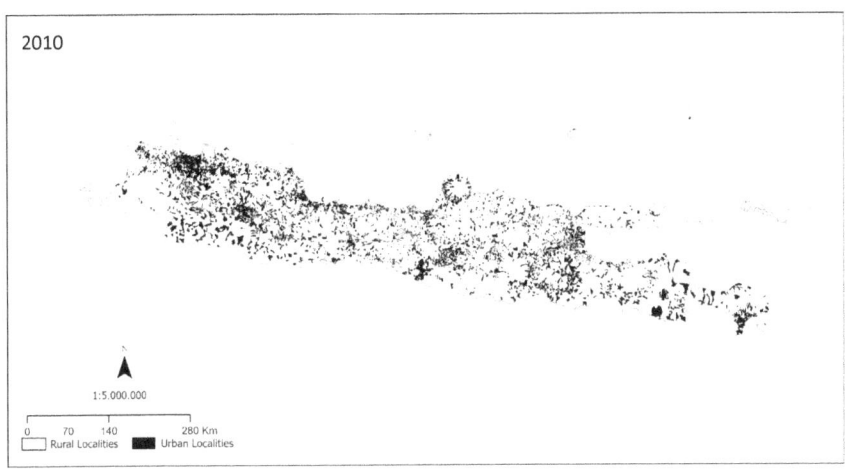

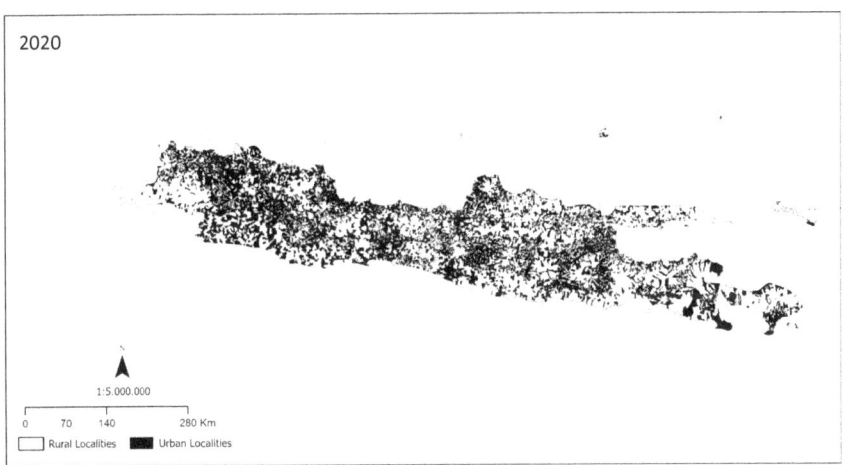

Source: Authors' drawing based on data from BPS (2010a, 2020); map boundaries are extracted from geospatial data from Indonesia's Geospatial Information Agency (BIG).

Appendix 3.3 Distribution of urban localities in Kalimantan region, 2010 and 2020

Source: Authors' drawing based on data from BPS (2010a, 2020); map boundaries are extracted from geospatial data from Indonesia's Geospatial Information Agency (BIG).

Chapter 3 Demographic changes and spatial patterns, 2000–2020   73

Appendix 3.4 Distribution of urban localities in Sulawesi region, 2010 and 2020

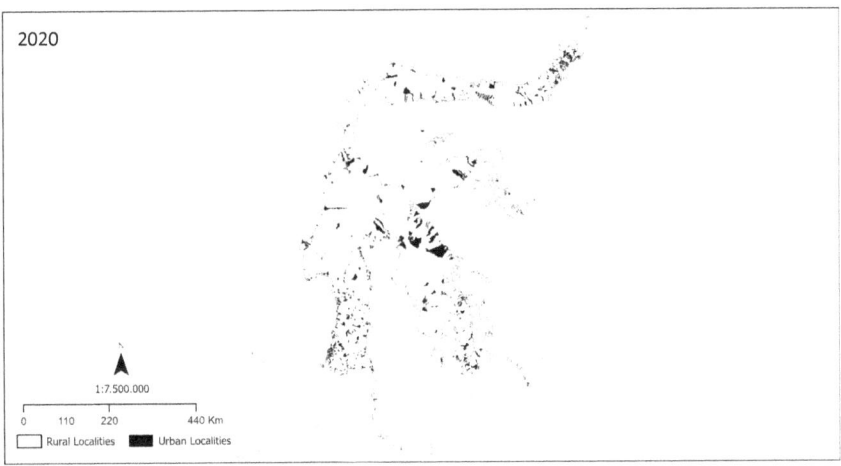

Source: Authors' drawing based on data from BPS (2010a, 2020); map boundaries are extracted from geospatial data from Indonesia's Geospatial Information Agency (BIG).

Appendix 3.5 Distribution of urban localities in Eastern Indonesia region, 2010 and 2020

Source: Authors' drawing based on data from BPS (2010a, 2020); map boundaries are extracted from geospatial data from Indonesia's Geospatial Information Agency (BIG).

4 Urban planning in Indonesia and its contribution to Southern Planning

Sonia Roitman

Urbanisation in Indonesia has accelerated since the country became independent. Currently, more than half of Indonesia's population live in cities. Consequently, urban planning, the discipline managing urban growth and responding to the service and infrastructure needs of the population so that they may have good quality lives, has a significant role to play in Indonesia. In this chapter, I discuss historic and current conditions of urban planning in Indonesia, and how 'Indonesian Planning' has contributed to the conceptual and empirical development of what is often called 'Southern Planning' (Watson 2016)—the theory and practice of urban planning as it has developed in the Global South.

I argue that three structural conditions have significantly affected the growth of Indonesian cities, namely, poverty, informality and the growth of the middle class. In addition, as I discuss later, the role of the private sector, whose actions have been targeted towards the demands of upper-middle and middle groups, has shaped the character of the Indonesian planning system. Lately, a second group of challenges linked to the provision of infrastructure and environmental impacts has become critical in urban areas. These are a consequence of urbanisation and economic development, and include provision of housing, managing vulnerability to disasters and providing adequate solid waste disposal. They are not the only challenges faced in cities, but overcoming them is important for moving towards resilient, safe, inclusive and sustainable cities (as expressed in Sustainable Development Goal 11, adopted by the United Nations in 2015).[1] I show that, despite all the problems, actors within

---

1 www.un.org/sustainabledevelopment/cities

the Indonesian planning system, especially particular communities as critical stakeholders within that system, have opportunities to address these challenges. In this chapter, I discuss these challenges and how the Indonesian planning system helps illustrate the conditions of Southern Planning.

The chapter is organised into seven sections. The next two sections look at the meaning of Southern Planning, and provide an in-depth discussion of the Indonesian planning system. In the fourth section, I elaborate on structural challenges experienced in Indonesian cities, focusing on poverty, informality and the growth of the middle class. The fifth section examines the most recent challenges in cities linked to infrastructure provision and environmental impacts. A sixth section looks at the opportunities that the current planning system can use to improve Indonesian cities. Finally, the conclusion reflects on the contribution of Indonesian planning to a broader analysis of Southern Planning.

What is Southern Planning?

Urban planning as a practice and discipline aims to improve the quality of life of people who live in cities and urban settlements. As an intervention in cities, it requires the involvement of a broad range of actors who are part of urban settings, namely government, private sector, civil society organisations, communities and lay residents. In the past, this practice was considered an exclusive domain of 'experts', while over the past 50 years, common agreement has emerged that, to be successful, urban planning needs to be inclusive, democratic and participatory, aiming for 'cities for all', where different groups and sectors feel represented (UN-Habitat 2009). Inclusive cities require policies and actions within a framework based on the values of social justice, the public good, respect, diversity and democracy. Various stakeholders are responsible for city-making; however, the government has a steering role, providing a vision for the city and the design and implementation of the instruments that can make this vision possible.

Urban planning as a practice developed in the Global North,[2] where planners worked on how to solve city problems, including lack of adequate

---

2 The Global North and Global South refer to a political division of countries based on socioeconomic characteristics and political history. The Global South includes Latin America and the Caribbean, Africa, Asia (excluding Japan, South Korea, Singapore and Israel) and Oceania (excluding Australia and New Zealand). The visualisation of North and South is based on the Brandt line separating what used to be seen as 'developed' and 'developing' countries.

housing, lack of sanitation, air pollution and unplanned urban growth. A standard approach was to develop city master plans that mainly aimed to 'beautify' cities without addressing the root causes of these problems (poverty, inequality and polluting industrial practices). Plans followed a top-down approach, directed by the central government, in collaboration with the private sector. As the practice evolved, from around the 1980s, a revision of planning occurred based on a 'collaborative turn', with a new emphasis on more inclusive approaches that recognise the contributions of a diverse set of actors in city-making (Watson 2016).

Over the past 30 years, informed by postcolonial discourses, the urban planning discipline started to question the validity of mainstream planning ideas. Historically, planners were educated in the Global North and examined the problems of cities in that region. However, the Global South (formerly labelled 'developing countries') presented different historical trajectories and sociopolitical conditions that made it impossible for concepts and practices from the North to translate to the context of the South.

Following a postcolonial critique of the city, Southern Planning (or Global South Planning) argues that the concepts of Northern Planning are not appropriate and useful to understanding the conditions and realities of the South (Watson 2009, 2016), and that cities in the South cannot be examined using explanations developed for the North. Southern Planning theory 'starts from different premises and different sets of assumptions' than Northern Planning (Watson 2016: 33). Thus, this approach demands a change of position to look at 'ordinary cities' (Robinson 2002) and to think 'off the map' (ibid.) so that we may understand planning 'from the South' (Watson 2009). This change of position allows the creation of new analytical categories and theories that explain the realities of the South (Roy 2011). It provides value and visibility to the 'epistemologies of the South', which are new processes of production and valorisation of both scientific and non-scientific knowledge drawing on the practices of groups oppressed and discriminated against by capitalism and colonialism (Santos 2012).

Southern Planning also gives rise to 'new types of responses to urban realities and urban processes' (Bishop et al. 2003: 3) on the premise that existing global or general theoretical paradigms have their own limitations. This perspective acknowledges the existence of 'conflicting interests and trends in contemporary geopolitical relations' between the North and the South (ibid.: 4). It criticises notions of development elaborated in the North that exclude 'other ways of seeing and doing' (Escobar 1992: 22). The rise of Southern Planning as a new approach has been informed by discussions of post-development or 'alternatives to development' that reinforce the need to adopt a critical stance vis-a-vis scientific knowledge, recognise the importance of local autonomy, culture and knowledge, and defend grassroots movements (ibid.).

Using the category 'Southern Planning' requires understanding the specific conditions of the South. Drawing from several scholars, Gillespie and Mitlin (2023) identify four critical characteristics of Southern urbanism: the production of space through both formal and informal practices; urbanisation without large-scale manufacturing and dislocation of capital and labour in urban economies; infrastructures that are incremental, heterogenous and dependent on the everyday practices of residents; and auto-construction practices as a critical method to satisfy housing needs.

Despite some problems (such as poverty) being present in both North and South, the different historical trajectories of, and the different approaches to solving, these problems in the two regions mean that their magnitude and visibility greatly differ. Using the Global North and Global South as an analytical lens does not mean using a 'deficit perspective' in which the North is good and the South is bad. On the contrary, these categories provide opportunities for discussion and sharing of experiences between North and South, but also encourage North-North and South-South dialogue and opportunities for horizontal collaboration.

The Indonesian planning system

Indonesian planning contributes to the conceptual and empirical development of Southern Planning, as I explain in this section that reviews the key features of the Indonesian planning system. Since Indonesia's independence, the urban planning system has been dictated by the national government. The first Town Planning Act was approved in 1948 following the ideas of Thomas Karsten, a Dutch engineer and town planner who was influential in the Netherlands East Indies (Cowherd 2005). Karsten incorporated principles of local indigenous knowledge. President Sukarno (1945–1967) aimed to develop a postcolonial model for the country, breaking away from the influence of Europe and other Northern countries. Later, as a counteractive movement, President Suharto (1966–1998) established strong links with the United States and tried to import some of the urban planning models from there. During these 50 years the main actors driving city-making were the national government and the private sector. Only since *reformasi* (i.e. the post-1998 period) have opportunities expanded for civil society organisations and communities to participate in urban planning, generating a hybrid planning system. Indonesia's planning system is described by government as being guided by a clear vision of urban growth based on population needs and environmental conditions, according to an evidence base and technocratic knowledge. However, it is a system that is heavily politicised. Indonesia is not alone in this, as urban planning worldwide is influenced by political context.

During the New Order regime of President Suharto, the Indonesian planning system was characterised by a top-down and authoritarian approach. Initially, Indonesian urban planning had been greatly influenced by the planning principles inherited from the Netherlands and the Dutch colonial government. Under the New Order, ideas promoted by the World Bank and originating in the United States, including an emphasis on middle-class consumption and the prevalence of road infrastructure over railway, became more influential (Cowherd 2005; see also Kusno, this volume).

The planning system has thus always involved an element of centralised control. Since the early New Order years, the National Development Planning Agency (Badan Perencanaan Pembangunan Nasional, Bappenas) has been responsible for the design and implementation of development policies, programs and guidelines, including those that pertain to urban planning. The first Spatial Planning Law (Law 24/1992), however, did not come into being until 1992. This law established guidelines on spatial planning across the country and required local governments to develop their own master plans. However, these guidelines were seldom effectively implemented (Rukmana 2015).

The private sector has also played a major role in urban planning in Indonesia since the Suharto era, when there were strong connections between private developers and the Suharto family (Dieleman 2011; Pratiwo and Nas 2005; Winarso and Firman 2002). These connections facilitated the growth of a handful of private developers who have accumulated wealth as part of a 'politico-business oligarchy' (Hadiz and Robison 2013). Strong connections with politicians helped big private developers to 'negotiate' around planning regulations and 'the most well-connected developers profited the most' (Dieleman 2011: 71).

During the Suharto period, both government and private actors routinely circumvented planning regulations, with these violations justified in terms of the 'development agenda' and the promotion of private investment (Cowherd 2005). Suharto issued several presidential decrees to approve large new developments (e.g. housing and road infrastructure projects) that actually violated planning regulations, but were run by members of his family or people close to him (Cowherd 2005; Dieleman 2011). Thus, non-observance of planning regulations helped dominant actors in the regime consolidate their power, as observed by Cowherd

(2005: 190): 'the preference for market forces over state-guided planning presented what was perceived by its political and business elite as the best opportunities for extending their power and influence'. Overall, the New Order government performed an enabling role, facilitating actions of the private sector, including through public-private partnerships (Herlambang et al. 2019). Developers took the initiative to build numerous large-scale projects, such as transport infrastructure or large private housing estates, providing an urban governance model based on private delivery of services and infrastructure (Dieleman 2011).

This model has survived into the *reformasi* era, though this period has also brought changes in decision-making processes on urban planning. In 2007, the government passed a new spatial planning law (Law 26/2007). This gave greater responsibilities and authority to provincial and district governments to make decisions concerning urban planning. In particular, district-level governments, including cities (*kota*), had authority over new developments within their jurisdiction, and according to their own spatial plans (*rencana tata ruang wilayah*, RTRW) (though the 2020 job creation or 'omnibus' law involved an element of recentralisation). There are also spatial plans at the provincial (RTRW *propinsi*) and national (RTRW *nasional*) levels. The national government still plays a role in planning, largely through Bappenas and the General Directorate of Spatial Planning within the Ministry of Agrarian Affairs and Spatial Planning (Kementerian Agraria dan Tata Ruang). Thus, although since *reformasi* local governments have had more power to make planning decisions, they are still bound by national regulations, policies and development plans.

Law 26/2007 on Spatial Planning not only describes the responsibilities of local governments in managing their spatial plans, but also provides for sanctions for planning violations, stipulates minimum standards of services, and requires public participation and accountability in urban planning processes (Rukmana 2015). However, not all aspects of this law are enforced. For example, the law requires that 30 per cent of urban areas be used for open space, but this is clearly not the case in most heavily populated Indonesian cities. Other planning instruments are also not enforced, such as the 'balanced housing ratio 1:2:3' (*lingkungan hunian berimbang*, LHB). This is a national policy requiring new private housing developments to provide housing supply for high, medium and low-income families following a distribution of 1:2:3 (1 house for high-income families, 2 for medium-income and 3 for low-income; the requirement was originally 1:3:6 when introduced in 1974 but was changed to 1:2:3 in 2011). This policy is rarely enforced because it is not profitable for developers, land is scarce in most cities, and local governments have poor enforcement and weak technical capacity (in terms of a lack of staff and/or a clear understanding of what relevant regulations mean) (Roitman 2018; Yuniati 2013).

Similar to other countries in both the Global North and Global South, access to land is a contentious and heavily politicised issue. In several Indonesian cities, such as Jakarta and Yogyakarta, no more urban land is available to continue to expand the city and much of the remaining urban land is owned by a handful of powerful national developers. Land is not only an expensive commodity, it can also be subject to unlawful actions conducted by 'land mafias'. These are networks of actors including landowners, investors, government officials, lawyers and politicians who use tactics such as coercion and manipulation of documents to gain control over land and to get financial benefits from this commodity (Bachriadi and Aspinall 2023).

Within this context, various problems undermine the effectiveness of the formal planning system in Indonesia. One problem is lack of coordination across different government levels (Datta et al. 2011), which creates unclear division of responsibilities and lack of enforcement of regulations at the local level. Lack of enforcement partly arises from lack of technical capacity (in terms of human resources and/or expertise) on the part of local governments. In this regard, Indonesia is similar to many countries of the Global South. Corruption and lack of application of planning norms are also common (Dieleman 2011; Rukmana 2015). Collusion among local politicians, bureaucrats, property developers and other powerful interests sometimes means local governments are reluctant to enforce their own regulations (see Permana, this volume). Developers often build new housing estates or other developments without the required planning permissions, or build in areas that are gazetted as green areas (Pratiwo and Nas 2005). Before *reformasi*, it was largely the national government that was responsible for ignoring planning regulations; after *reformasi*, as local governments took on greater authority over development decisions, they also became more responsible for violations (Rukmana 2015). As during the New Order era, elite partnerships between developers (including national and local companies, now increasingly backed by international investors) are central to the growth strategies of most urban areas, but now it is often city governments that drive these partnerships (Herlambang et al. 2019).

One significant change since *reformasi*, however, has been increased involvement by communities in planning processes—a result of the emphasis on democracy and participation (*partisipasi*) that underpinned the *reformasi* movement. The government provides for community participation via its *musrenbang* (*musyawarah perencanaan pembangunan*, development planning deliberation) process. *Musrenbang* meetings are held at all levels when local governments formulate their development plans, and involve not just communities but also other stakeholders, including government agencies (Datta et al. 2011). The purpose is to integrate top-down (government) planning with bottom-up (community) perspectives when establishing priorities for development planning and budget allocation (Purba 2011). *Musrenbang* are thus one instrument whereby communities can express their preferences about local development, and they are intended to be an efficient tool for creating awareness of community needs and preferences among government decision-makers. However, critics often say the *musrenbang* involve only tokenistic participation, with local leaders and government officials often dominating these processes, and little evidence that communities are able to influence decision-making processes through them. Moreover, *musrenbang* tend to be dominated by men, with less active participation by women, and few poor people (ibid.). According to Purba (2011: 272), 'the hierarchical and paternalistic nature of the process serves to curb active participation by more marginal members'.

In sum, Indonesia's planning system can be considered a hybrid system, in which a variety of government, business and community actors engage with differing sets of resources and authority to shape the urban environment. There is still a strong legacy of centralised, top-down and even authoritarian planning, but this has been disrupted by the shift to decentralisation over the past 25 years. Private business interests, especially property developers, often achieve their goals through informal relations with political power-holders. Informality is also present at the community level, as I describe in the next section. The participation of ordinary citizens, including poor urban residents, is formally recognised but practically constrained through the formal planning system. At the same time, poor groups continue to self-build their homes through what Bayat (1997: 56) calls 'the often quiet practices of the ordinary'.

The structural context: Poverty and informality

The Indonesian planning system has arisen in the context of rapid urbanisation and significant structural constraints. When Indonesian independence was declared in 1945, only 12 per cent of the population lived in cities (Roitman and Rukmana 2023: 3). By 2019, 56 per cent of the population lived in urban areas (Roberts et al. 2019: 1), increasing to 59 per cent in 2023.[3] Population-wise, two major groups deserve special

---

3 Worldometer (www.worldometers.info/world-population/indonesia-population), accessed 18 August 2023.

attention in relation to their contribution to urban growth: middle-class Indonesians and low-income families, mainly those living in more disadvantaged locations.

According to the World Bank (2019a), Indonesia's middle class, that group which is economically secure and able to absorb economic shocks, represented 20 per cent of the total Indonesian population by 2019. They spend their disposable income on non-food related items such as health, education and other services. They are the group spending the most on housing. About three-quarters of the middle class live in urban areas (ibid.: 18). Since 2002, 'middle class consumption has grown at 12 per cent annually' and in 2016 it represented 'close to half of all household consumption in Indonesia' (ibid.: 13). Middle-class families have benefited from the economic growth and development of the country, but have also 'helped to sustain Indonesia's enviable record of economic growth' (ibid.: 12).

The idea of an emerging new middle class guided by consumption practices was encouraged from the 1980s and 1990s by Suharto's approach of opening the Indonesian economy. Although at that time the social group that could afford a middle-class lifestyle was very small (around 7–10 per cent of the total population), the group that aspired to do this was already growing (Cowherd 2005). This trend was also encouraged through television, music, and fashion from Europe and the United States (Cowherd and Heikkika 2002, cited in Cowherd 2005). The promotion of consumption practices was used as a strong tool for the economic recovery after the 1997–1998 Asian financial crisis (Herlambang et al. 2019).

The growth of the middle class has created demand for new services and infrastructure in urban areas, including shopping malls and private housing in gated communities (or private 'clusters'), driving the growth of suburban areas where 'new towns' (gated communities, some of them self-contained, with services and infrastructure) were built by the private sector (Dieleman 2011; Roitman and Recio 2020; Elyda, this volume). Through the provision of housing and infrastructure, the private sector has consolidated its role as a key actor in the making of Indonesian cities.

Simultaneously, this growth of the middle class has contributed to an increase in income inequality in the country, as evidenced by the Gini ratio.[4] This indicator has increased from 0.31 in 1990 to 0.39 in 2023, with a peak of 0.41 in 2014 (BPS 2020, 2023b). Inequality has become a prominent topic in the political agenda (Negara 2017; Roberts et al. 2019) and has

---

4   The Gini ratio is a measure of income distribution across a population, and ranges from 0 (full equality) to 1 (no equality).

become visible in Indonesian cities through stark contrasts in housing options for upper- and middle-class groups versus those for poorer citizens (Roitman and Recio 2020).

The poor have also been a major driving force in urbanisation, and they have shaped the face of Indonesia's towns and cities. The poor once constituted a large majority of the Indonesian population, but in 2019, according to the World Bank, they comprised just 11 per cent (the groups classified by the World Bank as 'vulnerable' and 'aspiring middle class', based on consumption, represented 24 per cent and 44 per cent respectively; World Bank 2019a: 9, 43). The poor have moulded Indonesia's urban landscape above all by giving rise to the *kampung*, or self-built settlements, which are a distinctive feature of Indonesian's urban landscape (Jellinek 1991). *Kampung* typically arose as a result of people engaging in self-help housing, in unplanned locations, with insecure land tenure. Overall, living conditions in *kampung* have improved over recent decades, as the government has implemented several programs to improve these settlements. However, many *kampung* residents face daily challenges, especially those who live in disaster-prone areas, and their insecurity of tenure means they face regular eviction threats (see Siagian, this volume).

Within this context, it is evident that three structural conditions—poverty, informality and a growing middle class—have been major factors shaping the development of both Indonesian urban life and Indonesian planning. Indonesia is then similar to other countries in the Global South. Although not unique to the Global South, the impact and magnitude of poverty and informality are more significant there than in the Global North. Moreover, while both poverty and informality are challenges to the Indonesian planning system, they have shaped how the urban space has been produced by government, private sector and residents, including poor groups.

Poverty has long been a serious global problem. However, it is worth noting a significant shift in the conceptualisation of poverty among academics and policymakers in recent decades, from a merely income-based definition to a more comprehensive and multidimensional understanding. In this broader view, poverty is defined not only in relation to people's wages, but also to basic needs and involvement in decision-making processes. Multidimensional poverty consists of several dimensions including inadequate and unstable income, limited or no safety net, overcrowding, poor-quality housing, inadequate provision of public infrastructure and basic services, limited opportunities to express voice or exercise power, limited protection of rights, a limited asset base and having to pay high prices for necessities (Mitlin and Satterthwaite 2013).

In Indonesia, poverty is still considered based mainly on a monetary or quantitative definition. In 2023, 7 per cent of residents in urban areas in Indonesia were considered poor, according to the government (BPS 2023a). However, there is growing recognition of the multidimensional nature of poverty. Therefore, government poverty programs have expanded their focus beyond income to incorporate other aspects such as housing, sanitation, capacity building and, most importantly, the involvement of poor people in the design and implementation of these programs. Involving them directly enables poor people to make decisions on what the programs should aim to achieve, based on their own understanding and experience of poverty. For example, the National Program for Community Empowerment (Program Nasional Pemberdayaan Masyarakat, PNPM) was implemented countrywide in urban and rural areas between 2007 and 2014 and included funding to build community infrastructure, improve housing, develop microcredit programs, provide scholarships and provide training for capacity building. It included participatory principles (Roitman 2016). More recently, the Kotaku program (Kota Tanpa Kumuh, City without Slums) focused on 100 per cent access to drinking water, 0 per cent slums and 100 per cent access to adequate sanitation. Similarly to the PNPM, organised communities were able to submit proposals for housing and neighbourhood improvement, and training and activities to support their livelihoods.

Thus, while historically, especially in the New Order period, poor Indonesians were largely excluded from the planning system, these and other poverty programs in the post-1998 period have incorporated community engagement as a principle, enabling poor Indonesians to articulate their own development needs and play a role in planning the development of their communities. PNPM was a pioneer in this regard, and is generally seen as being more successful than the *musrenbang* process, discussed earlier, in encouraging community participation. Such programs require communities to be able to organise themselves, and make decisions about projects they would like to prioritise and how to do this. Communities at the neighbourhood level (*rukun tetangga*) have received advice and support from local governments and non-government organisations about how to plan and run their own priorities. As a result, organised communities have become important actors in the Indonesian policy governance structure (Roitman 2019; Sari et al. 2023). However, it has become clear that while some communities have been successful in becoming more active and making decisions about how to improve their living conditions, others have not. Some obstacles include the continuation of top-down approaches, where government or community leaders dictate what to do, without communities owning the decision-making process; dependence on external sources of funding; and limited community capacity to build networks and relationships with other stakeholders (Roitman 2019). The inclusion of groups that were historically marginalised from decision-making processes is aligned with postcolonial theories and the principles of Southern Planning, as I explained earlier in this chapter.

Informality, meanwhile, is a condition more prevalent in the Global South than in the Global North, with the informal economy contributing 30 per cent of the combined gross domestic product (GDP) of the Global South, and 70 per cent of all employment (World Bank 2019b). As a condition, informality refers to 'a way' to act, 'a logic' of intervention, and a 'dominant mode of existence in the city' (Roitman and Walters 2024), based on organic, random and unstructured practices and responses. Similarly, informality can be defined as 'lack of conformity' with established and recognised regulations and practices (Das and Susantono 2022: 1). Although sometimes misconceptually associated exclusively with poor groups, informality is embedded in the practices of all social groups in the Global South.

Within planning, informality refers mainly to informal tenure and informal provision of services. In the context of urban Indonesia, when we talk about informality, we typically refer to the *kampung* or informal settlements that developed historically as largely self-governed spaces only loosely ruled by the colonial and then postcolonial state (see Kusno, this volume). In Indonesian *kampung*, tenure insecurity remains one of the main problems faced by the poor, though due to the sensitivity of the problem and lack of data, it is difficult to know how many households do not have land tenure security. However, while informality affects the poor more than the middle classes, informality also shapes many gated communities built by the private sector and where middle-class people live—for example, in the form of collusion between private developers and government officials to circumvent planning regulations. Informality in the form of such circumvention of regulations is thus commonplace, both because it is not easy to control development and because of the influence of political factors and competing interests underpinning the expansion of the city.

While informality is often viewed negatively, if we think of it neutrally, we can see that informality in fact provides opportunities for 'out-of-the-box' and innovative responses to urban challenges. This non-deficit view of informality allows us to break with a colonial view whereby areas not following colonial planning norms are illegal or informal. As I discuss below, the creativity of many Indonesian urban communities attests to the vibrancy of many 'informal' parts of Indonesian cities.

Planning challenges

Having reviewed key structural conditions facing Indonesian planning, I now discuss three additional planning challenges that, while not novel, have certainly become more serious in recent times as cities continue to grow. They are associated with the provision of infrastructure and environmental impacts.

Housing shortages

Housing affordability for low- and middle-income groups is a significant challenge in Indonesia. The National Medium Term Development Plan (Rencana Pembangunan Jangka Menengah Nasional, RPJMN) 2015–2019 aimed to reduce the housing backlog from 13.5 million to 6.5 million (KPUPR and World Bank 2023: 5). However, in 2023, there were still 12.7 million households who did not have a house and 1.13 million new households needing housing annually (ibid.: 3). The housing sector suffers from both quantitative and qualitative deficits. The first deficit refers to affordable housing and is measured through the number of housing units available. The qualitative deficit refers to the adequacy of the housing provided, measured in terms of structural integrity, space adequacy (overcrowding) and access to basic services such as water and sanitation (ibid.: 2, 4). Overcrowding is usually an invisible problem but a major cause of qualitative deficit. When more than one household lives in the same dwelling, or when the space is too small, this is considered overcrowding. The RPJMN 2015–2019 aimed to reduce substandard housing from 3.4 million to 1.9 million households (ibid.: 5). However, in 2023, there was a change in the definition of substandard housing, incorporating United Nations Sustainable Development Goals indicators, leading to a large increase in the number of households considered to be living in substandard houses to 29.6 million (ibid.: 2, 4, 5). Thus, a main aim of the RPJMN 2020–2024 is to reduce this high qualitative deficit.

President Joko Widodo (2014–2024) implemented some policies and programs to address the housing crisis. One of these programs was the National Affordable Housing Program (NAHP, Program Nasional Perumahan Terjangkau), overseen by the Ministry of Public Works and Housing, with a budget of US$450 million provided by the World Bank. The NAHP has three components: first, financial assistance for down payments to help first-time buyers enter the housing market, addressing the quantitative deficit; second, home improvement assistance to help households living in inadequate housing, addressing the qualitative deficit; third, technical assistance to build capacity on housing policy reform provided by local governments. As a result, 32,000 new housing units have been purchased and 823,000 units have been improved in the country (KPUPR and World Bank 2023). Although this is a good achievement, it remains limited in contrast to the magnitude of the housing crisis in the country.

This housing challenge shows how the formal Indonesian planning system is aiming to address the quantitative and qualitative housing deficits that exist as a result of a significant number of households under the poverty line being unable to afford housing. A positive aspect of the NAHP is that citizens who are informal workers can access the program to retrofit and improve the quality of their housing. Rather than excluding informal workers, NAHP acknowledges their working conditions as a key feature of the Indonesian economy. NAHP is a centralised program, designed and managed by the national government, with program facilitators working with communities. NAHP also aims to address disaster vulnerability, a critical challenge in Indonesia.

Disaster vulnerability

Indonesia faces high vulnerabilities to disaster due to its island morphology and its location in the 'ring of fire' region of high volcanic activity. It is considered one of the most disaster-prone countries on the planet (Djalante and Garschagen 2017). The country suffers from regular floods, droughts, earthquakes and volcanic eruptions, as well as occasional typhoons and tsunamis; the most common disasters are floods and earthquakes (ibid.).

After the devastating Indian Ocean tsunami of December 2004, the national government passed Law 24/2007 on Disaster Management, which establishes a national system for managing disasters and disaster risks in the country, and outlines the shared responsibilities of all government levels to achieve this, while providing more authority and responsibility to local governments within Indonesia's decentralised framework. District-level governments have Regional Disaster Management Agencies (Badan Penanggulangan Bencana Daerah-Kota/Kabupaten, BPBD-K) that are responsible for managing local disasters. The government encourages stakeholders from the private sector, civil society and universities to participate in the implementation of disaster management processes. However, there are still obstacles to communities fully participating in and implementing community-based disaster risk management. For example, in the case of Bandung, spatial planning at the local level does not incorporate processes of community-based disaster risk management and there is a lack of coordination between different stakeholders (Kent et al. 2023).

Das and Luthfi (2017) argue that although decentralisation facilitates a governance structure able to manage disasters at the local level, there is lack of clarity about different agencies' roles and responsibilities. The government of Joko Widodo addressed disaster risk management as a central policy area. It focused on infrastructure, such as flood mitigation systems, better warning systems and social support for affected communities (Djalante and Garschagen 2017). At the same time, as Permana (this volume) argues, problems of informality in local government, notably collusion between officials and developers and other investors, can undermine the enforcement of regulations (such as those governing drainage) designed to prevent and mitigate disasters.

Cities are considered 'hotspots' for disasters and therefore require more attention than other areas to reduce vulnerabilities and provide resilient environments (Joerin and Shaw 2010). In terms of the effects of the structural challenges discussed above, there are higher risks for poor urban residents, who are usually located in areas prone to disasters as these areas have lower land prices and attract little from private developers (Kent et al. 2023). In Yogyakarta, for example, the poorest *kampung* are located along the three main rivers that cross the city (Murwani et al. 2023). These riverside *kampung* get flooded regularly and communities have built their own retention walls using their own funding because, lacking formal land tenure, they have not been able to get government support to do so. Urban disasters not only damage the housing of the urban poor, they also disrupt their livelihoods, which are often based on small businesses conducted at home.

Disaster management in Indonesia illustrates key features of Southern Planning and Indonesian planning. First, it shows that areas with informal land tenure need to be included in both the disaster management formal and informal systems due to their high vulnerability. Second, due to the lack of government capacity (lack of financial and human resources, and high demand for support), informal and spontaneous responses from local communities provide support that saves lives after disasters. With regard to the Indonesian planning system, disaster management is currently highly decentralised, although there are still inconsistencies in the distribution of responsibilities at the different government levels. Finally, the field shows how the private sector can exercise its power against local governments, getting away with noncompliance with planning regulations.

Solid waste management

Driven by increasing consumption, solid waste is a major concern worldwide. In Indonesia, it is a severe problem in both urban and rural areas. Indonesian cities produce about 200,000 tonnes of waste every day and nearly half of this is produced by households (Wijayanti and Suryani 2015: 172). Household waste disposal is limited. Most city governments provide a limited waste collection service, with communities typically organising their own collection, and a large proportion of the population relying also on informal waste collection by scavengers or the burning of waste.

Scavenging is a widespread practice usually conducted by residents of informal settlements. Although it constitutes an important livelihood source, it exposes people to high health risks (Colon and Fawcett 2006). It has a limited impact on the waste cycle, as only about 9–15 per cent of solid waste is reduced through the recycling done in Indonesia by scavengers (MacRae and Rodic 2015: 311). Scavengers typically extract the valuable and recyclable items from the waste they collect and sell it to intermediate dealers, who later take the residue to formal or informal dumping sites.

The re-use of solid waste to create handicrafts and building materials has become a successful practice in some places. For example, in Sukunan, a village on the outskirts of Yogyakarta metropolitan area, solid waste is managed by the community. People there use an innovative process with success driven by strong community engagement, clear local leadership and commitment, and a communication strategy that promotes the village nationally (Iswanto et al. 2018). Despite its success and sustainability over time, this and similar community initiatives have had a limited impact in terms of scale.

At the city scale, while many cities still struggle to deal with their waste, Surabaya is widely recognised within the country as a city that is successfully managing its solid waste (see Azizah, this volume). Several policies and programs at the local level have been implemented since the 1980s, with a major turning point in local governance coming in the early 2000s (see Mustafa, this volume). The success of the Surabaya model is based on a strong partnership built by the city government with several stakeholders, including a local government in Japan that has provided valuable technical expertise and ideas, the local private sector in Surabaya, the media, and local researchers (Feliciani 2023).

Waste management in Indonesia shows the importance of decentralisation in allowing local governments to manage their own program implementation. However, the system only functions as a combination of formal and informal initiatives. The successful management of solid waste requires a collaborative effort by several stakeholders within the planning system, including the private sector. Participatory efforts where communities take responsibility, and even leadership, are providing strong positive outcomes that can be scaled up to mitigate the lack of material resources from local governments to provide a better service. Similarly, even if at a low scale, informal practices of scavengers and their recycling and re-using of materials provide livelihood opportunities in the informal economy.

Opportunities within Indonesian planning

Considering the challenges discussed in this chapter and the responses that stakeholders involved in Indonesia's planning system have developed, there are many opportunities within contemporary urban Indonesia to build upon and develop more inclusive and participatory approaches to planning that could in turn make an important contribution to Southern Planning more broadly. There are several areas where Indonesia has positive experiences to contribute, both in terms of evolving discussions on how to improve urban governance and in terms of the proactive and innovative character of many of its grassroots urban communities.

Reformasi provided the opportunity to transform urban governance in the country, through more transparent, democratic and inclusive practices. This has been translated into the devolution of power to local governments, with clearer responsibilities and the explicit commitment to design and implement more inclusive social programs. Examples include the PNPM and Kotaku program discussed earlier that require the involvement of several government levels, community facilitators and local communities. The private sector has been involved in some initiatives, such as waste management in Surabaya. However, these initiatives are limited, and it is important that the private sector understands that in addition to profit-making, it needs to be committed to building inclusive cities, where poor groups and informal workers are not left out.

The idea that for urban planning to be effective it must be participatory, inclusive, open and transparent (UN-Habitat 2009) constitutes a key understanding of Southern Planning, as adopting this approach allows for local needs to be considered, and local knowledge and practices to be implemented, while bringing to the discussion table a broad range of actors, including those who have historically been marginalised. The Indonesian experience demonstrates progress in this area. In at least some parts of Indonesia, urban poor grassroots communities have become more active in decision-making processes to improve their neighbourhoods. Examples of this are the work of community group Kalijawi in Yogyakarta over the past 12 years (Murwani et al. 2023) and recent work by the community in

Kampung Akuarium, North Jakarta, to upgrade their housing units, resist eviction and establish a collaborative process between the community, a supporting non-government organisation and the local government (Sari et al. 2023).

Reformasi has also opened the door to incipient conversations about processes that need to be improved. One of these is *musrenbang*, which has lately been examined as a process that needs to be revised to become fully inclusive and democratic (Datta et al. 2011; Purba 2011). These conversations are mostly driven by non-government organisations, local communities that have managed to become 'visible' actors, and academics and universities (Murwani et al. 2023; Roitman 2019). Some local governments, even if slowly, have become more receptive to these criticisms. While there is still a long way to go in opening up decision-making processes, reducing the domination of top-down approaches and addressing corruption and noncompliance with planning guidelines by developers, the vibrancy of the discussions shows there is still an appetite for improving Indonesia's urban governance.

A second way in which Indonesia provides a positive example to the wider world of Southern Planning is in the proactive and organised nature of its grassroots urban communities. The history and contemporary experience of many urban *kampung* in Indonesia shows they can find their own solutions when government lacks the capacity or will to provide support. In this regard too, Indonesia's experience resonates with those of many countries in the Global South where governments often lack the financial and human resources needed to solve urban planning issues. In such circumstances, communities often step up and provide their own solutions. In Indonesia, many urban communities are proactive and well prepared when it comes to solving their own problems, as a consequence of strong social bonds that exist at the local level. Practices such as *gotong-royong* (mutual cooperation) that are embedded in the social structure of low-income residents are the foundation for strong social solidarity, enabling communities to take action in response to emerging problems at the grassroots whenever required.

As a result, Indonesian communities are creative and innovative. This applies to responses to improve housing and living conditions, as well as in terms of individual and community businesses. There are numerous success stories that illustrate these characteristics, such as Sukunan, the ecovillage in Yogyakarta where community members recycle their own waste (Iswanto et al. 2018), and Kampung Warna-Warni Jodipan in Malang (Sutikno 2023), a *kampung* that has become financially self-sufficient and able to fund community activities and address community needs by developing a 'slum-tourism' project.

The strong organisation many urban *kampung* communities have achieved has led to them developing the resilience to absorb the shocks of health and financial crises. The example of Kalijawi in Yogyakarta (Murwani et al. 2023) shows the range of strategies communities can develop in becoming resilient. Over a decade of organised actions, this community has established a Community Development Fund of US$50,000 to support communal and individual initiatives, created a social enterprise that provides food at low cost, conducted mapping processes to understand the needs and resources in each part of the community, and built communication channels with local governments to advocate for change and inclusion. This is just one example of the many success stories of community participation and of how the exchange of experiences and lessons learned is happening within the country.

Conclusion

The analysis of Indonesian planning I have provided in this chapter shows that Indonesian planning shares many of the features identified in the scholarly literature as being characteristic of Southern Planning. From a historical perspective, the national government tried to imitate successful practices from the Global North, and has provided strong direction on development planning countrywide. But the decentralisation of urban planning responsibilities, and the encouragement of community participation, have provided opportunities for bottom-up approaches, creating a hybrid urban planning system. Groups that had been previously left out have become more active in moulding their own cities. At the same time, non-observance of planning regulations, corruption and informal connections between government and an elite private sector have also shaped the character of Indonesia's urban centres since independence, and continue to do so today.

It is important not simply to view Southern Planning in general, and Indonesian planning in particular, in terms of a 'deficit perspective'. The improvements of the system need to be highlighted since, over the past two decades, democratisation has provided avenues for grassroots participation, giving ordinary residents of urban areas more opportunities to engage and create change in their urban environments. Although obstacles still stand in the way of a fully participatory system, around the country there are many success stories of community engagement showing that positive change from the grassroots is possible. There is a diversity of responses, rich and varied, each with unique potential. Success stories can be shared and scaled up, but need to be adapted to local conditions. Planning practices need to be elaborated according to the local environment and in ways that involve local communities.

References

Bachriadi, Dianto and Edward Aspinall. 2023. 'Land mafias in Indonesia'. *Critical Asian Studies* 55(3): 331–53. doi.org/10.1080/14672715.2023.2215261

Bayat, Asef. 1997. 'Un-civil society: The politics of the "informal" people'. *Third World Quarterly* 18(1): 53–72. doi.org/10.1080/01436599715055

Bishop, Ryan, John Phillips and Wei-Wei Yeo. 2003. 'Perpetuating cities: Excepting globalization and the Southeast Asia supplement'. In *Postcolonial Urbanism: Southeast Asian Cities and Global Processes*, edited by Ryan Bishop, John Phillips and Wei-Wei Yeo, 1–36. Routledge.

BPS (Badan Pusat Statistik, Statistics Indonesia). 2020. 'Berita resmi statistik Gini coefficient ratio provinsi 2002–2017 [Official provincial Gini coefficient ratio statistics, 2002–2017]'. BPS. www.bps.go.id/website/materi_ind/materiBrsInd-20200115120531.pdf

BPS (Badan Pusat Statistik, Statistics Indonesia). 2023a. Berita Resmi Statistik No. 47/07/Th. XXVI, 17 July. BPS. www.bps.go.id/pressrelease/2023/07/17/2016/profil-kemiskinan-di-indonesia-maret-2023-html

BPS (Badan Pusat Statistik, Statistics Indonesia). 2023b. Berita Resmi Statistik No. 48/07/Th. XXVI, 17 July. BPS. www.bps.go.id/pressrelease/2023/07/17/2035/gini-ratio-maret-2023-tercatat-sebesar-0-388-html

Colon, Marine and Ben Fawcett. 2006. 'Community-based household waste management: Lessons learnt from EXNORA's "zero waste management" scheme in two south Indian cities'. *Habitat International* 30(4): 916–31. doi.org/10.1016/j.habitatint.2005.04.006

Cowherd, Robert. 2005. 'Does planning culture matter? Dutch and American models in Indonesian urban transformations'. In *Comparative Planning Cultures*, edited by Bishwapriya Sanyal, 165–92. Routledge.

Das, Ashok and Asrizal Luthfi. 2017. 'Disaster risk reduction in post-decentralisation Indonesia: Institutional arrangements and changes'. In *Disaster Risk Reduction in Indonesia: Progress, Challenges, and Issues*, edited by Riyanti Djalante, Matthias Garschagen, Frank Thomalla and Rajib Shaw, 85–125. Springer. doi.org/10.1007/978-3-319-54466-3_4

Das, Ashok and Bambang Susantono. 2022. 'Introduction: Urban informality and the COVID-19 pandemic'. In *Informal Services in Asian Cities: Lessons for Urban Planning and Management from the COVID-19 Pandemic*, edited by Ashok Das and Bambang Susantono, 1–37. Asian Development Bank.

Datta, Ajoy, Harry Jones, Daniel Harris, Leni Wild and John Young. 2011. *The Political Economy of Policy-making in Indonesia: Opportunities for Improving the Demand for and Use of Knowledge*. ODI Working Paper 340. Overseas Development Institute.

Dieleman, Marleen. 2011. 'New town development in Indonesia: Renegotiating, shaping and replacing institutions'. *Bijdragen tot de Taal-, Land- en Volkenkunde* 167(1): 60–85. www.jstor.org/stable/41203121

Djalante, Riyanti and Matthias Garschagen. 2017. 'A review of disaster trend and disaster risk governance in Indonesia: 1900–2015'. In *Disaster Risk Reduction in Indonesia: Progress, Challenges, and Issues*, edited by Riyanti Djalante, Matthias Garschagen, Frank Thomalla and Rajib Shaw, 21–56. Springer. doi.org/10.1007/978-3-319-54466-3_2

Escobar, Arturo. 1992. 'Imagining a post-development era? Critical thought, development and social movements'. *Social Text* 31/32: 20–56. doi.org/10.2307/466217

Feliciani, Fitria Aurora. 2023. 'Path leading to urban sustainability: Reflections from solid waste management in Surabaya'. In *Routledge Handbook of Urban Indonesia*, edited by Sonia Roitman and Deden Rukmana, 352–66. Routledge. doi.org/10.4324/9781003318170-30

Gillespie, Tom and Diana Mitlin. 2023. 'Global development and urban studies: Tactics for thinking beyond the North–South binary'. *Environment & Urbanization* 35(2): 433–49. doi.org/10.1177/09562478231172057

Hadiz, Vedi R. and Richard Robison. 2013. 'The political economy of oligarchy and the reorganization of power in Indonesia'. *Indonesia* 96(1): 35–57. doi.org/10.5728/indonesia.96.0033

Herlambang, Suryono, Helga Leitner, Liong Ju Tjung, Eric Sheppard and Dimitar Anguelov. 2019. 'Jakarta's great land transformation: Hybrid neoliberalisation and informality'. *Urban Studies* 56(4): 627–48. doi.org/10.1177/0042098018756556

Iswanto, Sita Rahmani and Sonia Roitman. 2018. 'Sukunan village, Yogyakarta, Indonesia: Environmental sustainability through community-based waste management and eco-tourism'. In *Global Planning Innovations for Urban Sustainability*, edited by Sébastien Darchen and Glen Searle, 90–105. Routledge. doi.org/10.4324/9781351124225-7

Jellinek, Lea. 1991. *The Wheel of Fortune: The History of a Poor Community in Jakarta*. Allen & Unwin.

Joerin, Jonas and Rajib Shaw. 2010. 'Climate change adaptation and urban risk management'. In *Climate Change Adaptation and Disaster Risk Reduction: Issues and Challenges*, vol. 4, edited by Rajib Shaw, Juan M. Pulhin and Joy Jacqueline Pereira, 195–215. Emerald Publishing. doi.org/10.1108/S2040-7262(2010)0000004015

Kent, Anthony, Saut Sagala, Danang Azhari, Jeeten Kumar and Amesta Ramadhani. 2023. 'Planning for resilience in Bandung: Case studies of local disaster management strategies'. In *Routledge Handbook of Urban Indonesia*, edited by Sonia Roitman and Deden Rukmana, 311–23. Routledge. doi.org/10.4324/9781003318170-27

KPUPR (Kementerian Pekerjaan Umum dan Perumahan Rakyat) and World Bank. 2023. *Building Safe, Adequate and Affordable Housing in Indonesia*. KPUPR and World Bank.

MacRae, Graeme and Ljiljana Rodic. 2015. 'The weak link in waste management in tropical Asia? Solid waste collection in Bali'. *Habitat International* 50: 310–16. doi.org/10.1016/j.habitatint.2015.09.002

Mitlin, Diana and David Satterthwaite. 2013. *Urban Poverty in the Global South: Scale and Nature*. Routledge.

Murwani, Ainun, Atik Rochayati, Surati, Wulan Utami, Susilah, et al. 2023. 'Community organisation and neighbourhood improvement through collective action and bottom-up gender planning in Yogyakarta'. In *Routledge Handbook of Urban Indonesia*, edited by Sonia Roitman and Deden Rukmana, 102–16. Routledge. doi.org/10.4324/9781003318170-10

Negara, Siwage Dharma. 2017. 'Promoting growth with equity: Indonesia's 2018 budget'. *Perspective* 68: 1–13. ISEAS – Yusof Ishak Institute. www.iseas.edu.sg/wp-content/uploads/2017/09/ISEAS_Perspective_2017_68.pdf

Pratiwo and Peter J.M. Nas. 2005. 'Jakarta: Conflicting directions'. In *Directors of Urban Change in Asia*, edited by Peter J.M. Nas, 68–82. Routledge.

Purba, Rasita Ekawati. 2011. 'Public participation in development planning: A case study of Indonesian *musrenbang*'. *International Journal of Interdisciplinary Social Sciences: Annual Review* 5(12): 265–78. doi.org/10.18848/1833-1882/CGP/v05i12/51964

Roberts, Mark, Frederico Gil Sander and Sailesh Tiwari, eds. 2019. *Time to ACT: Realizing Indonesia's Urban Potential*. World Bank. doi.org/10.1596/978-1-4648-1389-4

Robinson, Jennifer. 2002. 'Global and world cities: A view from off the map'. *International Journal of Urban and Regional Research* 26(3): 531–54. doi.org/10.1111/1468-2427.00397

Roitman, Sonia. 2016. 'Top-down and bottom-up strategies for housing and poverty alleviation in Indonesia: The PNPM programme in Yogyakarta'. In *Dynamics and Resilience of Informal Areas: International Perspectives*, edited by Sahar Attia, Shahdan Shabka, Zeinab Shafik and Asmaa Ibrahim, 187–210. Springer. doi.org/10.1007/978-3-319-29948-8_11

Roitman, Sonia. 2018. 'How to use the power of urban planning to tackle inequality'. *The Conversation*, 9 February. https://theconversation.com/how-to-use-the-power-of-urban-planning-to-tackle-inequality-91010

Roitman, Sonia. 2019. 'Urban poverty alleviation strategies in Yogyakarta, Indonesia: Contrasting opportunities for community development'. *Asia Pacific Viewpoint* 60(3): 386–401. doi.org/10.1111/apv.12229

Roitman, Sonia and Redento B. Recio. 2020. 'Understanding Indonesia's gated communities and their relationship with inequality'. *Housing Studies* 35(5): 795–819. doi.org/10.1080/02673037.2019.1636002

Roitman, Sonia and Deden Rukmana. 2023. 'Urban Indonesia: Challenges and opportunities'. In *Routledge Handbook of Urban Indonesia*, edited by Sonia Roitman and Deden Rukmana, 3–14. Routledge. doi.org/10.4324/9781003318170-2

Roitman, Sonia and Peter Walters. 2024. 'The logic of informality in shaping urban collective action in the Global South'. In *Research Handbook on Urban Sociology*, edited by Miguel A. Martinez, 538–51. Edward Elgar Publishing.

Roy, Ananya. 2011. 'Postcolonial urbanism: Speed, hysteria, mass dreams'. In *Worlding Cities: Asian Experiments and the Art of Being Global*, edited by Ananya Roy and Aihwa Ong, 307–35. Wiley-Blackwell. doi.org/10.1002/9781444346800

Rukmana, Deden. 2015. 'The change and transformation of Indonesian spatial planning after Suharto's New Order regime: The case of the Jakarta metropolitan area'. *International Planning Studies* 20(4): 350–70. doi.org/10.1080/13563475.2015.1008723

Santos, Boaventura de Sousa. 2012. 'Public sphere and epistemologies of the South'. *Africa Development* 37(1): 43–67. www.jstor.org/stable/24484031

Sari, Amalia Nur Indah, Andesha Hermintomo, Dian Tri Irawaty and Vidya Tanny. 2023. 'Participation within the insurgent planning practices: A case of Kampung Susun Akuarium, Jakarta'. In *Routledge Handbook of Urban Indonesia*, edited by Sonia Roitman and Deden Rukmana, 58–72. Routledge. doi.org/10.4324/9781003318170-7

Sutikno, Fauzul Rizal. 2023. 'Community action and legibility of the state: The case of Malang'. In *Routledge Handbook of Urban Indonesia*, edited by Sonia Roitman and Deden Rukmana, 88–101. Routledge. doi.org/10.4324/9781003318170-9

UN-Habitat. 2009. *Planning Sustainable Cities: Global Report on Human Settlements 2009*. Earthscan. https://unhabitat.org/planning-sustainable-cities-global-report-on-human-settlements-2009

Watson, Vanessa. 2009. 'Seeing from the South: Refocusing urban planning on the globe's central urban issues'. *Urban Studies* 46(11): 2259–75. doi.org/10.1177/0042098009342598

Watson, Vanessa. 2016. 'Shifting approaches to planning theory: Global North and South'. *Urban Planning* 1(4): 32–41. doi.org/10.17645/up.v1i4.727

Wijayanti, Dyah Retno and Sri Suryani. 2015. 'Waste bank as community-based environmental governance: A lesson learned from Surabaya'. *Procedia: Social and Behavioral Sciences* 184: 171–79. doi.org/10.1016/j.sbspro.2015.05.077

Winarso, Haryo and Tommy Firman. 2002. 'Residential land development in Jabotabek, Indonesia: Triggering economic crisis?' *Habitat International* 26(4): 487–506. doi.org/10.1016/S0197-3975(02)00023-1

World Bank. 2019a. *Aspiring Indonesia: Expanding the Middle Class*. World Bank. www.worldbank.org/en/country/indonesia/publication/aspiring-indonesia-expanding-the-middle-class

World Bank. 2019b. *Global Economic Prospects: Darkening Skies*. World Bank. https://pubdocs.worldbank.org/en/431501542818370186/Global-Economic-Prospects-Jan-2019-Europe-and-Central-Asia-analysis.pdf

Yuniati, Vera. 2013. 'Inclusionary housing in Indonesia: The role of balanced residential ratio 1:3:6 in Makassar'. Magister Perencanaan Kota dan Daerah, Universitas Gadjah Mada, Yogyakarta.

5 Local budgets in urban Indonesia: Different characteristics need different policies

Erman Rahman, Ihsan Haerudin and Ronaldo Octaviano

Hand-in-hand with the rapid urbanisation of Indonesia over recent decades, the number of regions officially designated as cities (*kota*, sometimes also translated as 'municipalities') has risen sharply. At the outset of the post-Suharto period, in 1998, there were only 59 *kota* in Indonesia; by 2023 there were 93 autonomous *kota*. The number of rural districts or regencies (*kabupaten*), meanwhile, increased from 234 to 415 in the same period.[1] However, despite the different names, the central government generally treats *kota* and *kabupaten* as if they are the same. For example, it applies the same policies concerning local governance and public services, such as minimum service standards, performance reporting and evaluation methods, accountability systems and complaints handling management, to both *kota* and *kabupaten*. Likewise, the government applies fiscal policies and transfer formulas, which determine the size of local government budgets, on the basis of various demographic and development indicators without differentiating whether a district is a *kota* or a *kabupaten*.[2]

---

1 In addition, five administrative *kota* and one administrative *kabupaten* are part of the Special Capital Region of Jakarta. Different from autonomous *kota* and *kabupaten*, administrative *kota* and *kabupaten* are led by mayors appointed by the governor and do not have their own regional legislative council (Dewan Perwakilan Rakyat Daerah, DPRD).
2 To be sure, there are a few differences. The regulatory framework governing rural areas was significantly strengthened by Village Law 6/2014 that

In this chapter, we examine how district governments in urban Indonesia are performing in terms of delivering development and public service outcomes, in the context of the budgetary resources available to them. Government spending at this level is important. Since the introduction of decentralisation in 1999, districts budgets have accounted for almost one-third of overall spending, and are especially important in the health and education sectors, where they contribute more than half of spending (World Bank 2020: 27).

Analysts have had longstanding concerns about district budgets, development and public services in regional Indonesia, including the low contributions of own-source revenue to district budgets, high personnel spending and low capital expenditures, each of which has been seen as a major inhibitor of economic and social development in the regions (see, for example, Lewis and Smoke 2017; Patunru and Rahman 2014). Lewis (2017) found that district spending has positive impacts on public services. He argues that good financial management performance (which presumably primarily means less corrupt management), although moderated by a district's dependence on intergovernmental transfers, has a positive impact on public service access. More recently, USAID ERAT (2022: 6) identified that decentralisation has improved access to public services and reduced interdistrict disparity.

This chapter aims to build on these earlier studies by analysing variations in development outcomes, public services, and budgetary revenue and expenditure patterns among different kinds of districts based on their urban characteristics. In the first section, we start by more clearly differentiating among types of districts, devising seven separate categories based not simply on administrative type (i.e. *kota* versus *kabupaten*) but also on the basis of key urban characteristics (population size, and density and proportion of urbanised villages/wards). We identify that many (supposedly rural) *kabupaten* in fact have urban characteristics while many (supposedly urban) *kota* in fact look more rural: we call these, respectively, 'Urban Kabupaten' and 'Rural Kota' (though we might also think of them as 'fake *kabupaten*' and 'fake *kota*'). In the second section we

---

mandates central and district governments to transfer significant amounts of funds to rural villages (*desa*). In contrast, urban areas are governed only by a government regulation (*peraturan pemerintah,* PP). The most recent PP (59/2022) on urban areas (*perkotaan*) acknowledges the existence of urban areas within *kabupaten* in addition to *kota* and promotes the adoption of smart city policies aimed at improving public services. However, the regulation is mostly normative, adding administrative requirements for local governments to develop 'urban area development plans', but without additional empowerment measures or resources, as with the Village Law.

use this categorisation to show that, in general, more-urbanised districts have better development and service outcomes, although their rate of improvement is slower than in less-urbanised districts. In the third section we analyse local government revenues that show per capita government revenues are generally lower in more-urban districts, even though their ability to raise their own revenue is much greater.

We discuss district government spending patterns in the fourth section. In general, we find that higher development and public service outcomes do not primarily result from more public spending in these urban areas: on the contrary, more-urban districts have lower government budgets per capita. While we detect some variation in government spending (e.g. more-urbanised districts generally spend less on personnel and more on housing and public facilities), public spending patterns are generally similar across regions with different characteristics. This finding indicates that uniform directives from the central government are playing a more significant role in influencing budget policies than the voices of citizens of the districts and local technocratic planning process—despite Indonesia's decentralised governance framework. This is likely caused by the high dependency of districts on fiscal transfers from the central government. We conclude by arguing that it is important for the central government to start implementing asymmetric decentralisation policies to allow for different functional authorities, fiscal policies and monitoring priorities based on the different needs of different types of districts.

Classifying urban districts

In Indonesia, subnational development databases, such as development outcomes databases managed by BPS (Badan Pusat Statistik, Statistics Indonesia), and budget databases managed by the Ministry of Finance, are organised based on the distinction between *kota* and *kabupaten* as administrative units. We follow this approach in this chapter too, but we also need to emphasise that there are other ways to classify and distinguish among urban areas, as in other countries. The OECD (Organisation for Economic Co-operation and Development), for example, classifies cities into four categories based on population size: large metropolitan areas (more than 1.5 million people); metropolitan areas (between 500,000 and 1.5 million); medium-sized urban areas (200,000–500,000); and small urban areas (50,000–200,000).[3]

---

3 https://data.oecd.org/popregion/urban-population-by-city-size.htm, accessed 28 October 2023.

With the OECD criteria in mind, an initial scan of the characteristics of various *kota* and *kabupaten* indicates there is a need to develop a new classification system for Indonesia, one that goes beyond the sometimes arbitrary (in demographic terms) distinction between *kota* and *kabupaten*. Take, for example, the capital of Papua province, Jayapura: this *kota* had a population of 299,000 in 2020 and can therefore be classified in OECD terms as a medium-sized urban area. However, it covers a large area of 833 km^2, which makes its population density in 2020 only 360 people per km^2, much lower than the average *kota* density of 3,808 people per km^2 at that time. Another example is Subulussalam in Aceh province, a *kota* that had a population of 81,000 in 2020. Its population density was 69 people per km^2, with only 7 per cent of its villages (*desa*) and wards (*kelurahan*) categorised as urban areas according to BPS criteria.[4] In contrast, several supposedly rural *kabupaten* have strongly urban characteristics. For example, Kabupaten Tangerang in Banten province, part of the sprawling peri-urban zone surrounding Jakarta, had in 2020 a population of 3.77 million, a population density of 3,672 people per km^2, and 69 per cent of its villages and wards classified as urban. Kabupaten Sidoarjo in East Java, on the outskirts of Surabaya, had a population of 2.24 million, a population density of 3,085 people per km^2, and 84 per cent of its villages and wards classified as urban. In short, these *kabupaten* have demographic (population size and density) and spatial (proportion of urbanised villages/wards) characteristics that are more similar to large metropolitan areas than to rural districts, just as some *kota* resemble rural districts more than cities.

Combining the OECD criteria with population statistics and the BPS criteria used to classify whether a village or ward has urban or rural characteristics, we reclassify Indonesia's 415 *kabupaten* and 93 *kota* (2014–2023) into seven categories based on their administrative type, population size, population density and proportion of urban villages/wards. Our findings are summarised in Table 5.1. Using this approach, we refer to *kota* that have population densities of less than 1,000 people per km^2 or that have fewer than half of their villages and wards classified as urban as 'Rural Kota'—these are locations that are administratively classified as municipalities or cities (i.e. as *kota*) but that have the social characteristics

---

4 These criteria can be seen in BPS Regulation 37/2010 on Classification of Urban and Rural Areas in Indonesia. According to this regulation, a village or ward is classified as urban or rural based on its population density, proportion of agriculture-based households and access to urban facilities (schools, markets, hospitals, electricity, etc.). See chapter by Malamassam and Katherina, this volume, for more discussion. We use aggregated data for each *kota/kabupaten*.

Table 5.1 Seven district types

District category	Admin. type	Population density and % of urbanised villages/wards	Population
1. Rural Kabupaten	Kabupaten	<1,000 people/km² or <50% urbanised villages	
2. Rural Kota	Kota	<1,000 people/km² or <50% urbanised villages	
3. Urban Kabupaten	Kabupaten	≥1,000 people/km² and ≥50% urbanised villages	
4. Small Kota	Kota	≥1,000 people/km² and ≥50% urbanised villages	<0.3 million
5. Medium Kota	Kota	≥1,000 people/km² and ≥50% urbanised villages	≥0.3 to <0.5 million
6. Metropolitan Kota	Kota	≥1,000 people/km² and ≥50% urbanised villages	≥0.5 to <1.5 million
7. Large Metropolitan Kota	Kota	≥1,000 people/km² and ≥50% urbanised villages	≥1.5 million

Source: Classification by the authors based on OECD urban population criteria (https://data.oecd.org/popregion/urban-population-by-city-size.htm) and BPS Regulation 37/2010 on Classification of Urban and Rural Areas in Indonesia.

of rural areas. We classify other *kota* using the four population-based categories developed by the OECD. Meanwhile, we classify as 'Urban Kabupaten' those *kabupaten* with population densities of 1,000 people or more per km² and in which half or more villages and wards are categorised as urban. We call the remaining *kabupaten* 'Rural Kabupaten'. Figure 5.1 shows the distribution of the 415 *kabupaten* and 93 *kota* based on our new categories.

Table 5.2 describes general characteristics of these seven categories of districts, including their regional distribution. Among the seven categories, more than two-thirds of the total population (excluding those living in Special Capital Region Jakarta) in 2020 lived in Rural Kabupaten (68.7 per cent), followed by 11.9 per cent in Urban Kabupaten, 8.6 per cent in Large Metropolitan Kota and 5.2 per cent in Metropolitan Kota, while the rest were distributed in other categories. The table shows some clear regional patterns. For example, all 24 of the Rural Kota are located outside Java-Bali (71 per cent of them were established after decentralisation); all 15 Urban Kabupaten are located in Java and Bali, and are mostly located within the suburban sprawl surrounding major metropolitan areas. Most of the Small Kota and Medium Kota are located outside Java and Bali,

Figure 5.1 Categorisation of districts by population density and per cent of urbanised villages/wards

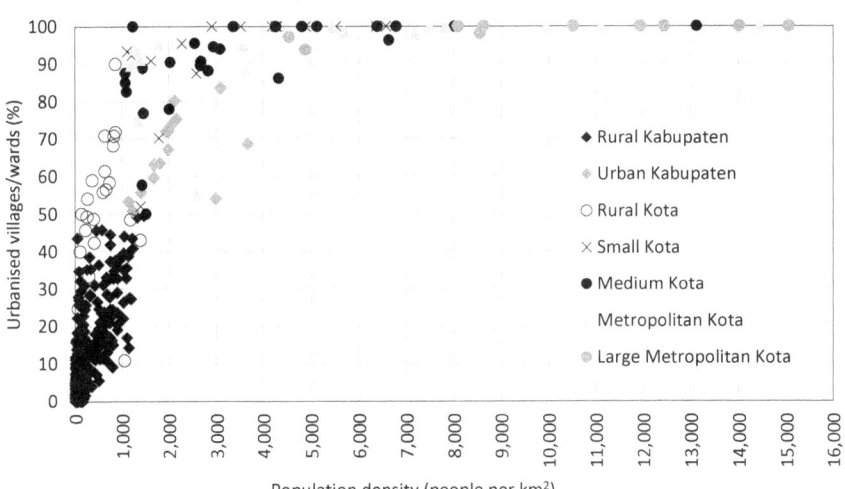

Source: Calculated by the authors from Susenas (Survei Sosial Ekonomi Nasional, National Socioeconomic Survey) data for relevant years produced and published by BPS (Badan Pusat Statistik, Statistics Indonesia), raw data of 2021 Podes (Potensi Desa, Village Potential) and Minister of Home Affairs Regulation 050-145/2022 on Code Identification and Update, Government Administration Regional Data and Islands, 2021.

whereas most of the Metropolitan Kota and Large Metropolitan Kota are either located in Java and Bali, or are provincial capitals outside those islands. Generally speaking, therefore, these patterns reflect the higher rate of urbanisation in Java and Bali compared to other parts of Indonesia (see chapter by Malamassam and Katherina, this volume). Table 5.2 also shows that Urban Kabupaten often have very large populations, but also large geographical areas, making their average population density less than even Small Kota. By contrast, Rural Kota generally have higher populations than Small Kota, but are spread over larger geographical areas with significantly lower population densities.

Development and public service outcomes

Having developed a new classification framework for analysing Indonesia's districts, we are now in a position to examine the variation in several development and public service outcomes among different district types. In Indonesia's post-Suharto decentralised model of government, district-level governments have considerable leeway to develop their own policies in many areas of development and public services, so we would expect to see considerable variation (Hill 2014).

Table 5.2 Seven district types, general characteristics

District category	Number of districts	Regional distribution	Average population	Proportion of total population* (%)	Average population density (people/km^2)	Average proportion of urbanised villages/wards (%)
1. Rural Kabupaten	400	All regions in Indonesia	440,762	68.7 (65.9)	234	11.7
2. Rural Kota	24	All outside Java-Bali	166,123	1.6 (1.5)	544	48.9
3. Urban Kabupaten	15	All in Java-Bali, mostly suburbs of metropolitan areas	2,032,520	11.9 (11.4)	2,060	66.2
4. Small Kota	16	Mostly outside Java-Bali, plus Kota Banjar, Kota Magelang, Kota Salatiga, Kota Blitar, Kota Madiun and Kota Mojokerto	140,644	0.9 (0.8)	3,409	92.6
5. Medium Kota	27	In all regions (outside Java, mostly provincial capitals)	310,619	3.3 (3.1)	3,778	90.1
6. Metropolitan Kota	16	All in Java-Bali, Sumatra and Kalimantan (outside Java-Bali, mostly provincial capitals)	835,751	5.2 (5.0)	5,366	92.5
7. Large Metropolitan Kota	10	Mostly in Java plus Kota Medan, Kota Palembang and Kota Makassar	2,199,038	8.6 (8.2)	9,867	98.9

* Excludes the population of Special Capital Region Jakarta. Values in parentheses indicate proportion of the total population including Special Capital Region Jakarta of 10.62 million people.

Source: Calculated by the authors from Susenas (Survei Sosial Ekonomi Nasional, National Socioeconomic Survey) data for relevant years produced and published by BPS (Badan Pusat Statistik, Statistics Indonesia), raw data of 2021 Podes (Potensi Desa, Village Potential) and Minister of Home Affairs Regulation 050-145/2022 on Code Identification and Update, Government Administration Regional Data and Islands, 2021.

Development outcomes

In Tables 5.3, 5.4 and 5.5 we compare the seven district types in terms of their performance across three key development indicators: human development index (HDI), poverty rate, and per capita regional gross domestic product (RGDP). As might be expected, these tables show that the general pattern is that more-urbanised districts perform better, and that larger cities do better than smaller cities. However, the rate of improvement of development outcomes in more-urbanised districts from 2016 to 2022 was generally worse than in rural districts, particularly on HDI and poverty, which indicates a reduction of interdistrict disparities. Part of the explanation might be that the COVID-19 pandemic affected urbanised districts more than rural districts; in particular, Urban Kabupaten (mostly suburbs of metropolitan areas in Java-Bali) were the hardest hit by the pandemic.

This pattern is particularly apparent with the HDI. As shown in Table 5.3, the average HDI in 2016 was by far the lowest in Rural Kabupaten and increased as districts became more urbanised. However, the trends over 2016–2022 worked against this pattern, with less-urbanised districts improving more. Again, we suspect the greater impact of COVID-19 in more-urbanised districts was a major contributor: Large Metropolitan Kota even experienced a decrease in HDI in the 2019–2020 period, while the HDI in other district categories marginally increased during the same period.

Table 5.3 Average human development index (HDI) based on district category, 2016–2022

District category	HDI		Average annual HDI change (index points)				
	2016	2022	2016–22	2016–19	2019–20	2020–21	2021–22
1. Rural Kabupaten	65.38	68.39	0.50	0.64	0.12	0.29	0.69
2. Rural Kota	72.48	75.15	0.45	0.59	0.05	0.25	0.60
3. Urban Kabupaten	73.63	76.48	0.47	0.61	0.07	0.32	0.62
4. Small Kota	75.95	78.48	0.42	0.49	0.06	0.30	0.71
5. Medium Kota	76.57	79.11	0.42	0.51	0.07	0.31	0.62
6. Metropolitan Kota	77.48	79.91	0.40	0.50	0.05	0.37	0.51
7. Large Metropolitan Kota	79.46	81.88	0.40	0.55	-0.06	0.34	0.50

Source: Calculated by the authors from BPS (Statistics Indonesia) data (https://bps.go.id/indicator/26/413/4/-metode-baru-indeks-pembangunan-manusia.html, accessed 2 September 2023).

Table 5.4 Average poverty rate based on district category, 2016–2022 (%)

District category	Average poverty rate		Average annual poverty reduction (percentage points)				
	2016	2022	2016–22	2016–19	2019–20	2020–21	2021–22
1. Rural Kabupaten	14.71	13.01	0.28	0.43	0.10	-0.31	0.63
2. Rural Kota	9.64	8.32	0.22	0.32	0.13	-0.32	0.57
3. Urban Kabupaten	8.40	7.62	0.13	0.47	-0.68	-0.50	0.56
4. Small Kota	7.64	6.64	0.17	0.30	-0.08	-0.34	0.53
5. Medium Kota	8.12	7.30	0.14	0.28	-0.15	-0.33	0.47
6. Metropolitan Kota	6.28	5.79	0.08	0.29	-0.31	-0.38	0.32
7. Large Metropolitan Kota	5.47	5.16	0.05	0.25	-0.40	-0.34	0.29

Note: A negative poverty reduction rate indicates an increasing poverty rate over time.

Source: Calculated by the authors from BPS (Statistics Indonesia) data (https://bps.go.id/indicator/23/621/4/persentase-penduduk-miskin-p0-menurut-kabupaten-kota.html, accessed 2 September 2023).

There is a similar pattern in poverty (Table 5.4), with more-urbanised districts having relatively low poverty rates in 2016 but also lower rates of reduction over the following six years. However, more-urbanised districts also face higher (and growing) income inequality (Roberts et al. 2019). The pandemic had a greater and more immediate impact on poverty reduction in more-urbanised districts, especially in Urban Kabupaten, Metropolitan Kota and Large Metropolitan Kota from 2019 to 2020. In comparison, Rural Kabupaten and Rural Kota were relatively resilient and able to slightly reduce poverty in 2020, indicating the pandemic had not fully reached rural districts at that time. Hypothetically, if the 2016–2019 poverty reduction continued without any COVID-19 interruption, the poverty rates of Urban Kabupaten, Metropolitan Kota and Large Metropolitan Kota would be 1.2–2.0 per cent lower than the actual 2020 rates, while the other district types would be around 0.6–0.9 per cent lower. Hence, the pandemic can be seen as contributing to the convergence of urban-rural poverty rates.

Patterns and trends with per capita RGDP are a little different (Table 5.5). Not only did more-urbanised districts have significantly higher per capita RGDP in 2016, they also had higher per capita RGDP growth in the pre-pandemic period of 2016–2019, suggesting that the urban-rural wealth gap was widening. The average 2016 per capita RGDP of Large Metropolitan Kota was almost double that of Rural Kabupaten and Rural Kota. The annual growth in the former was 3.4 per cent per annum during

Table 5.5 Average per capita regional gross domestic product (RGDP) based on district category, 2016–2022 (constant prices 2010)

District category	Per capita RGDP (Rp million/person)		Annual per capita RGDP growth (%)				
	2016	2022	2016–22	2016–19	2019–20	2020–21	2021–22
1. Rural Kabupaten	39.94	36.13	3.2	2.8	-2.0	3.4	3.8
2. Rural Kota	38.95	34.47	2.9	2.8	-2.3	3.1	3.4
3. Urban Kabupaten	43.24	35.38	2.3	2.9	-5.1	1.9	4.2
4. Small Kota	62.42	51.33	2.7	2.9	-2.6	1.9	3.6
5. Medium Kota	67.07	58.51	2.6	2.8	-4.1	3.4	3.5
6. Metropolitan Kota	58.71	52.10	2.8	3.0	-3.9	3.1	4.4
7. Large Metropolitan Kota	73.18	66.32	3.2	3.4	-4.0	3.4	4.1

Source: Calculated by the authors from BPS (Statistics Indonesia) data (https://bps.go.id/indicator/171/2194/4/-seri-2010-pdrb-atas-dasar-harga-konstan-2010-100-menurut-pengeluaran-kabupaten-kota.html, accessed 2 September 2023).

2016–2019, while all other districts grew by 2.8–3.0 per cent. The COVID-19 pandemic initially had a negative impact on economic growth across all district types (2019–2020), although all recovered in 2021–2022 with higher growth rates than pre-pandemic levels. In particular, Urban Kabupaten experienced the largest economic contraction in 2020 and the lowest growth the year after. Overall, if we compare growth rates for the entire 2016–2022 period with the average pre-pandemic growth in 2016–2019, we see that the divergence of RGDP growth was slightly interrupted by the pandemic: actual average 2016–2022 growth in all urban district types was lower than the average 2016–2019 growth, while in the two rural district types RGDP growth was higher.

Public service outcomes

Similar to development outcomes, public service outcomes in general are positively correlated with district urbanisation levels, based on four indicators: school enrolment rate (SER) for students aged 13–15 years (hereafter '13-15 SER'), percentage of births attended by professional workers ('attended births'), access to clean water and access to sanitation. We show that Rural Kabupaten have significantly lower performance on these measures compared to all the more-urbanised district types. Generally, more-urbanised districts have worse performance in terms of their rate of improvement of public service outcomes, but this is most

Table 5.6 School enrolment rate for students aged 13–15 years (13-15 SER) based on district category, 2016–2022 (%)

District category	Average 13-15 SER		Average annual change (percentage points)				
	2016	2022	2016–22	2016–19	2019–20	2020–21	2021–22
1. Rural Kabupaten	92.92	94.32	0.23	0.40	0.19	0.12	-0.11
2. Rural Kota	97.14	96.76	-0.06	-0.04	0.04	0.31	-0.62
3. Urban Kabupaten	96.58	97.56	0.16	0.23	0.17	0.58	-0.44
4. Small Kota	97.24	97.30	0.01	0.07	-0.04	0.00	-0.12
5. Medium Kota	97.15	97.83	0.11	0.15	-0.03	-0.08	0.34
6. Metropolitan Kota	96.50	97.02	0.09	0.17	0.36	0.34	-0.69
7. Large Metropolitan Kota	96.24	97.56	0.22	0.39	0.08	0.24	-0.18
Overall average	93.77	94.96	0.20	0.34	0.17	0.14	-0.14

Source: Calculated by the authors from Susenas data for the relevant years published by BPS.

likely due to the fact that, being closer to 100 per cent coverage, they find it harder to cover the 'last mile'. As a result of this rural catch up, however, interdistrict disparity on access to public services has been narrowing.

With regard to 13-15 SER, Rural Kabupaten have the worst performance, with only 93 per cent 13-15 SER in 2016 (Table 5.6). In the same year, the 13-15 SER in the six other district categories was in the 96–97 per cent range. Over the following six years, however, Rural Kabupaten achieved the greatest improvement; Large Metropolitan Kota were something of an anomaly, also achieving a similar level of improvement. In general, the negative impact of the pandemic in decreasing 13-15 SER occurred only in 2022, particularly in Rural Kota, Urban Kabupaten and Metropolitan Kota.

Attended births were generally high across all districts, except in Rural Kabupaten (Table 5.7). However, Rural Kabupaten significantly improved their performance from 84.7 per cent of births attended in 2016 to 91.5 per cent in 2022. Urban districts had better baseline performance, with Small Kota and Large Metropolitan Kota standing out by having almost 100 per cent of births attended by professional health workers in 2016. These strong results may have different causes: Small Kota governments may perform better due to having relatively small populations and high population densities, while citizens in Large Metropolitan Kota have better access to private health services. The impact of COVID-19 on attended births was again worse in the most-urbanised districts, especially in Java-Bali—that is, in Urban Kabupaten, Metropolitan Kota and Large Metropolitan Kota.

Table 5.7 Proportion of births attended by professional health workers (attended births) based on district category, 2016–2022 (%)

District category	Average attended births		Average annual change (percentage points)				
	2016	2022	2016–22	2016–19	2019–20	2020–21	2021–22
1. Rural Kabupaten	84.68	91.50	1.14	1.49	1.20	1.01	0.15
2. Rural Kota	95.63	97.65	0.34	0.50	-0.39	0.45	0.47
3. Urban Kabupaten	96.28	97.29	0.17	0.46	0.42	-0.54	-0.25
4. Small Kota	99.84	99.96	0.02	-0.03	-0.11	0.02	0.30
5. Medium Kota	96.83	98.42	0.27	0.52	-0.05	-0.16	0.24
6. Metropolitan Kota	96.86	97.10	0.04	0.38	0.53	-0.49	-0.95
7. Large Metropolitan Kota	99.10	99.11	0.00	0.09	-0.11	0.40	-0.56
Overall average	87.33	92.93	0.93	1.35	0.95	0.79	0.12

Source: Calculated by the authors from Susenas data for the relevant years published by BPS.

Access to clean water includes piped water supply and also wells, springs and rainwater reservoirs. When it comes to provision of access to clean water for citizens, districts are divided into three main groups: Rural Kabupaten had the worst performance, serving only 74 per cent of their populations in 2016, although this figure increased annually by 1.6 per cent across 2016–2022; Rural Kota, at 86 per cent in 2016, had a moderate increase of 0.8 per cent annually; and the remaining, more-urbanised districts had 95–98 per cent coverage in 2016 and the lowest increases (Table 5.8).

Access to sanitation was similar: Rural Kabupaten in 2016 provided the lowest coverage, at only 57 per cent; Large Metropolitan Kota provided the highest (86 per cent); and the five other urban districts fell in between, with 80–84 per cent coverage (Table 5.9). Six years later, Rural Kabupaten had significantly improved access to 75 per cent (an annual increase of 2.9 percentage points), closing the gap with Rural Kota at 83 per cent. Meanwhile, slow improvement in Large Metropolitan Kota and high improvement in Urban Kabupaten created convergence across the five urban district categories to 88–90 per cent coverage in 2022.

In general, with the exception of economic growth, all of the development and public service outcome measures analysed indicates that they are positively correlated with district urbanisation level. We also see that less-urbanised districts are 'catching up' with urbanised districts, indicating convergence of development and public service outcomes. With regard to economic growth, however, the gap remains wide (Table 5.5).

Table 5.8 Access to clean drinking water based on district category, 2016–2022 (%)

District category	Access to clean water		Average annual change (percentage points)				
	2016	2022	2016–22	2016–19	2019–20	2020–21	2021–22
1. Rural Kabupaten	74.30	83.71	1.57	1.58	1.38	1.52	1.76
2. Rural Kota	85.78	90.35	0.76	0.77	2.47	0.60	-0.81
3. Urban Kabupaten	95.22	95.88	0.11	0.53	-0.12	-0.43	-0.39
4. Small Kota	95.98	97.73	0.29	0.24	0.64	-0.08	0.47
5. Medium Kota	95.52	97.77	0.37	0.59	-0.47	1.12	-0.16
6. Metropolitan Kota	95.78	97.42	0.27	0.28	0.84	0.34	-0.39
7. Large Metropolitan Kota	97.85	98.05	0.03	0.16	0.02	0.49	-0.80
Overall average	78.41	86.29	1.31	1.35	1.23	1.29	1.31

Source: Calculated by the authors from Susenas data for the relevant years published by BPS.

Table 5.9 Access to proper sanitation based on district category, 2016–2022 (%)

District category	Access to proper sanitation		Average annual change (percentage points)				
	2016	2022	2016–22	2016–19	2019–20	2020–21	2021–22
1. Rural Kabupaten	57.42	74.98	2.93	4.14	3.07	1.23	0.84
2. Rural Kota	79.74	83.40	0.61	0.47	0.70	1.35	0.22
3. Urban Kabupaten	80.56	88.93	1.40	1.88	0.38	0.26	2.10
4. Small Kota	83.00	87.87	0.81	1.12	1.35	-0.10	0.27
5. Medium Kota	83.66	88.86	0.87	1.65	0.55	1.60	-1.90
6. Metropolitan Kota	81.42	86.17	0.79	1.14	1.36	2.19	-2.24
7. Large Metropolitan Kota	86.25	89.64	0.57	1.25	-0.54	1.22	-1.04
Overall average	62.68	77.57	2.48	3.52	2.56	1.22	0.55

Source: Calculated by the authors from Susenas data for the relevant years published by BPS.

More-urbanised districts not only have high per capita RGDP, they also enjoyed higher economic growth (although it was interrupted by the COVID-19 pandemic that hit them worse than rural districts). Specifically on two 'miscategorised' district types—Urban Kabupaten and Rural Kota—the former had similar development and public service outcomes to other types of *kota*, rather than to Rural Kabupaten, and was the hardest hit by the pandemic. Meanwhile, with the exceptions of the economy and access to water, Rural Kota have similar development and public service outcomes to other types of *kota*.

Local budget revenues

Under Indonesia's decentralised system of government, district governments contribute a large share of overall public spending, including in basic education, health care and infrastructure that are so crucial to social welfare and economic development. District government spending is thus critical to addressing both longstanding and emerging problems of urban governance: public transport, waste management, housing, slum areas, and flood prevention and other disaster risks. This section explores what magnitude of resources district-level governments have available to them, and how far they vary across different types of districts.

Based on 2017–2021 local budget data provided by the Directorate General of Fiscal Balance of the Ministry of Finance, the average per capita budget revenues (nominal) of all 508 districts in Indonesia increased from Rp 5.8 million (US$390) per person in 2017–2018 to Rp 6.3 million (US$419) per person in 2019. This was due to increasing intergovernmental transfers from the central government, and not driven by increasing own-source revenue (OSR). The COVID-19 pandemic reduced revenues to about Rp 5.8 million (US$386) per person in 2021–2022; by the time of writing they had not yet returned to pre-pandemic levels. Among our seven district types, Rural Kabupaten, Rural Kota and Small Kota had the highest and relatively similar per capita budget revenues, around Rp 6.1–6.8 million (US$405–454) per year in the 2017–2021 period (Figure 5.2). In contrast, high population Urban Kabupaten, Metropolitan Kota and Large Metropolitan Kota had the lowest per capita budget revenues, at around Rp 2.0–2.6 million (US$133–176) per year—about one-third of the richest three district categories. As discussed in the following paragraphs, more than half of district revenues are sourced from intergovernmental transfers, in which the General Allocation Grant (Dana Alokasi Umum, DAU) is the main transfer instrument. The DAU formula is biased against more-urbanised districts, based on formulas used prior to the issue of new Law 1/2022 on Central-Subnational Government Fiscal Relations ('Fiscal Balance Law'). More-urbanised districts tended to have smaller geographic areas, higher HDI and higher per capita RGDP that 'penalised' them in terms of the DAU allocation prior to 2022, despite their higher populations. Furthermore, the formula created disincentives for more-urbanised districts to generate higher OSR, since this would reduce their DAU allocation.

Figure 5.2 Per capita budget revenues, 2017–2021

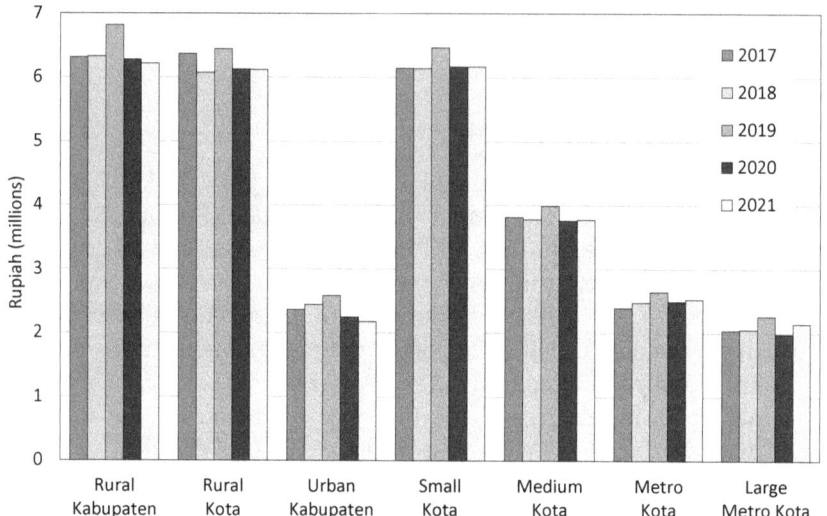

Source: Calculated by the authors from data from the Directorate General of Fiscal Balance, Ministry of Finance (https://djpk.kemenkeu.go.id/?p=5412, accessed 10 May 2023) and Susenas data.

Intergovernmental transfers from the central government are the main revenue source for all types of districts, while the contribution of OSR is limited, although increasing. OSR is potentially very important, because if districts raise considerable revenue locally, they will have much greater capacity to fund their own development and welfare activities. Most districts, however, have very limited achievements in this regard. Patunru and Rahman (2014) identified that the average contribution of OSR in 2013 was only 6 per cent in *kabupaten* and 13 per cent in *kota*. In 2017–2021 our own analysis indicates that the average OSR contribution in Rural Kabupaten and Rural Kota ranged from 8 to 12 per cent, in Small Kota and Medium Kota the figures were 16–21 per cent, in Urban Kabupaten and Metropolitan Kota they were 29–33 per cent, and the highest figures were in Large Metropolitan Kota at 41–45 per cent.

However, given that since 2015 the OSR category has included reimbursements paid to districts from the national health insurance scheme, OSR is no longer a good indicator of a district's fiscal autonomy because district governments are required to spend these reimbursements on their health facilities. The other components of OSR are local taxes and levies (*pajak daerah dan retribusi daerah*, PDRD) and revenues from locally owned assets. PDRD has various components, including land and property taxes, advertisement taxes, food and beverage taxes, hotel taxes, cultural and entertainment taxes, waste management levies, parking levies and market levies (Government Regulation 35/2023 on General Provisions on Local Taxes and Local Levies; Ketentuan Umum Pajak Daerah dan Retribusi Daerah).

Table 5.10 shows massive variation in the contribution of these local taxes and levies to local government revenues, ranging from just 3 per cent in Rural Kabupaten to over one-third in Large Metropolitan Kota. Rural Kabupaten, Rural Kota and Small Kota, given their very low rates of PDRD, are still highly dependent on intergovernmental transfers. Using RGDP as a proxy for the potential for local districts to raise their own taxes and charges, we devise a 'local tax-levy ratio' (PDRD : RGDP) that shows how effective districts are at raising revenue from their local economies. Table 5.10 shows that Urban Kabupaten and Large Metropolitan Kota had the highest ratios of 1.1 per cent and 1.0 per cent, respectively (2017–2021 average). These findings suggest that both types of district have higher property values than other district types. In addition, Urban Kabupaten seem to have better endowments in terms of large geographic areas and high populations, while Large Metropolitan Kota have higher population densities and more concentrated economic activities that allow them to better collect local taxes and charges. In contrast, the local tax-levy ratio in Rural Kabupaten was only 0.4 per cent in the same period, indicating extremely low capacity to generate revenue.

Table 5.10 Composition of local taxes and levies (PDRD) and contributions to total budget revenue and regional gross domestic product (2017–2021 average)

District category	Per capita PDRD (Rp/person/year)	% PDRD of OSR	% PDRD of total revenue	% PDRD of RGDP
1. Rural Kabupaten	144,991	34.54	3.29	0.36
2. Rural Kota	266,253	44.64	5.02	0.62
3. Urban Kabupaten	620,889	57.31	20.27	1.11
4. Small Kota	315,063	31.34	5.24	0.52
5. Medium Kota	395,522	53.39	10.38	0.62
6. Metropolitan Kota	492,123	72.27	20.11	0.76
7. Large Metropolitan Kota	745,918	81.96	35.24	1.03

Note: PDRD = *pajak daerah dan retribusi daerah* (local taxes and levies), OSR = own-source revenue, RGDP = regional gross domestic product.

Source: Calculated by the authors from data from the Directorate General of Fiscal Balance, Ministry of Finance (https://djpk.kemenkeu.go.id/?p=5412, accessed 10 May 2023) and Susenas data.

Overall, what these figures tell us is that, generally, the more urban a district, the greater its ability to generate its own revenue from local taxes and charges. Large Metropolitan Kota and Urban Kabupaten—particularly those located around Jakarta—are especially advanced in maximising their PDRD potential. While the greater capacity of urban governments to collect PDRD may be caused by relatively lower clientelism in urban areas than in rural areas, as argued by Berenschot (2018) (in this argument, less-clientelist governments would be better at raising taxes, because they are less affected by corruption), it may also be driven by better endowments. PDRD are mostly levied on economic activities that are more likely to be concentrated in urban areas. Cities also have greater access to the internet and technology and higher potential for adopting more efficient tax collection and administration. However, in a detailed look at the three cities analysed by Mustafa in this volume, the local tax-levy ratio is highest in South Tangerang (1.9 per cent), followed by Bogor (1.4 per cent) and Surabaya (0.7 per cent). This is negatively correlated with Mustafa's argument that strong civil society and government leadership is required for governance reforms, with the worst governed district of the three having the highest local tax-levy ratio. This outcome may reflect, in contrast to Berenschot's (2018) argument, that more-corrupt district governments are incentivised to increase their PDRD because this will enlarge public resources that allow leaders to introduce welfare programs to shore up their popularity while also expanding their ability to act corruptly.

Local budget expenditure

The Indonesian government provides various classifications to distinguish among the major expenditure items of district governments. These classifications include personnel, capital, goods and services, and transfers (mainly to villages). Transfer spending is the most significant difference between *kabupaten* (and Rural Kota) and urban districts given that the 2014 Village Law (article 72) requires district governments to transfer 10 per cent of the discretionary transfers they receive from the central government and 10 per cent of their local taxes and levies to villages. This policy applies to both *kabupaten* and *kota* that have rural villages (*desa*). As a result, Rural Kabupaten, Urban Kabupaten and Rural Kota spend a relatively high proportion of their local budgets on these transfers, which is not the case with other urban district categories (Figure 5.3).

To see different spending patterns among the district categories, we removed transfer spending from our analysis. When we used the government's economic classification of expenditure types, there was

Figure 5.3 Local budget spending (%) by economic classification and district category, 2017–2021

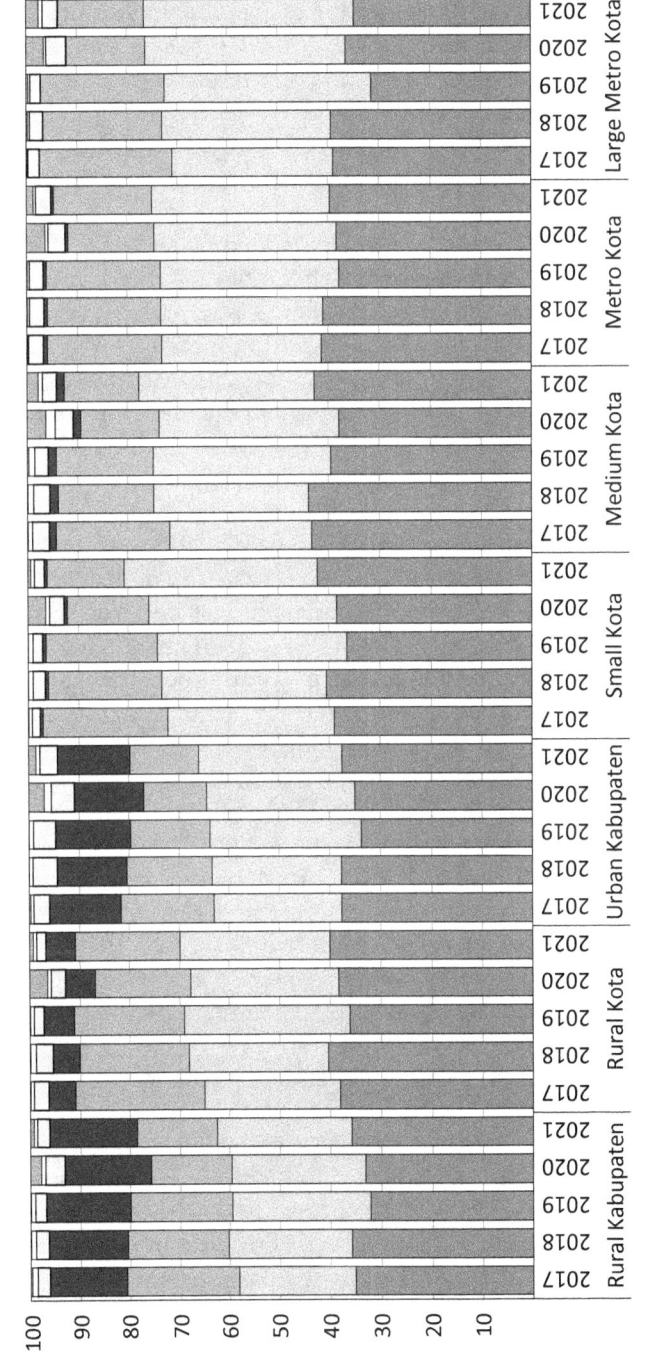

Source: Calculated by the authors from data from the Directorate General of Fiscal Balance, Ministry of Finance (https://djpk.kemenkeu.go.id/?p=5412, accessed 10 May 2023).

no major difference in spending patterns among the district categories, except that Rural Kabupaten and Rural Kota spent a higher proportion of their budgets on capital expenditure, while Large Metropolitan Kota spent more on goods and services and less on personnel (Figure 5.4). This pattern makes sense since the need for infrastructure development in less-urbanised districts is higher, while Large Metropolitan Kota prioritise operation and maintenance of existing infrastructure through goods and services spending.

The impacts of COVID-19 on local budget spending appear to be similar across the different district categories. This indicates the changes were driven primarily by the central government's instruction to reallocate capital spending towards operational spending (notably on goods and services) for health, education, and social and economic services. In general, local governments in all types of districts responded similarly to the instruction, although there was high regional variation in the scale of the pandemic.

Specifically on personnel spending, our analysis finds significant improvement across different district types. In 2013, personnel and administrative expenditure comprised more than half of district budget spending (Patunru and Rahman 2014), while it was between 35 and 43 per cent among the seven district categories in 2021 (Figure 5.3). However, districts still find it difficult to meet the maximum personnel spending required by the new Fiscal Balance Law (article 146) of 30 per cent of total expenditures. A detailed look at local budgets in 2021 shows that only 79 districts met this requirement (Table 5.11). With the exceptions of South Tangerang (Large Metropolitan Kota) and Subulussalam and Tual (both Rural Kota), all of the compliant districts were Rural Kabupaten, with the vast bulk located outside Java-Bali. By contrast, more than 60 per cent of districts in the Small Kota and Medium Kota categories spent over 40 per cent of their budgets on personnel. Moreover, based on the 2019–2021 trend, the proportion spent on personnel generally increased, suggesting it will be very difficult for most districts to comply with the 2027 target date set down in the law.

We can also analyse expenditure patterns based on local government functions (in addition to the above economic classifications, the Indonesian government tags local budgets according to nine functions: general services, order and security, economic activities, environmental protection, housing and public facilities, health, tourism, education and social protection). Our analysis (Figure 5.5) shows that, in general, district governments across different levels of urbanisation spend the most on general services (most of which is government administration), education, health, housing and public facilities (including water supply) and

Figure 5.4 Local budget spending (%) by economic classification and district category, adjusted (without transfers), 2017–2021

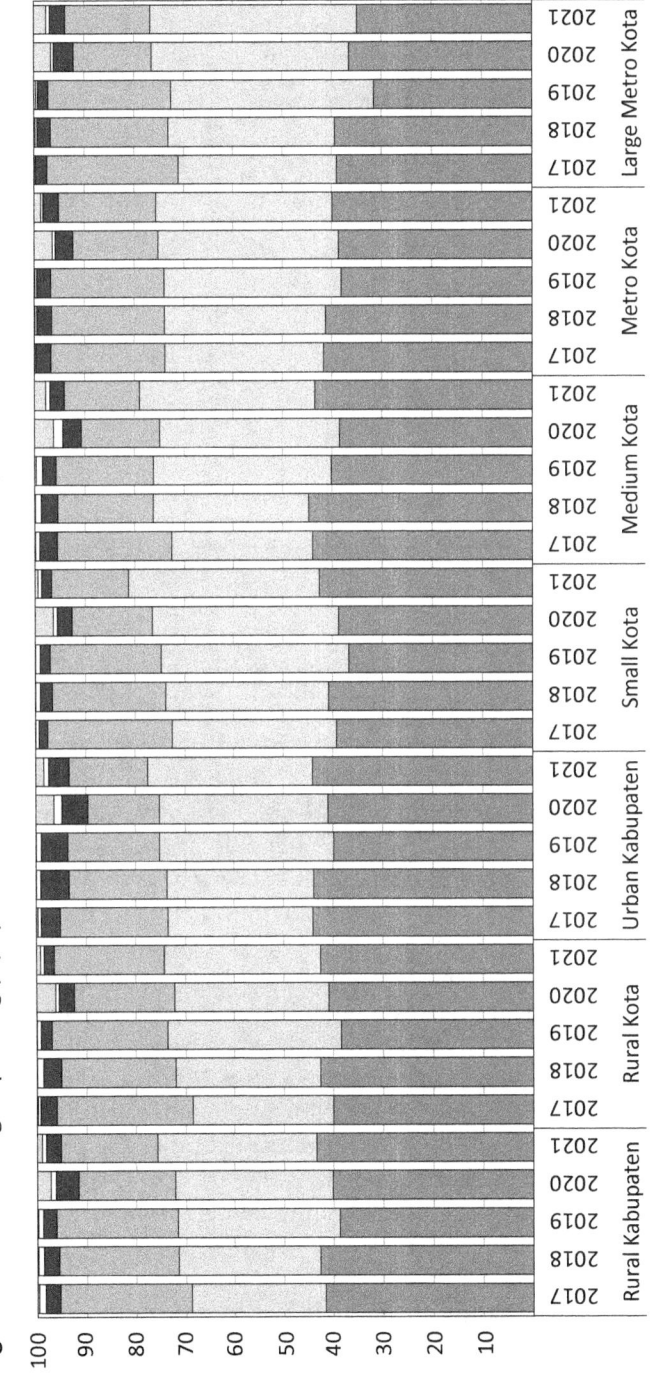

Source: Calculated by the authors from data from the Directorate General of Fiscal Balance, Ministry of Finance (https://djpk.kemenkeu.go.id/?p=5412, accessed 10 May 2023).

Table 5.11 District compliance with mandatory personnel spending, 2017–2021

District category	Number of districts complying with mandatory personnel spending					Number of districts with 30–40% personnel spending, 2021
	2017	2018	2019	2020	2021	
1. Rural Kabupaten	89	78	131	101	76	214
2. Rural Kota	2	1	2	1	2	9
3. Urban Kabupaten	2	2	3	3	0	10
4. Small Kota	0	0	2	1	0	6
5. Medium Kota	0	0	0	2	0	9
6. Metropolitan Kota	0	0	0	1	0	8
7. Large Metropolitan Kota	0	1	3	1	1	9
Total	93	82	141	110	79	265

Source: Calculated by the authors from data from the Directorate General of Fiscal Balance, Ministry of Finance (https://djpk.kemenkeu.go.id/?p=5412, accessed 10 May 2023) and Susenas data.

economic activities (including transport). It is likely that citizen demand and electoral pressures (as well as central government instructions) are driving high spending in these sectors, except general services.

In 2017–2019, before COVID-19, less-urbanised districts spent more on general services and less on housing and public facilities compared to more-urbanised districts such as Metropolitan Kota and Large Metropolitan Kota. Relatively higher proportions of general spending in Rural Kabupaten may indicate worse budget policies or even be driven by higher clientelism, as argued by Berenschot (2018). On the other hand, higher pre-pandemic spending on housing and public facilities in more-urbanised districts may be driven by sound technocratic budget planning, stronger citizen voices or less-clientelist governments. All district types spent a significant proportion of their budgets on the education and health sectors, driven by the central government's mandatory spending, discussed below. Small Kota had a particularly interesting spending pattern in 2017–2019, as they stand out as the highest spender on health and social protection functions among the seven district categories (Figure 5.5). The COVID-19 pandemic changed spending priorities similarly across districts, with central government instructions being a main driver. Spending on health increased dramatically in 2020–2021, as did spending on the economic activity function, reflecting government efforts to protect the economy. These increases came at the expense of housing and public facilities.

Figure 5.5 Local budget spending (%) by government function and district category, 2017–2021

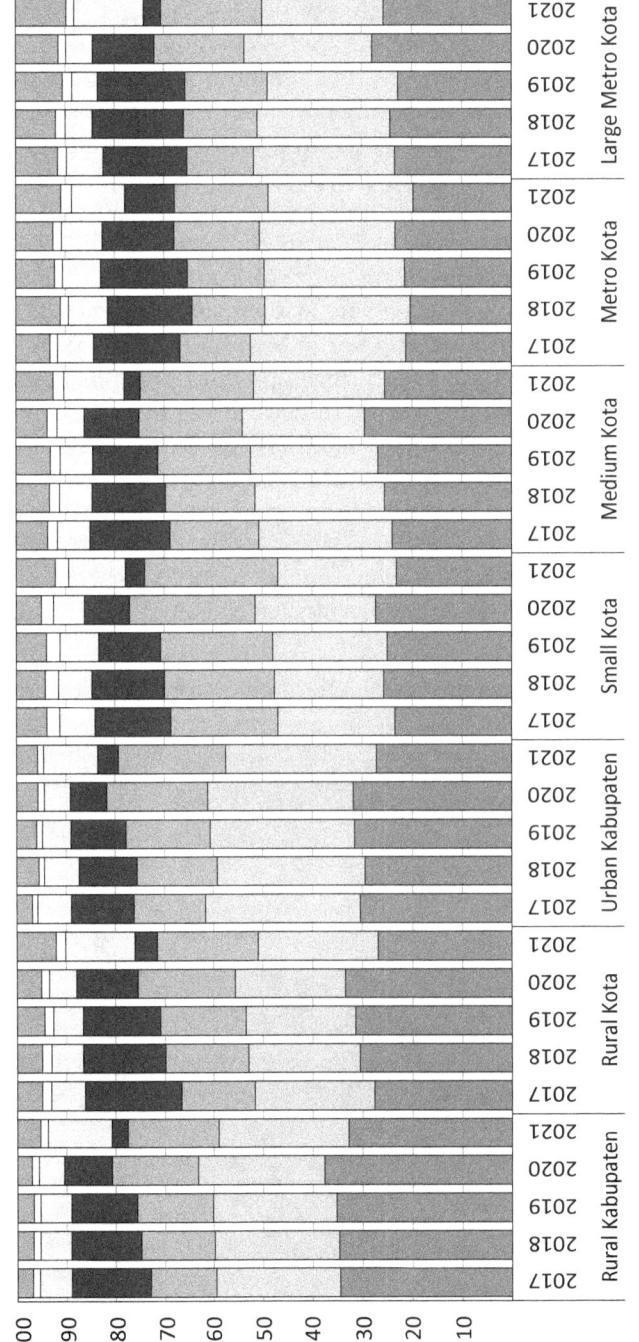

Source: Calculated by the authors from data from the Directorate General of Fiscal Balance, Ministry of Finance (https://djpk.kemenkeu.go.id/?p=5412, accessed 10 May 2023).

When we compare per capita spending among district categories (Figure 5.6), we find that the spending of Rural Kabupaten, Rural Kota and Small Kota is greatest, reflecting their generally higher per capita revenues, discussed earlier. The relatively high population densities of Small Kota mean their local governments have greater opportunities to deliver services to their citizens compared to the governments of the two rural district types. These three types of districts also spend more per capita on general services, mainly on government administrative functions, indicating less-efficient government in service delivery and, possibly, more-clientelist forms of government. The three types of district where per capita spending is lowest are also the most urbanised (Urban Kabupaten, Metropolitan Kota and Large Metropolitan Kota). They are able to achieve the relatively high development outcomes discussed above largely because the private sector contributes more to delivering services in these districts. It is important, however, to pay more attention to Medium Kota that have less private sector participation, but also significantly lower per capita public funding to serve their citizens than Small Kota.

All district types spent on average more than 20 per cent of their budgets on education in 2017–2021, as mandated by Indonesia's constitution

Figure 5.6 Per capita spending based on functions and district categories, 2021 (Rp million per person)

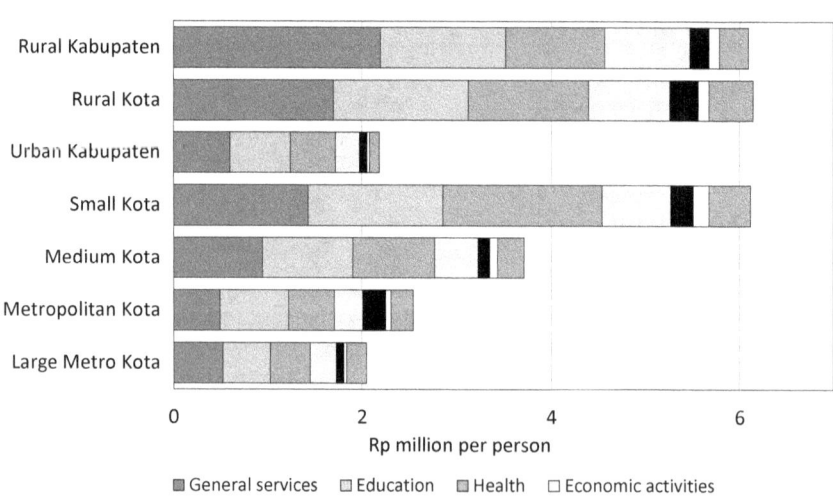

Source: Calculated by the authors from data from the Directorate General of Fiscal Balance, Ministry of Finance (https://djpk.kemenkeu.go.id/?p=5412, accessed 10 May 2023) and Susenas data.

amendment (article 31) and Law 20/2003 on the National Education System (article 49). However, 61 district governments still spent less than 20 per cent of their budgets on education in 2021. Most non-compliant districts were Rural Kabupaten, but the list also included two Rural Kota (Pagar Alam and Tual) and one Large Metropolitan Kota (Makassar). The eastern islands region (covering two provinces in Nusa Tenggara, two provinces in Maluku and six provinces in Papua) was most problematic, with about half of the districts not complying with the mandate. Considering the low presence of private education services in the area, it is not surprising that the quality of education in the region is lower (World Bank 2020: 180). Although the proportion of education spending is similar across different types of districts, per capita spending varies widely. Based on 2021 budget figures, Urban Kabupaten, Metropolitan Kota and Large Metropolitan Kota spent only Rp 0.5–0.7 million (US$32–49) per person on education, while Rural Kabupaten, Rural Kota and Small Kota spent Rp 1.3–1.4 million (US$89–95). The high per capita spending likely contributed to the improvement of 13-15 SER in less-urbanised areas discussed earlier (Table 5.6).

With regard to the health function, Law 36/2009 on Health (article 171) mandates 10 per cent of total budget expenditure be spent on the health sector, excluding personnel (this requirement was abolished, however, by Law 17/2023 on Health, passed in August 2023). Based on 2018–2021 budget data, until 2019, around half of district governments had not complied (Table 5.12). However, increased health spending during the COVID-19 pandemic helped to reduce non-compliance to only 22 per cent of districts in 2021, most of them Rural Kabupaten and Rural Kota, and mostly outside Java-Bali. Ten urban districts—four Medium Kota, five Metropolitan Kota and one Large Metropolitan Kota, all located outside Java—also did not comply. Given the welfare disparity between Java-Bali and outer islands and between more- and less-urbanised areas, such low health spending in less-urban areas and off-Java-Bali districts is concerning. Similar to the education sector, our analysis identifies a large gap in per capita health spending. Urban Kabupaten, Metropolitan Kota and Large Metropolitan Kota spent only Rp 0.4–0.5 million (US$29–33) per person in 2021, while Rural Kabupaten and Rural Kota spent more than twice as much. Small Kota spent even more on health, at Rp 1.7 million (US$112) per capita. However, relatively low per capita health spending in more-urbanised districts may be compensated by relatively higher numbers of private health providers in those areas.

Infrastructure spending on capital and housing and public facilities (the sources of financing for water supply, sanitation and neighbourhood facilities, all crucial for urban areas) decreased post-pandemic across all district types. Although spending for economic activities increased

Table 5.12 Proportion of non-personnel health spending to total spending, and non-compliant districts, 2018–2021

District category	Non-personnel health as % of total spending				Number of non-compliant districts				Total number of districts
	2018	2019	2020	2021	2018	2019	2020	2021	
1. Rural Kabupaten	9.90	10.38	11.67	12.71	224	201	135	94	400
2. Rural Kota	10.70	11.02	12.36	12.83	13	13	13	8	24
3. Urban Kabupaten	11.47	11.93	14.07	14.48	6	3	2	0	15
4. Small Kota	15.13	15.04	16.61	17.80	3	4	2	0	16
5. Medium Kota	11.30	11.86	13.34	15.05	13	12	9	4	27
6. Metropolitan Kota	9.32	9.90	10.77	12.18	11	9	6	5	16
7. Large Metropolitan Kota	10.16	12.09	12.38	14.98	6	6	4	1	10
Total	10.21	10.70	12.00	13.08	276	248	171	112	508

Source: Calculated by the authors from data from the Directorate General of Fiscal Balance, Ministry of Finance (https://djpk.kemenkeu.go.id/?p=5412, accessed 10 May 2023).

significantly in all types of districts in 2021 (Figure 5.5), most likely it was not used for roads and public transport infrastructure, since capital spending remained low. It can thus be inferred that district budget policy trends are not conducive to financing programs to address these urban issues. The situation was worst in Urban Kabupaten and Large Metropolitan Kota, where local governments spent less than Rp 0.36 million (US$24) per person in total on the housing and public facilities and economic activity functions in 2021. Although slightly better, the 2021 spending of Metropolitan Kota on these two categories was only Rp 0.54 million (US$36) per person. In contrast, the 2021 total per capita spending of Medium Kota and Small Kota for these two categories was, respectively, 63 per cent and 171 per cent higher than that of Large Metropolitan Kota.

The Fiscal Balance Law further mandates a minimum of 40 per cent of total expenditures (excluding transfer spending) on 'public service infrastructure' (article 147) with a five-year grace period. We estimate public service infrastructure by using total capital expenditures excluding those under the general service function (which focuses mainly on internal government affairs), dividing this by total non-transfer expenditures. Worsened by the post-pandemic trend of decreasing capital expenditures, only four Rural Kabupaten and one Rural Kota complied with this requirement in 2021 (Table 5.13), indicating a very steep challenge for full compliance by 2027, particularly in the more-urbanised districts. Therefore, it is crucial for these types of districts to find alternative financing, including through private sector engagement, to address urban infrastructure challenges.

Conclusion

In this chapter we have shown that different types of Indonesian districts, especially urban districts, have different development needs and challenges that are more complicated than indicated by the simple administrative classification of *kota* and *kabupaten* that is usually used to understand district variation in Indonesia. Reclassifying urban districts based on population density, proportion of urbanised villages/wards, and population size helps to identify urban districts' varied development characteristics and needs. It turns out that, in some ways at least, even Indonesia's urban districts have very different features, with there being a major gulf between, for example, Small Kota (and Rural Kota)—most of which are located outside Java-Bali and which lag considerably behind the larger metropolitan areas in Java-Bali—and the large Urban Kabupaten that surround the major metropolises in that region.

Table 5.13 Public service infrastructure spending by district category, 2019 and 2021

District category	Public service infrastructure spending (Rp million/km²)		Public service infrastructure as % of non-transfer spending		Number of districts with 30–40% public infrastructure of non-transfer spending		Number of districts with >40% public infrastructure of non-transfer spending	
	2019	2021	2019	2021	2019	2021	2019	2021
1. Rural Kabupaten	133.28	101.30	22.9	18.6	44	21	6	4
2. Rural Kota	614.60	557.71	21.6	20.9	0	2	0	1
3. Urban Kabupaten	702.87	578.70	17.0	15.2	0	0	0	0
4. Small Kota	4,388.05	3,137.87	20.3	14.3	0	0	0	0
5. Medium Kota	2,402.88	1,741.71	17.4	14.2	0	1	0	0
6. Metropolitan Kota	2,851.74	2,302.70	21.7	18.3	1	1	0	0
7. Large Metropolitan Kota	4,803.63	3,063.12	22.7	15.8	1	0	0	0
Total	605.03	447.42	22.2	18.2	46	25	6	5

Source: Calculated by the authors from data from the Directorate General of Fiscal Balance, Ministry of Finance (https://djpk.kemenkeu.go.id/?p=5412, accessed 10 May 2023) and Susenas data.

With regard to outcomes, the general pattern is clear: more-urbanised districts perform better, although their improvement rates are slower. This goes both for economic and welfare measures, such as the human development index and poverty rates, and for public service outcomes (access to education, health, clean water and sanitation). The trend is a little different for the economic outputs (i.e. RGDP). Not only do urbanised districts have higher per capita RGDP in general, but they also had a higher pre-pandemic growth rate, which was increasing interdistrict disparity. However, the pandemic hit urbanised districts harder than others in 2020.

With local budgets, we have a mixed assessment. In terms of the big picture, such as per capita revenue sources and overall spending levels, there is considerable variation. In general, total per capita revenue and spending by Rural Kabupaten, Rural Kota and Small Kota were the highest, while highly populated Urban Kabupaten, Metropolitan Kota and Large Metropolitan Kota had the smallest per capita budgets. While more-urbanised districts face a diminishing rate of return that makes it more difficult for them to increase development and public service outcomes, higher per capita budget spending contributes to higher improvement rates in less-urbanised areas and helps reduce the gaps discussed above.

More-urbanised districts were also much more effective at raising their own revenues. However, even for the most-urbanised district type, Large Metropolitan Kota, central government transfers contribute to more than half their revenues. Since fiscal equalising is the main objective of Indonesia's intergovernmental transfers, particularly the General Allocation Grant (DAU), the pre-2022 formula was biased against urbanised areas that had higher own-source revenue, smaller geographic areas and better development outcomes. The village fund policy also creates bias against urban districts. However, the 2022 Fiscal Balance Law has corrected the bias to some extent. The new law allocates DAU based on local service needs (e.g. numbers of students, population size and length of roads), adjustment factors that include population density, and fiscal capacity based on revenue potential (in 2022 RGDP was used as a proxy for tax or revenue potential, as in this chapter) rather than own-source revenue. All of these have reduced the rural bias in the previous intergovernmental transfer regime. The fact that an increasingly high proportion of the population lives in urban areas may have driven this policy—both for technocratic and political reasons.

In terms of quality of spending, in general we can see several improvements. Although most of the districts have not met the government's target of a maximum of 30 per cent of spending on personnel, this spending is significantly lower than a decade ago. Relatively high capital spending in less-urbanised areas, as well as higher goods and services and housing and public facilities spending in more-urbanised areas, indicates that budget policies are relatively responsive to different needs. Decreasing non-compliance with mandatory health and education spending also indicates improved local spending policies, although we identify lower quality in more-rural districts and smaller urban centres outside Java-Bali, which may reflect higher levels of clientelism (Berenschot 2018).

However, our analysis also shows similar spending patterns, by both economic classification and government function, across different district types. Mandatory spending policies—although not fully followed— contribute to similar levels of spending regardless of districts' different needs. While taking up a similar proportion of their total budgets, per capita education and health expenditures in Rural Kabupaten, Rural Kota and Small Kota were about twice those in Metropolitan Kota and Large Metropolitan Kota. The governments of different types of districts also responded remarkably similarly to the COVID-19 pandemic, despite the fact that the impacts of the pandemic varied greatly across districts. Basically, all district types increased health and economic activity spending at the cost of housing and public facilities, while education and general services spending was stable and high.

These are good examples of centrally driven (and uniform) policies driving local budgetary spending priorities, despite Indonesia's decentralised framework. It seems that upward accountability to the central government plays a more dominant role in determining district government spending policies than downward accountability to local populations. While the new Fiscal Balance Law to some extent reduces the bias against urban areas, it also strengthens central government control over spending, reducing the discretion of subnational governments by introducing mandatory spending requirements and earmarking allocations of DAU to finance temporary civil servants and education, health and infrastructure services (Lewis 2023).

As top-down accountability seems to be driving local budget spending policies, while bottom-up accountability will take some time to develop, customising central government policies regarding local budgets will be important. Governments of Metropolitan Kota and Large Metropolitan Kota—with relatively high private sector investment—should be incentivised to create an enabling environment for private sector engagement and economic development, while addressing metropolitan challenges such as traffic congestion, housing, air pollution and water supply. With limited per capita budget spending, provision of basic services should be targeted only at the poor to reduce inequality. In contrast, the governments of Rural Kabupaten and Rural Kota need to prioritise their budgets for provision of basic services for their populations. Meanwhile, increasing the quality of public services in Small Kota and Medium Kota to enable them to act as 'service hubs' for the neighbouring rural areas should be a priority. The most complicated challenges are faced by Urban Kabupaten. On one hand they need to address the challenges of metropolitan cities as discussed above, but they also need to have different priorities for their remnant rural areas. With relatively low per capita budgets, expansive service areas and relatively low private sector participation compared to metropolitan cities, these Urban Kabupaten need special attention.

One option would be to gradually implement asymmetric decentralisation, in which different rules could be applied to different regions with different needs. While there has been public discussion of this option in Indonesia, its implementation has been limited to special autonomy arrangements in Aceh and Papua and the special regions of Yogyakarta and Jakarta. The final draft of the National Long-Term Development Plan 2025–2045 indicates the government has a long-term commitment to adopt asymmetric decentralisation and sees this as one way to reduce inter-regional inequality.[5]

Several asymmetric decentralisation policies could be developed gradually. For example, in 2014 the government transferred the secondary education function from district to provincial governments; our analysis shows it may be possible to re-decentralise this function to Large Metropolitan Kota that have high fiscal capacity and strong commitments to twelve years of compulsory education. By the same token, the authority to manage primary education in non-performing districts (e.g. those that spend less than 20 per cent on education and have poor development outcomes) could be transferred to their provincial government. Establishing greater incentives for district governments to increase their local taxes and levies (as a ratio of their RGDP), including by authorising districts that are Large Metropolitan Kota and their suburbs to keep a larger portion of the income taxes they generate (Roberts et al. 2019), might also be desirable. So might developing new targeted grant schemes, such as specific public service grants for Medium Kota with low administrative personnel spending and low private sector participation in service provision.

---

5   Ministry of National Development Planning, January 2024 (https://drive.google.com/file/d/1JSZp1Oz37KWktxi-hi0okVXxEsKuaU-I/view?usp=sharing). See pages 127, 141, 207.

Above all, our analysis suggests there is a need for scholars and policymakers alike to recognise that Indonesia's districts are highly varied and, in some ways, becoming increasingly so. Urbanisation is changing the face of contemporary Indonesia, but urban Indonesia itself is highly varied, with small, medium, metropolitan, large metropolitan and suburban urban areas having highly varied endowments, resources and needs. In both academic analysis and policy formulation, we need to start moving beyond the simple binary of *kota* versus *kabupaten* assumed by Indonesia's standard system of administrative classification and recognise better the huge diversity of urban (and, indeed, rural) Indonesia.

References

Berenschot, Ward. 2018. 'The political economy of clientelism: A comparative study of Indonesia's patronage democracy'. *Comparative Political Studies* 51(12): 1563–93. doi.org/10.1177/0010414018758756

Hill, Hal, ed. 2014. *Regional Dynamics in a Decentralized Indonesia*. ISEAS Publishing.

Lewis, Blane D. 2017. 'Local government spending and service delivery in Indonesia: The perverse effects of substantial fiscal resources'. *Regional Studies* 51(11): 1695–707. doi.org/10.1080/00343404.2016.1216957

Lewis, Blane D. 2023. 'Indonesia's new fiscal decentralisation law: A critical assessment'. *Bulletin of Indonesian Economic Studies* 59(1): 1–28. doi.org/10.1080/00074918.2023.2180838

Lewis, Blane D. and Paul Smoke. 2017. 'Intergovernmental fiscal transfers and local incentives and responses: The case of Indonesia'. *Fiscal Studies* 38(1): 111–39. www.jstor.org/stable/26605586

Patunru, Arianto A. and Erman A. Rahman. 2014. 'Local governance and development outcomes'. In *Regional Dynamics in a Decentralized Indonesia*, edited by Hal Hill, 156–85. ISEAS Publishing.

Roberts, Mark, Frederico Gil Sander and Sailesh Tiwari, eds. 2019. *Time to ACT: Realizing Indonesia's Urban Potential*. World Bank. doi.org/10.1596/978-1-4648-1389-4

USAID ERAT. 2022. *National Local Governance and Public Service Assessment Report*. Asia Foundation. www.program-erat.or.id/wp-content/uploads/2023/09/USAID-ERAT-National-LGPSA-Report.pdf

World Bank. 2020. *Indonesia Public Expenditure Review: Spending for Better Results*. World Bank. www.worldbank.org/en/country/indonesia/publication/indonesia-public-expenditure-review

6 Patterns of urban government in Indonesia: The role of civil society coalitions and mobilisation

Mochamad Mustafa

Following the fall of the authoritarian New Order regime in 1998, Indonesia embarked on a path of democratic decentralisation. However, more than two decades since it began, the results of this reform have been mixed. While some local governments have shown enhanced capacity to deliver effective governance, others remain mired in inefficiency and corruption. The outcomes appear to depend on specific features of the local political landscape, in a general context of greater fragmentation of local political actors and heightened competition among local elites to control government resources than during the New Order era.

Two analytical lenses have dominated academic discussion of the drivers of these mixed outcomes. The first lens focuses on the destructive roles played by elites, whether remnants of the old New Order governing coalition or new elites that have emerged alongside democratic decentralisation. Some authors, such as Hadiz (2004, 2010) and Heryanto and Hadiz (2005), argue that old predatory elites continue to wield influence, resulting in weak democracy and poor policy performance at both national and local levels. This perspective, however, is largely unable to explain variation in patterns of local governance, though others, such as Aspinall (2013) and Buehler (2014), have examined the interplay between old and new elites in the heightened competition for local power and resources in local politics.

The second lens emphasises the role of local leadership. Many studies focusing on this aspect contend that democratic decentralisation incentivises local political leaders to pursue popular welfare-oriented and developmental policies in order to boost their political support and keep winning elections. These policies may either hinder or promote good governance, but the key is that the willingness and effectiveness of leaders to implement them varies. Bunnell et al. (2013), for example, suggest that the individual agency and quality of local government leaders is crucial in determining how well particular districts and cities perform. Von Luebke (2009, 2012) asserts that ambitious leaders are more likely to pursue reformist policies and implement them than unambitious ones. Rosser et al. (2011) and Rosser and Sulistyanto (2013) suggest that local leadership lies along a spectrum, ranging from 'political entrepreneurship'—that is, the mobilisation of poor voters by the introduction of popular policies—to patronage distribution—that is, the mobilisation of both the poor and non-poor through the cultivation of clientelist networks (Rosser et al. 2011: 15).

This chapter broadens the analytical scope to highlight the critical role played by civil society, encompassing non-government organisations (NGOs), media, academics, active citizens, social organisations and other civic-based movements, in promoting local government reform in Indonesian cities. The role of civil society has generally been underexplored in understanding local politics in Indonesia in the context of democratic decentralisation. This neglect might be due to perceptions of civil society as being generally too weak, and characterised by fragmentation, depoliticisation and disorganisation, to challenge entrenched predatory elites.

To be sure, some scholars have highlighted the potential influence of a wider array of players, including progressive civil society activists and organisations, in local politics and decision-making (e.g. Antlov et al. 2010; Aspinall 2013; Tans 2012). Aspinall (2013), for example, affirms that post-Suharto local politics are no longer exclusively the domain of predatory elites, even though their penetration of the political system is still high. Tans (2012) demonstrates that societal mobilisation can constrain predatory networks, using the case of Serdang Bedagai district, North Sumatra, to show that civil society and social mobilisation can affect local elections. In particular, he shows how certain modes of electoral coalition-building can affect local government performance, with civil society components pressuring an elected politician to pursue various pro-poor developmental programs.

My chapter contributes to this evolving literature by emphasising the role of civil society in shaping local politics and good governance. In it, I argue that the presence or absence of a robust local civil society constitutes a critical determinant of whether local politics drives effective reform or ineffective and corrupt governance. In particular, a robust civil society can provide political support to local government leaders who seek to reform local governance and purge it of corrupt elements, while leaders who lack such support can experience political frustration and achieve, at best, partial reform. In short, I suggest that while leadership clearly still matters, the impact of democratic decentralisation is equally contingent on whether a strong local civil society offers support to local government leaders to take action against predatory interest groups.

I make this argument by presenting case studies from three Indonesian cities in which different patterns of interplay between civil society and government had very different impacts on the extent of good governance reform. The first case is Surabaya, the capital of East Java province. The story of post–New Order Surabaya is one in which a strong local civil society energised reformist leaders of the city to bring about reform, turning Surabaya into a showcase of successful decentralisation. The second case, Bogor, located not far from Jakarta, shows how the absence of civil society forces can frustrate a reform-minded leader, compromising a good governance agenda. Finally, the third case, from South Tangerang on the periphery of Jakarta, highlights the detrimental impact of dynastic control and predatory political practices on governance and development in the absence of strong civil society forces.

Surabaya: Transformative good governance reform

Surabaya, the capital city of East Java and second-largest city in Indonesia, faced significant challenges in the early period of democratic decentralisation. Locals often joked that KMS, the initialism for Kota Madya Surabaya or Surabaya City Region, stood for Kota Maling Surabaya or Surabaya Thieves City, reflecting a legacy of dysfunctional governance that had persisted since the New Order era. Unprofessionalism, lack of discipline and corruption featured at all levels of the city administration. Severe urban problems, including frequent flooding during the wet season, an inadequate drainage system, poor waste management, disorderly public spaces and a chaotic transportation network, were a challenge for government. Unmanaged waste inundated the city's waterfront areas, and there were numerous slums with inadequate sanitation and limited access to clean water. Illegal semi-permanent housing and informal businesses occupied the city's riverbanks, and unruly street vendors took over public spaces, contributing to the overall disorderly state of the city (Dick 2002; Marijan 2008; Mustafa 2017).

However, Surabaya has since undergone a remarkable transformation, evolving into a highly advanced city, famous throughout the country for having made substantial improvements in governance, particularly in bureaucratic reform, financial management and service delivery.

These reforms have brought about transformative changes in urban development, addressing longstanding issues such as flooding, waste management, disordered public spaces and inadequate public services.[1] Surabaya is now celebrated as a hub for governance best practices and is frequently cited as a reference point by other regions and central government bodies aiming to elevate their governance standards.

As extensively discussed in my PhD dissertation (Mustafa 2017), this progress in governance reform can be attributed to the sustained presence of vibrant progressive actors from civil society. These actors, including university academics, NGO activists and local media, have exercised considerable influence over local policymaking in Surabaya, creating a conducive environment for the emergence of good governance reforms. The role of civil society, particularly NGOs, was crucial during the nationwide protests against Suharto in 1998 in Surabaya and elsewhere, but one factor that distinguished Surabaya from many other locations in the aftermath of this regime change is that these civil society actors subsequently played an important part in forming new pro-reform alliances aimed at challenging local-level political influence of both the predatory elites from the New Order era and the new predatory elites that emerged during the *reformasi* era.

In fact, civil society engagement has long been widely recognised as a driving force behind successful urban development initiatives in Surabaya, such as the Kampung Improvement Program, which was initiated in the 1960s,[2] or various community-based waste management initiatives and the 'green and clean' program run since 2005. The City Chamber (Dewan Kota), formally established in 2003 and comprising around 160 professional associations, has also been active in addressing urban issues related to vulnerable citizens, including riverbank settlement improvement, waste management and slum settlement improvements (Mustafa 2017: 103–6).

Particularly important in Surabaya's local civil society landscape is the prominent role played by local and national media. Jawa Pos, the country's second-largest media group and one of its oldest, operates 40 local newspapers across Indonesia and actively supports regional autonomy. In 2001 it established the Jawa Pos Institute for Pro-Otonomi, which researches and promotes good local governance and presents annual awards for innovative local government policies and programs.

---

1 On flooding and waste management, see chapters by Permana and Azizah, respectively, this volume.
2 See also footnote 6 in the chapter by Kusno, this volume.

Local radio stations like Suara Surabaya (Voice of Surabaya), meanwhile, play a crucial role in providing daily reports on city issues and offering discussion forums and talkback programs that address the local population's concerns, such as traffic, crime and other pressing problems (Mustafa 2017: 106).

In Surabaya, the downfall of the New Order regime and the introduction of democratic decentralisation in the early *reformasi* era generated high public expectations for improved governance in response to the city's challenges. However, this transformation did not immediately change local leadership or bureaucratic structures. The incumbent mayor, Sunarto Sumoprawiryo, who had a military background, secured his position in the 2000 mayoral election (then carried out within the local parliament) by aligning with new political parties. However, his re-election and inability to effectively address urban challenges triggered widespread opposition.

Civil society responded by organising frequent mass demonstrations, reflecting strong dissent against Sunarto's rule and indicating the population's ability to mobilise collectively. Various progressive activists, intellectuals and professionals consolidated their position by establishing the City Chamber to engage in political activism in response to the continuation of the New Order mayor, and to guard against a military resurgence. Working with the University Rectors Forum, Kamar Dagang Indonesia (Kadin; Indonesian Chamber of Commerce), Wahana Lingkungan Hidup (Environmental Watch) and other civil society organisations, they succeeded in removing Sunarto Sumoprawiryo from the mayor's position in 2002, replacing him with the PDI-P (Partai Demokrasi Indonesia-Perjuangan, Indonesian Democratic Party of Struggle) politician, Bambang DH, who was widely viewed as an ally of the activists (Marijan 2008: 95; Mustafa 2017: 105).

The transition from Sunarto to Bambang DH did not immediately translate into a strong administration. Despite Bambang's endorsement by civil society groups, he had limited support within the bureaucracy and inherited a corrupt system from the previous regime. His backing in the local legislative body (Dewan Perwakilan Rakyat Daerah, DPRD) was fragile. Though his party, PDI-P, held a significant number of DPRD seats, it was split into two rival camps, with Bambang belonging to the minority camp that supported his replacement of Sunarto. This situation led to conflict with his bureaucrats and the DPRD, hindering Bambang's reform efforts.

With strong support from civil society allies, Bambang took steps to gain control of the bureaucracy by replacing M. Yasin, the city's regional secretary, who held significant influence in the bureaucracy and had ties to old politicians in the DPRD. Consequently, DPRD members rejected

Bambang's accountability report and voted to impeach him (something made possible by local government rules at the time). Civil society once again mobilised in support of Bambang, protesting the DPRD's decisions and campaigning for a public boycott of the next legislative general election. This pressure led the Ministry of Home Affairs to reject the DPRD's decision, marking a significant turning point in Surabaya's struggle for governance reform (Ashadi 2012: 17–23; Mustafa 2017).

Bambang's victory over the DPRD illustrated the power of civil society to mobilise and drive effective change in the face of strong elite resistance. It also bolstered Bambang's popularity among the local population while eroding public trust in the DPRD, political parties and politicians, particularly those with links to the New Order. However, this political crisis also pressured Bambang DH to bring about change in Surabaya.

In the aftermath of the crisis and with continued support and expectations from civil society and the public, Bambang embarked on a journey to cultivate pro-reform allies within the bureaucracy. He strategically rotated staff in crucial agencies involved in addressing corruption. He revitalised the City Supervisory Agency (Badan Pengawas Daerah, Bawasda), an oversight bureau for public officials that had been inactive during Sunarto's administration. Bambang also pursued a bureaucratic professionalisation program, introducing large-scale staff improvement programs with reward and punishment mechanisms. Staff members with excellent performance were rewarded with opportunities for career promotion, while those who failed to demonstrate the required level of professionalism faced demotion. At least 200 public officials were demoted during Bambang's administration (Ashadi 2012: 37). This concerted effort at bureaucratic reform and professionalisation had far-reaching implications for the city.

On the basis of these bureaucratic reforms, the city government was able to address pressing public concerns. Improvements encompassed modernising waste management, overhauling drainage systems to prevent flooding, and reclaiming public spaces from illegal street vendors and slum dwellers. A 30 per cent green open space policy was launched to safeguard the environment and enhance the city's landscape. It involved revoking permits from businesses that were unlawfully occupying spaces such as streets and parks. Notably, the city cancelled permits for fourteen petrol stations on public land that had been sanctioned by the previous administration. Additional measures included enforcing billboard taxation, registering billboards and ensuring tax compliance. Crucially, during this period the city also introduced procurement reform, dramatically innovating how it spent its money, and introducing a model that was widely copied in other parts of Indonesia (Mustafa 2017: 108).

The successes of this early period bore fruit during the tenure of Bambang DH's successor, Tri Rismaharini (Risma), who led the city from 2010 to 2019. Under Risma, Surabaya was to reap the benefits of the transformation that had occurred during Bambang DH's mayoralty, and to pursue further reform. Risma was well known for her strong leadership, which further advanced the city's reform trajectory. Under her leadership, her administration solidified the city's reputation as a trailblazer in governance reform and a hub for innovative governance practices, and she built a personal reputation as a dedicated and clean bureaucrat. Importantly, Risma capitalised on the bureaucratic reforms initiated by Bambang's administration, leveraging the presence of well-functioning bureaucratic structures and a cadre of young, skilled and committed officials within city management (Mustafa 2017: 132–34).

But civil society remained important under Risma, too. The crux of her success lay in the broad support she received from progressive actors in her elections. Risma's nomination itself was a result of strategic efforts by influential intellectuals and media figures in Surabaya, especially those associated with Jawa Pos, Suara Surabaya and Enciety, an urban research centre run within the Surabaya Institute of Technology. They viewed Risma as a leader with the potential to sustain the program of change in the city, since she had already played a role supporting key reforms as a bureaucrat under Bambang DH (Anisah 2015: 75–76). Risma had established a close relationship with Suara Surabaya, the city's most popular radio station, since 2002 by actively responding to issues raised by members of the public who called into the radio station. She was also supported by many community-based associations, including the traditional market traders' association, the stall vendors' association and Gerakan Rakyat Surabaya (GRS, Surabaya Citizens' Movement) (Mustafa 2017: 33).

Robust support from civil society bolstered Risma's confidence in tackling challenges posed by local predatory elites who had vested interests in obstructing her government. Notably, Risma resisted a PDI-P proposal to promote 362 bureaucrats affiliated with the party to higher-ranking positions, which could have granted the party substantial control over the bureaucracy. In December 2010 she directly confronted local predatory elites by dramatically raising local billboard taxes (potentially a major source of revenue), even though she knew these companies were primary funders of political parties and politicians in Surabaya. Despite this knowledge, her action led the DPRD to attempt her impeachment, but this move met with strong opposition from civil society. Grassroots networks, NGOs and local intellectuals, particularly from the Surabaya

Institute of Technology network, mobilised substantial opposition to the DPRD in support of Risma (Mustafa 2017: 134–36).

Predictably, these confrontations strained Risma's relationship with local politicians and set the stage for frequent clashes between her and members of the local legislature and other predatory elites. However, these confrontations also provided a favourable political landscape for procurement reform, reducing the likelihood of the new procurement measures (which involved more transparent online procedures) falling under the influence of predatory elites (specifically, contractors and their allies in the bureaucracy and legislature). They also generated broad public support and energised civil society networks, intellectuals, media and reformist elements within the bureaucracy to rally behind Risma's leadership at the expense of the DPRD and anti-reform actors' influence.

As a result, Risma's administration gained increasing confidence to implement more daring good-governance policies in the city, buoyed by strong public support. Risma expanded the previous administration's efforts to cleanse the bureaucracy, introducing various mechanisms to oversee performance accountability. In numerous cases, she appointed young and dynamic civil servants to senior roles as part of a broader reorganisation of the city administration, leading to most department heads in Surabaya being officials aged between 38 and 45, many of whom had previously collaborated with her in various capacities before she was elected mayor (Mustafa 2017: 137).

Risma pursued further reforms to reduce corruption and enhance transparency, focusing on the most contentious aspect of the city's resources: the local budget. This had previously been a major target of rent-seeking by members of the legislature, bureaucrats and businesspeople who had used various measures to introduce favoured projects and facilitate skim-offs. Risma achieved her goal of cleaning up budgetary management by advancing e-procurement reform and expanding it to establish the Government Resource Management System (GRMS). This comprehensive electronic system integrated various aspects of the city government's budget processes, encompassing budgeting, project planning, procurement, contracting, monitoring, payment and performance assessment, all online. The GRMS provided Risma and her administration the tools to ensure consistency and accountability in the government's budget, effectively countering the legislature's interests in local budgetary matters and facilitating early detection of abuses. Additionally, Risma enforced a policy preventing her officials from using non-budgetary funds to support any policymaking involving parliamentary members (Mustafa 2017: 153, 160).

This brief summary helps contextualise how it is that Surabaya has become something of a role model for local governance reform in Indonesia. Under both Bambang DH's and Risma's administrations there was consistent alignment of pro-democratic actors within the government and civil society. Risma's confrontations with local predatory elites, especially those in the legislature, highlight the resilience of this network in enabling reform and programmatic delivery, propelled by a broad network of support that extended from the bureaucracy to civil society, intellectuals and the media.

Bogor: Compromised good governance reform

Bogor city is a medium-sized city in West Java, located approximately 60 kilometres south of the national capital, Jakarta. It is part of the greater Jakarta metropolitan area and ranks as the fourteenth-largest city in Indonesia. In the early *reformasi* era, democratic decentralisation did not bring about a fundamental transformation in Bogor's governance landscape. Instead, the city's governance was characterised by clientelist practices that fostered corruption and collusion. Over the past decade, by contrast, the city has made significant strides in fulfilling some promises of decentralisation, particularly in service delivery. Still, it has made less progress in the fight against corruption and clientelism. This mixed picture provides a telling contrast with Surabaya, because it is the product of an interplay between a reforming elected leader and dominant predatory elites in the relative *absence* of a robust civil society.

Compared to Surabaya, civil society in Bogor is relatively weak and apolitical. The dominant civil society groups there focus on pursuits such as promotion of local culture and products, hobbies and professional activities, though there is also a large number of religious-based associations, as in all parts of Indonesia. As I have argued elsewhere (Mustafa 2017: 204–5), only a few civil society organisations in the city actively engage in pro-democratic activism. Most such groups are local chapters of student-based national organisations. An influential local NGO, LBH Keadilan Bogor (Legal Aid Foundation – Justice Bogor), emerged in 2012 and uncovered several corruption allegations. However, its influence remains limited. Local media in Bogor only began to flourish after the New Order period. The oldest and most famous local newspaper is *Radar Bogor*, established in 1998, and various online media outlets have appeared in the past decade, but the local media landscape is far less rich than in Surabaya (ibid.: 203).

Established local political actors adapted to the transformed political landscape adeptly during the initial post-Suharto transition phase (1999–2004). A former New Order–era official, a career bureaucrat in the

Ministry of Home Affairs, Iswara Natanegara, secured the mayoralty in 1999 through legislative means. He was succeeded by Diani Budiarto, a former local assistant secretary who served as mayor for two terms from 2004 to 2013. Under Iswara's and Diani's leadership, there was little governance reform and only incremental progress in local development, primarily in physical infrastructure. Both mayors made sporadic efforts to address road infrastructure, disorderly traditional markets and traffic congestion. They also made some attempts to improve governance; for instance, Iswara established a 'One Roof' system to streamline business licensing, a policy that was upheld by Diani. Additionally, an electronic procurement system was introduced in 2007. However, few local actors believed these initiatives did much to promote transparency and accountability or reduce corruption (Mustafa 2017: 214, 226).

Meanwhile, progressive civil society forces in Bogor city remained weak and disorganised during this period. While some demonstrations criticised the local government, most were too small to constitute a consolidated public movement or present forceful demands for change. An illustrative case occurred in 2003, centring on the so-called 'APBD Gate' scandal (where APBD refers to the *anggaran pendapatan dan belanja daerah*, the local government revenue and expenditure budget). This scandal implicated all of the city's DPRD members. The city attorney-general's office investigated cases of illegal expenditure made by the DPRD in the 2002 financial year and eventually prosecuted all 45 members of the DPRD for corruption. However, none of the bureaucrats involved in allocating the DPRD budget and facilitating the misuse were investigated as suspects or sentenced (Hidayat 2010).

Civil society groups responded to the case by organising street protests, pressuring the local attorney-general's office to investigate the bureaucrats. It seems unlikely that these protests significantly influenced how local prosecutors handled the case, as no bureaucrat was prosecuted. Additionally, the civil society protests did not appear to markedly influence broader public opinion. This was evident in the general election results in June 2004 when many DPRD members involved in the APBD Gate scandal were re-elected. Two even went on to serve as the speaker and the deputy speaker of the DPRD (Mustafa 2017: 211).

From 2014 to 2023, a new reformist leader, Bima Arya Sugiarto (Bima), took over the leadership of the city as mayor (see Sugiarto, this volume, for his reflections on this period in office). With his career experience, expertise and idealistic personal outlook, many locals believed he would challenge incumbent political elites and thoroughly reform local politics. Bima had a background as an activist, lecturer and national political analyst. He completed his PhD in politics at the Australian National

University in 2005 and subsequently ran a prominent national political research and campaign consultancy, developing a high media profile as a political expert on numerous national TV shows and other media platforms. In 2009, he joined PAN (Partai Amanat Nasional, National Mandate Party) and was appointed head of the party's national political communications department.

Given high public expectations that his leadership would bring changes to the city's administration and given his own campaign promises to do so, Bima was highly motivated to address corruption within the bureaucracy, which the previous mayors had entrenched. Shortly after his inauguration in April 2014, he introduced a new online taxation processing system and made local budget documents accessible to the public via the city's official website. He frequently conveyed in public events and internal meetings that he would not tolerate or protect corrupt practices. Bima also refused to build personalised and clientelist connections with the media, civil society, politicians, prosecutors and police officers by providing them with unbudgeted financial support—a common practice in most regions of Indonesia (Mustafa 2017: 230).

The mayor stood firmly against corrupt and collusive relationships with other local actors, prompting resistance from his political counterparts both within and outside his administration. As Bima cut off the flow of financial support to bureaucrats, legislators and other influential political actors, there was increasing pressure outside his administration to undermine his popularity. For example, in response to Bima's unbending approach, oversight authorities in the city, especially the local attorney-general's office, intensified their investigatory activities. They conducted aggressive investigations of emerging problems and complaints, and followed up diligently on rumours of maladministration publicised by local civil society groups and the media, all of whom had rent-seeking motivations to pressure the mayor. Within the bureaucracy, Bima's anti-corruption message had even more significant consequences. There were reports of growing worry and uncertainty among the local apparatus. They saw that Bima's decision not to engage in corrupt practices and provide slush funds to them placed local bureaucrats in a vulnerable position—not only depriving them of informal sources of income but also exposing them to law enforcement investigations and political attack—demotivating them from supporting their mayor (Mustafa 2017: 230–35).

Fundamentally, these circumstances placed the mayor in a significant dilemma. He was facing significant internal pushback and even resistance against his agenda from within the administration and from hostile law enforcement bodies. At the same time, a robust civil society to pressure such forces and support the mayor in prioritising the fight against corruption and clientelism had not emerged. The mayor thus faced a choice between strongly pursuing his idealistic vision of clean governance while lacking support or stalling on his anti-corruption agenda in order to focus on other less politically risky goals, such as expediting tangible public development outcomes. Ultimately, he chose a middle way. He adopted a soft approach by continuing to demonstrate his personal commitment to clean leadership and intensifying his communication and lobbying efforts with all elite actors to reduce their demands for financial kickbacks in exchange for supporting his agenda (Mustafa 2017: 279). He also avoided outright confrontation with the DPRD and the bureaucracy on issues of governance reform and, rather than focusing on rooting out corruption, instead turned his attention to service delivery.[3] In parallel, he nurtured a new generation of young, pro-reform bureaucrats. He placed them in various strategic positions at the echelon II (heads of departments), subdistrict (*camat*) and ward (*lurah*) levels to strengthen his pro-reform coalition within the bureaucracy.

Bima's strategy worked well, and he succeeded in his first term. He delivered on pledges to develop infrastructure, create new parks, introduce a 'smart city' framework, improve traffic management and provide support to social, cultural and local business groups. He also delivered on his commitment to good governance, but did so narrowly, translating that commitment into a soft approach involving measures such as introducing a new online taxation system, publishing the government's local budget documents, establishing a merit system for government officials, creating an online complaints handling mechanism, and introducing online business licensing. These accomplishments and his ability to communicate effectively via social media earned him popularity and secured his re-election in 2018.

In his second term, he gained more confidence. The preceding five-year struggle to consolidate support was now delivering him expanded backing within the city bureaucracy and from local political actors. Between 2018 and 2023, he thus improved the city's performance in various areas of development, expanding infrastructure development and enhancing service delivery in education, social protection, health, water and sanitation, improving environmental management, encouraging state-private sector collaboration, promoting tourism, improving city transportation facilities, providing more public spaces, and enhancing

---

3 In this and subsequent paragraphs, my analysis of Bima's tenure as mayor is primarily drawn from personal observations made during my interactions with the mayor and his administration; between 2017 and 2023 I worked closely with the mayor on various governance issues.

the tidiness of the city. In short, over the five years, the city significantly evolved and became a leading site for various innovations, as indicated by around 200 awards granted to the city and its mayor by national, provincial and international institutions, media and private sector bodies. Through his various campaigns and innovations, the mayor also firmly instilled public awareness of the importance of city government and what it means to have a good mayor and well-functioning city administration, which generated increasing public expectation of and demand for reform.

Overall, this increasing support for the mayor resulted from his softening of his strategy, especially his turning away from his earlier policy of directly confronting and eliminating clientelist and corrupt elites from the city, especially within his bureaucracy. To some extent, this approach in practice meant turning a blind eye to the continuation of clientelist and corrupt practices among his bureaucrats. He had made a calculation that he needed to secure the support of the bureaucracy, especially in the absence of more robust external support, such as from an energised civil society. Arguably, while this approach helped the mayor to survive, and to perform in most cases, it also ran the risk of perpetuating and even amplifying clientelism and corrupt practices. In a discussion with the mayor, he noted that 'while corruption committed in previous eras had the purpose of benefiting the mayor, during my tenure, bureaucrats were driven by self-interest, and possibly reaped greater personal benefits than before—presumably because they no longer needed to provide a gratification to the mayor' (interview with Bima Arya Sugiarto, 14 September 2024). As Bima's term concludes, a pressing concern is thus the sustainability of his good governance reforms and the potential resurgence of clientelist and corrupt actors in future city governance. The Bogor case thus demonstrates the limits of what an individual reforming leader can achieve in the absence of sustained pressure from civil society and the public.

South Tangerang: Predatory capture

Tangerang Selatan (South Tangerang) was established as a city in 2008, separating from Tangerang district (*kabupaten*). Located in Banten province, South Tangerang is an economically prosperous municipality due to its proximity to Jakarta (it is located about 30 kilometres from central Jakarta), which positions it firmly within the capital's commuter zone (see chapter by Elyda, this volume), attracting many middle-class urbanites and creating numerous social and economic opportunities for residents. However, instead of experiencing the development of urban civic engagement and civil society activism since the city's foundation,

South Tangerang has instead seen the deep penetration of a major predatory dynasty into virtually all aspects of local governance.

South Tangerang lacks a vibrant public sphere despite the presence of many registered mass organisations and NGOs, significant offline and online media presence, and twenty universities in the city. Some local chapters of national student organisations, such as HMI (Himpunan Mahasiswa Islam, Islamic Students Association) and PMII (Persatuan Mahasiswa Islam Indonesia, Indonesian Islamic Students Association), have sporadically engaged in street demonstrations, but their focus on city issues is limited. Among the few progressive civil society organisations, two local NGOs, Forum Masyarakat Serpong Peduli (Serpong Caring Community Forum) and Truth, have actively monitored governance and service delivery issues, especially in health and waste management. However, these groups are too small to mobilise significant pressure on the city administration, and lack the capacity and networks to effectively advocate for policy reform. Meanwhile, most local media outlets rely heavily on government support through advertisement programs or funding from government events (Mustafa and Rahman 2019).

Overall, citizen participation in local politics in South Tangerang is generally weak and plays little role in promoting good governance. The character and origins of the local population is one explanation for this situation. Many citizens, especially those from the middle and upper classes, live in private real estate complexes that cater to most of their needs. They are also mostly migrants who feel a greater attachment to Jakarta's social and economic life than to South Tangerang's. As a result, many of these middle-class residents lack a sense of ownership over local community affairs, and lack motivation to engage in local-level civic activism (see chapter by Flyda, this volume). In the 2015 and 2020 mayoral elections, the voter participation rate was low, at 57 per cent and 60 per cent, respectively. Paradoxically, then, despite the fact that many national politicians, researchers, academics and staff members of international NGOs and donor organisations live in the city, their presence has little impact on how the city is run.

The political landscape of Tangerang city has instead largely been shaped by the influential Chasan Sochib family, one of the most prominent political dynasties in Indonesia. This dynasty's influence has been discussed in various reports (see, for example, Agustino 2010; Kenawas 2015; Kusumaningtyas et al. 2017; Muhammad 2016; Sutisna 2018; Yandri 2017). The family holds considerable sway throughout the province of Banten. Led by the late Chasan Sochib, an important player in local business and government affairs during the New Order, family members have secured positions in the executive and legislative branches at central, provincial and district levels. Capitalising on his longstanding political investment in the Golkar Party, Chasan facilitated his daughter, Ratu Atut Chosiyah (Atut), to gain the vice-governorship of Banten in 2001 and, later, the governorship in the 2006 and 2011 elections. This consolidation of power allowed the family to exert significant control over local politics and business throughout the province and its constituent districts and municipalities (Kenawas 2015; Sutisna 2018).

The dynasty's ambition to seize control of the government of South Tangerang was evident from the time the city was formed. Its efforts began with the appointment of Muhammad Saleh, a member of Atut's inner circle, as the caretaker mayor upon the formation of the city in 2008. The dynasty's grip tightened during the first mayoral election in 2010, even as civil society struggled to present a united front. The dynasty backed Airin Rachmi Diany (Airin), the wife of Tubagus Chaeri Wardana (Wawan), the son of Chasan Sochib; Wawan had from the start been a significant player in the dynasty's rise to power (Kusumaningtyas et al. 2017; Muhammad 2016). Some civil society groups, concerned about the dynasty's influence, attempted to oppose Airin's candidacy. Under the banner of JPTS (Jaringan Pemilih Tangerang Selatan, South Tangerang Voter Network), these activists aimed to block Airin's election by supporting a candidate who they believed could defeat her. Unfortunately, their efforts faltered, resulting in Airin's victory (Mustafa and Rahman 2019).

Soon after Airin became mayor of the city, the Chasan family network, through Airin's husband Wawan, quickly took control of various government functions. Wawan shadowed Airin and the bureaucracy when it came to determining key strategic policies, from appointing officials to critical bureaucratic posts to controlling the distribution of government projects (Mustafa and Rahman 2019). Under Wawan's influence, the recruitment and promotion of public officials and the running of the bureaucracy were based on clientelist processes whereby what really counted were the contributions individuals had made to supporting Airin's election and their personal loyalty. By placing trusted individuals in key posts, meanwhile, Wawan was able to secure access to essential projects for his own businesses and those of allies. Consequently, from the time the city was founded, low capacity, corruption and clientelism in the bureaucracy all became major and chronic problems (ibid.).

It became common knowledge that Wawan was securing projects on a grand scale through his family's companies. In 2013, Indonesia Corruption Watch reported that his family owned 24 companies managing projects issued by national, provincial and local governments. In South Tangerang, Wawan even regularly attended official meetings and directed the work of programs in four key strategic government offices: the education, health, spatial planning and employment bureaus. He also served as a 'broker' for other businesses and regulated who received what (Kusumaningtyas et al. 2017: 254; Mustafa and Rahman 2019).

At the same time, Airin (shadowed by Wawan) also strengthened her position by establishing collusive and clientelist relations with institutions and groups that had the potential to challenge her and her family. For example, her government distributed largesse in the form of government funding, positions and projects in order to coopt actors such as mass organisations, government-oriented NGOs and local media. As a result, such groups formed a kind of *uncivil* society in the city, competing for government projects and for control over lucrative territory such as parking zones and street vendor areas (this is especially the case for mass organisations of *preman*, or gangsters), in the process building clientelist relationships with the local government (Mustafa and Rahman 2019). While some of these groups occasionally express critical views on local government matters, either through articles in the local media or through street demonstrations, they often do so in pursuit of a pay-off in the form of increased access to government resources. By the same token, Airin also built patronage relationships with DPRD members, with the result that DPRD members generally lacked the confidence and integrity to challenge the executive's performance or promote strategic policy reforms (ibid.).

In 2013, the Corruption Eradication Commission (Komisi Pemberantasan Korupsi, KPK) arrested Wawan for corruption in the construction of the South Tangerang regional hospital and fraudulent medical equipment procurement under the city's 2012 budget. However, the corruption court proceedings did not yield strong evidence implicating Airin, though it clearly indicated that several high-level bureaucrats were under Wawan's influence. While a coalition of civil society groups called on the KPK to investigate Airin's involvement, the effort proved unsuccessful (Mustafa and Rahman 2019). Despite the scandal, the DPRD did not actively seek to remove Airin from her position, likely due to their involvement in and benefit from the corrupt system that had emerged under her leadership. Despite being perceived as responsible for city governance, Airin was able to distance herself from her husband's actions, maintaining that she did not consent to them. Meanwhile, even Wawan's imprisonment failed to diminish his influence, as he continued to wield power over local government affairs from inside jail (ibid.).

Despite this generally predatory context, South Tangerang's local government did implement various development and welfare programs. Substantial infrastructure projects were delivered, especially road networks, public health centres, schools, drainage systems and irrigation facilities (Kusumaningtyas et al. 2017: 254–57; Mustafa and Rahman 2019). While these projects ostensibly addressed the city's essential needs, they also conveniently aligned with the interests of the elite players who derived resources from government projects and budgets, opening opportunities for predatory actors to exploit and profit from them through kickbacks, mark-ups and similar mechanisms. In terms of welfare policies, the city government offered free education up to junior high level and introduced a program for free medical treatment, mainly through community-based integrated health service posts (*posyandu*) that promote infant health. However, concerns remain about the quality of the education and healthcare services provided, including issues with patient care and implementation (Kusumaningtyas et al. 2017: 257; Mustafa and Rahman 2019).

Despite lacking substantive performance in good governance, Airin was nevertheless able to secure her second term in 2015 by winning a commanding 60 per cent of the vote, propelled by her dynastic networks, mobilisation of the bureaucracy, and the patronage connections she had nurtured through various mass organisations. During her second term, she continued to focus on infrastructure and essential services, including health care and education. However, her efforts faced multiple challenges. The prevalence of rent-seeking practices among all interest groups in the city, including the DPRD, law enforcement agencies, bureaucrats and mass organisations, posed a significant obstacle. The composition of the bureaucracy, largely shaped by political and patronage considerations, meant it was unable to perform well, hindering the achievement of substantial outcomes beyond symbolic projects. Informants noted that Wawan's grip on project distribution and strategic appointments persisted, while Airin continued to accommodate her political allies and potential opponents by providing them and their allies with posts in the public apparatus and with positions as contract staff.

In 2020, after Airin's second term ended, the mayoral election saw a transition to a new administration that was seemingly aligned with the dynasty's influence. The winning pair consisted of Benyamin Davnie, who had served as Airin's deputy mayor for two terms, and Pilar Saga Ichsan, the nephew of Atut. This was a succession that looked likely to perpetuate the dynasty's control over the city's politics. The continued absence of a strong civil society coalition advocating reform in the city meant that the dynasty's favoured candidates faced little serious competition in the election. Unfortunately, it also means there is unlikely to be substantial pressure for governance reform in the city, at least in the short term.

Conclusion

As in previous studies of democratic decentralisation in Indonesia, the case studies I have presented in this chapter suggest that predatory elites continue to exert a powerful, enduring and negative influence over the quality of local governance, including in some of Indonesia's most advanced urban areas where we would expect pressure in favour of reform to be greatest. To some extent, this influence has been mitigated by the incentives created through democratisation, which have encouraged local elites—even predatory elites—to promote development and welfare policies that attract popular support. However, these three cases provide evidence to suggest that the presence or absence of progressive forces in civil society at the local level also significantly influence the nature of local governance.

Progressive forces within civil society have played a vital role in challenging the dominance of predatory elites in local political systems. They do so both by directly opposing these elites and supporting rival reformist leaders and public officials who usher in governance reforms and, through their public advocacy work, promoting a public demand for reform. This chapter has focused on three patterns in the politics of local government. First, as the case of Surabaya demonstrates, transformative reforms are more likely to occur when civil society is strong enough to energise reformist leaders, enabling them to challenge predatory elites. Second, in cities with reformist leaders but where civil society pressure and support is lacking, these leaders are more likely to compromise on good governance reform by negotiating with incumbent elites to maintain political stability and support. The story of Bogor under Mayor Bima Arya Sugiarto illustrates this pathway. Third, as South Tangerang demonstrates, achieving genuine good governance reform is an uphill battle in cities with both predatory leaders and weak civil society. The chapter did not discuss another possible pattern: a city with a robust civil society and predatory leader, though such a combination is surely also possible. Overall, my analysis demonstrates that it is important to look beyond government leadership factors to understand the progress (or lack thereof) of governance reform at the local level, and to focus also on the role of civil society and its complex interactions with local government.

The analysis also helps to shed light on one important feature of local governance reform in Indonesia: many of the most far-reaching experiments in such reform over the past two decades have occurred in cities, rather than in rural areas. Generally speaking, robust local civil societies able to drive local reform are more likely to arise in cities than in rural areas, given the greater economic diversity, higher education levels and stronger middle classes of cities (see, for example, Aspinall and Berenschot 2019: 203–27). Certainly, Surabaya fits that pattern. But the cases of Bogor and South Tangerang also show that it cannot be taken for granted that urban centres will have strong and independent civil societies; indeed, the case of South Tangerang indicates that middle-class residents might become apathetic about city affairs as they withdraw into the private worlds of their gated communities (see also Elyda, this volume).

As an active member of Indonesia's civil society, long engaged in the effort to promote local governance reform, this is a topic that is close to my heart. The analysis I have presented in this chapter provides valuable insights into strategies to promote improved local governance within the context of democratic decentralisation in Indonesia. First, proponents of good local governance should focus on fostering the development of progressive civil society actors at the local level, rather than simply assuming that institutional reform and support for local government leaders will themselves drive change. This process can begin with identifying groups, actors and organisations with the potential to bring about positive change in local governance. Second, advocates of good local governance should explore avenues for building coalitions among progressive civil society forces at the local level. Collaborative efforts allow these forces to wield more influence than they can achieve alone. The formation of such alliances depends on the extent to which they can unite around a shared democratic and governance agenda. Third, local progressive forces should refine their strategies for advocating local governance reform.

Fourth, it is the interaction between local civil society and reforming government leaders that drives change; local civil society groups thus need to identify and support potentially reformist politicians to win elections and, in doing so, create channels for the articulation of their agendas within the local government apparatus. Fifth, it is essential to recognise that politicians seldom rely solely on the support of progressive civil society forces to win elections. Given that political pressure from predatory elites and rent-seeking groups often persists beyond elections, progressive forces should continue to monitor government and exert pressure on local politicians after they are elected to ensure that they fulfil their promises. Simultaneously, members of progressive coalitions should enhance their capacity to provide technical advice related to policymaking, program implementation and oversight processes, ensuring that their influence remains strong in the post-election period. The story of Surabaya presented in this chapter indicates that far-reaching local government reform *is* possible in Indonesian cities, but it also indicates that complex and lasting coalitions are needed to ensure that this goal is achieved.

References

Agustino, Leo. 2010. 'Dinasti politik Pasca-Orde Baru: Pengalaman Banten [Post-New Order political dynasties: The Banten experience]'. *Prisma: The Indonesian Indicator* 29: 10–116.

Anisah, Laili N. 2015. 'Tri Rismaharini: Wajah pemimpin populis Indonesia? [Tri Rismaharini: The face of a populist leader in Indonesia?]'. In *Berebut Kontrol Atas Kesejahteraan Kasus-Kasus Politisasi Demokrasi di Tingkat Lokal* [Competing for control over welfare cases of politicising democracy at the local level], edited by Caroline Paskarina, Mariatul Asiah and Otto Gusti Madung, 70–87. PolGov Fisipol UGM.

Antlov, Hans, Derick W. Brinkerhoff and Elke Repp. 2010. 'Civil society capacity building for democratic reform experience and lessons from Indonesia'. *Voluntas: International Journal of Voluntary and Non-Profit Organizations* 21(2): 417–39. doi.org/10.1007/s11266-010-9140-x

Ashadi, Saiful R. 2012. *Bambang DH Mengubah Surabaya* [Bambang DH changes Surabaya]. Indonesia Berdikari.

Aspinall, Edward. 2013. 'Popular agency and interest in Indonesia's democratic transition and consolidation'. *Indonesia* 15: 101–21. doi.org/10.1353/ind.2013.0021

Aspinall, Edward and Ward Berenschot. 2019. *Democracy for Sale: Elections, Clientelism, and the State in Indonesia*. Cornell University Press. doi.org/10.7591/9781501732997

Buehler, Michael. 2014. 'Elite competition and changing state-society relations: Shari'a policymaking in Indonesia'. In *Beyond Oligarchy: Wealth, Power, and Contemporary Indonesian Politics*, edited by Michele Ford and Thomas Pepinsky, 157–75. Cornell University Press.

Bunnell, Tim, Michelle Ann Miller, Nicholas A. Phelps and John Taylor. 2013. 'Urban development in a decentralized Indonesia: Two success stories?' *Pacific Affairs* 86(4): 857–76. doi.org/10.5509/2013864857

Dick, Howard W. 2002. *Surabaya, City of Work: A Socioeconomic History, 1900–2000*. Ohio University Press.

Hadiz, Vedi R. 2004. 'Decentralization and democracy in Indonesia: A critique of neo-institutionalist perspectives'. *Development & Change* 35(4): 697–718. doi.org/10.1111/j.0012-155X.2004.00376.x

Hadiz, Vedi R. 2010. *Localizing Power in Post-Authoritarian Indonesia: A Southeast Asian Perspective*. Stanford University Press.

Heryanto, Ariel and Vedi R. Hadiz. 2005. 'Post-authoritarian Indonesia: A comparative Southeast Asian perspective'. *Critical Asian Studies* 37(2): 251–75. doi.org/10.1080/14672710500106341

Hidayat, Rachmat. 2010. 'Inilah kronologi APBD Gate DPRD kota Bogor tahun 2002 [Chronology of the Bogor city regional parliament budget misuse 2002]'. *Tribunnews.com*, 19 July. http://m.tribunnews.com/regional/2010/07/19/inilah-kronologi-apbd-gate-dprd-kota-bogor-tahun-2002

Kenawas, C. Yoes. 2015. 'The rise of political dynasties in a democratic society'. Paper presented to the 2014 Arryman Fellows' Symposium, 16 May. Northwestern University, Illinois.

Kusumaningtyas, Atika Nur, Kurniawati Hastuti Dewi, Esty Ekawati and Fathimah Fildzah Izzati. 2017. 'Resume penelitian perempuan kepala daerah dalam jejaring oligarki lokal [Research summary: Female local leaders in local oligarchic networks]'. *Jurnal Penelitian Politik* 14(2): 243–64.

Marijan, Kacung. 2008. 'The 1999 decentralization policy, local politics, and local capacity of the port city of Surabaya'. In *Port Cities in Asia and Europe*, edited by Arndt Graf and Chua Beng Huat, 86–104. Routledge. doi.org/10.4324/9780203884515-11

Muhammad, E. Saputro. 2016. 'Tumbuhnya oligarchy local: Kekuasaan ekonomi dan politik Tubagus Chaeri Wardana di Kota Tangerang Selatan [The growth of local oligarchy: The political and economic power of Tubagus Chaeri Wardana in South Tangerang city]'. Graduate thesis. Universitas Islam Syarif Hidayatullah Jakarta.

Mustafa, Mochamad. 2017. 'Democratic decentralisation and good governance: The political economy of procurement reform in decentralised Indonesia'. PhD thesis. University of Adelaide. https://hdl.handle.net/2440/117256

Mustafa, Mochamad and Erman Rahman. 2019. 'Urban politics and service delivery in South Tangerang'. Urban Politics in South Asia Project: Local government and public goods in four Southeast Asian countries—Thailand, Indonesia, Malaysia, Philippines. Unpublished paper.

Rosser, Andrew, Ian Wilson and Priyambudi Sulistyanto. 2011. 'Leaders, elites, and coalitions: The politics of free public services in decentralised Indonesia'. Research Paper 11. Developmental Leadership Program.

Rosser, Andrew and Priyambudi Sulistyanto. 2013. 'The politics of universal free basic education in decentralised Indonesia: Insights from Yogyakarta'. *Pacific Affairs* 86(3): 539–60. doi.org/10.5509/2013863539

Sutisna, Agus. 2018. 'The proliferation symptoms of political dynasties in Banten under the era of Governor Ratu Atut Chosiah'. *Diponegoro Law Review* 3(2): 182–98. doi.org/10.14710/dilrev.3.2.2018.182-198

Tans, Ryan. 2012. 'Mobilizing resources, building coalitions: Local power in Indonesia'. *Policy Studies* 64. East-West Center. www.jstor.org/stable/resrep06516

von Luebke, Christian. 2009. 'The political economy of local governance: Findings from an Indonesian field study'. *Bulletin of Indonesian Economic Studies* 45(2): 201–30. doi.org/10.1080/00074910903040310

von Luebke, Christian. 2012. 'Striking the right balance, economic concentration and local government performance in Indonesia and Philippines'. *European Journal of East Asian Studies* 11: 17–44. doi.org/10.1163/15700615-20120005

Yandri, Pitri. 2017. 'The political geography of voters and political participation: Evidence from local election in suburban Indonesia'. *Indonesian Journal of Geography* 49(1): 57–64. doi.org/10.22146/ijg.11315

7 Citizens into consumers: The impact of gated communities on Jakarta's periphery

Corry Elyda

Commentators often enthusiastically point to the growth of Indonesia's middle class as a major force of social and political change in Indonesia. Yet, alongside the growth of the middle class, striking changes have occurred in middle-class lifestyles, especially in urban areas. Arguably one of the most dramatic developments in urban life and landscapes in Indonesia over recent decades has been the growth of privately run real estate complexes, commonly referred to as gated communities, where middle-class residents sequester themselves from the sometimes chaotic urban landscapes that surround them, enjoying amenities that can only be dreamed of by the *kampung*[1] residents beyond their walls. As I argue in this chapter, the growing physical separation of urban middle-class people in such communities points also to their growing social and political separation, even withdrawal, from broader Indonesian society, with potentially far-reaching consequences.

I present this argument by studying the municipality of South Tangerang (Tangerang Selatan), which is located about 30 kilometres south-west of central Jakarta. This municipality is home to some of the most extensive and famous private real estate developments in Indonesia, such as Bintaro Jaya, Bumi Serpong Damai (BSD) city and Alam Sutera, housing hundreds of thousands of middle-class people. The residents of these communities not only have access to comfortable and often

---

1   A *kampung* is an unplanned neighbourhood, mostly occupied by low income and middle income residents.

luxurious private housing, they also get most of their basic needs such as electricity and water from the private companies that run them, and they can enjoy sports facilities, shopping malls and other facilities there, rarely having to leave their estates except to work. As I explain, many of the residents of these gated communities have little interaction with, or concern for, the wider municipality of South Tangerang within which they live. This situation may help to explain why South Tangerang has been dominated by one of Indonesia's most notorious and scandal-prone political dynasties, despite having some of the country's wealthiest and best-educated inhabitants.

In this chapter, I analyse the growth of these gated communities, the character of life within them, and their social and political effects. First, I provide a picture of the private housing market in Jakarta and explain how this drives many middle-class consumers, especially first home buyers, to Jakarta's outskirts. Next, I briefly introduce the municipality of South Tangerang, the main focus of the chapter and a site of especially intensive development of private housing estates. A third section introduces the main private housing estates in the municipality, drawing a contrast between large- and small-scale developments. The remainder of the chapter focuses on the differences between life inside and outside these estates, outlining the gaps in facilities provided to residents of private gated communities compared to the general public in South Tangerang, followed by discussion of the political and social consequences of this form of housing inequality.

Jakarta's housing market and the pressures of middle-class housing

Jakarta is a booming city, and has been for a long time. Year by year, the workforce is growing rapidly. According to the Jakarta branch of Statistics Indonesia (BPS Jakarta), the number of workers in Jakarta in 2023 was 5.07 million people, an increase of 5.3 per cent from the preceding year's 4.8 million workers (Ningsih 2023). The same cannot be said for the city's population. BPS Jakarta reported that the annual population growth rate in Jakarta was only 0.64 per cent in 2020–2022, the lowest in the country (Ahdiat 2023b). One of the main reasons for Jakarta's sluggish population growth, despite the city being a magnet for employment, is housing unaffordability.

Decent housing in Jakarta is unaffordable for most workers, especially young first home buyers. The World Bank revealed in 2019 that Jakarta's property price to income ratio was higher than many of the most expensive cities in the world, such as New York and Singapore. The ratio in Jakarta was 10.3 while the ratio in New York was 5.7 and Singapore was 4.8 (Roberts et al. 2019: 94). One main reason for this unaffordability is low housing supply. Jakarta suffers from a severe housing backlog. According to one recent analysis, the city currently lacks 1.38 million housing units (Purwanti 2023).

The backlog is a result of many longstanding problems in Indonesian housing and urban policy, including escalating land prices and lack of public housing. Instead of itself trying to fulfil the housing needs of citizens, the government has long handed over the management of Indonesia's housing supply, especially for middle-class citizens, to private developers. This policy orientation was cemented in the early 1970s, when the national government introduced a liberal market–oriented housing policy that focused on growth-oriented urban development (Santoso 2020). The policy was triggered in part by the inability of the Indonesian government to fulfil its own public housing supply targets (Kusno 2012). As a result, over the past half century, most residents, including in big cities, have either independently built their own houses (consistent with longstanding practice) or they have relied on private developers.

As land prices in the city centre are very high and the land supply is scarce, many private developers in Jakarta opt to build apartments. According to Lamudi, which describes itself as Indonesia's largest property technology company, the land price in Jakarta's residential areas ranges from Rp 20 million (US$1,200) to Rp 60 million (US$3,700) per square metre (Novriyadi 2024). Meanwhile, the price in high-end locations, such as Menteng in central Jakarta, is around Rp 100 million (US$6,200) per square metre (Sandi 2023). The number of apartment buildings has grown rapidly in Jakarta. According to a report by the real estate agency Colliers, Jakarta had 220,451 apartment units in 2022 with the number having cumulatively increased by 9.23 per cent since 2018 (Ahdiat 2023a).

However, the apartment option is not attractive for many citizens, especially first home buyers, who lack experience of vertical living. A digital survey conducted by the telecommunication company Telkomsel in 2022 showed that 93 per cent of millennials in Jakarta would prefer to own a house over an apartment (Annur 2023). There are several reasons for this preference. The first is that people think of owning an apartment as temporary, compared with owning a landed house. Under Government Regulation 18/2021 on Management Rights, Land Rights, Vertical Housing and Land Registration, the government provides owners of an apartment unit a Hak Guna Bangunan (HGB, Right to Build) certificate, which lasts for 80 years. Meanwhile, landed houses are permanently owned in the form of a Surat Hak Milik (SHM, Certificate of Ownership). An SHM is considered the highest level of individual land ownership in Indonesia.

This means buying an apartment is out of the question for many middle-class people, who tend to think of their home not only as a place to live but also as an investment and asset that they will pass on to their children.

A second reason many middle-class Jakartans are reluctant to buy an apartment is the size. Apartments with price ranges of Rp 500 million (US$32,000) to Rp 1 billion (US$64,000) are typically very small. With that money, typical middle-class buyers can only afford units of 25 to 50 square metres. According to Colliers Indonesia, the price of an apartment in the Jakarta central business district in late 2021 was around Rp 52.3 million (US$3,300) per square metre while in non-prime areas it was around Rp 26.6 million (US$1,700) per square metre (Laksono and Alexander 2021). Meanwhile, Jakarta's minimum wage was Rp 4.9 million (US$310) per month in 2023—putting owning an apartment completely out of reach of minimum wage earners.

A third, and arguably the most important, disincentive is the many problems associated with apartment ownership in Jakarta. These include stalled development (such that buyers purchasing an apartment off the plan may have to wait years before they can occupy it) and violations of tenants' rights, such as the refusal of the developer or building management to hand over the certificates once the apartment is ready. Residents in Green Pramuka apartment in 2015, for instance, staged a protest after the building management refused to hand over the certificates of land and buildings to the Tenants and Owners Association (P3SRS) as promised. The protest turned ugly, resulting in four tenants being charged with collective assault (Elyda 2015). Other problems include embezzlement by P3SRS committees and high costs of maintenance and services.

For all these reasons, many home buyers in Jakarta avoid apartment living. Those who move into apartments are often newlyweds, or people who are starting out in their careers, and they typically treat their apartment as a temporary or transit abode before buying a landed house. As one put it to me:

> I rented an apartment for a while after getting married and I did not like it. The space was so small, making me feel claustrophobic and the parking space was limited although I had paid for it. I also felt secluded and alone. I finally decided to move to a landed house in Bintaro. (Interview with Bintaro resident, 1 July 2023)

Houses with a garden or yard are still the first choice of most middle-class Jakartans. But buying a landed house is not easy. The high prices referred to above mean that it is almost impossible for ordinary middle-class residents to buy an affordable house in Jakarta. Instead, they look for alternatives in the municipalities that ring Jakarta, from where they can commute daily to their workplaces in the city—in 2015 it was estimated that 1.38 million people commuted into Jakarta daily from these outlying districts (Budiari 2015). The municipality of South Tangerang is one of the favoured choices of such people, as it is connected to Jakarta by toll roads and a train line.

South Tangerang and dynastic politics

South Tangerang is a relatively new municipality. It was formed when it split from the district (*kabupaten*) of Tangerang in 2008. Its population in 2021 was 1.37 million, almost one-tenth of that of Jakarta, and the population grew by 0.94 per cent between 2021 and 2022 (BPS 2023). Partly because its population is made up of so many middle-class commuters, it is one of the most prosperous regions in the country. Its human development index score, for instance, is one of the highest in the country.[2] It is also a relatively wealthy municipality in terms of local government income. Robust development of new residential areas and a growing population have allowed the municipality to generate significant local income from taxes and charges (ANRI 2013). It generated Rp 1.5 trillion (US$98.6 million) in local taxes in 2022, with the biggest single contributor, at Rp 634 billion (US$41.7 million), being from property transfer fees (Bisnis Metro 2022). This figure is higher even than that of other municipalities neighbouring Jakarta, such as Depok, which had locally generated revenue of Rp 1.2 trillion (US$78.3 million) in the same year (Lantara 2023).

Despite this steady stream of income and despite its prosperous middle-class population, politics in South Tangerang have been dominated—as with politics in many districts of Banten, the province of which is it part—by one of Indonesia's most powerful (and notorious) local political dynasties. This dynasty was established by businessman-cum-politician Chasan Sochib who, during the New Order period, 'acted as a bridge between the military, bureaucracy, and Golkar [the state political party], and to Banten's society, including the underground (criminal) world' (Masaaki and Hamid 2008: 117; see also Mustafa, this volume). After the collapse of the New Order, his daughter, Ratu Atut Chosiyah, served as Banten governor from 2007 to 2017. Many of her relatives assumed influential leadership positions in the province and its component districts (Iqbal 2018; Sukri 2020). The political dynasty is notorious for its 'shadow state' (Hidayat 2007) connections. Ratu Atut

---

2 https://tangselkota.bps.go.id/indicator/26/45/1/indeks-pembangunan-manusia.html

herself was sentenced in 2014 to four years and seven years in jail, to be served consecutively, for a health equipment procurement corruption case and a case of bribery in a local election dispute (Farisa 2022).

In South Tangerang the mayor from 2011 to 2021 was Airin Rachmi Diany, Ratu Atut's sister-in-law. She was able to rely on her family connections, and the political and financial resources these delivered, to easily win two direct elections for the post, in 2010 and 2015. Many people viewed the real power behind the throne during her period in office as her husband (and Ratu Atut's brother), Tubagus Chaeri Wardana (Wawan). Like his sister, he was also imprisoned for corruption in 2014 (Ni'am and Rostika 2022). After Airin served her maximum of two terms in office she passed the baton of power to her former deputy, Benyamin Davnie, who, alongside Pilar Saga Ichsan (a nephew of Ratu Atut) as his running mate, won the mayoral election in 2020. Benyamin is widely seen as a close ally of the dynasty and as serving its political ambitions. Meanwhile, the Golkar party announced it would support Airin as a governor candidate for Banten in the 2024 provincial election (CNN Indonesia 2023).

Private housing estates in South Tangerang

One of the striking features of South Tangerang is that the physical landscape is dominated by private housing estates. Driven by the pressures of the Jakarta housing market described above, private property developers began to open new residential estates in the area as early as the 1970s. One of the main private developments in South Tangerang is Bintaro Jaya housing complex, built in 1979. With the supporting amenities that Bintaro had, many smaller housing complexes began to mushroom nearby, such as Bukit Nusa Indah, which opened in 1985. Meanwhile, in Serpong subdistrict, the expansion of BSD commenced with a more than 6,000 hectare plot in 1984. The development of private housing in South Tangerang became more and more intense after the development of a toll road connecting Serpong and Pondok Aren (Bintaro) with Jakarta in 1999 as well as the revitalisation, in 2009, of the local commuter line connecting South Tangerang to the city centre.

According to South Tangerang Regional Secretary Herman Suwarman, as of 2020 there were 1,160 private housing complexes in the municipality (Ferdiansyah 2020). These included hundreds of small housing complexes, but also several giant estates and even a new fully fledged privately run town. The three biggest housing complexes are Bintaro Jaya, BSD and Alam Sutera.

Bintaro Jaya

South Tangerang might be a relatively new municipality, but it is predated by some of the private housing complexes located there. As noted above, their development began in the 1970s. One of the most famous and largest housing complexes is Bintaro Jaya. It was built by Jaya Real Property, a subsidiary of PT Pembangunan Jaya, a company established by the Jakarta administration in cooperation with various businessmen, including the man who became one of Indonesia's main real estate developers, Ciputra, who back in the 1960s owned an architect firm (Lo 2010). As of 2022, Jaya Real Property's shares were majority owned by PT Pembangunan Jaya at 63.59 per cent, with BNP Paribas Wealth Management Singapore owning 14.03 per cent.[3]

Established in 1979, Bintaro Jaya was in many ways a prototypical middle-class housing estate in Indonesia, being developed at the leading edge of the boom in private estate construction. Today it covers almost 2,000 hectares and is home to over 17,000 households as well as the headquarters of several major corporations. Bintaro Jaya is actually situated across two provinces: Banten and Jakarta (Bintaro itself is the name of a subdistrict in South Jakarta). Bintaro Jaya is therefore widely viewed as being one of the most prestigious housing complexes in the greater Jakarta area, in part due to its proximity to the capital city and in part due to its status as a relatively early, and relatively luxurious, housing development.

Bintaro Jaya is divided into thirteen sectors. Some of these are named after elite areas of Jakarta, such as Senayan and Menteng, underlining the fact that most residents work in Jakarta, and providing them with a sense that they still live in Jakarta. It has various advanced facilities, including hospitals, markets and shopping centres. The estate is famous for its good quality international private schools, such as Pembangunan Jaya School, High Scope, Sekolah Alam Bintaro and Al-Azhar Bintaro—another important drawcard for many middle-class families. However, given it is seen as such a desirable location, Bintaro Jaya has become barely affordable for first home buyers. For example, in 2023 prices started at Rp 1 billion (US$63,500) for a unit of 33 square metres in the newly built U-Ville cluster, whereas freestanding homes in the older parts of the development are extremely expensive. As a result, Bintaro is an ageing community. The children of the residents who moved into the area decades ago and newcomers cannot afford to buy property in the area. The developer is currently building more affordable apartments and superblocks, as well as hangout places, to attract younger buyers.

---

3 www.jayaproperty.com/investor?year=2022&id_select=shareinfo-tab

BSD city

Unlike other housing complexes in South Tangerang, BSD (Bumi Serpong Damai) was intended from the start to become a fully fledged city complete with commercial, educational, healthcare and business facilities. One of the most important private property developers of the New Order period, Ciputra Group, founded BSD in 1989 (see Dieleman 2011). Ciputra Group, however, was hit hard by Indonesia's economic crisis of 1997–1998. In order to survive, it was forced to divest itself of some major projects, including BSD, and renegotiate with its creditors (Leaf 2015).

Sinar Mas Group (one of Indonesia's biggest business conglomerates) acquired the development in 2004. According to its official website (bsdcity.com), the township covers more than 6,000 hectares and has 40,000 houses with a population of around 450,000 people. BSD is continuing to expand, as it keeps acquiring land and extending its township to incorporate parts of nearby Tangerang district.

Initially, Ciputra built BSD with the goal of attracting customers from various social classes and income categories. Accordingly, it offered different housing types ranging from 60 square metres to 150 square metres. Some of the housing complexes located within the greater BSD area were not gated (Firzandy 2018). Under Sinar Mas, however, BSD has aimed more squarely at higher income brackets. In pursuit of this approach, Sinar Mas built more high-end facilities such as shopping malls, hospitals and modern grocery markets to lure upper middle-class families. BSD is also well known for housing several major corporate headquarters, as well as private universities, notably Multimedia Nusantara University and Prasetya Mulya University, and a campus of Australia's Monash University. The provision of all these facilities, along with the 1999 construction of the Serpong-Pondok Indah toll road that connects BSD to the centre of Jakarta, has made BSD a highly attractive location for many middle-class home buyers. As a result, BSD is perhaps the best known of all the recent new towns to have sprung up on Jakarta's outskirts.

Alam Sutera

Alam Sutera housing complex is built and managed by PT Alam Sutera Realty. Its first project began in 1994 on an 800 hectare plot. As of 2016, the company had launched 37 residential clusters and 2 apartment buildings in its township. Each cluster comprises 150–300 houses and is supported with a range of premium facilities, including education, entertainment, healthcare centres and advanced security systems with a command centre.[4]

---

[4] www.alam-sutera.com/about/about.html

Unlike Bintaro and BSD, both of which rely heavily on the local train system to provide mobility for residents to Jakarta, Alam Sutera's access is strictly through private cars and buses. One of the factors that has made Alam Sutera an option for commuters despite its relatively far distance from Jakarta was the opening of the Jakarta-Merak toll road exit in 2009 that connects the township to nearby areas, including BSD, Tangerang and Jakarta. Alam Sutera township targets consumers with high incomes. Its landed houses are typically large, starting from 200 square metres. Its prices are also high; for example, units in its new cluster, the Gramercy, start at Rp 16 billion (US$1 million).[5]

Small housing complexes

In addition to the large gated housing complexes, South Tangerang has more than 1,000 smaller private housing complexes. Most of these are enclaved in organic residential settlements called *kampung*. These housing complexes usually have a small number of units, ranging from 8 to 50 houses. Their size and the facilities they offer vary. A cluster with 8 to 15 houses, for example, will have only basic facilities, such as a security post, road and small green spaces. Those with dozens of houses will have more extensive facilities, such as a park, a playground, a sports field and a small prayer house.

While some of these small communities were established decades ago, their development has continued to be rapid, and has occurred hand-in-hand with the development of the larger estates with all their modern facilities. For instance, between 2008 and 2014, the South Tangerang government granted at least 450 permits for small complexes to be built in the area around BSD city (Rita Rita 2017).

Most of the small housing complexes are located near the three giant complexes in order for residents to be able to access the facilities provided by them, a phenomenon that leads to them being labelled 'free riders' (Diningrat 2018). For small-scale developers, the facilities provided by BSD and Bintaro are highly beneficial. They not only use those facilities as a selling point to buyers; it also means they can get away with building small-scale housing complexes with only basic infrastructure.

Part of the context here is that national housing regulations are far less onerous for small-scale developments than for larger estates. According to Regulation 11/2008 on Guidelines for Housing and Settlement Compatibility, the public facilities developers are required to provide depend on the population of a complex. Complexes with 250 people

---

5 https://alam-sutera.com/product/product.html?product=The%20Gramercy

or fewer are required to have only a prayer house (*mushala*), shops and playground. Those with 2,500 people or fewer must have a mosque, a playground, a kindergarten, an elementary school, a community hall and a garbage disposal centre. With more than 2,500 residents, a complex requires comprehensive facilities similar to those of a small town, such as junior and senior high schools, a health clinic, shops, a maternity clinic and a bus station. Therefore, most of the 'free riders' around the larger housing developments in South Tangerang are small gated complexes, with only 10 to 20 houses. Diningrat (2018: 363) points out that these can pose major infrastructure challenges:

> those who have the obsession of consuming things but refuse to pay for the supply, in the long term, will create what we call public goods undersupply. It is marked with the emergence of problems such as congestion, floods, clean water crises, environmental damage and urban sprawl.

Of course, for many middle-class buyers, especially those with relatively limited means, the presence of so many small-scale complexes is advantageous. They can buy a less-expensive house in a small complex (the price of a house in Bintaro and BSD starts at around Rp 1 billion (US$63,500), while buyers can still find similarly sized houses under Rp 1 billion outside the big complexes) and are still able to enjoy the facilities offered by the larger estates. Many buyers in these small complexes view the facilities in BSD and Bintaro as a deciding factor when making a purchase.

Infrastructure gaps

Over recent decades private developers have transformed not only the physical landscape but also the social landscape of South Tangerang. As I argue in this and the next two sections, the creation of so many gated housing complexes has given rise to gaps that separate the residents of these communities from the general population that surrounds them.

A starting point for investigating these gaps is to examine the reasons why middle-class consumers find these locations attractive. As many as 25 years ago, Richard Robison argued that one of the visible signs of the growth of Indonesia's middle class was the appearance of 'mushrooming new housing estates ranging from the comfortable to the luxurious, all replete with security guards and various forms of enclosure' (Robison 1996 cited in Leisch 2002: 342). Robison's comment hints at the key to these places' attractiveness: it is not only the physical comforts they provide, but also the sense of security and exclusivity they offer that make them so appealing to would-be residents. The developers of South Tangerang's gated communities, especially Sinarmas Land and Jaya Realty, have provided high-quality infrastructure and facilities to lure buyers. These facilities range from basic infrastructure, such as roads, water systems, internet connectivity, parks, education facilities and hospitals, to those oriented to entertainment and lifestyle, such as fashionable restaurants, shopping malls and theme parks.

The South Tangerang government, despite the relatively healthy income streams it enjoys, is unable to keep up, resulting in a deep contrast between the facilities residents enjoy inside Bintaro and BSD, and those they experience once they step outside. Most South Tangerang residents, notably poor and lower middle income residents, still live in unplanned and unregulated settlements, both urban *kampung* and semi-rural settlements that survive from an earlier stage in the region's development. South Tangerang residents have created separate terms— Tangsel *swasta* (private South Tangerang) and Tangsel *negeri* (public South Tangerang)—to showcase the gap in facilities separating these two spaces, with the former referring to areas managed by the developers and the latter referring to the territory managed by the municipal government. In fact, the gap is so obvious that residents often make jokes about it, both online and offline, in daily conversation. One common meme, for example, that circulates on social media uses a picture of the Taj Mahal, with this landmark and an area of lush park surrounding it labelled as Alam Sutera and BSD; meanwhile, the densely populated and messy area outside the gate is labelled as Pamulang and Ciputat, two districts in South Tangerang that do not belong to the giant housing complexes.

The consequences of this infrastructure gap are profound. It means that residents of the gated communities, especially the more exclusive locations such as BSD city and Bintaro, are socially and psychologically separated from the *kampung* around them, and from the wider South Tangerang community. In particular, their enjoyment of the comprehensive facilities built and managed by the private entities that run their living spaces frees them from being dependent on the local government. Although the residents of these communities live in South Tangerang, they have little need to interact with locals outside their communities, or with the local government. This independence has resulted in other gaps—political and socioeconomic.

Before I go on to consider these political and socioeconomic consequences, let me briefly illustrate the infrastructure gap by considering three areas of provision that people in the region often point to as highlighting the distinction between the gated communities and the wider South Tangerang community: roads, water and security. In order to understand these gaps, I interviewed residents living in different housing complexes, including BSD, Bintaro and other smaller complexes.

All the interviewees agreed that the infrastructure and facility gap is apparent. Those who live outside the big estates still prefer living in South Tangerang to other locations because they can access the facilities in the estates. It is also the reason why they are not concerned with the gap as they can still enjoy the facilities in the big estates.

Roads

Residents in gated communities acknowledge that the most obvious difference between areas managed by developers and those managed by the city administration is in the quality of the roads. The roads managed by the developers are typically wider, better maintained, neat and orderly. Residents of Bintaro and BSD city I spoke to praised the developers for maintaining these facilities well. It typically takes only one to two weeks for the complex management to fix a damaged road or patch a pothole. Roads in BSD are especially known for their width, ease of traffic flow and orderliness, but even more modest roads, such as those in Bintaro, for example, are in better condition than those outside the complexes.

Roads outside the complexes are typically smaller, lack footpaths, and are often damaged, inundated and unorganised. Footpaths barely exist even on the roads near train stations that require pedestrian facilities the most. As a resident who lives in Green Aleena, a small housing complex in Serpong near BSD, explained:

> The roads are one of the saddest [things we can see] when we go outside BSD. BSD has well maintained roads but in Ciputat and Pamulang [nearby ordinary residential and *kampung* areas], the roads are bad. The market is also chaotic. The roads are often clogged by traffic, without any particular reason. (Interview, 26 July 2023)

Although the rapid growth of South Tangerang as a commuter hub means that roads throughout the municipality are increasingly congested (including some in the private estates), the worst congestion typically occurs in bottlenecks where the wide and generally smooth-flowing roads of the gated communities connect to the outside: in other words, where these private and public worlds meet.

Residents also see significant differences on roads near train stations in private and public South Tangerang. Sinarmas Land and Jaya Realty have been revamping the train stations that are situated in their areas, such as Pondok Ranji and Jurang Mangu stations in Bintaro and Cisauk in BSD. Such stations look modern and are integrated with markets, drop-off areas and nearby bus shelters. Meanwhile, stations on the same lines that service ungated communities tend to provide a much less comfortable commuter experience: they lack lanes for drop off and pick up, and there is little or no regulation of street vendors and feeder public minivans (*angkot*) that wait for passengers nearby. Although most of these stations are situated near traditional markets, they are not integrated with them via pedestrian access paths. As a result, these stations are choke points for congestion on a daily basis.

Water

Besides roads, another severe infrastructure gap is in clean water provision. BSD and Bintaro residents are guaranteed piped water into their houses and rarely experience disruptions in supply. These complexes, as well as Alam Sutera, source their water from Tirta Kerta Raharja (TKR), the water supply company owned by the district of Tangerang (the district from which South Tangerang split more than a decade ago). TKR's raw water supply is from the Cidurian and Cisadane Rivers that pass through Banten province. According to its website, the water is processed in its thirteen water treatment plants before being distributed to customers. Initially, for big housing complexes, including BSD and Bintaro, TKR only supplied water to the complex, and water distribution and maintenance of pipelines within the estates were managed by other parties on behalf of estate management. However, over time BSD has transferred its water treatment facilities as well as its household customers to TKR (Iqbal 2023). But BSDE, a subsidiary of Sinarmas Land, recently won the bidding for a Rp 162.67 billion (US$10.36 million) drinking water supply project from Tangerang district government. BSDE will build, rehabilitate, operate and maintain the raw water supply and TKR's water treatment plants for the next 25 years (Nityakanti 2023).

In contrast, the provision of piped water to the rest of South Tangerang is hit and miss. According to an attachment to Tangerang Mayoral Regulation 37/2019 on the Drinking Water Provision System Master Plan for 2019–2039, South Tangerang has 11,559 household connections to the piped water system, which represents only 12.08 per cent coverage excluding the three private developments. Older housing complexes, such as Bukit Nusa Indah in Ciputat (built in 1985), are connected with TKR's piped water system. However, most of the new small housing complexes rely on groundwater, as do most residents of *kampung* and private houses outside the complexes. The attachment to the mayoral regulation mentioned above states that 43.77 per cent of households in South Tangerang use groundwater judged as meeting drinking water quality standards, while 34.22 per cent use unsafe groundwater. The same source also points out that 'non-technical' issues hinder the development of piped water in South Tangerang, including 'the lack of budgeting commitment from the local government for drinking water provision' (p. 33).

In addition to supply concerns, many residents of South Tangerang outside the major gated communities complain about water quality. Many who do not have access to piped water rely on bottled water for drinking, adding significantly to household expenditure. Most households in smaller gated communities and in *kampung* use individual wells for their water needs. However, many residents are doubtful about the quality, and believe the water is unsafe for consuming even after being boiled (traditionally, Indonesians boil water from groundwater or springs in order to ensure it is safe to drink). A resident in Cluster Pratama Paradise housing complex, for instance, considers that the groundwater from his well has a strong smell of iron and causes reddish stains. Hence, he uses it only for washing and other activities and buys containers of water for consumption (interview, 1 June 2023). Meanwhile, in other clusters, the water is not clear, making residents afraid to consume it although there is no laboratory proof that it is unsafe.

Security

Another gap that separates residents of the gated communities from people living in surrounding areas is in the ways they ensure security for their homes. As Ian Wilson explains in his chapter in this volume, security provision has played an important role in the development of Jakarta's physical and social landscape. The same applies to the provision of housing. Twenty years ago, one observer of Indonesia's gated communities noted:

> The security aspect is very important when making the decision to buy a house. Residents of Jakarta always appear to be anxious. In the upper class quarter of Menteng in central Jakarta, which was first inhabited by the Dutch colonial rulers and later by the Chinese upper class and acolytes of the former president Soeharto (also a resident), the walls have grown with the years from less than two to more than four meters in height today. Whenever a thief managed to get in, the wall was extended. (Leisch 2002: 343)

Similar concerns and fears guide middle-class office workers from Jakarta who choose to live in South Tangerang's gated housing communities. In my informal discussions with residents, they often stated that security was the main consideration when choosing where to live.

In fact, the nature of the security provided in these gated communities varies greatly. The large-scale private complexes provide more complex security systems, including CCTV, multiple portals and security officers. Upper middle-class communities in BSD and Bintaro usually have especially high security standards, including 24-hour security guards on site and one-gate systems controlling entry to and exit from the community. Some clusters in Bintaro and BSD city require outsiders to register and leave their identification cards with guards before entering a compound. In contrast, many of the small-scale communities scattered around South Tangerang have more minimal systems. Although they still implement a one-gate system, some small clusters do not have security officers but instead rely on CCTV and community security officers (*hansip*) in their area.

In my research, I found that residents are often highly sensitive to reported incidents of crime in their vicinity. Some residents of gated communities said they had decided to improve security measures in their communities following (sometimes very minor) criminal incidents. For example, one resident of a small housing complex in Jombang, Ciputat said that the residents in his compound agreed to hire a security officer after one of the houses was robbed in the middle of the day. A resident in another small gated housing complex in the same area said that community members decided to close the gate to their compound after several pairs of shoes went missing from outside residents' homes. Previously, they had left the gates open to allow children from surrounding *kampung* to freely use their roads to play.

All residents I spoke to agreed that the police could not be relied on to either prevent crime or catch perpetrators. Recorded criminal cases in South Tangerang are the highest in all of Banten province: according to official BPS statistics, 1,402 of 6,454 criminal cases reported to the Banten Police in 2020, or about 22 per cent, occurred in the municipality (Dihni 2021). Such figures contribute to fears of insecurity among residents, driving the introduction of increasingly restrictive security measures in the private communities. Meanwhile, residents who live in *kampung* and non-gated residential areas largely have to rely on their own resources to guard against crime, for example, building fences, walls or iron grids around their homes, and organising *hansip* to patrol their neighbourhoods.

Political gaps

In Indonesia, as in many other countries, the middle class is often viewed as being a potential driver of political change. However, it is arguable that the social conditions of their lives in gated communities is blunting that potential in Indonesia. Gated communities are resulting in the withdrawal of the middle class from broader society. Many middle-class residents in such communities consider involvement in public matters to be unnecessary; after all, the private entities that built their homes and manage their communities are responsible for fulfilling many of their daily needs. For them, as long as those private entities repair their roads, keep their parks clean and guarantee supply of piped water and other utilities, they have little need to rely on the local government. Paying more for the services they need is far more convenient than protesting against the local government's poor performance, or engaging in civic action in order to clean up the local government's management of city infrastructure. Most such residents make contact with the local government only when taking care of unavoidable administrative matters, such as registering for identity cards or registering a new family member who has moved into the area (though many middle-class residents actually pay agents to take care of such matters, rather than dealing with the local administration themselves).

Certainly, most residents of South Tangerang's private housing complexes I interviewed in my research seem apathetic about local political affairs. Indeed, many said they do not even consider themselves to be citizens of South Tangerang. As one resident of BSD put it: 'I am not a citizen. I am a consumer who lives in BSD. My relationship is between consumer and developer. I do not have a sense of citizenship' (interview, 20 May 2023). The backgrounds of many residents of South Tangerang's gated communities also militates against them developing a sense of belonging to South Tangerang, even when they have lived there for many years, and plan to live out their lives there. Most of them have moved to South Tangerang from elsewhere, and many of them work in Jakarta and identify much more with the capital than with South Tangerang. Some residents even refuse to register as residents of South Tangerang by changing their identity cards to include their current address.[6] As one resident of Bintaro, who was in fact raised and still lives there, explained, he prefers to keep his registered domicile as his grandmother's address in East Jakarta:

> Although it is a hassle to visit my grandmother's house in East Jakarta [around a one hour drive from Bintaro, in order to register his residence there], it is still worth it because I can skip the bureaucracy in South Tangerang. It will also be good for my son in the future if he wants to study in Jakarta. (Interview, 1 June 2023)

While residents who have not acquired ID cards with South Tangerang addresses are ineligible to vote in municipal government elections, others who have registered as South Tangerang residents told me they

---

6 In Indonesia, you can move to another domicile but not change the information in your ID card to the new address. So, many people who move to South Tangerang are not registered as citizens there.

still barely pay attention to local government affairs and do not vote (indeed, I encountered quite a few who did not remember the name of the current mayor). Some who did vote said they were either indifferent to or pessimistic about the results. These middle-class citizens were aware that South Tangerang has been under the control of the Ratu Atut dynasty and feel that their votes will not make a difference.

This situation helps to explain why, despite being a relatively prosperous part of Indonesia, South Tangerang generally has low levels of voter participation in its elections. In the 2020 mayoral election, the voter participation rate of South Tangerang residents was only 60 per cent (Sutrisna and Carina 2020). Gated community residents form a large proportion of the abstentions. Table 7.1 shows the voter participation rate in various locations in the 2020 mayoral elections, demonstrating relatively low turnout in gated communities compared to those in a poor community located not far from the municipal garbage dump. Lower voter turnout, it should be noted, is not a new phenomenon in South Tangerang: in the 2015 mayoral election, participation was only 57 per cent (Setiawan 2019).

Arguably, this context is one of the explanations for why the Ratu Atut dynasty has been able to maintain its hold over South Tangerang, despite the municipality being, on average, a prosperous and well-educated part of Indonesia. While Mayor Airin and her supporters have been able to rely on traditional clientelist mobilisation strategies to win support in poor *kampung*, they have had little need for votes from middle-class gated communities—and little reason to fear them given their low participation rate. Table 7.1 also shows that the Benyamin–Pilar candidate pair gained relatively few votes in the gated community polling stations compared to the *kampung*.

Social gaps

In addition to having a political impact, the gaps in provision of infrastructure and public facilities separating residents of private gated communities from those of *kampung* also creates social gaps that are arguably more profound. Despite living in relatively close physical proximity, it is as if these two groups inhabit entirely separate social worlds. The price of housing in the gated communities means residents are generally homogeneous in terms of their socioeconomic backgrounds and income levels. Sharing similar social mores, and with little need to rely on the local government, they tend to live in a social bubble that contains neighbourhoods and facilities that only they—and people with similarly high income levels—can access.

Table 7.1 Voting in South Tangerang mayoral election, 2020

Location	Polling booth number	Registered voters	Ballots used	Participation rate (%)	Vote for Benyamin Davnie and Pilar Saga Ichsan (%)
De Latinos, BSD city					
Rawa Buntu ward, Serpong	060	307	120	39.1	22.9
Rawa Buntu ward, Serpong	061	405	141	34.8	23.6
Rawa Buntu ward, Serpong	058	198	107	54.0	28.2
Serpong ward, Serpong	041	324	152	46.9	38.0
Bintaro Jaya Sector 5 (Jl Perkici)					
Jurang Mangu Timur ward, Pondok Aren	062	351	105	29.9	26.7
Jurang Mangu Timur ward, Pondok Aren	061	255	90	35.3	20.0
Pondok Ranji ward, Ciputat Timur	052	145	42	29.0	21.4
City landfill area, Cipeucang					
Serpong ward, Serpong	018	325	202	62.2	34.7
Lengkong Wetan ward, Serpong	019	308	185	60.1	54.8

Source: South Tangerang City General Elections Commision (https://sipangsi.id and https://pilkada2020.kpu.go.id/#/pkwkk/tungsura/3674031011062).

In my research, I found that the bigger the housing complex, the less the connection its residents have with people who live beyond its gates. In fact, residents' relationships with locals, especially with locals from lower income groups, tend to occur only in the context of service provision and employment. Many locals who live near gated communities work for residents, usually as maids, gardeners and security officers. Members of the two groups, to the extent that they connect, do so in the context of employer–employee or consumer–service provider relations, with little opportunity for serious social or personal intimacy or friendship to develop.

One area that illustrates the social gap separating gated community and *kampung* residents is schooling. The two groups tend to send their children to different schools, meaning that their children have little opportunity to socialise with children from the other group. Despite historical issues with the quality of public schooling, there are many excellent public schools in Indonesia, especially in wealthy neighbourhoods of larger cities. South

Tangerang has several good public schools, especially its senior high schools. SMAN 2 senior high school and SMAN 3, for example, are ranked at 152 and 412 nationally in scores for state university entrance selection (Putra 2023). Nonetheless, middle-class parents increasingly send their children to elite private schools (World Bank 2019: 42). This is certainly the case in South Tangerang, where most gated community parents put their children in private schools. Most of these parents have small families—just one or two children—and place a premium on education. Indeed, they often chose where to live based on the availability of high-quality private schools. Most of them assume that public schools in South Tangerang are subpar. But some, in their interviews with me, also expressed concern with the potential social mixing their children would be exposed to at public schools: 'Public schools are too diverse. Many children are rude. Private school is more cultured. They focus on character building' (interview with a parent from a small gated community in Ciputat, 31 May 2023).

In this context, school tuition fees are a major expenditure item for many residents of gated communities. South Tangerang is a haven for high-quality private and alternative schools: the municipality had, in 2023, 157 public elementary schools and 185 private elementary schools. While public schools are free, better-quality private schools charge parents between Rp 1 million (US$65) and Rp 8 million (US$520) per month. While some parents I interviewed complained about these fees and the quality of education provided, others were happy with the abundant number of prestigious schools in Bintaro and BSD. Given the high cost of these schooling options, schools in South Tangerang cannot serve as a melting pot in which children get to know others from different social classes and diverse backgrounds. While most residents of gated communities are not concerned about this issue, and even see it as a positive, a few express worries about it. Some of them take their children to play in public parks in order to provide them with opportunities to interact with children from poor families.

In fact, it is not only that residents of gated communities lack social interactions with people from beyond their communities; they also struggle to build relationships with their neighbours. Spending most of their days commuting and working in Jakarta, most are unable to invest time in social interactions in their new neighbourhoods. As a result, most lack social support networks, even when they have lived in their gated community for many years (though many try to get around this problem by buying a home close to that of a relative who has already moved into the area). As Leisch (2002: 346) explained:

although the population structure is comparatively homogenous, the term 'gated community' is not really appropriate for this form of settlement. At the least, the connotation that it is a group of people with social contacts is misleading. Most residents do not know their neighbours in their own neighbourhood and do not have any contact with them at all.

Thanks to technology, many residents these days are able to connect with one another through WhatsApp groups or similar social network mechanisms that keep them updated with news and information regarding their neighbourhood. Overall, however, rather than representing closely integrated communities, these gated communities generally are highly atomised social settings.

Conclusion

This chapter has provided an overview of what is rapidly becoming a dominant mode of living for the wealthiest segments of the urban middle class of Indonesia's capital city. The municipality of South Tangerang is at the cutting edge of the development of private gated communities, but such urban environments are either already growing, or have the potential to grow, in and around all of Indonesia's major cities and, increasingly, in and around small towns as well. Nevertheless, we should not exaggerate how many Indonesians live in gated communities: according to official statistics in 2022, the percentage of Indonesians who buy houses from developers is extremely small, at only 0.6 per cent; most Indonesians (82.7 per cent) still build their own houses and 2.6 per cent buy from other individuals (Kuncaraning et al. 2022). But many Indonesians aspire to live in such locations and, as I have shown in this chapter, the mode of living they produce is already generating potentially far-reaching social and political consequences.

Gated communities, especially those that provide full amenities, encourage the middle class to opt out of public services and public involvement. The bubble they experience within these spaces provides an attractive lifestyle and a relief from the excruciating traffic, long working hours and stressful jobs. Gated-community residents find it convenient to have their daily needs handled professionally by private entities rather than by public officials, whom they view as less capable. The high-quality facilities they enjoy in these bubbles make them reluctant to leave and, increasingly, middle-class people are living almost their entire social lives within such spaces.

This situation places barriers in the way of the middle class playing the role that is often expected of it by social scientists. Middle-class residents of private housing estates in South Tangerang are better educated, better resourced and, potentially, have greater bargaining power in their dealings with public officials than the average Indonesian citizen; however, they have little incentive to engage with local government, let alone to make efforts to improve it. The dependence of residents of gated communities on private rather than public entities to meet their daily needs creates a distance between them and the local government, and the local people who live outside their communities. The resulting lack of a sense of belonging causes political apathy, represented by the low participation rates of private housing estate residents in local elections.

One result is the relative political stagnation of the municipality, which, deprived of the active citizenship of many of its middle-class residents, has been governed by members or supporters of the same political dynasty since its foundation. Meanwhile, typical urban problems such as traffic congestion, flooding and crime continue to accumulate in the municipality. While residents of gated communities can, to an extent, protect themselves from these problems, they still encounter them when they leave their protected enclaves. Some problems—air pollution, for example—cannot be prevented from seeping into their communities. Individual or private solutions thus ultimately have limited utility, but it remains to be seen whether the retreat of the middle class from public life in gated communities will give way to more active forms of citizen participation aimed at tackling urban issues.

References

Ahdiat, Adi. 2023a. 'Ini pertumbuhan apartemen di Jakarta 5 tahun terakhir [Growth of apartments in Jakarta over the past 5 years]'. *Katadata*, 26 January. https://databoks.katadata.co.id/datapublish/2023/01/26/ini-pertumbuhan-apartemen-di-jakarta-5-tahun-terakhir

Ahdiat, Adi. 2023b. 'Laju pertumbuhan penduduk Jakarta terendah se Indonesia [Population growth rate of Jakarta lowest in Indonesia]'. *Katadata*, 2 March. https://databoks.katadata.co.id/datapublish/2023/03/02/laju-pertumbuhan-penduduk-jakarta-paling-rendah-se-indonesia

Annur, Cindy Mutia. 2023. 'Mayoritas milenial di Indonesia lebih memilih rumah tapak ketimbang apartemen [Most millennials in Indonesia prefer landed houses over apartments]'. *Katadata*, 14 March. https://databoks.katadata.co.id/datapublish/2023/03/14/mayoritas-milenial-di-indonesia-lebih-memilih-rumah-tapak-ketimbang-apartemen

ANRI (Arsip Nasional Republik Indonesia). 2013. *Citra Kota Tangerang Selatan Dalam Arsip* [A picture of South Tangerang city from the archives]. ANRI.

Bisnis Metro. 2022. 'Pendapatan pajak tahun 2022 di Tangsel lampaui target, BPHTB tertinggi [South Tangerang's tax revenue for 2022 passes targets, highest land transfer tax]'. *Binis Metro*, 28 December. http://bisnismetro.id/pendapatan-pajak-tahun-2022-di-tangsel-lampaui-target-bphtb-tertinggi/

BPS (Badan Pusat Statistik, Statistics Indonesia). 2023. 'South Tangerang municipality in figures 2023'. BPS.
Budiari, Indra. 2015. '1.38 million commute into Jakarta daily'. *Jakarta Post*, 17 February. www.thejakartapost.com/news/2015/02/17/138-million-commute-jakarta-daily.html
CNN Indonesia. 2023. 'Golkar akan usung Airin jadi cagub Banten, Andika Hazrumy cabup Serang [Golkar will put forward Airin as gubernatorial candidate for Banten, Andika Hazrumy as district candidate for Serang]'. CNN Indonesia, 15 May. www.cnnindonesia.com/nasional/20230515032356-617-949490/golkar-akan-usung-airin-jadi-cagub-banten-andika-hazrumy-cabup-serang
Dieleman, Marleen. 2011. 'New town development in Indonesia: Renegotiating, shaping and replacing institutions'. *Bijdragen tot de Taal-, Land- en Volkenkunde* 167(1): 60–85. www.jstor.org/stable/41203121
Dihni, Vika Azkiyah. 2021. 'Tindak kejahatan di Tangerang Selatan tertinggi di Banten pada 2020 [Crime numbers in South Tangerang highest in Banten for 2020]'. *Katadata*, 26 November. https://databoks.katadata.co.id/datapublish/2021/11/26/tindak-kejahatan-di-tangerang-selatan-tertinggi-di-banten-pada-2020
Diningrat, Rendy Adriyan. 2018. 'Fenomena pembonceng gratis (free riders) di sekitar kota baru Bumi Serpong Damai (BSD city) [The phenomenon of free riders around new city Bumi Serpong Damai (BSD city)]'. *Tataloka* 20(4): 362–72. doi.org/10.14710/tataloka.20.4.362-372
Elyda, Corry. 2015. 'Tenants, owners take high risks in apartment disputes'. *Jakarta Post*, 18 November. www.thejakartapost.com/news/2015/11/18/tenants-owners-take-high-risks-apartment-disputes.html
Farisa, Fitria Chusna. 2022. 'Kilas balik kasus korupsi dan suap Ratu Atut Chosiyah hingga bebas dari penjara [Looking back on the corruption and bribery case of Ratu Atut Chosiyah until her release from jail]'. *Kompas.com*, 7 September. https://nasional.kompas.com/read/2022/09/07/13522061/kilas-balik-kasus-korupsi-dan-suap-ratu-atut-chosiyah-hingga-bebas-dari?page=all#google_vignette
Ferdiansyah, Bernardy. 2020. 'KPK: Banyak pengembang belum serahkan fasos-fasum di Tangerang Raya [KPK: Many developers have not delivered social and public facilities in Greater Tangerang]'. *Antara*, 17 September. www.antaranews.com/berita/1732042/kpk-banyak-pengembang-belum-serahkan-fasos-fasum-di-tangerang-raya
Firzandy, Hendrico. 2018. 'BSD city: Menuju world class city [BSD city: Becoming a world class city]'. *Ultimart: Jurnal Komunikasi Visual* 10(1): 67–79. doi.org/10.31937/ultimart.v10i1.765
Hidayat, Syarif. 2007. '"Shadow state"? Business and politics in the province of Banten'. In *Renegotiating Boundaries: Local Politics in Post-Suharto Indonesia*, edited by Henk Schulte Nordholt and Gerry van Klinken, 203–24. Brill. www.jstor.org/stable/10.1163/j.ctt1w76x39.14
Iqbal, Muhammad. 2018. 'Mencengangkan! Ini trah Ratu Atut di birokrasi: Anak, adik, mantu [Astonishing! This is the Ratu Atut lineage in the bureaucracy: Children, siblings, in-laws]'. *Detikcom*, 18 July. https://news.detik.com/berita/d-4120938/mencengangkan-ini-trah-ratu-atut-di-birokrasi-anak-adik-mantu

Iqbal, Muhammad. 2023. 'BSD serahkan instalasi pengelolaan air ke perumdam TKR Tangerang [BSD transfers water processing installation to regional public water company TKR Tangerang]'. *IDN Times*, 20 June. https://banten.idntimes.com/news/banten/muhammad-iqbal-15/bsd-serahkan-instalasi-pengelolaan-air-ke-perumdam-tkr-tangerang

Kuncaraning, Ririn, Mayang Sari and Syari'ati Rizqi Nafi. 2022. 'Housing and settlement statistics 2022'. Badan Pusat Statistik.

Kusno, Abidin. 2012. *Politik Ekonomi Perumahan Rakyat dan Utopia Jakarta* [Political economy of public housing and Jakarta's utopia]. Ombak Publishers.

Laksono, Muhdany Yusuf and Hilda B. Alexander. 2021. 'Berapa harga apartemen di Jakarta saat ini? Berikut rinciannya [How much do apartments cost in Jakarta? Here's the breakdown]'. *Kompas.com*, 22 December. www.kompas.com/properti/read/2021/12/22/153000721/berapa-harga-apartemen-di-jakarta-saat-ini-berikut-rinciannya?page=all

Lantara, Feru. 2023. 'Pemkot Depok targetkan pendapatan daerah tahun 2023 sebesar Rp 1,297 triliun [Depok city government targets regional revenue of Rp 1.297 trillion in 2023]'. *Antara News*, 25 January. https://megapolitan.antaranews.com/berita/228498/pemkot-depok-targetkan-pendapatan-daerah-tahun-2023-sebesar-rp1297-triliun

Leaf, Michael. 2015. 'Exporting Indonesian urbanism: Ciputra and the developmental vision of market modernism'. *South East Asia Research* 23(2): 169–86. doi.org/10.5367/sear.2015.0260

Leisch, Harald. 2002. 'Gated communities in Indonesia'. *Cities* 19(5): 341–50. doi.org/10.1016/S0264-2751(02)00042-2

Lo, Benny. 2010. *Properti Moderat (Modal Dengkul dan Urat)* [Moderate property (it takes sweat and networks)]. CV Andi Offset.

Masaaki, Okamoto and Abdul Hamid. 2008. 'Jawara in power, 1999–2007'. *Indonesia* 86: 109–38. www.jstor.org/stable/40376462

Ni'am, Syakirun and Icha Rostika. 2022. 'Sang "Pangeran Banten", Tubagus Chaeri Wardana bebas bersyarat [Tubagus Chaeri Wardana, the 'Prince of Banten', on conditional release]'. *Kompas.com*, 7 September. https://nasional.kompas.com/read/2022/09/07/14014071/sang-pangeran-banten-tubagus-chaeri-wardana-bebas-bersyarat?page=all

Ningsih, Dwi Saputri. 2023. 'Keadaan ketenagakerjaan provinsi DKI Jakarta [Employment situation in Jakarta province]'. Berita Resmi Statistik No. 63/11/31/Th.XXV. 6 November. Badan Pusat Statistik.

Nityakanti, Pulina. 2023. 'BSDE bakal garap proyek air minum di Tangerang, begini prospeknya [BSDE will run a drinking water project in Tangerang, here are the prospects]'. *Kontan.co.id*, 31 August. https://investasi.kontan.co.id/news/bsde-bakal-garap-proyek-air-minum-di-tangerang-begini-prospeknya

Novriyadi. 2024. 'Daftar harga tanah per meter Jakarta dan Bodetabek tahun 2024 [Price of land per square metre in Jakarta and surrounds in 2024]'. *Lamudi.co.id*, 5 January. www.lamudi.co.id/journal/harga-tanah-per-meter-jakarta

Purwanti, Agustina. 2023. 'Peliknya memiliki hunian di kawasan megapolitan Jakarta [The difficulty of owning a residence in the megapolitan region of Jakarta]'. *Kompas*, 7 August. www.kompas.id/baca/riset/2023/08/05/peliknya-memiliki-hunian-di-kawasan-megapolitan-jakarta

Putra, Ilham Pratama. 2023. '10 sekolah dengan nilai UTBK 2022 tertinggi di Tangsel, ada peringkat 1 nasional! [10 schools with highest computer-based test scores in South Tangerang are ranked 1st nationally!]'. *medcom.id*, 27 April. www.medcom.id/pendidikan/news-pendidikan/0k8m48LK-10-sekolah-dengan-nilai-utbk-2022-tertinggi-di-tangsel-ada-peringkat-1-nasional

Rita Rita, Achmad Rusli. 2017. 'Pola perkembangan urban sprawl di sekitar kota baru: Studi kasus BSD Tangerang Selatan [Pattern of development of urban sprawl around a new town: Case study of BSD, South Tangerang]'. Masters thesis. Tarumanagara University, Jakarta. http://repository.untar.ac.id/2953

Roberts, Mark, Frederico Gil Sander and Sailesh Tiwari, eds. 2019. *Time to ACT: Realizing Indonesia's Urban Potential*. World Bank. doi.org/10.1596/978-1-4648-1389-4

Robison, Richard. 1996. 'The middle class and the bourgeoisie in Indonesia'. In *The New Rich in Asia: Mobile Phones, McDonald's and Middle-Class Revolution*, edited by Richard Robison and David S.G. Goodman, 79–101. Routledge.

Sandi, Ferry. 2023. 'Harga tanah DKI susah turun: Tertinggi Rp 150 juta/M di sini [Land prices in Jakarta won't fall: Highest is 150 million rupiah per metre]'. CNBC Indonesia, 20 July. www.cnbcindonesia.com/news/20230720172725-4-455973/harga-tanah-dki-susah-turun-tertinggi-rp-150-juta-m-di-sini

Santoso, Jo. 2020. 'Indonesian housing policy in the era of globalization'. In *Housing and Human Settlements in a World of Change*, edited by Astrid Ley, Ashiq Ur Rahman and Josefine Fokdal, 47–64. Transcript Verlag. https://library.oapen.org/handle/20.500.12657/47124

Setiawan, Zaki Ari. 2019. 'Partisipasi politik di Tangerang Selatan menjadi yang paling rendah [Political participation in South Tangerang is low]'. *WartaKotalive.com*, 9 January. https://wartakota.tribunnews.com/2019/01/09/partisipasi-politik-di-tangerang-selatan-menjadi-yang-paling-rendah

Sukri, Mhd Alfahjri. 2020. 'Dinasti politik di Banten: Familisme, strategi politik dan rendahnya partisipasi politik masyarakat [Political dynasty in Banten: Familialism, political strategy and low public political participation]'. *JISPO: Jurnal Ilmu Sosial dan Ilmu Politik* 10(2): 169–90. https://journal.uinsgd.ac.id/index.php/jispo/article/view/8316

Sutrisna, Tria and Jessi Carina. 2020. 'Meski naik 4 persen, tingkat partisipasi pemilih pilkada Tangsel masih di bawah target [Despite rising 4 per cent, participation rate of voters in South Tangerang mayoral election still below target]'. *Kompas.com*, 16 December. https://megapolitan.kompas.com/read/2020/12/16/16520361/meski-naik-4-persen-tingkat-partisipasi-pemilih-pilkada-tangsel-masih-di

World Bank. 2019. *Aspiring Indonesia: Expanding the Middle Class*. World Bank. www.worldbank.org/en/country/indonesia/publication/aspiring-indonesia-expanding-the-middle-class

8 Housing at an impasse: Living in a state of protracted transit in rental social housing in Jakarta

Clara Siagian

> In the *kampung*, I had a desire to live. But here? I don't know. If we think about this *rusunawa*, really, how long will it last? It's fifteen, maybe twenty years until it has to be demolished. It's hard to build a binding culture [*membangun adat budaya yang melekat*] here because [the *rusunawa*] will be demolished anyway.

This comment was made by Pak Suro, a resident of a rental social housing (*rumah susun sederhana sewa, rusunawa*) unit in Jakarta. The government evicted him, his wife, two small children and an ailing parent from their *kampung* (low-income self-built urban neighbourhood) in 2016. After a few months of living in a makeshift tent among the rubble of his and his neighbours' homes, he reluctantly agreed to relocate to a unit in a *rusunawa* some 20 kilometres away. Witnessing his parent's deteriorating health and his daughter's frequent bouts of pneumonia caused by living amid the dust and debris near the ruins of their former home had become too much. Yet, instead of rebuilding a new life in the *rusunawa*, Pak Suro felt deprived. He felt he had become poorer, but what he lamented most was the precarity of his new life. For Pak Suro, as for many other residents after their *kampung* is demolished, a *rusunawa* is not, and cannot be, a home.

Rusunawa emerged into the public debate amid the intense period of *kampung* evictions that occurred in Jakarta during 2013–2017 under the combined leadership of Joko Widodo (governor of Jakarta in 2012–2014, president of Indonesia 2014–2024) and his deputy, Basuki Tjahaja Purnama or Ahok, who himself later became governor in 2014–2017, with Djarot

Saiful Hidayat as his deputy.[1] In total, Jakarta's Legal Aid Institute (Lembaga Bantuan Hukum, LBH) documented around 495 cases of *kampung* evictions, displacing 15,319 households, from 2015 to 2018 (LBH Jakarta 2016a, 2017, 2018a, 2018b).[2] While this chapter focuses on *rusunawa* as a housing alternative provided to evicted residents, it should be noted that government policy intends *rusunawa* primarily to benefit lower-income urban households more generally.

The removal of *kampung* did not unfold without resistance. *Kampung* residents in some locations physically confronted security personnel enforcing the evictions (LBH Jakarta 2016a); other residents, with the assistance of non-government organisations (NGOs), challenged the provincial government in court (Putri 2020). Some *kampung* dwellers also formed an alliance with the Urban Poor People's Network (Jaringan Rakyat Miskin Kota, JRMK), an advocacy group representing the interests of Jakarta's urban poor. This group managed to sign a political contract with Anies Baswedan, the ultimately victorious candidate in the 2016–2017 gubernatorial elections; this contract included a clause prohibiting further evictions of *kampung* members affiliated with the group (Savirani and Aspinall 2017; Savirani and Guntoro 2020). Throughout the period of intense evictions, there was heated debate and public criticism of the policy. NGOs such as LBH Jakarta, Rujak and Islam Bergerak criticised the evictions as an attack on the urban poor and their rights to housing (Firdaus 2015; Kampung Kota Merekam 2019; Savirani and Guntoro 2020).

This is where rental social housing (*rusunawa*) came into the picture. The government presented relocation to *rusunawa* as its response to these critiques, framing relocation—and thus *kampung* evictions—as a fulfilment of residents' rights to housing and as an improvement in their lives. Government leaders evoked widespread stereotypes about *kampung* as comprising derelict, unruly and semi-permanent houses along rubbish-choked rivers and contrasted this picture with *rusunawa* as clean and sleek, with finely delineated shapes and uniformity of design. Ahok, for instance, frequently defended evictions to the media, on one occasion saying, 'in fact, we are protecting the poor. We are relocating them to better places

---

1 Because Ahok was prosecuted for blasphemy for something he said during his re-election campaign, Djarot Saiful Hidayat assumed the governor seat on 15 June 2017. According to an LBH Jakarta report, in his 159 days in the role, Djarot conducted at least fourteen *kampung* evictions (LBH Jakarta 2018a).
2 This figure from LBH Jakarta includes *kampung* evictions conducted during the initial period of the Anies Baswedan – Sandiaga Uno administration (16 October 2017 – 30 September 2018). From 1 January 2018 to 30 September 2018, Anies–Sandiaga evicted 277 households (LBH Jakarta 2018b).

with better living conditions. We provide them with newly built and fully furnished *rusunawa* [low-cost apartments]. And you're telling me this is inhumane?' (Wardhani 2014). It is important to note that although there is no complete data, LBH Jakarta observed that not all evicted households could be resettled in *rusunawa* as there were insufficient units to house them all (LBH Jakarta 2016b). Nevertheless, promoting *rusunawa* was a way to ameliorate unease among middle-class residents about the harshness of *kampung* evictions and to cement public support for the policy.

Based on ethnographic fieldwork among relocated residents I conducted in three *rusunawa* in Jakarta from 2019 to 2021, I argue in this chapter that, rather than having their lives improved, residents of this social housing model have become ensnared in a life characterised by precarity and impermanence. As a form of temporary housing, *rusunawa* fail to serve as a launching pad for residents to move out and on to more secure forms of housing as envisioned by the government, despite the considerable burden they impose on Jakarta provincial expenditure. While eviction strips *kampung* residents of their major assets and livelihood base, living in *rusunawa* puts them in a downward spiral of debt they find impossible to escape. Furthermore, their prolonged impermanence engenders a feeling of anxiety that undermines their ability and desire to make *rusunawa* a home. As a result, both the residents and the government are locked in a stalemate, without a clear pathway to move onward.

This chapter is structured as follows. I start by describing contemporary housing problems in Indonesia and Jakarta to situate the presence of *kampung* as self-built informal settlements. I then provide a brief overview of how the problematisation of *kampung* leads to eviction. Next, I describe *rusunawa* as a policy and as a form of housing, before elaborating on the ongoing impasse in *rusunawa* and how both residents and government perceive this situation. Following this discussion, I explore the dynamic of affect engendered by this impasse among the residents—a state I describe as 'residential anxiety'—and the ensuing consequences of this anxiety in their everyday lives. I conclude by considering the broader meaning of the *rusunawa* policy.

Indonesian housing issues at a glance

Housing is a longstanding problem in Indonesia, especially in cities like Jakarta. Recent figures in 2023 show that around 12.7 million households do not own a house, of which 7 million neither own, rent or lease a house (MPWH and World Bank 2023: 3). However, this figure excludes around 29.6 million households living in housing deemed inadequate (ibid.: 4). On top of these numbers, each year Indonesia is expected to require between 780,000 (World Bank 2020: 230) and 1.13 million houses until 2045 (MPWH and World Bank 2023: 3). The dire need for housing is especially pertinent and prevalent in cities, since 70 per cent of Indonesians are predicted to live in urban areas by 2045 (World Bank 2020).

Yet, 2018 figures show that housing constitutes only 2.2 per cent of government expenditure, and public expenditure on housing is only around 0.4 per cent of total gross domestic product (GDP) (World Bank 2020: 234). Most of this expenditure goes on several housing subsidy schemes. However, land scarcity and high land prices in cities mean that the government tends to build subsidised housing outside cities, and especially away from city centres. Despite the strong and persistent trend of urbanisation, it is estimated that 57 per cent of government-subsidised housing is in rural areas (Roberts et al. 2019: 255). In Surabaya and Bandung, meanwhile, around 99 per cent and 98 per cent of subsidised houses respectively are located more than 10 kilometres from the city centres (ibid.). Overall, the World Bank (2020) has argued that the government's housing subsidy schemes do not seem to meet the needs of the poorest and rather benefit banks and developers. A 2020 report by the organisation shows there is a huge vertical inequality in access to housing subsidies and amounts of subsidy given, with beneficiaries from higher-income brackets tending to get two to four times the amount of subsidy given to beneficiaries from lower brackets (ibid.: 241–42). Meanwhile, in general, only Indonesians in the highest 20 per cent income bracket can afford houses from the commercial market (ibid.: 231). While the rental market does meet some housing needs, it is virtually unregulated and unsupported, and tenants are largely unprotected.

The housing situation in Jakarta illustrates the severity of the problem. Not only is there scarcely any new land available in Jakarta for housing construction, but among remaining plots, 60 per cent are owned by several large-scale developers, with the capacity to convert this land into approximately 980,000 houses (Roberts et al. 2019: 254). These developments are unlikely to meet the housing needs of poorer Jakartans. In terms of poverty, officially in 2022 only 477,000 of Jakarta's population of 10 million, or around 4.4 per cent, were classified as poor (Theodora 2023). However, this number should be considered with a grain of salt as the poverty line in Indonesia is primarily set based on calorie needs. In Jakarta this translates to roughly US$53 per person per month in 2023. Set too low, the poverty line does not reflect the real cost of basic needs or the multidimensional nature of poverty (Artha and Dartanto 2018; Cook and Pincus 2014; Firdausy and Budisetyowati 2022; Theodora 2023). Furthermore, it also misses a significant portion of the population who are considered as 'vulnerable', meaning they can slide into poverty from any kind of economic shock (Adji et al. 2020; Sumner et al. 2014).

Nevertheless, housing affordability is not only a challenge for the poorest. The current housing stock and prices also do not match the needs and financial capacity of the non-poor, especially the vulnerable (i.e. those who are slightly above the poverty line) and the lower-middle class. A study by the newspaper *Kompas* in 2021 found that the average price of a landed house of 36 square metres in Jakarta was more than half a billion rupiah. Average households on Jakarta's minimum wage of around Rp 4.9 million (US$310) per month could only reasonably buy a house at a cost of around Rp 160–200 million, which means a small house 30–50 km away from the city centre (Rosalina et al. 2021).

Self-built houses in informal settlements (or *kampung*) have continued to be the major, or even the only, housing option for most Indonesians, particularly, but not limited to, the poor and the vulnerable (Rukmana 2018; Sutanudjaja et al. 2018). While they are much more affordable, houses in *kampung* often lack proper land certificates from the National Land Agency (Badan Pertanahan Nasional, BPN), which are the ultimate form of secure tenure in Indonesia. *Kampung* residents typically possess other legal deeds, such as affidavits from *kelurahan* (urban village administrative unit) offices or receipts for regular payments of land and property tax (Zhu and Simarmata 2015), but these documents provide inadequate protection when facing eviction or a legal dispute over ownership. Furthermore, many *kampung* houses are poorly built, and many *kampung* are increasingly prone to hazards, especially flooding induced by climate change, and lack proper water, sanitation and other connections to city-wide public infrastructure (Padawangi 2019; on urban flooding, see Permana, this volume).

The *kampung* question and evictions

The presence of informal settlements, or *kampung*, in cities of Indonesia, especially Jakarta, has raised complex political questions dating back to late colonial times, when in the 1920s several prominent Dutch bureaucrats, architects and philanthropists raised issues of hygiene, disease and disorder that were said to plague *kampung* (Colombijn 2013: 181–87; Versnel and Colombijn 2015). Then, as now, most *kampung* residents worked in the informal economy. As such, outsiders have long associated *kampung* with poverty and often considered them to be slums (Irawaty 2018). In the eyes of contemporary state officials, such associations render *kampung* an anachronism in their quest to transform Indonesian cities, especially Jakarta as the nation's 'exemplary centre', into modern world-class cities (Kusno 2000: 62).

Governments have used different tools to pursue their vision of urban renewal and deal with the 'problem' of *kampung*. They have tried to 'upgrade' *kampung*, most notably through the renowned Kampung Improvement Program (KIP) in the 1970s and 1980s (Das 2015; Silver 2008). The idea of *kampung* upgrading persists, and governments have expanded it to other cities in Indonesia, under various programs such as the ongoing Kota Tanpa Kumuh (Kotaku, or City without Slums) program that is partly funded by the World Bank.

But in Jakarta, *kampung* upgrading is no longer the dominant approach in the government's toolbox. Instead, the government in Jakarta has increasingly turned to removing certain targeted *kampung*, demolishing structures and evicting residents. The rationale behind such *kampung* eviction varies, and can include land disputes, beautification programs and making space for infrastructure development like toll roads or ports. Governments usually buttress these justifications with legal arguments suggesting that the targeted *kampung* dwellers are occupying their land illegally (even when they have lived there for generations) as they rarely own formal BPN-issued certificates.

In 2013, Joko Widodo (Jokowi), the then governor of Jakarta, oversaw the eviction of around 1,500 households living in *kampung* next to two water reservoirs, despite a campaign promise that he would not evict people from *kampung* (Muhammadi 2013).[3] After Jokowi became president, his former deputy and replacement as governor, Ahok, oversaw a number of *kampung* evictions, including some that prompted strong resistance by *kampung* dwellers (e.g. in Kampung Pulo, Bukit Duri, Kali Jodo and Kampung Akuarium). The topic of *kampung* evictions entered public debate and became a major issue during the gubernatorial election in 2017 during which Ahok and his deputy, Djarot, lost to Anies Baswedan and Sandiaga Uno. According to my calculation drawing on various sources, at least 18,000 households were evicted from 2013 to 2018 (LBH Jakarta 2016a, 2017, 2018a; Megantara 2014; Muhammadi 2013).[4]

While the grounds for eviction varied from one *kampung* to another, several occurred as part of the government's efforts to minimise and mitigate flooding. Jokowi, for instance, explained that removing *kampung* settlements was crucial to restoring the function of water reservoirs as part of Jakarta's flood prevention infrastructure. Several settlements were

---

3 The campaign slogan was *'digeser bukan digusur'* ('moved but not removed').
4 In 2013 Jokowi also oversaw several other evictions including in Kampung Pedongkelan, near Ria-Rio Water Reservoir, but I cannot find any estimate on the numbers of households removed at that time.

also demolished as part of the Ciliwung River normalisation program and the coastal embankment component of the National Capital Integrated Coastal Development program, both joint projects of the provincial and national governments (Pane et al. 2023).

The narrative that *kampung*, especially ones by riverbanks, are causing flooding and contaminating river water garnered public, especially middle-class, support for demolition. As in the past, the Jakarta government was able to say that because the targeted *kampung* dwellers lacked BPN certificates, they were occupying their lands illegally. It also said the *kampung* dwellers were violating zoning regulations by building along riverbanks. Effectively, the government thus buttressed its policy of demolitions with public order and law enforcement justifications (LBH Jakarta 2016b). Although *kampung* is actually an elusive term that captures a highly diverse and heterogeneous range of Indonesian urban neighbourhoods (Newberry 2006; Simone and Fauzan 2013), many Jakartans bought into the government's portrayal of *kampung* as squalid, run down, dirty, unruly and poor settlements of semi-permanent houses by riverbanks. In contrast to this image, the government promotes *rusunawa*, with their uniformity, orderliness, and sleek and modern designs, as not only a solution to the flooding problem, but also as an upgraded form of settlement for evicted residents.

Rusunawa

Rental social housing or *rusunawa* are typically owned and managed by government at either the national or subnational (provincial or district) level.[5] While this chapter focuses on Jakarta (Figure 8.1), *rusunawa* also exist in other cities, such as Batam, Surabaya, Bandung, Medan, Makassar and Mataram. While most are intended for low-income households, they are also built to house students, low-level civil servants and workers. In Jakarta, *rusunawa* usually take the form of mid- to high-rise apartment complexes (five to sixteen floors) that house residents from low socioeconomic backgrounds. These apartment blocks are typically equipped with cleaning services and around-the-clock security, engineers and electricians. Rents in *rusunawa* are subsidised, and in 2023 ranged from Rp 341,000 (US$22) to Rp 1,500,000 (US$96) per month, depending on the size of the apartment, location, amenities and age of the building. Most residents qualify for a place by earning below a certain income

---

5   A few *rusunawa* are either owned and/or managed by private organisations, such as Rusunawa Buddha Tsu-Chi (managed by Buddha Tsu-Chi Foundation) in north and west Jakarta.

Chapter 8 Living in a state of protracted transit in rental social housing in Jakarta   181

Figure 8.1   Distribution of *rusunawa* (social housing) in Jakarta

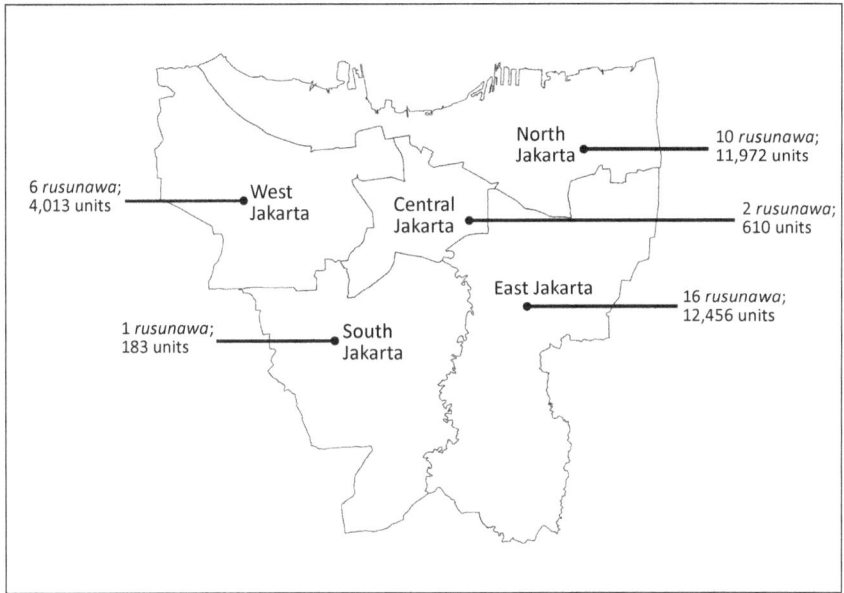

Source: Author's calculation based on information on the official website of the Jakarta Department of Public Housing and Settlement Areas (DPRKP), accessed 10 September 2023.

threshold.[6] In addition, *rusunawa* host households who have been evicted from *kampung*. This group of evictee residents are officially called *warga terprogram* (programmed tenants). I focus on the latter group.

As programmed tenants, *kampung* evictees are provided with additional rent subsidies, on top of those provided to regular low-income residents, making their rents vary between Rp 156,000 and Rp 300,000 per month (2023 rates, around US$10–19), excluding utilities. The units they occupy are fairly small, usually not more than 30 square metres of floor space. As a result, evictee families of five to eight persons often have to squeeze in a dwelling unit consisting of two small bedrooms, with no

---

6 In 2023, to apply for residence, applicants had to prove that their monthly household income was below a certain threshold, either below Rp 4,500,000 (US$287) or Rp 7,500,000 (US$480) for more recent units in *rusunawa* towers with modern amenities such as elevators. According to information provided on the official website of DPRKP (Dinas Perumahan Rakyat dan Kawasan Pemukiman, Jakarta's Department of Public Housing and Settlement Areas), in 2023 there were 8 *rusunawa* management units that oversaw 41 *rusunawa* complexes with a total of 19,135 dwelling units (DPRKP 2023). The oldest complex, Rusunawa Flamboyan, was built in 1991. The majority of the current complexes were built in the 2001–2007 and 2013–2023 periods.

possibility of alteration, subdivision or expansion (Nizomi et al. 2022; Siagian et al. 2023).

Upon relocating to a *rusunawa*, evicted residents sign a lease agreement that stipulates a contract of two years. According to Gubernatorial Decree 111/2014 on Rusunawa, which was issued during Ahok's tenure, this agreement can be renewed, and the decree does not stipulate a limit on how many times the contract can be renewed. The decree also stipulates that failure to pay rent for three months will result in an official warning (*surat peringatan*). After two official warnings, the government reserves the right to void the contract, expel the occupants and vacate the unit. Furthermore, if any member of the household is implicated in a particular crime, especially one involving drug use, then the whole household must move out of the *rusunawa*.

The provincial government envisions *rusunawa* to serve as a kind of incubator where evicted residents are provided with support and assistance to improve their economic status and 'graduate' from *rusunawa*, ready to progress to the next step in their housing career (DPRKP 2022). As indicated in Table 8.1, the Jakarta government views low-income Jakarta residents as part of a structured housing system in which all can eventually transition to the private market. Relevant government officials and *rusunawa* managers see their tasks as not only maintaining and overseeing the daily operation of the *rusunawa*, but also providing pastoral care for the evicted residents by disciplining, educating and dispensing advice to them. Aside from the subsidised rent, these programmed residents also have access to in-kind assistance such as *pangan murah* (cheap foodstuffs), dispensed at fortnightly subsidised food markets, on top of standard social assistance programs from national and local governments.[7] During the COVID-19 pandemic, the provincial government waived the rent for all *rusunawa* tenants.

Partnering with philanthropists, community service organisations and private companies through corporate social responsibility schemes, the government also organises entrepreneurial and vocational skills training sessions, known by the Indonesian term *pemberdayaan* (empowerment), on topics such as air-conditioning repair, cooking, handicrafts and batik manufacture. The idea is that residents will be able to use these skills to start profitable small businesses and save up money to apply for other housing schemes once they 'graduate' from their status as programmed residents.

---

7 The subsidised food market is not only for programmed tenants but also for all households holding Kartu Jakarta Pintar (Smart Jakarta Card)—a social assistance program to support families with school-aged children.

Table 8.1 Housing career scheme as envisioned by the Jakarta Department of Public Housing and Settlement Areas

Monthly income	Housing type	Housing suppliers
Less than or equal to the provincial minimum wage (Rp 4.9 million; US$310)	*Rusunawa* (rented social housing)	Provincial budget (APBD): 13,798 units National budget (APBN): 2,444 units Developers' obligation: 2,664 units
Less than or equal to Rp 14.8 million (US$952)	*Rusunami* (owner-occupier flat)	Provincial state-owned enterprise (BUMD): 6,971 units (e.g. Sarana Jaya, JakPro, Pasar Jaya) National state-owned enterprise (BUMN): 3,489 units
More than Rp 14.8 million (US$952)	Market	Private developers

Note: APBD = *anggaran pendapatan dan belanja daerah* (local or subnational government budget); APBN = *anggaran pendapatan dan belanja negara* (Indonesian central government budget); BUMD = *badan usaha milik daerah* (region-owned enterprise); BUMN = *badan usaha milik negara* (state-owned enterprise).

Source: Author's translation from the Jakarta Department of Public Housing and Settlement Areas (DPRKP 2022: 36).

Other Global South countries, such as Turkey (Civelek 2017) and South Africa (Scheba and Turok 2023), offer similar schemes, in which social housing is depicted as a temporary residence for poor citizens during which they are empowered and then helped to move to more permanent forms of housing. The idea that residents will be able to graduate from *rusunawa* also echoes the 'graduation model' used in social assistance programs, especially cash transfer schemes, in Indonesia and elsewhere. According to the model, after beneficiaries receive cash benefits and other support, enabling them to improve their livelihoods, learn financial management skills, invest and accumulate assets, they will be able to pursue decent lives without government support: they 'graduate' from the program. This model has been criticised for various reasons, including for assuming that most people follow a linear trajectory out of poverty and for underestimating the role of social structures and macroeconomic factors in pushing people back into poverty (Sabates-Wheeler and Devereux 2013). In Indonesia, an evaluation survey conducted by the World Bank estimates that only 26.7 per cent of 'graduated' recipients of PKH (Program Keluarga Harapan, the Family Hope Program, a major conditional cash transfer program) had improved their socioeconomic status (Syamsulhakim and Khadijah 2021: 14), echoing the suggestion that the graduation model is often unrealistic (Sabates-Wheeler et al. 2018).

What does the impasse consist of?

Many *rusunawa* residents who were removed from their *kampung* during 2013–2017 have experienced *rusunawa* life, and the associated interventions, for six to ten years. But there is little sign that the program has improved the life of evicted residents, let alone helped them to 'graduate' from *rusunawa*. Instead, *rusunawa* are burdened with mounting arrears that, by June 2020, had reached Rp 71.2 billion (US$4.58 million) (Yuliani 2020). The government estimated that more than 60 per cent of these arrears came from programmed tenants (Velarosdela and Patnistik 2020). Even before the COVID-19 pandemic, Jakarta's Bureau of Statistics reported total arrears of Rp 32 billion (US$2.1 million) in 2017 (BPS 2017). In several interviews with me, both provincial government officials and officials from *rusunawa* management units shared their frustration with a situation in which, as one manager put it, 'we give so much subsidy, but we receive peanuts from the rent'.

Analysts have found that residents experienced significant economic impoverishment not only immediately after eviction but also years after being resettled in *rusunawa* (Adianto et al. 2023; Savirani and Wilson 2018; Sholihah and Shaojun 2018; Tilley et al. 2019). In my fieldwork, many residents experienced eviction as a form of material dispossession: they lost their lands and houses, the major and perhaps the only significant assets they had owned in their lifetimes. For others, their *kampung* houses were not only dwelling places, they were also primary sources of income, either from rooms they rented out or from kiosks or cottage industries they operated from home. Most residents also depended on the *kampung* as a dense network of people who provided patrons and sources of information for income opportunities (Guinness 1999; Jellinek 1991; Peters 2010). The fact that many *kampung* were located in proximity to economic hubs such as markets, terminals or ports further increased their economic vibrancy.

Such conditions cannot be emulated in *rusunawa*. The remote locations of *rusunawa* isolate the residents from potential economic opportunities (Savirani and Wilson 2018). Residents who try to start any commercial endeavour within a *rusunawa* compound have to rely on the already economically deprived residents whose purchasing power has been greatly diminished by their own eviction and relocation. Furthermore, the units are generally too small to rent out spare rooms or set up businesses, and the management prohibits residents from turning their units into commercial spaces anyway.

Provincial government officials in charge of *rusunawa*, and members of *rusunawa* management teams, are fully aware that evictions and relocation have impoverished residents by removing them from the *kampung* where they derived their livelihoods. Their answer to this impoverishment is the so-called empowerment programs that provide residents with tradeable skills. However, in my observation, these programs are generally conducted in a piecemeal manner with little to no follow-up. The workshops are small, and they focus only on skills provision without further support in terms of start-up capital, supervision, marketing or consistent coaching. Most thus lead nowhere. The few initiatives I have found that survive tend to involve the residents functioning as piece-rate workers who produce commodities such as batik, bags or vegetables for outside buyers without being involved in the design, marketing and distribution of these goods, let alone providing an overall business strategy. Even for these workers, the income they derive is far from enough to lift their family's economic condition to the level where they can graduate from the *rusunawa*. The initiatives also struggle to retain workers, as residents often move on to other occupations whenever they find more promising economic opportunities.

As a result, while managers hope that residents will progress out of *rusunawa* into the subsidised housing market, there are currently few realistic prospects for most of them doing so. Currently, residents can make this transition via the Rumah DP Nol Persen (Zero Down Payment) scheme, which is accessible to Jakartans with a maximum monthly income of Rp 7 million (US$450). While the residents are aware of this scheme, they understand there is little likelihood that precarious and low-income informal workers like them will be trusted with a 20- to 30-year mortgage, especially when that involves competing with citizens with formal employment and higher incomes. Their greatest fear, however, is that they will be unable to pay the monthly mortgage, which ranges from Rp 2.1 to 2.6 million (US$135–167). With this pathway thus blocked for most, they remain in the *rusunawa*.

Despite such challenges, and despite the impossibility of the workshops they offer truly helping residents to generate new income, *rusunawa* managers tend to put the weight of responsibility for failure on residents. Managers say that residents' 'mindset' is still entrenched in a '*kampung* mentality' characterised by a lack of grit, perseverance and industriousness. The following comments are typical:

> It's typical of programmed tenants. They are all lazy. Just stroll around in a slum *kampung*, you can see how lazy they are, they are just sitting around with no intention to improve. (Interview with head of management of a *rusunawa* complex, 13 October 2021)

> They actually enjoy living in a *rusunawa* with all the facilities. They don't want to exit although they can if they want to. They are spoiled, like

children who are spoon-fed. (Interview with provincial government official, 24 February 2021)

Such officials, also thinking of the high cost of running and maintaining *rusunawa*, end up viewing the programmed residents as no longer deserving government largesse—even within just a few years of being evicted from their *kampung* homes. Instead, officials think of these residents as hogging resources that other more deserving and disciplined Jakartans should be accessing. At the same time, even in the face of mounting arrears (which on paper justifies removing such residents), the management cannot evict these residents for political reasons. The provincial-level officials and the management predict that such a move would be extremely unpopular and could eventually lead to uproar among the residents as well as political backlash from Jakarta's urban poor in general, especially if made without a strong legal basis. The government, nevertheless, is preparing to remove residents with outstanding arrears by drafting an amendment to the Gubernatorial Decree on Rusunawa to specify tenancy limits of a total of six years for regular tenants and ten years for programmed tenants (interview with provincial-level official, 24 February 2021).

Rent as a loss of control over one's home

While eviction and relocation have resulted in livelihood and income precarity among residents of *rusunawa*, these factors are not the only explanation for the mounting arrears experienced by *rusunawa*. During my fieldwork, I also detected a generalised sense of indignation among some of the residents. Many remained angry that the state had dispossessed them of their houses and land without providing proper monetary compensation. Some residents liked to underscore that, during his governorship, Jokowi had visited their *kampung* where he listened to their aspiration for fair compensation and promised to seek a solution that both government and residents could agree on (Pemprov DKI Jakarta 2012). As Pak Lingga, a former resident of Kampung Pulo, recalls:

> It was when Jokowi was still the governor. He said the government would pay. It's in the laws. Not only our houses and lands, any form of physical structure on a land that we owned would be compensated. We heard it ourselves when they gathered us at the *kelurahan* [urban village administrative unit] office, [from the] subdistrict, and even [from] Jokowi himself when he visited our *kampung*. Now, we are tricked and trapped, aren't we? The government too. It's as if we are telling the government, 'why the heck did you move us to *rusun* [apartments]?! I've told you I can't

pay rent and you insist that I pay. You didn't pay for my [demolished] house, so of course I'm not going to pay for your house!'[8]

Both the residents and the management understand that such resentment motivates some residents to refuse to pay their rent even when the rental price is low compared to that in *kampung*. For the management, the notion of heartache or *sakit hati* also explains the residents' lack of commitment to maintaining amenities and keeping the *rusunawa* clean. It is, however, important to note that not all residents express a similar level of indignation. There are residents who agree that eviction is a state prerogative and who accept the government's claim that they had occupied their lands illegally. Others accept such arguments but also maintain they have rights to at least some compensation for their demolished homes.

The struggle with rent signifies another transformation in the residents' lives after relocation: loss of control over something very personal—their home. The feeling of loss is especially pronounced among older men whose masculinity is attached to their ability to provide shelter and to bequeath a house as a tangible inheritance to their children (Siagian et al. 2023).

This loss of control itself points to the acute reality that *rusunawa* are only a temporary form of housing. The residents in my study frequently used the phrase *menumpang di rumah pemerintah* ('lodging [temporarily] in the government's house') to express the temporariness of their lives in *rusunawa*. The term 'lodging' (*menumpang*) positions residents as guests in someone else's house and as people who will eventually have to move out, something that, as I mentioned before, the government is also keen to emphasise. Existing regulations provide legal background for this temporariness, stipulating that if and when the government decides to change the purpose of the land of a *rusunawa*, residents will have to vacate their units without compensation.

Permanent impermanence and residential anxiety

The temporariness of housing in *rusunawa* is reminiscent of the experience of refugees, either internally displaced persons (IDPs) or international asylum seekers. While the magnitude of suffering and the extent of dislocation relocated *rusunawa* residents experience may pale in comparison to that experienced by refugees, both groups are forcefully

---

8 Pak Lingga is likely referring to Jokowi's visits to Kampung Pulo, a few months after he was elected as Jakarta's governor. On the official YouTube account of the Provincial Government of Jakarta, there were two videos recording Jokowi's visits and conversations with residents of Kampung Pulo on 23 October 2012 and on 7 December 2012.

uprooted from their homes and required to live in a new transitory location. Most people in both groups do not know how long they will live in this temporary space, while maintaining hope they will move on to their next, more permanent home. Yet very often, both refugees and *rusunawa* residents end up living in what is supposed to be a temporary space for long periods, even indefinitely. What is supposed to be a transitory phase of a couple of years becomes a life of protracted displacement.

The protracted displacement of refugees and IDPs is often understood as an experience of being 'betwixt and between', of being caught in a liminality between a past and future home (Brun and Fábos 2015). Ghassan Hage (2009: 98) further conceptualises this feeling as 'stuckedness', which he defines as the 'sense of existential immobility' that arises from the inability to move on to a better space 'that constitutes a suitable launching pad for their social and existential self'. This concept of 'stuckedness' aptly captures the situation of *rusunawa* residents who feel unable to move out or on from *rusunawa* even when wishing to do so. One resident explicitly equates their experience with IDPs in a natural disaster setting:

> I feel like we're like victims of a disaster who live in a refugee place. If victims of a disaster are placed in tents, we are placed in *rusunawa* because this is a disaster that the government created. There's a limit to how long we can live in this transitory place. We keep asking ourselves, 'Are you sure you want to stay here for the rest of your lives, renting?'

There is an understanding among the residents that *rusunawa*, as temporary housing, will lead to yet another displacement. However, this state of temporariness in fact started for most residents long before they moved to the *rusunawa*. Although most of my informants had lived in *kampung* for years, decades or even generations, the status of *kampung* as informal settlements with contestable tenure and as unwanted remnants of backwardness has always rendered *kampung* people insecure and prone to removal by the state. Some residents told me they had experienced decades of recurrent rumours that their *kampung* was about to be bulldozed, with such rumours eventually acquiring something like the status of permanent myth. Yet, as eviction proved, the state ultimately has the power to turn myth into reality (Maqsood and Sajjad 2021). In her study of three *kampung* in Java, including one in Jakarta, Rita Padawangi (2019) demonstrates how this myth then turns into a tool that leads residents to change and improve their *kampung* on their own to fit with the state's vision of modernity, in the hope that this will prevent eviction.

In *rusunawa*, meanwhile, temporariness underpins the logic of the settlement and its governance. Not only do the residents have to renew their lease every two years; their mounting arrears and the legal uncertainty of their status in *rusunawa* create a heightened sense of impermanence.

While advancing a moral claim on the government by keeping alive the idea of *sakit hati*, the residents understand that in essence they have no legal claim over their units and they also have no way of knowing or controlling when their tenure will end. This situation produces a structure of feeling that I call 'residential anxiety' among the residents. Residential anxiety captures the general restlessness in regard to the precarity of their housing status, as Pak Suro expresses it at the beginning of this chapter, or as other residents frequently put it: 'you can be kicked out anytime'.

Should this place become home?

Residential anxiety undercuts any attempt or even desire to build a community in *rusunawa*. 'Why bother', says an informant, 'if we're going to leave this place anyway?'. While people generally socialise with their neighbours, ask each other for favours now and then, and help each other out when needed, they still express doubt over the value of investing time and effort in creating a sense of communal belonging in a *rusunawa*. The feeling that their settlement could end at any time is further reinforced by their mounting arrears, which legally enable the government to expel them, and the lack of legal clarity on the number of times their contract can be renewed. All of these factors create a looming fear among residents which lead them to believe that the management is creating excuses and justification to evict programmed tenants one unit at a time. For instance, the residents point to the frequent drug raids conducted by the National Narcotics Agency (Badan Narkotika Nasional) in *rusunawa* as a ploy to vacate units occupied by evicted households. The residents also insist that their status as a programmed tenant should be able to be passed on to their next of kin, as promised verbally by Ahok when he evicted them.[9] *Rusunawa* managers reject this claim and maintain that when the head of a household who first signed the agreement dies, the left-behind household members will become regular tenants paying regular rent.

Although residents and the government in fact share a desire to see programmed tenants move out of *rusunawa*, the situation at the time of writing resembles a bind that is difficult to disentangle. Though most residents strongly wish to leave, they understand that they cannot exit in the absence of official support to facilitate their leaving. Most lack the financial resources to relocate and will find it impossible to immediately

---

9   While I cannot find a source to confirm such a promise by Ahok, Djarot Saiful Hidayat, in July 2017 when he was acting governor following Ahok's imprisonment, stated that *rusunawa* units could be passed on to members of a nuclear family (i.e. children or parents) (Suranto 2017).

recreate in a new location the social conditions that sustained them during their previous life in the *kampung*. Thus, while residents often joke about escaping *rusunawa*, they recognise the disadvantages and impracticality of this idea. Upon relocation to *rusunawa*, the government changed all the residents' personal ID cards and family cards to reflect their physical address in *rusunawa*. For all administrative purposes (making new IDs or adding new members to family cards), the residents need an endorsement letter not only from their *rukun tetangga* (neighbourhood association) or *rukun warga* (citizens' association) but also from the *rusunawa* management. However, the management will refuse to provide a recommendation to change the address on their IDs if they have not paid off their arrears. Therefore, while they may be able to 'escape' *rusunawa*, they will not be able to change their address in their legal documentation, which will prevent them accessing state welfare benefits.

Meanwhile, their feeling of not being at home and lacking control in their new surroundings, and the precarious nature of their settlement in *rusunawa*, generate a feeling of nostalgia for the *kampung*. Residents imagine their *kampung* as an ideal space where they felt at home. This feeling is especially prevalent among residents who identify as Betawi, Jakarta's local ethnic group. Betawi residents describe their former *kampung* as their *kampung halaman* or home town, where they were born and spent their childhood, where they had their first friendships and romance, and where they started their own families.[10] *Kampung halaman*, as Emily Hertzman (2017: 90) notes in her ethnography among Chinese Indonesians who migrated from Singkawang, is not only a physical space but also 'a social space in which one's understandings of the world are shared with and valued by others. Home comes into being through people's experiences, memories, imaginings, activities, and social relationships'. Unlike in *rusunawa*, where residents are conditioned to live as a nuclear family, in the *kampung* many people lived in intergenerational households or next to their extended families, making *kampung* a more personal place. They thus contrast the lack of communal belonging and identity in *rusunawa* with the social bonds that they had in the *kampung*. When I asked why they wanted to return to the *kampung*, many residents responded: 'it is where my *ari-ari* (umbilical cord) was buried', suggesting that their *kampung* bonds go beyond nostalgia but are also corporeal and spiritual.

---

10 Among non-Betawi residents, the idea of returning to *kampung halaman* is still prominent although they usually refer to their home town in Java, where they were born and where their extended families live, rather than *kampung* in Jakarta from where they were forcibly evicted. Typically, they cultivated this desire even before they were relocated to the *rusunawa*.

Conclusion

It should be stressed that in addition to programmed residents, there are large numbers of other low-income residents for whom *rusunawa* provide an essential and affordable housing service. Given the amount of unmet housing needs and the lack of inexpensive options for the poor and vulnerable, building more *rusunawa* units and improving their condition could become a critically important government policy. However, the precarious job market and lack of affordable housing means the idea that, after living a few years in *rusunawa*, low-income residents will be able to improve their financial conditions and move on to home ownership is still a challenging, if not unattainable, vision.

The extent of the challenge is evident from the experience of the residents who are the focus of this chapter: evicted former residents of *kampung*, who remain unable to move on to the next steps in their housing trajectory despite, at the time of writing, having lived in *rusunawa* for six to eleven years. Instead, *rusunawa* have become a place of prolonged 'stuckedness', and residents are held in a limbo with neither the ability to make *rusunawa* a permanent home nor to know with certainty what will happen to them next. While their arrears keep mounting and the government keeps spending money on maintaining *rusunawa*, the residents are living in a state of impoverishment, indignation and anxiety that elevates their vision of the *kampung* as an ideal home to which they yearn to return.

While there are alternatives to break through this housing impasse, none of them will fix the issue on its own. The pathway forward is likely to involve several measures together, in which a solution for one resident or household will be different to the next. Some families might want to stay in *rusunawa* under existing arrangements, while others might want to receive more financial support to start on the path towards more permanent housing. Other families wish to run their *rusunawa* according to owner-occupier schemes in which residents manage their buildings themselves. While this alternative might take even more commitment and resources from the government, the government of Jakarta is actually experimenting with this scheme in several *kampung* (so-called *kampung susun*) in Kampung Akuarium, Kampung Kunir and Kampung Susun Produktif (Dovey et al. 2019; Pane et al. 2023; Putri 2020). The key, however, is to start formulating these alternatives in close and respectful conversation with the residents and with a commitment to treat housing as a human right.

References

Adianto, Joko, Rossa Turpuk Gabe, Rini Kurniawati and Suciyhuma Armenda. 2023. 'From shelters for numbers to shelters for welfare: Rectifying the social housing provision programme in Jakarta'. *Housing Policy Debate* 33(3): 662–80. doi.org/10.1080/10511482.2021.1981423

Adji, Ardi, Taufik Hidayat, Hendratno Tuhiman, Sandra Kurniawati and Achmad Maulana. 2020. *Measurement of Poverty Line in Indonesia: Theoretical Review and Proposed Improvements*. Working Paper 48-e-2020. National Team for the Acceleration of Poverty Reduction (TNP2K).

Artha, Dwi Rani Puspa and Teguh Dartanto. 2018. 'The multidimensional approach to poverty measurement in Indonesia: Measurements, determinants and its policy implications'. *Journal of Economic Cooperation and Development* 39(3): 1–38.

BPS (Badan Pusat Statistik , Statistics Indonesia). 2017. *Potensi Pengembangan Perekonomian di Rumah Susun DKI Jakarta* [The prospect of economic development in Jakarta *rusunawa*]. Pusat Pelayanan Statistik Dinas Komunikasi, Informatika dan Statistik Pemerintah Provinsi DKI Jakarta.

Brun, Cathrine and Anita Fábos. 2015. 'Making homes in limbo? A conceptual framework'. *Refuge: Canada's Journal on Refugees* 31(1): 5–17. doi.org/10.25071/1920-7336.40138

Civelek, Cansu. 2017. 'Social housing, urban renewal and shifting meanings of "welfare state" in Turkey: A study of the Karapınar Renewal Project, Eskişehir'. In *Social Housing and Urban Renewal,* edited by Paul Watt and Peer Smets, 391–429. Emerald Publishing. doi.org/10.1108/978-1-78714-124-720171011

Colombijn, Freek. 2013. *Under Construction: The Politics of Urban Space and Housing during the Decolonization of Indonesia, 1930–1960*. Brill.

Cook, Sarah and Jonathan Pincus. 2014. 'Poverty, inequality and social protection in Southeast Asia: An introduction'. *Journal of Southeast Asian Economies* 31(1): 1–17. www.jstor.org/stable/43264696

Das, Ashok. 2015. 'Slum upgrading with community-managed microfinance: Towards progressive planning in Indonesia'. *Habitat International* 47: 256–66. doi.org/10.1016/j.habitatint.2015.01.004

Dovey, Kim, Brian Cook and Amanda Achmadi. 2019. 'Contested riverscapes in Jakarta: Flooding, forced eviction and urban image'. *Space and Polity* 23(3): 265–82. doi.org/10.1080/13562576.2019.1667764

DPRKP (Dinas Perumahan Rakyat dan Kawasan Permukiman; Department of Public Housing and Settlement Areas). 2022. *Laporan Kinerja Instansi Pemerintah Tahun 2021* [Government agency performance report 2021]. DPRKP Jakarta.

DPRKP (Dinas Perumahan Rakyat dan Kawasan Permukiman; Department of Public Housing and Settlement Areas). 2023. 'Produk: Informasi Ketersediaan Unit Sewa Rusunawa [Product: Information on *rusunawa* unit availability]'. DPRKP Jakarta. https://dprkp.jakarta.go.id/?cmd=product-rusunawa_unit

Firdaus, Febriana. 2015. 'Pengamat: Penggusuran warga Kampung Pulo bukan solusi atasi banjir Jakarta [Observer: Eviction of Kampung Pulo residents is not a solution to the Jakarta floods]'. *Rappler Indonesia*, 20 August. www.rappler.com/world/indonesia/103210-penggusuran-kampung-pulo-bukan-solusi-banjir-jakarta

Firdausy, Carunia Mulya and Dwi Andayani Budisetyowati. 2022. 'Variables, dimensions, and indicators important to develop the multidimensional poverty line measurement in Indonesia'. *Social Indicators Research* 162(2): 763–802. doi.org/10.1007/s11205-021-02859-5

Guinness, Patrick. 1999. 'Local community and the state'. *Canberra Anthropology* 22(1): 88–110.

Hage, Ghassan. 2009. 'Waiting out the crisis: On stuckedness and governmentality'. In *Waiting*, edited by Ghassan Hage, 97–106. Melbourne University Press.

Hertzman, Emily Zoe. 2017. '*Pulang kampung* (returning home): Circuits of mobility from a Chinese town in Indonesia'. PhD thesis. University of Toronto. https://search.proquest.com/openview/e697069e66483c02da1f60574fa9de3e/1?pq-origsite=gscholar&cbl=18750

Irawaty, Dian Tri. 2018. 'Jakarta's *kampungs*: Their history and contested future'. PhD thesis. University of California, Los Angeles. https://search.proquest.com/opeview/5ce8bea4456b0fa5d15f3720f06ba93c/1?pq-origsite=gscholar&cbl=18750

Jellinek, Lea. 1991. *The Wheel of Fortune: The History of a Poor Community in Jakarta*. Allen & Unwin.

Kampung Kota Merekam. 2019. 'Menyalakan harapan di Kampung Akuarium [Kindling hope in Kampung Akuarium]'. Kampung Kota Merekam, 11 November. https://medium.com/kampung-kota-merekam/menyalakan-harapan-di-kampung-akuarium-68eae6d91669

Kusno, Abidin. 2000. *Behind the Postcolonial: Architecture, Urban Space, and Political Cultures in Indonesia*. Routledge.

LBH (Lembaga Bantuan Hukum; Legal Aid Institute) Jakarta. 2016a. 'Atas nama pembangunan: Laporan penggusuran paksa di wilayah DKI Jakarta tahun 2015 [In the name of development: Report on forced evictions in DKI Jakarta, 2015]'. LBH Jakarta.

LBH (Lembaga Bantuan Hukum; Legal Aid Institute) Jakarta. 2016b. 'Mereka yang terasing: Laporan pemenuhan hak atas perumahan yang layak bagi korban penggusuran paksa Jakarta yang menghuni rumah susun [Abandoned: Report on the rights to adequate housing for Jakarta's victims of forced evictions relocated to social housing]'. LBH Jakarta. www.bantuanhukum.or.id/web/wp-content/uploads/2016/12/Laporan-Penelitian-Rumah-Susun_LBH-Jakarta_2016.pdf

LBH (Lembaga Bantuan Hukum; Legal Aid Institute) Jakarta. 2017. 'Seperti puing: Laporan penggusuran paksa di wilayah DKI Jakarta tahun 2016 [Like debris: Report on forced evictions in DKI Jakarta, 2016]'. LBH Jakarta. www.bantuanhukum.or.id/web/wp-content/uploads/2017/04/Laporan-Penggusuran_LBHJAKARTA_2016.pdf

LBH (Lembaga Bantuan Hukum; Legal Aid Institute) Jakarta. 2018a. 'Mengais di pusaran janji: Laporan penggusuran paksa di wilayah DKI Jakarta tahun 2017 [Scrapping in the graveyard of promises: Report on forced evictions in DKI Jakarta, 2017]'. LBH Jakarta.

LBH (Lembaga Bantuan Hukum; Legal Aid Institute) Jakarta. 2018b. 'Masih ada: Laporan penggusuran paksa di wilayah DKI Jakarta Januari-September 2018 [Still here: Report on forced evictions in DKI Jakarta, January–September 2018]'. LBH Jakarta. www.bantuanhukum.or.id/web/wp-content/uploads/2018/10/laporan-penggusuran-jakarta-2018.pdf

Maqsood, Ammara and Fizzah Sajjad. 2021. 'Victim, broker, activist, fixer: Surviving dispossession in working class Lahore'. *Environment and Planning D: Society and Space* 39(6): 994–1008. doi.org/10.1177/02637758211029290

Megantara, Aditya. 2014. 'Pemkot Jakarta Barat renggut tempat tinggal warga di Kali Apuran, Kedaung Kali Angke [West Jakarta municipality robs Kedaung Kali Angke residents of their houses]'. LBH Jakarta, 23 December. https://bantuanhukum.or.id/pemkot-jakarta-barat-renggut-tempat-tinggal-warga-di-kali-apuran-kedaung-kali-angke

MPWH (Ministry of Public Works and Housing) and World Bank. 2023. *Building Safe, Adequate and Affordable Housing in Indonesia: A Partnership of the Government of Indonesia and the World Bank through the National Affordable Housing Program (NAHP)*. Kementerian Pekerjaan Umum dan Perumahan Rakyat and World Bank.

Muhammadi, Fikri Zaki. 2013. 'Resistance to eviction in Muara Baru from only a few'. *Jakarta Post*, 21 May. www.thejakartapost.com/news/2013/05/21/resistance-eviction-muara-baru-only-a-few.html

Newberry, Jan. 2006. *Back Door Java: State Formation and the Domestic in Working Class Java*. University of Toronto Press.

Nizomi, Fiona Alexandra, Joko Adianto and Rossa Turpuk Gabe. 2021. 'Habitus in habitation: Case study in Jatinegara rental apartment, Jakarta'. *International Journal of Design in Society* 16(1): 59–76. doi.org/10.18848/2325-1328/CGP/v16i01/59-76

Padawangi, Rita. 2019. 'Forced evictions, spatial (un)certainties and the making of exemplary centres in Indonesia'. *Asia Pacific Viewpoint* 60(1): 65–79. doi.org/10.1111/apv.12213

Pane, Annisa, Budhi Gunawan and Susanti Withaningsih. 2023. 'Development of Kampung Susun Akuarium based on sustainable housing principles'. *Sustainability* 15(11): 8673. doi.org/10.3390/su15118673

Pemprov (Pemerintah Provinsi) DKI Jakarta. 2012. '07 Des 2012 Gub Bpk. Jokowi berdialog dengan warga Kampung Pulo, Kampung Melayu, Jatinegara [7 December 2012, Governor Jokowi's dialogue with residents of Kampung Pulo, Kampung Melayu, Jatinegara]'. YouTube, 7 December. www.youtube.com/watch?v=nN-gq9PvznM

Peters, Robbie. 2010. 'The wheels of misfortune: The street and cycles of displacement in Surabaya, Indonesia'. *Journal of Contemporary Asia* 40(4): 568–88. doi.org/10.1080/00472336.2010.507044

Putri, Prathiwi Widyatmi. 2020. 'Insurgent planner: Transgressing the technocratic state of postcolonial Jakarta'. *Urban Studies* 57(9): 1845–65. doi.org/10.1177/0042098019853499

Roberts, Mark, Frederico Gil Sander and Sailesh Tiwari, eds. 2019. *Time to ACT: Realizing Indonesia's Urban Potential*. World Bank. doi.org/10.1596/978-1-4648-1389-4

Rosalina, Puteri, Satrio Wisanggeni, Albertus Krisna and Fransiskus Wisnu. 2021. 'Milenial kian sulit gapai rumah impian' [Millenials are increasingly struggling to achieve a dream home]. *Kompas*, 1 October. www.kompas.id/baca/ekonomi/2021/10/01/milenial-kian-sulit-gapai-rumah-impian

Rukmana, Deden. 2018. 'Upgrading housing settlement for the urban poor in Indonesia: An analysis of the Kampung Deret Program'. In *Metropolitan Governance in Asia and the Pacific Rim: Borders, Challenges, Futures*, edited by Bligh Grant, Cathy Yang Liu and Lin Ye, 75–94. Springer. doi.org/10.1007/978-981-13-0206-0_5

Sabates-Wheeler, Rachel and Stephen Devereux. 2013. 'Sustainable graduation from social protection programmes'. *Development and Change* 44(4): 911–38. doi.org/10.1111/dech.12047

Sabates-Wheeler, Rachel, Ricardo Sabates and Stephen Devereux. 2018. 'Enabling graduation for whom? Identifying and explaining heterogeneity in livelihood trajectories post–cash transfer exposure'. *Journal of International Development* 30(7): 1071–95. doi.org/10.1002/jid.3369

Savirani, Amalinda and Edward Aspinall. 2017. 'Adversarial linkages: The urban poor and electoral politics in Jakarta'. *Journal of Current Southeast Asian Affairs* 36(3): 3–34. doi.org/10.1177/186810341703600301

Savirani, Amalinda and Ian Wilson. 2018. 'Distance matters: Social housing for the poor'. *Inside Indonesia*, 28 April. www.insideindonesia.org/distance-matters-social-housing-for-the-poor

Savirani, Amalinda and Guntoro. 2020. 'Between street demonstrations and ballot box: Tenure rights, elections, and social movements among the urban poor in Jakarta'. *PCD Journal* 8(1): 13–27. doi.org/10.22146/pcd.v8i1.414

Scheba, Andreas and Ivan Turok. 2023. 'The role of institutions in social housing provision: Salutary lessons from the South'. *Housing Studies* 38(6): 1132–53. doi.org/10.1080/02673037.2021.1935765

Sholihah, Puput Ichwatus and Chen Shaojun. 2018. 'Impoverishment of induced displacement and resettlement (DIDR) slum eviction development in Jakarta Indonesia'. *International Journal of Urban Sustainable Development* 10(3): 263–78. doi.org/10.1080/19463138.2018.1534737

Siagian, Clara, Ariane Utomo, Muhammad Insan Kamil and Brian Cook. 2023. 'Unravelled homes: Forced evictions and home remaking in Jakarta'. *International Journal of Urban and Regional Research* 47(3): 386–404. doi.org/10.1111/1468-2427.13170

Silver, Christopher. 2008. *Planning the Megacity: Jakarta in the Twentieth Century*. Routledge.

Simone, AbdouMaliq and Achmad Uzair Fauzan. 2013. 'On the way to being middle class'. *City* 17(3): 279–98. doi.org/10.1080/13604813.2013.795331

Sumner, Andy, Arief Yusuf and Yangki Suara. 2014. *The Prospects of the Poor: A Set of Poverty Measures Based on the Probability of Remaining Poor (or Not) in Indonesia*. Working Paper in Economics and Development Studies No. 201410. Department of Economics, Padjadjaran University. https://EconPapers.repec.org/RePEc:unp:wpaper:201410

Suranto, G. 2017. 'Rusunawa tidak bisa jadi hak milik [*Rusunawa* cannot be privately owned]'. *InfoPublik*, 13 July. https://infopublik.id/kategori/nasional-sosial-budaya/210796/rusunawa-tidak-bisa-jadi-hak-milik

Sutanudjaja, Elisa, Marco Kusumawijaya, M. Zul Qisthi and Inten Gumilang. 2018. *Strategy for a Social City in Indonesia: Case Studies in Malang, Cirebon, and Jakarta*. Friedrich Ebert Stiftung and Rujak Center for Urban Studies. https://library.fes.de/pdf-files/bueros/indonesien/14610-20180827.pdf

Syamsulhakim, Ekki and Nurzanty Khadijah. 2021. *Graduating from a Conditional Cash Transfer Program in Indonesia: Results of a Household Survey of Prosperous-Independent Graduates of the Family Hope Program (PKH) in 2020*. World Bank. doi.org/10.1596/36784

Theodora, Agnes. 2023. 'Sudah tidak relevan, saatnya garis kemiskinan dievaluasi' [No longer relevant, time to evaluate the poverty line]. *Kompas*, 15 May. www.kompas.id/baca/ekonomi/2023/05/15/sudah-tidak-relevan-saatnya-garis-kemiskinan-dievaluasi

Tilley, Lisa, Juanita Elias and Lena Rethel. 2019. 'Urban evictions, public housing and the gendered rationalisation of *kampung* life in Jakarta'. *Asia Pacific Viewpoint* 60(1): 80–93. doi.org/10.1111/apv.12209

Velarosdela, Rindi Nuris and Egidius Patnistik. 2020. 'Tunggakan sewa rusunawa hingga Juni 2020 mencapai Rp 71 miliar [*Rusunawa* rental arrears to June 2020 reach Rp 71 billion]'. *Kompas*, 7 July. https://megapolitan.kompas.com/read/2020/07/07/12594541/tunggakan-sewa-rusunawa-hingga-juni-2020-mencapai-rp-71-miliar

Versnel, Hans and Freek Colombijn. 2015. 'Rückert and Hoesni Thamrin: Bureaucrat and politician in colonial kampong improvement'. In *Cars, Conduits, and Kampongs: The Modernization of the Indonesian City, 1920–1960*, edited by Freek Colombijn and Joost Coté, 121–51. Brill.

Wardhani, Dewanti A. 2014. 'Governor Ahok defends eviction policy'. *Jakarta Post*, 24 December. www.thejakartapost.com/news/2014/12/24/governor-ahok-defends-eviction-policy.html

World Bank. 2020. *Indonesia Public Expenditure Review: Spending for Better Results*. World Bank. www.worldbank.org/en/country/indonesia/publication/indonesia-public-expenditure-review

Yuliani, Putri Anisa. 2020. 'Tunggakan rusunawa capai Rp71 M, pemprov DKI tanggung Rp44,8 M [*Rusunawa* arrears reach Rp 71 billion, Jakarta provincial government pays Rp 44.8 billion]'. *Media Indonesia*, 7 July. https://mediaindonesia.com/megapolitan/326149/tunggakan-rusunawa-capai-rp71-m-pemprov-dki-tanggung-rp448-m

Zhu, Jieming and Hendricus Andy Simarmata. 2015. 'Formal land rights versus informal land rights: Governance for sustainable urbanization in the Jakarta metropolitan region, Indonesia'. *Land Use Policy* 43: 63–73. doi.org/10.1016/j.landusepol.2014.10.016

9 Drainage politics: The political economy of flood management in Indonesian cities[1]

Yogi Setya Permana

Indonesia is one of the most disaster-prone countries globally, being frequently exposed to various geophysical and climate-related hazards (Lin 2015). Increasing sea-surface temperatures contribute to growing risks of hydrometeorological hazards such as storms, tropical cyclones, floods and landslides. In 2022, flooding was the most frequent type of natural disaster in Indonesia, with floods also having increased in intensity over the preceding decade (Annur 2022). While geophysical disasters like earthquakes and volcanoes have caused more deaths than floods in Indonesia, flooding occurs more often, affects more people, and causes more damage (Djalante et. al. 2017). Flooding is a particular problem in urban areas, both for those along coasts and those located inland in or near water catchments. Rising sea levels are a particular problem for the first group: the newspaper *Kompas* reported that almost 200 cities in Indonesia's coastal areas will be more frequently exposed to destructive tidal flooding in coming years (Rosalina et al. 2021). Meanwhile, inland urban centres are endangered by a trend of increasingly frequent and intense floods and landslides that have occurred in the 893 inland watershed areas in Indonesia over the past ten years (Wisanggeni et al. 2023).

City governments in Indonesia deal with disasters and disaster risks—particularly flooding—differently. As I show in this chapter, some cities succeed relatively well at managing or even averting floods while

---

1 Material for this article is mostly taken from the in-progress PhD dissertation of the author at KITLV, University of Leiden, the Netherlands.

others fail. How is it possible that cities operating within the same national context, and often dealing with similar risk factors (such as topography and rainfall patterns), perform very differently in terms of outcomes of flood management? This question becomes even more puzzling when we observe that cities that do not invest heavily in massive technical interventions sometimes do equally well or even better than cities that depend on such interventions.

In this chapter, I draw on my research in three urban regions of Indonesia to propose that the best explanation for how and why cities cope so differently at dealing with floods lies in the local politics of flood risk management. Floods are physical occurrences, but their form, magnitude and location, and the number of people affected by them, are all shaped by political processes (Pelling 1999). Previous studies in Indonesia and beyond have contributed to identifying how flooding intertwines with politics (Coates and Nygren 2020; Padawangi and Douglass 2015). Such studies emphasise that it is necessary to uncover how power relations and political economy factors affect flooding events. For example, patterns of neoliberal development can undermine flood planning by allowing expansion of deep groundwater wells in pursuit of capitalist urbanisation, as has happened in Jakarta (Batubara et al. 2023). Likewise, the powerlessness of underprivileged communities living in *kampung* areas (self-built settlements) can make them vulnerable to floods (van Voorst 2016). Despite these studies, we know little about how local political patterns shape variations in flood management outcomes in Indonesia.

The three urban areas I draw upon in this chapter to compare the political dimensions of flood management practices are Surabaya, Semarang and Bandung district, all on Java Island. Bandung district is included in the analysis because although formally it is a district (*kabuputen*) rather than a city or municipality (*kota*), it has urban demographic and infrastructure features due to its proximity to Bandung city (see chapters by Malamassam and Katherina, and by Rahman, Haerudi and Octaviano, this volume, on the fuzzy boundary between rural and urban districts in Indonesia). Surabaya is selected because it shows impressive performance in terms of relatively low numbers of flood events and impacted people. Semarang and Bandung district have much less impressive performance, though both locations have implemented numerous large-scale flood prevention infrastructure projects.

Looking carefully at these locations, I examine how varying levels of state capacity in urban areas in Indonesia intersect with and shape flood defence infrastructure and how this intersection shapes flood management outcomes. I argue that success and failure in flood management is fundamentally related to the varying enforcement capacity of local governments, and their willingness to enforce their own regulations, both of which shape how effective they are at implementing regulations that enable effective use of flood defence infrastructure. A key here concerns the nature of the local political economy. Where there are extensive collusive relationships linking state actors and economic elites, local governments are much less effective at building the regulatory enforcement capacity necessary for effective flood defence. In such settings, companies frequently evade or ignore drainage and flood prevention rules. City governments that are able to tame or bypass such collusive relationships are much better at managing floods, reducing both the number of flood events and the number of people impacted by them.

My findings also suggest that linkages between local government and civil society are crucial to enabling enforcement of flood defence measures. In locations where what I call a progressive state-society linkage model is in force, such as Surabaya, the character of local politics supports enforcement of drainage regulations. By 'progressive', I mean a pattern whereby civil society engages actively in local governance. In such settings, members of the government apparatus cannot easily collude with companies that violate drainage regulations. Moreover, because the local government is open to input from the citizenry, it is more likely to be responsive to the needs of a larger segment of society, including their need for protection from flooding. I thus draw on the Surabaya case to show how successful enforcement of drainage regulations can involve more than a city government drawing on its own resources: in Surabaya the local government also relies on information and knowledge from the community in order to effectively enforce drainage regulations. There is, in short, 'co-produced enforcement' of flooding regulations. In contrast, I draw on the cases of Semarang and Bandung to show that worse outcomes arise in local government regions that lack progressive state-society linkages and where instead a patten of 'forbearance' prevails (Holland 2016)—that is, tolerance of companies and other economic actors that routinely violate drainage and flood prevention regulations.

I present these arguments through four sections. The first provides an overview of flood defence infrastructure and policies in the three observed regions, and lays out statistics on flood cases in them. Section two elaborates on implementation of flood mitigation regulations on the ground in the three regions, and how this implementation links to the varied outcomes. Section three explains variation of regulatory enforcement capacity across the three case-study locations and connects this variation with local political dynamics, including the nature of local civil society and the degree of collusion between political and economic actors. This section also employs two different terms—'co-produced enforcement' and 'forbearance'—to show why Surabaya has been relatively successful, and the other two governments relatively unsuccessful, at mitigating floods. In section four I present concluding remarks.

Flood defence infrastructure in three urban areas: Overview and outcomes

The critical infrastructure for preventing and mitigating floods is drainage. The Ministry of Public Works Regulation 12/2014 on the Drainage System in Indonesia, article 1, defines drainage as a 'water channel on the surface or under it, artificial or natural, that functions to drain excess water from an area to a receiving water body'. Urban drainage systems in Indonesia normally comprise a nested system of channels at three levels: primary, secondary and tertiary. These three drainage types are in turn equipped with water absorption facilities, storage facilities and other complementary equipment such as pumping stations and water gates. All these separate types of infrastructure in turn connect to form a drainage system (Regulation 12/2014, article 5). Drainage channels, meanwhile, can be natural or artificial. Natural drainage occurs as a result of topographical conditions and the earth's gravity, generating water flow that functions without facilities such as concrete installations. Artificial drainage is made by humans to drain water and involves supporting facilities such as pipes, tunnels and other installations.

Indonesian local governments at the district (*kabupaten*) and city (*kota*) levels have the authority to manage drainage. Under Regulation 12/2014, article 20, they are empowered to manage the operation, maintenance, rehabilitation and supervision of primary, secondary and tertiary drainage channels. They can determine drainage system policy, formulate drainage management plans, and issue (or withhold) permits for activities that have an impact on the system. They are expected to ensure that the drainage system, including its components such as pumping stations, floodgates and sedimentation cleaning, functions smoothly to enable the unimpeded flow of surface water. Importantly, cities and districts have the authority to require private entities, such as companies that run industrial or housing estates, to adhere to regulations governing the drainage system, and to provide adequate drainage and flood control facilities on land they control—important given that run-off and waste from such locations are frequent contributors to flooding in Indonesia (Kodoatie 2021: 2).

Each of the local governments that are the subject of this chapter has developed a regulatory framework for drainage and flood prevention. The Surabaya city government has issued several regulations in the area. For instance, it requires industrial and real estate developers to build proper drainage facilities, channels and retention ponds through Surabaya Mayor Regulation 14/2016. It empowers government personnel to monitor and enforce drainage regulations as they apply to such companies. The city of Semarang also has an established legal framework governing the city's drainage system. Its regional government regulation (Perda) 7/2014 requires developers of industrial, residential and commercial areas to provide drainage facilities and integrate them into existing drainage systems. Parties that convert land from open space to built-up purposes are required to compensate for any resulting increase in water discharge. The goal is that the construction of new buildings does not increase the water volume entering the drainage system. The regulatory landscape in Bandung district is similar to those in the two cities. The local government has the right to issue warnings, suspend private construction processes and even demolish constructions if it finds violations of drainage provisions. The district's authority also covers industrial waste disposal (a particular challenge in the district given that waste from the many textile factories there, if disposed of without proper processing, can cause sedimentation resulting in river overflow and flooding). The Bandung district government thus requires factories to provide wastewater treatment plants (*instalasi pengolahan air limbah*, IPAL) to treat their wastewater before it is discharged into waterways. The local government has the authority to supervise, monitor and test the quality of wastewater discharged into waterways or drainage channels. The government can issue warnings to owners and managers of factories who violate the rules, suspend their activities, demolish their buildings and revoke their operating permits.

On paper, it appears that the three governments have equally strong regulations in place to enable them to defend their populations from flood hazards. However, the outcomes are varied. Indicators I use to assess the effectiveness of flood defence infrastructure are the number of flood cases and number of people affected. 'Case' here means an event or 'occurrence' (*kejadian*) where an area of land is submerged by water, as recorded in the Indonesian Disaster Information Database (Data Informasi Bencana Indonesia, DIBI), managed by the National Agency for Disaster Management (Badan Nasional Penanggulangan Bencana, BNPB). The number of people affected includes those who died, were physically hurt, displaced and/or suffered property damage as a result of flooding, with data also derived from DIBI.

The number of flood cases experienced in each of the three locations (from 2010 to 2020 for Surabaya and Semarang, 2014–2021 for Bandung district) is shown in Figure 9.1. Despite both having large-scale flood

Figure 9.1 Flood cases: Surabaya, Semarang and Bandung district, 2010–2021

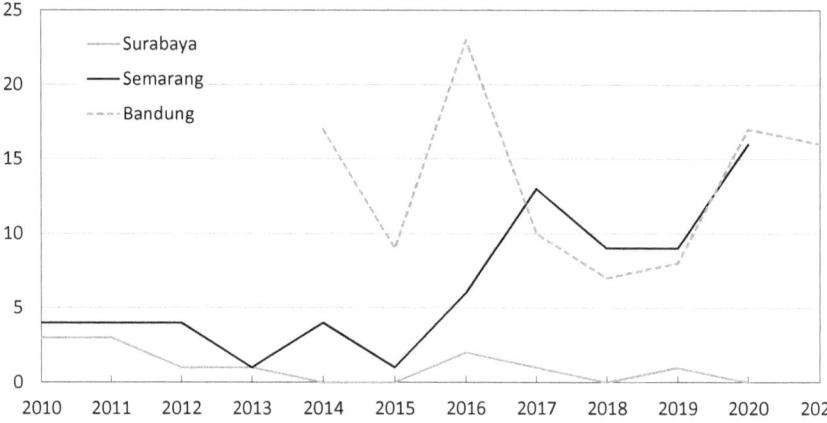

Source: Compiled by the author from data available in the Indonesian Disaster Information Database (https://dibi.bnpb.go.id).

prevention infrastructure, the figure shows relatively high and increasing numbers of flood cases in Semarang and Bandung. In Semarang, flooding peaked in 2020 with sixteen cases. The number of people affected by floods in Semarang in 2020 reached more than 16,000 with, cumulatively from 2013, a total of 60,974 people affected out of Semarang's population of 1.65 million. Between 2010 and 2020, Semarang spent more than US$200 million on improving its drainage system, with the rate of expenditure accelerating. Semarang has also benefited from flood defence infrastructure projects provided by the national government.

Bandung district's situation is similar. The year 2015 marked the beginning of construction of massive flood defence infrastructure in Bandung in the form of the Cisangkuy Floodway. This is an artificial canal used to reduce Cisangkuy River water discharge in southern Bandung, which frequently overflowed during the rainy season. Between 2015 and 2021 more than US$100 million was invested on flood defence infrastructure in the district. Not only has Bandung invested large sums of money on flood management infrastructure (much more than was invested in Surabaya), it also seems to have invested more in terms of human capacity, particularly through the deployment of military forces in law enforcement. The government involves the military, along with police, the prosecutor's office and local government, to accelerate the project's effectiveness in improving the river quality. This organisational structure is now called the 'Citarum Harum Taskforce' (where *harum* means fragrant). More than 7,000 military personnel have been deployed in the taskforce, with the Citarum watershed divided into 23 sectors, each with its own team headed by a local military officer, from upstream in Bandung district to downstream in Karawang district (Iqbal 2018). There are nine sectors in Bandung district, each of which is headed by a colonel. The military can ask for information from factory managers and inspect factory facilities to examine waste processing. They are also granted formal authority to suspend any activities that contribute to pollution of the Citarum River, including operation of factories that dump raw waste.

These flood management efforts in Bandung district occur as part of a nationally organised and endorsed Citarum River revitalisation project, established by Presidential Regulation (Perpres) 15/2018 (articles 8 and 9 enable military involvement in the taskforce and provide it with the powers mentioned above). The goal of this project is to improve the quality of the Citarum River by reducing pollution and floods; it does so primarily by funding new infrastructure. However, the Bandung district controls flood policies as they pertain to secondary and tertiary drainage channels and waterways. The district is also responsible for managing people and their activities along the water catchment. However, despite all this investment, flood cases have not significantly declined (Figure 9.1). In fact, the problem is even worse when we look at DIBI data on the number of people affected by floods, which show an increase in the five years following 2018, with the number peaking in 2020 at over 500,000.

Surabaya presents a very different picture. The city has been able to reduce cases of floods and the total number of people affected, while minimising expenditure on flood mitigation. The city spent only US$12 million between 2010 and 2021 (around 10 per cent of Semarang's allocation), and yet produced a better result with fewer floods. According to the assessment by the BNPB, Surabaya is exposed to high flood risk in all corners of the city, especially the east, south-west and north-west (https://inarisk.bnpb.go.id). However, this hazard does not lead to flood disasters. Moreover, between 2005 and 2019 Surabaya, Semarang and Bandung had similar average rainfall. Based on data from Statistics Indonesia (Badan Pusat Statistik, BPS), average monthly rainfall in Surabaya is 181 mm, Semarang is 181 mm and Bandung district is 176.3 mm. Nevertheless, Surabaya performs better in managing floods than the other two regions. Figure 9.1 shows that flood cases in Surabaya have been declining. In 2020, there was no recorded flood case in Surabaya, despite a heavy rainy season that year and a great deal of localised puddling of water. Since 2010, there has never been more than five flood cases in Surabaya annually. The highest number of people affected by floods in Surabaya occurred in 2017, with only 2,800 affected (of a total population of 3 million).

Same regulations, different results

My fieldwork findings suggest that Surabaya's positive record of flood control results largely from its local government's serious enforcement of its regulations on drainage system usage. Over the past decade or so, the Surabaya government demonstrated a high level of commitment to implementing its drainage regulations. In particular, it does not hesitate to take action against violations that occur, even if doing so requires it to confront large and powerful business interests. Moreover, the government does not tolerate interference in its enforcement measures, such as site inspections by members of Satgas Banjir, the government's flood taskforce.

Let me illustrate with an anecdote drawn from my fieldwork. In mid-November 2022, I had the opportunity to personally accompany the Surabaya Flood Taskforce commander as he inspected drainage facilities and managed his team members during the rainy season. He drove around the city in a four-wheel drive command car equipped with a communication radio through which he monitored the movement of taskforce members in the field. At one point, a team member reported via walkie-talkie radio that the Grand Palma (a big housing complex managed by Citraland, a subsidiary of Ciputra Group, one of Indonesia's major property developers), was refusing them access to the complex's housing area. The night before, the taskforce had received a report that the drainage channel from the Grand Palma area was overflowing and causing flooding in nearby *kampung*.

The commander negotiated with the housing management directly, seeking access to inspect the drainage system. When management still refused to grant permission, citing various excuses, the commander became visibly angry. He threatened to close the drainage channel outside the housing complex, which would have caused the water to back up and flood the complex itself—a site with exclusive and high-end housing. The complex managers were obviously surprised by this threat and immediately backed down, providing access to the taskforce to inspect the drainage system.

As expected, when they inspected them, the taskforce members found that the retention ponds in the housing complex were neither built nor operating according to regulations. They were not only too shallow, and some too small; the operation of the main retention ponds was also not following procedures. Some ponds were full of water even though it had not rained yet; they should have been emptying via existing drainage channels in periods when it was not raining, allowing them to absorb run-off when it did rain. The housing manager argued that draining the retention ponds would spoil the aesthetic of the area, given that they were using them as a decorative artificial lake in the middle of the housing area. The flood taskforce commander immediately ordered the housing manager to repair the retention ponds and restore their function according to original specifications. He also emphasised that during the repair of the retention ponds, members of the flood taskforce had to be given full access to the housing area.

In contrast to Surabaya, the Semarang government seems not to be so seriously committed to enforcing its drainage regulations. My fieldwork findings indicate that property companies in Semarang generally fail to build and maintain drainage and water retention facilities as required by regulations. The city government, for its part, seems reluctant to confront big property companies and has made few efforts to enforce its regulations. A field officer at the Public Works Agency responsible for dealing with floods told me about the flooding in a *kampung* in the Mijen subdistrict in early February 2021 (confidential interview, 27 April 2022).[2] The flood was caused by the overflow of the Dau River when high-intensity rains occurred. The river received additional water drainage from BSB (Bukit Semarang Baru) city, an exclusive housing complex jointly owned and managed by the Korompis Family through PT KAL and Ciputra Group through one of its subsidiaries, Citraland. The field officer reported this situation to the superiors. The superior only warned the BSB management to provide a proper drainage system, such as a retention pond and drainage channels. However, there was no follow-up from BSB.

As a result of lax enforcement, Semarang's public drainage system frequently fails to accommodate the high-volume flows of surface water that come from private housing complexes during periods of heavy rain. High-level bureaucrats themselves are reluctant to confront the companies responsible, apparently because they see them as having strong positions in the local political economy and access to local authorities. As one high-ranking bureaucrat within the Semarang city government explained:

> You already know that those involved in this business [real estate/housing property] are primarily top people. So, to change the function of [land] from [previously being] water catchment, there should be a reservoir there, but making it so there is no reservoir, it's possible. Well, many violations should not be committed but in fact they can be committed … getting rid of those people, that's what we have to do [if we want to fix the problem]. (interview, 15 February 2022)

---

2 Interviewees are occasionally named, with permission; in all other cases names are withheld to maintain confidentiality.

Weak enforcement of regulations has contributed to ineffective flood management, as indicated by the increasing number of flood cases and impacted people, despite the city's sizeable investments in flood defence infrastructure.

In Bandung, though real estate companies also contribute, the main source of the district's drainage and flood hazard problems is industrial companies. The Bandung District Environmental Agency noted in 2019 that the district hosted around 1,000 such companies, with 600 of them in the textile industry (Oktora 2019). Many of these companies dispose of their industrial waste into the Citarum River and its tributaries, with only 10 per cent having wastewater treatment plants (IPAL). This raw waste contributes to high turbidity levels in the Citarum River network (interview, Chandra, water expert, University of Padjajaran, 5 December 2022). Industrial waste also sinks to the river floor, turning into a thick jelly-like material over time, and thus contributing to the flooding problem.

Representatives of the industry do not deny that some textile companies violate IPAL regulations in the Citarum watershed. Ade Sudrajat, chair of the Indonesian Textile Industry Association (Asosiasi Pertekstilan Indonesia), has said that many textile factories avoid installing IPAL in order to reduce operating costs; factories without IPAL can reduce their costs by around Rp 200 to 300 million or US$19,000 per month (*kumparanNEWS* 2018). He also said that officials were involved in allowing companies to keep disposing their industrial waste without processing, and that they turned a blind eye to the practice in exchange for payments:

> [There are companies] who are allowed to dump as much waste as they like by just giving money to certain individuals [within the government]. Whether it's a lot or a few [companies that commit violations] is something we need to investigate. But, such companies exist, that's for sure. (*kumparanNEWS* 2018)

There seem to be two main sets of state actors involved in these collusive arrangements. The first is elements from the military—in keeping with what we know about patterns of informal military fundraising in other industries and parts of Indonesia. In 2000, the International Crisis Group reported that the Indonesian military raised its funds through various informal means to cover around 75 per cent of its expenditure; these fundraising activities are generally not supervised by the public (ICG 2000: iii). By taking 'security' fees from companies or engaging directly in business, military officers can earn large amounts of money they can use to finance their future political activities. Barber and Talbott (2003: 131) concluded that the military is involved in illicit natural resource businesses, such as the illegal timber economy. While such activities may have declined over the past two decades, they persist. In 2021, a coalition of Indonesian non-government organisations issued a report alleging that the deployment of military personnel in Intan Jaya district, Papua province, was related to securing mining businesses linked to several leading military figures (Rakhman et al. 2021). Such informal fundraising practices impact negatively on both the quality of democracy and the professionalism of the military (Mietzner 2008: 227).

Retired General Doni Monardo, former commander of the Siliwangi Territorial Command covering western Java, and one of the initiators of the Citarum Harum project, has warned about collusive practices involving the military and companies in the district (Iqbal 2022). During one site visit in the upstream Citarum area, Doni met with soldiers working on the project and issued a blunt warning:

> If you want to retire with pride and honour one day, do not ever fall for the lure [of bribes]. There will always be people who come to you and offer lures. Especially those who often commit violations against the environment. Do not sacrifice the future of our children and grandchildren just for the sake of [short-term] rewards … Do not tarnish the achievements of Siliwangi soldiers. (Iqbal 2022)

General Doni's warning was not without reason. A Mongabay journalist who accompanied him on his visit to Wayang Mountain in 2022 heard that Doni said certain military members in the Citarum Harum Taskforce had already *'masuk angin'*, a term that more or less means 'caught a cold' (interview, 17 November 2022). The Mongabay journalist interpreted this to mean that Doni had heard of collusion between military personnel and factories that were violating waste processing regulations and dumping their raw waste into the river (ibid.). In short, military officers were offering protection in exchange for payments, weakening enforcement of pollution regulations.

Members of the Citarum River Patrol, a grassroots community group established to monitor pollution in the river, informed me in interviews that military personnel often intimidated them when they were monitoring factories suspected of dumping industrial waste into the river (interview, 17 November 2022). Local military commanders told members of the river patrol that they should always 'coordinate' with them if they wanted to inspect factory waste disposal pipes. However, patrol members said they were reluctant to do so because when they did, factories often seemed to know in advance of their arrival, with the result that they failed to obtain evidence of illicit waste disposal (something they could get when they did not inform the military). Also, when they conducted monitoring operations with army personnel present, factory managers and other senior factory staff would usually welcome them at the front gate, and the river patrol team would not be allowed to check inside the factory area; they would just be required to wait outside until the army personnel finished their 'inspection'. The team suspected there was widespread collusion between individuals within the local army command and factory owners.

The second set of state actors involved in collusion are officials from the local government. Rumours circulate locally that such officials regularly collude with factory owners. For example, the aforementioned river patrol members are equipped with devices to measure water quality and cell phones with cameras to take pictures of pollution. They send the samples and photos they collect to the West Java Province Environmental Agency, hoping the information can be used to mount legal cases against the companies they find polluting the waterways. However, the provincial government does not have the authority to prosecute factories that violate IPAL regulations; this authority resides with the district government. According to members of the Citarum River Patrol, the provincial environmental agency sometimes forwards the evidence they provide to the Bandung district government, only for individuals from within that government to take it to the polluting factories where they use it as a bargaining tool to extract monetary payments in exchange for closing the case. In other words, rather than leading to prosecutions, the data the river patrol collects is sometimes used by officials to extract corrupt payments (interview, members of the Citarum River Patrol, 17 November 2022).

Explaining variation in enforcement

My empirical findings thus suggest that cities whose local governments are willing to enforce their own regulations have better outcomes in terms of flood prevention and mitigation. In other words, dealing with floods depends more on social and political factors than it does on mere technical capacity. People often blame weak enforcement of regulations on the limited quality and quantity of the bureaucratic workforce; certainly bureaucrats I interviewed, especially in Bandung and Semarang, sometimes complained they had inadequate bureaucratic resources to deal properly with the flood problem (e.g. interview with head of Semarang Housing Agency, 15 February 2022). However, this explanation does not convey the whole story; it sounds more like a standard excuse for underperformance. In Surabaya, the Flood Taskforce and similar agencies are relatively better resourced only regarding the number of field personnel and equipment they have when compared to their counterparts in Semarang and Bandung district. However, Surabaya does not have numerous big flood defence installations like Semarang and Bandung.

Nor does it have the additional state resources provided to Semarang and Bandung by the central government in the form of infrastructure investment and additional workforce. The discussion above has already indicated that collusion between state and business actors is the critical factor. Collusive practices lead to weak regulatory enforcement, indeed they often aim at achieving precisely this outcome. Thus, local governments that can tame or bypass such collusive relationships will be better at building effective flood defence.

This is certainly the lesson to be learned from the relative success of Surabaya in flood management. A progressive form of state-society linkage has been a major feature of the Surabaya reform model since the early *reformasi* years (see chapter by Mustafa, this volume; also Bunnel et al. 2013; Mustafa 2017). Building on the work of her predecessor, Bambang DH, Mayor Tri Rismaharini (Risma) was elected in the 2010 local election on a platform that emphasised clean and responsive administration and that had the backing of civil society forces and progressive networks. When Risma was threatened with impeachment by the local legislature, a large civil society coalition called the Surabaya Citizen Movement (Gerakan Rakyat Surabaya, GBS) held a series of massive protests to defend her. She also won the backing of an important local radio station, Suara Surabaya (the Voice of Surabaya), which in turn asked Mayor Risma to show a serious commitment to meeting public demands (interview with editor-in-chief of Suara Surabaya, 8 November 2021). Working with Suara Surabaya in 2011, Mayor Risma created an online system and digital application through which the public could make complaints about problems they noticed or experienced with public infrastructure or government services, including by uploading videos or photos. Mayor Risma could personally monitor all complaints and intervene within the bureaucracy to ensure they were being acted upon. The system also enabled the public to monitor follow-up by the city government. In the case of flooding, residents could report instances of inundations in their neighbourhoods and then directly monitor what street-level officials were doing about it in the field. Public monitoring of this kind helped to secure the city government's commitment to serving the public, while Suara Surabaya (and other media outlets) responded by supporting Mayor Risma's leadership.

The linkages between local government and society constructed through such mechanisms helped to ensure regulatory enforcement, including in the area of flood defence. Engagement by residents and civil society in local governance makes it harder for members of the government apparatus to diverge from formal rules, such as by colluding with companies who violate drainage regulations. Furthermore, a government that is receptive to a broad popular base will be more likely to prioritise performance. In the case of Surabaya, the mayor mobilised against corruption within the bureaucracy by strengthening her relationships with civil society actors (non-government organisations, universities and media), and the media helped to broaden her base and to limit the influence of predatory elites.

In Semarang and Bandung district, there was very little evidence of progressive state-society linkages of the sort developed in Surabaya. Mayors who have led Semarang over the past two decades have not been interested in pursuing a far-reaching reform agenda, and have instead relied mostly on clientelist strategies. In 2012, Mayor Soemarmo was arrested by the Corruption Eradication Commission (Komisi Pemberantasan Korupsi, KPK) for colluding with politicians in the local parliament in corruption in the annual government budget (*Kompas.com* 2012). Soemarmo's deputy, Hendar Prihadi, took over and won election in 2015, serving until 2022. Soemarmo's arrest did not prompt substantial reform. Hendar was also entangled in controversy. A non-government organisation, Jaringan Pendidikan Pemilih untuk Rakyat (JPPR, Voter Education Network for the People), opposed his inauguration because it was suspected he had received illicit campaign funds (Gabrillin 2016). In particular, it believed that businesses had donated to him without these donations being recorded in the mayor's campaign finance report; JPPR activists also say that property companies assisted his campaign, such as by providing transport for members of the public to attend his rallies (interview with JPPR activist, 13 April 2022). According to JPPR's investigation, one company suspected of making campaign donations to Hendar was PT IPU, a company that was several times involved in violating drainage regulations without being subject to strict sanctions by the local government (interview with JPPR activist, 13 April 2022; Batubara et al. 2021). Furthermore, lawyers and others have publicly accused PT IPU's owner of being a prominent member of the so-called 'land mafia'—a shadowy network that gains access to land through methods such as fraud, deception and intimidation (see, for example, *Obor Keadilan* 2021).[3]

The local political picture in Bandung district is similarly murky. From 2000 to 2020, the district was ruled by members of one family. Obar Sobarna, a former middle-ranking military officer, served as *bupati* (district head) for two terms from 2000 to 2010. His son-in-law, Dadang Nasser, was then elected as *bupati* for a further two terms, from 2010

---

3 For further discussion of land mafias in Indonesia, see Bachriadi and Aspinall (2023).

to 2020. This political dynasty's control of the district came to an end when Dadang Nasser's wife, Kurnia Agustina, who ran in the 2020 direct local election, lost to Dadang Supriatna. But Dadang did not clean up the district's government; in early July 2023, he was investigated by the KPK for allegedly accepting bribes in return for approving development projects in the district (CNN Indonesia 2023).

It was widely rumoured in the district that members of the Obar dynasty received money from business actors such as factory and industry owners around the Citarum watershed (interview with members of community-based river patrol, 17 November 2022). Local observers believed that this connection explains the absence of enforcement of drainage and IPAL requirements. In the 2020 direct local election, for example, the commissioner of the Bandung District Election Supervisory Agency (Badan Pengawas Pemilihan Umum Kabupaten Bandung) heard rumours that each factory in the region had donated at least Rp 50 million (around US$3,000) to support candidates from the ruling family (interview with commissioner, Kahpiana, 21 November 2022). It was of course difficult to prove this allegation. However, it can certainly be confirmed that Dadang Nasser had a close relationship with factories in Bandung. Indeed, he was a manager at several Bandung textile factories in the 1990s before becoming a public official.[4]

What do these stories tell us about the nature of local governance in Indonesian cities and more broadly? Social scientists have traditionally seen effective enforcement of a state's formal laws and rules as being a product of high levels of state capacity. Indeed, classical definitions of state capacity refer to the ability of states to implement their policies and goals (Fukuyama 2004; Skocpol 1985), and scholars adopting this approach have thus scrutinised whether state authorities can create and enforce binding rules for society (Mann 1984). Adopting this approach, attempts to measure state capacity usually focus on the financial and institutional resources a state can mobilise. Strong, professional, well-financed and well-equipped bureaucracies are assumed to be capable of implementing the law, such that gaps between the content of formal regulations and their actual implementation on the ground is generally explained by a state's alleged lack of capacity (Amengual and Dargent 2020: 164).

The account of flood prevention in Indonesian urban areas presented in this chapter complicates this conventional approach in at least two ways. First, it indicates that enforcement of regulations does not simply depend upon the strength of the bureaucracy and state agencies. Society also plays

---

4 www.bandungkab.go.id/arsip/profil-bupati-kabupaten-bandung

a role. As I have argued, the history of progressive state-society linkages in Surabaya was the key to that city experiencing greater regulatory enforcement than the other two cities. The Surabaya case represents what Amengual (2016: 8) calls 'co-produced enforcement'. When elements from within the state apparatus and allies in society team up, mobilising significant state and societal resources to enforce regulations, enforcement is more likely to be sustained over time (ibid.: 15). As indicated above, the Surabaya government not only relied on its own resources to enforce drainage regulations, but also obtained resources such as information, knowledge, funds and volunteer labour from the community. Community input and vigilance also helped to limit the predatory collusion between authorities and business actors that sabotaged enforcement in the other locations. High community engagement in local politics more generally also provided important backing to reformist local political leaders when they faced attacks from the local parliament and other sources.

Second, these cases also show that lack of enforcement is not always caused solely by a lack of state capacity, but can reflect a political choice made by bureaucrats or politicians in pursuit of particular benefits (Amengual and Dargent 2020: 162; see also Holland 2016: 245). During my fieldwork, I did not detect any significant difference among the three locations in terms of the strength of local agencies devoted to flood prevention, at least in terms of the resources provided to them or the level of expertise they had at their disposal. In fact, the central government provided additional resources to Semarang and Bandung. But officials in Surabaya were more concerned to enforce regulations than those in the other two urban areas. In her study of urban politics in Latin America, Holland (2016: 233) introduces the concept of 'forbearance' to explain 'intentional and revocable government leniency toward violations of the law, as a distinct phenomenon from weak enforcement'. Forbearance is a useful tool by which politicians and bureaucrats can attain particular advantages from non-state actors—such as mobilising electoral support from those who would otherwise be disadvantaged by regulatory enforcement—in part because it is commonly conducted informally without legislative approval or formal budgetary allocations (ibid.: 245).

Local political conditions in Semarang and Bandung were conducive to this phenomenon of 'forbearance' in the enforcement of flood control regulations. Politicians' and bureaucrats' reluctance to enforce drainage regulations in both locations did not arise from problems with the financial posture or workforce of the local bureaucracy. Instead, lax enforcement arose from collusion between politicians and business people. In both locations, by deliberately choosing not to enforce rules on drainage, local politicians could win critical political support and material resources, including the funding they needed to win local elections, from business people. At the same time, in both locations civil society was relatively weak, meaning the progressive state-society linkages witnessed in Surabaya did not emerge. In both places, non-government organisations and similar groups were present, and some certainly did try to contribute to flood defence (such as the members of the Citarum River Patrol in Bandung). However, civil society networks in Semarang and Bandung lacked the political weight needed to pressure the local government to enforce its own rules on flood prevention, and they also lacked the political channels for accessing the local government that their counterparts in Surabaya enjoyed. In the case of Bandung district, the role played by the military in backing local businesses made predatory collusion especially difficult to contain.

Conclusion

In this chapter I have tried to address puzzling questions about the varied outcomes produced by flood defence infrastructure in Indonesia's urban areas. In comparing Surabaya with Semarang and Bandung district, I have discussed why a city without expensive investment in flood prevention infrastructure was able to perform better than two urban areas that had larger-scale and much more costly technical interventions. While there may be some technical issues that help to explain Surabaya's better performance at flood management, overall I have argued that the key explanation lies in local political factors, especially in local governments' varying levels of capacity and willingness to enforce their own drainage regulations. Effective enforcement of drainage regulations is essential to preventing floods because it can ensure that key elements of flood defence infrastructure, such as drainage channels and retention ponds, are actually in place, are functioning properly and are not over capacity. Capacity and willingness to enforce regulations, in turn, is influenced by the extent to which local political conditions allow predatory collusion between public officials and business people. The more regularly such collusion facilitates violations of drainage regulations, the less successful flood defence outcomes will be. Conversely, if collusion occurs less frequently, then flood defence will likely be more successful. I have also argued that local state willingness to enforce drainage regulations does not just depend on the nature of the local state itself, but also on the nature of state-society linkages: places with greater engagement and input from civil society and the citizenry are more likely to experience better enforcement of drainage regulations.

This chapter also provides insights for scholars of disaster management and risk mitigation about how to rethink mainstream understandings of flood defence infrastructure. Such understandings tend to focus on physical installations and technical solutions. But the argument advanced in this chapter suggests that infrastructure for flood defence not only includes facilities such as canals, sea gates and pump stations but also complex assemblages of social and political actors and institutions, from both the public and private, or state and non-state, domains. Infrastructure to protect the population from flood hazards includes not only highly visible megaprojects. It also involves more than the (less visible) secondary and tertiary drainage channels. It incorporates such intangible political and social factors as the responsibility of real estate companies and factories to ensure that their activities do not cause flooding in surrounding areas. It requires an element of regulatory enforcement to ensure that the various components of the complex assemblage of social and political actors and institutions involved all play their part in flood prevention. Ensuring that water drains away from populated areas also means ensuring that rules are enforced on powerful actors in society.

Finally, in this chapter I have highlighted a similar need for analysts of urban Indonesia to emphasise political dimensions of urban planning and management. Such a political approach is particularly urgent given that cities in Indonesia are being increasingly threatened by climate-related disasters such as floods, with the result that climate change adaptation is becoming a mainstream topic of public discussion and an evolving focus of policymaking in the country. Social scientists need to insist that we include political analysis in these discussions and in preparing the policy landscape. As I have shown, hazards such as floods not only have natural causes and technical solutions, they also originate in political sources, such as politico-business collusion. Resilient urban areas will need more than technical interventions and sophisticated infrastructure; the effectiveness of such interventions and infrastructure will instead be contingent on the outcomes of contested political processes. As Indonesian urban studies face up to the challenges of climate change, we need to become even more adept at producing analysis that engages with city politics and power dynamics.

References

Amengual, Matthew. 2016. *Politicized Enforcement in Argentina: Labor and Environmental Regulation*. Cambridge University Press.

Amengual, Matthew and Eduardo Dargent. 2020. 'The social determinants of enforcement'. In *The Politics of Institutional Weakness in Latin America*, edited by Daniel. M. Brinks, Steven Levitsky and Maria Victoria Murilo, 161–82. Cambridge University Press.

Annur, Cindy Mutia. 2022. 'Hampir 3.500 bencana alam terjadi di Indonesia sepanjang 2022 [Nearly 3,500 natural disasters occurred in Indonesia throughout 2022]'. *Katadata*, 30 December. https://databoks.katadata.co.id/datapublish/2022/12/30/hampir-3500-bencana-alam-terjadi-di-indonesia-sepanjang-2022

Bachriadi, Dianto and Edward Aspinall. 2023. 'Land mafias in Indonesia'. *Critical Asian Studies* 55(3): 331–53. doi.org/10.1080/14672715.2023.2215261

Barber, Charles Victor and Kirk Talbott. 2003. 'The chainsaw and the gun: The role of the military in deforesting Indonesia'. *Journal of Sustainable Forestry* 16(3–4): 131–60. doi.org/10.1300/J091v16n03_07

Batubara, Bosman, Bagas Yusuf Kausan, Eka Handriana, Syukron Salam and Umi Ma'rufah. 2021. *Banjir sudah naik seleher: Ekologi politis urbanisasi DAS-DAS di Semarang* [The flood is already neck-deep: Political ecology of urbanisation of the Semarang watershed]. Cipta Prima Nusantara.

Batubara, Bosman, Michelle Kooy and Margreet Zwarteveen. 2023. 'Politicising land subsidence in Jakarta: How land subsidence is the outcome of uneven sociospatial and socionatural processes of capitalist urbanization'. *Geoforum* 139: 103689. doi.org/10.1016/j.geoforum.2023.103689

Bunnell, Tim, Michelle Ann Miller, Nicholas A. Phelps and John Taylor. 2013. 'Urban development in a decentralized Indonesia: Two success stories?' *Pacific Affairs* 86(4): 857–76. doi.org/10.5509/2013864857

CNN Indonesia. 2023. 'Bupati Bandung usai dilaporkan ke KPK: Biasa saja [Bandung head of district after being reported to KPK: Nothing extraordinary]'. CNN Indonesia, 7 July. https://www.cnnindonesia.com/nasional/20230707212005-12-970931/bupati-bandung-usai-dilaporkan-ke-kpk-biasa-saja.html

Coates, Robert and Anja Nygren. 2020. 'Urban floods, clientelism, and the political ecology of the state in Latin America'. *Annals of the American Association of Geographers* 110(5): 1301–17. doi.org/10.1080/24694452.2019.1701977

Djalante, Riyanti, Matthias Garschagen, Frank Thomalla and Rajib Shaw. 2017. 'Introduction: Disaster risk reduction in Indonesia: Progress, challenges, and issues'. In *Disaster Risk Reduction in Indonesia: Progress, Challenges, and Issues*, edited by Riyanti Djalante, Matthias Garschagen, Frank Thomalla and Rajib Shaw, 1–17. Springer. doi.org/10.1007/978-3-319-54466-3

Fukuyama, Francis. 2004. *State-Building: Governance and World Order in the 21st Century*. Cornell University Press.

Gabrillin, Abba. 2016. 'Wali kota Semarang akui terima uang Rp 300 juta dari Damayanti untuk kampanye [Semarang mayor admits accepting Rp 300 million from Damayanti for campaign]'. *Kompas.com*, 1 August. https://nasional.kompas.com/read/2016/08/01/13130951/wali.kota.semarang. akui.terima.uang.rp.300.juta.dari.damayanti.untuk.kampanye

Holland, Alisha C. 2016. 'Forbearance'. *American Political Science Review* 110(2): 232–46. doi.org/10.1017/S0003055416000083

ICG (International Crisis Group). 2000. 'Indonesia: Keeping the military under control'. ICG Asia Report No. 9. www.crisisgroup.org/asia/south-east-asia/indonesia/indonesia-keeping-military-under-control

Iqbal, Donny. 2018. 'Citarum Harum, langkah optimis pemerintah pulihkan kejayaan Sungai Citarum [Citarum Harum, the government's optimistic steps to revitalise Citarum River]'. *Mongabay*, 28 February. www.mongabay.co.id/2018/02/28/citarum-harum-langkah-optimis-pemerintah-pulihkan-kejayaan-sungai-citarum-bagian-3

Iqbal, Donny. 2022. 'Reuni para jenderal di kaki gunung Wayang [A reunion of generals at the foot of Wayang Mountain]'. *Mongabay.co.id*, 16 June. www.mongabay.co.id/2022/06/16/reuni-para-jenderal-di-kaki-wayang-bagian-2

Kodoatie, Robert J. 2021. *Rekayasa dan Manajemen Banjir Kota* [Engineering and management of urban flooding]. Penerbit Andi.

Kompas.com. 2012. 'Wali kota Semarang ditahan KPK [Mayor of Semarang detained by KPK]'. *Kompas.com*, 30 March. https://regional.kompas.com/read/2012/03/30/18245426/~Regional~Jawa

kumparanNEWS. 2018. 'Majalaya, Citarum, dan petaka limbah industri [Majalaya, Citarum, and the industrial waste disaster]'. *kumparanNEWS*, 23 March. https://kumparan.com/kumparannews/majalaya-citarum-dan-petaka-limbah-industri/full

Lin, Thung-Hong. 2015. 'Governing natural disasters: State capacity, democracy, and human vulnerability'. *Social Forces* 93(3): 1267–1300. doi.org/10.1093/sf/sou104

Mann, Michael. 1984. 'The autonomous power of the state: Its origins, mechanisms, and results'. *European Journal of Sociology* 25(2): 185–213.

Mietzner, Marcus. 2008. 'Soldiers, parties and bureaucrats: Illicit fund-raising in contemporary Indonesia'. *South East Asia Research* 16(2): 225–54. doi.org/10.5367/000000008785260446

Mustafa, Mochamad. 2017. 'Democratic decentralisation and good governance: The political economy of procurement reform in decentralised Indonesia'. PhD thesis. University of Adelaide. https://hdl.handle.net/2440/117256

Obor Keadilan. 2021. 'Kapolri: Usut tuntas mafia tanah tanpa pandang bulu, Andar: Minta tersangka Soedibejo alias Aciok dirut PT IPU ditangkap [National police chief: Investigate land mafia without discrimination; Andar: Requests Soedibejo, aka Aciok, director of PT IPU be arrested]'. *Obor Keadilan*, 18 February. https://www.oborkeadilan.com/2021/02/kapolri-usut-tuntas-mafia-tanah-tanpa.html

Oktora, Samuel. 2019. 'Pabrik masih buang limbah ke Citarum [Factory still dumps waste into Citarum]'. *Kompas.id*, 19 September. www.kompas.id/baca/utama/2019/09/19/pabrik-masih-buang-limbah-ke-citarum

Padawangi, Rita and Mike Douglass. 2015. 'Water, water everywhere: Toward participatory solutions to chronic urban flooding in Jakarta'. *Pacific Affairs* 88(3): 517–50. doi.org/10.5509/2015883517

Pelling, Mark. 1999. 'The political ecology of flood hazard in urban Guyana'. *Geoforum* 30(3): 249–61. doi.org/10.1016/S0016-7185(99)00015-9

Rakhman, Ode, Umi Ma'rufah, Bagas Yusuf Kausan and Ardi. 2021. 'Ekonomi-politik penempatan militer di Papua: Kasus Intan Jaya [The political economy of military deployment in Papua: The Intan Jaya case]'. #BersihkanIndonesia, YLBHI, WALHI Eksekutif Nasional, Pusaka Bentara Rakyat, WALHI Papua, LBH Papua, KontraS, JATAM, Greenpeace Indonesia and Trend Asia.

Rosalina, M. Puteri, Albertus Krisna and Satrio Pangarso Wisanggeni. 2021. 'Kota-kota yang terendam di masa depan [The submerged cities of the future]'. *Kompas.id*, 20 August. www.kompas.id/baca/nusantara/2021/08/20/kota-kota-yang-tenggelam-di-masa-depan

Skocpol, Theda. 1985. 'Bringing the state back in: Strategies of analysis in current research'. In *Bringing the State Back In*, edited by Peter B. Evans, Dietrich Rueschemeyer and Theda Skocpol, 3–38. Cambridge University Press.

van Voorst, Roanne. 2016. *Natural Hazards, Risk and Vulnerability: Floods and Slum Life in Indonesia*. Routledge.

Wisanggeni, Satrio Pangarso, M. Puteri Rosalina and Albertus Krisna. 2023. 'Sungai-sungai di Indonesia semakin membahayakan [Rivers in Indonesia are increasingly dangerous]'. *Kompas.id*, 23 February. www.kompas.id/baca/investigasi/2023/02/22/sungai-sungai-di-indonesia-semakin-membahayakan

10 Governing garbage: Solid waste management reform in Surabaya

Nur Azizah

The management of solid waste, or garbage, is a major problem confronting big cities in Indonesia. As the urban population expands, and as people living in cities consume more, cities produce more rubbish. Managing this garbage is fundamentally a responsibility of district-level governments, and there has been little in the way of nationwide initiatives or systematic strategies to deal with the problem. In towns and cities around the country, many residents continue to dump their garbage on the street, burn it or throw it into waterways, contributing to other problems such as air pollution and urban flooding. Community and city-organised garbage collection, meanwhile, ends up in ever-growing mountainous and insanitary landfills that dot the countryside around urban centres.

For these reasons, it is important to look at success stories of cities that are managing to get on top of their garbage problems. One such case is Surabaya, the capital of East Java province. Surabaya is currently more advanced than most other cities in Indonesia in terms of waste collection, transport and landfill management. In 2019 and 2022, the city received the Adipura Kencana award, the highest rank in the Adipura award, which is given to cities that can maintain city cleanliness and urban environmental management (including sanitation and green open spaces) consistently and sustainably for multiple years (Maulidiya 2019; Pemerintah Kota Surabaya 2023). In 2021, President Joko Widodo visited the Benowo landfill (Surabaya's dumping site) to inaugurate the first waste-to-electricity facility (*pengolahan sampah menjadi energi listrik*, PSEL) in Indonesia. In addition, waste management in Surabaya has involved a large degree of community participation, through waste banks and community-based recycling centres.

How has this success been achieved? In this chapter, I argue there were three key ingredients. First, waste management reform in Surabaya required a long period of effort by the city government. A major turning point came in the early 2000s, but success was built on a long history of efforts to develop a waste management system that can be traced as far back as the Dutch colonial era in the 1920s. The Surabaya experience thus suggests that successfully governing waste requires long-term commitment. Second, this effort required leadership, with a series of mayors in Surabaya, starting in the New Order era with Poernomo Kasidi (1984–1994), followed in the *reformasi* period by Bambang DH (2002–2010), Tri Rismaharini (2010–2019) and current Mayor Eri Cahyadi, having made a serious commitment to dealing with the city's waste. Previous studies affirm that local leadership is often a key factor in achieving better service provision and public sector reform in decentralised polities (Bunnell et al. 2013; Feliciani 2023; Grindle 2007; Puspitasari 2016; von Luebke 2007). Local government leaders have the capacity to mobilise resources for change in ways that other actors lack (Grindle 2007), and they can form coalitions with different actors and manage the bureaucracy in ways that enable local policies to be implemented (von Luebke 2007). Surabaya's waste management confirms these studies. A third ingredient in Surabaya's long-term success has been broad participation by varied stakeholders, including members of the community, non-government organisation (NGO) activists and private-sector actors. Participation in waste management is important not only because it encourages citizens, as one of the waste producers, to take responsibility for their own waste, but because it helps deal with limited government capacity (in terms of finances, resources and service coverage) to manage waste.

I also show in this chapter that the government in Surabaya has integrated three models for managing its waste. The first model relies on partnerships between the government and members of the community, the second involves partnerships with the private sector, while the third model is state driven, in which the city government is the main actor.

In the first partnership model, the city government cooperates with members of the community, and emphasises citizen participation at the grassroots level. This model operates at the level of door-to-door waste services, and the establishment and management of local recycling centres or *pusat daur ulang* (material recovery facilities, MRFs). The key actors in this model are the citizens and community-based organisations (*rukun warga* or *kampung*), environmental cadres (community members who are recruited as volunteers by the city government) and the city government. It also involves the environmental cadres educating citizens about waste sorting at the household level and about waste management in general.

In this model, the government provides physical, financial and human resources, including by developing the infrastructure required, such as buildings and waste processing machinery, and placing government staff as coordinators in each MRF. The implementation of this participatory model begins with the standpoint that both the government and citizens want a clean city.[1]

The second model involves the city government engaging in partnerships with for-profit actors in the private sector. Commercial actors are involved at various stages of the waste cycle in Surabaya. For example, numerous small and medium enterprises are involved in waste collection and transportation from commercial areas and apartments; large private companies such as Unilever and PT Telkom support waste management activities through their corporate social responsibility programs; local media group Jawa Pos has engaged in media campaigns to promote better waste management practices; and a large company, PT Sumber Organik, has been operating and managing the Benowo landfill. Under a long-term contract (2012–2032) with the city government, PT Sumber Organik has begun to implement a waste-to-energy program at the site. Building a waste-to-electricity plant (operational since 2015, then formally inaugurated by President Joko Widodo in 2021) produces benefits: it can transform waste into energy (a policy goal at the national level since 2018) and by doing so decrease the volume of waste that accumulates at the landfill. But it also requires massive investment. The Benowo waste-to-electricity plant cost approximately Rp 365 billion (US$23 million) (Hermana 2021), while the total investment for all the facilities at the landfill, including to develop a leachate control system, was around Rp 704 billion (US$45 million) (EBTKE 2021; Redaksi Asiatoday 2021). To recoup its investments, the site operator charges the city government tipping fees for every truckload of waste deposited at Benowo. As we shall see, despite the Surabaya city government's overall reputation for transparency and good governance, there were signs of informal politics in the form of rent-seeking in the procurement process that led to the issuing of the contract for the landfill management and power plant.

The third model is a state-driven waste management model; its key actors are bureaucrats and other government employees. The government applies this model after waste leaves the community level, by collecting

---

1 Nationally, opportunities for citizen participation in managing waste are recognised by Law 18/2008 on Solid Waste Management. However, implementation of participation works only when the (local) government provides necessary resources and citizens are willing to participate actively. Both ingredients have been present in Surabaya.

waste from both community-level recycling centres and from temporary dumping sites throughout the city and then transporting it to the Benowo landfill. Ensuring that this part of Surabaya's waste management system works smoothly, and that waste does not pile up at temporary landfills or recycling centres, requires speed and organisation. At this stage, the system shifts from one based on community resources to one that is increasingly based on technology and government employees. This model thus involves the use of heavy equipment such as waste compactors and arm-roll trucks, which have high maintenance costs. Most of the cost to run this model comes from the city budget, as I explain below.

In this chapter, I analyse the governance of garbage in Surabaya, sketching out the nature of Surabaya's approach to waste management, its origins and the ingredients that have contributed to its relative success. The chapter consists of five sections. The first discusses the broad context of the waste problem in urban Indonesia, noting that city (and other district) governments have historically underinvested in this sector. This is followed by an overview section on waste reform in Surabaya, emphasising the origins of reform in the intertwining of a waste crisis and political crisis in the early 2000s. The next three sections describe in detail how community participation, government investment and partnership with the private sector operate in Surabaya's system of waste management. In the conclusion, I consider what lessons from the Surabaya case can be applied to other towns and cities in Indonesia.

The waste problem in urban Indonesia

One of the major problems confronted by Indonesia as it urbanises is how to manage waste. In 2022, according to official figures, Indonesia produced well over 34.5 million tonnes of waste.[2] Waste generation in a particular locale is greatly influenced by household consumption and by population size. In cities, waste generation tends to be greater than in rural areas due to cities having both larger populations and higher levels of per capita daily consumption. In 2019, 56 per cent of Indonesia's total population lived in urban areas (Christy 2020), a figure that is predicted to grow to 73 per cent by 2045 (Finaka 2020). As the population in urban areas increases, waste management will become an even greater problem in Indonesia.

---

2 National Waste Management Information System (https://sipsn.menlhk.go.id/sipsn/). This data was accessed on 31 August 2023, and according to the information on the website, was accumulated from 289 districts/cities in 2022. This means that the total covers only about half of all districts and cities in Indonesia.

Recognising the severity of the problem, in 2008 the national government enacted Law 18/2008 on Solid Waste Management, an umbrella policy setting out broad guidelines on how garbage is to be managed. This law introduced a shift from an old paradigm—collecting, transporting and disposal—to a mechanism that includes the so-called 3Rs (reduce, reuse, recycle) (Kemenko Bidang Ekonomi 2015; UNDESA 2011). The shift also changed the official designation of landfills from *tempat pembuangan akhir* (final dumping site or landfill) to *tempat pemrosesan akhir* (final processing site), with the implication that landfills are now supposed to be sites to reuse waste, with only residues being deposited permanently. The law also requires involvement by more non-government actors in dealing with waste, starting with requiring waste producers (individuals, households and organisations) to treat their waste through the 3Rs prior to collection and transportation to landfill.

In Indonesia, waste management is considered part of environmental affairs, which is one of the authority areas that was transferred from the national to district governments at the start of decentralisation, more than twenty years ago. The national government establishes laws, regulations and standard operating procedures on waste management as a policy framework for district governments, but actual implementation, and to a large extent, design of waste management policies, is left to districts. Thus, local leaders, local branches of political parties, local bureaucracies and local communities largely determine the extent to which waste management succeeds.

However, previous studies indicate that local government has a poor record in managing waste in Indonesia. Explanations include 'lack of infrastructure and poor environmental awareness' (Concord Consulting 2015: 29) and 'absence of trained officials, and limited revenue' (Dethier 2017: 83). Funding is definitely a major challenge. By 2018, only 1 per cent of the national budget was allocated to protect the environment. At the provincial level, the highest budget allocation for the environmental sector in the same year was 2.8 per cent (this was in Jakarta province) (BPS 2018: vii). At the district/city level in 2023, an average of only 0.5 per cent of local budgets was allocated to waste management. According to the Ministry of Environment and Forestry, local governments need to allocate 3–4 per cent of their budgets to be able to effectively manage waste (Henry 2023).

As a result of low capacity and underfunding, many districts in Indonesia, especially urban areas (most of which are *kota* or municipalities), have experienced recurrent waste crises. A waste crisis is a condition in which waste growth cannot be controlled while waste management, including waste collection, transportation and dumping, occurs in a chaotic manner, causing problems such as overcapacity and overflow at landfills, which in turn leads to air and water pollution, leachate spread, waste avalanches and waste fires. Such problems occur frequently in and around some of Indonesia's major urban areas. In the middle of August 2023, for example, a waste fire lasted three weeks at Sarimukti landfill, which serves as the final dumping site for four metropolitan areas: Bandung district, West Bandung district, Cimahi district and Bandung city. An uncontrolled methane gas explosion ignited the fire, leading to severe air pollution and causing people living nearby to suffer acute respiratory and eye conditions (BBC News Indonesia 2023). In another example from 2023, between late July and early September, a waste crisis occurred in Yogyakarta city when the provincial government closed the Piyungan landfill, the final dumping site for Bantul and Sleman districts and Yogyakarta city. The landfill had exceeded capacity more than a decade earlier, in 2012, but local governments kept using it until it was no longer able to accept waste. The closure halted waste collection and transportation, causing garbage to pile up throughout Yogyakarta's urban areas (*detikJogja* 2023; Fallahnda 2023; Razak 2020). Given how common such problems are across contemporary Indonesia, it is important to look at relatively successful cases of waste management, which brings us to Surabaya.

Reforming waste governance in Surabaya

Surabaya is Indonesia's second-largest city. It is a densely populated city with 3.16 million inhabitants in 2019, and a population growth rate of 2 per cent (BPS Kota Surabaya 2020: 44). Surabaya's economy depends on trade and industry, with the city having been a significant hub for trade, transport and logistics in eastern Indonesia since the colonial era (Dick 2002; Marijan 2008). Its vast and growing population has also generated a massive waste problem. By 2020, waste production in Surabaya was more than 2,220 tonnes a day, of which 1,958 tonnes a day were brought to the Benowo landfill (Pemkot Surabaya 2021: II–84).

Over the past two decades, the city government has developed several programs to manage city waste. A major part of the government's approach has been designing and implementing community-based waste management, especially in waste collection and transportation. The government has also promoted citizen participation in waste management through formalising waste banks, mobilising environmental cadres, and organising green and clean competitions. At the same time, it has invested its own resources to manage waste.

The origins of waste management reform in Surabaya are highly political, and relate closely to a process of leadership change and political reform that occurred in the city during the early *reformasi* period in the early 2000s (see Mustafa, this volume). It should also be acknowledged, however, that the government inherited legacies that made it well placed to address the waste issue once this reform process began. There have been moments of progress in waste management in the past, although they were rarely sustained. In the colonial period, following a plague outbreak in 1911, the local colonial administration tried to improve waste collection services as part of its effort to reduce disease by improving sanitation (Dick 2002: 172). During the New Order era, the Surabaya city government was heavily engaged in the Kampung Improvement Program, which ran in several phases from the late 1960s to the late 1970s, with funding from the East Java provincial budget, a World Bank loan and community self-financing (Gervasi 2011; Prasetiyo et al. 2019). This program relied heavily on neighbourhood-level community participation and especially in its final phase focused on improving neighbourhood infrastructure, including pathways and drainage, making it easier to collect and transport waste from households (still largely organised by communities on the *swadaya*, self-reliance, principle). Finally, a late New Order mayor, Poernomo Kasidi (1984–1994), who had a background as a military doctor, was personally concerned about sanitation and environmental programs, including waste management. He introduced some important initiatives, notably the formation of a large team of city sweepers (see below), which was expanded by later mayors (the first time the city won the Adipura award was in 1988, under his leadership). Even so, around the turn of the century, as the *reformasi* era dawned, the city waste management system was moribund. As in most urban areas of Indonesia, collection and transport of waste was largely left to community self-management and private operators, with little attention paid to, or investment in, government-run parts of the service.

Years of neglect came to a head in 2000, when overuse of the Keputih landfill, in east Surabaya, which had been used since 1970 and had been over capacity for years, began to cause increasingly significant environmental problems for the people living near it. Although the city government had tried to install incinerators in the early 1990s to reduce the volume of waste accumulating at Keputih, these did not keep pace with the amount of garbage entering the landfill. People around the landfill suffered from the odour and from groundwater pollution. As the problem escalated in 2001, residents around the landfill started protesting by blocking the entrance gate (*Liputan6* 2001). They were led by Dewan Kota (City Council), a coalition of NGO activists, academics and professionals established in

1999 as 'a response to the return of military power and the inheritance of the New Order Mayor' (Mustafa 2017: 105)—the mayor in question was Sunarto Sumopawiro, a former military officer who had taken office in 1994 when the New Order was still at its height. The protest action by the residents effectively closed the landfill, bringing waste collection and transport to a halt. Garbage piled up throughout the city. As a result, the waste crisis at the landfill developed into a major cause of public discontent with the mayor, with most residents feeling the adverse effects of the city's mismanagement of its waste. As a circuit breaker, the city council (DPRD) deemed Mayor Sunarto to be absent from his duties as he had travelled to Australia for medical treatment without seeking the permission of the council. Citing his absence, but also the waste crisis, in 2002 the DPRD formally removed Sunarto from his position and appointed his deputy, Bambang DH, as the new mayor (*Liputan6* 2002).

Soon after his inauguration, Bambang DH made tackling the waste crisis a political priority. The city government under his leadership worked with experts from the Surabaya Institute of Technology (Institut Teknologi Surabaya, ITS) to design a better waste management system for the city. ITS academics worked with officials from the government of Kitakyushu city in Japan, with which Surabaya entered a sister-city relationship. Together they designed a new waste management program for the city that integrated several components, including community-based waste management, introduction of the 3Rs approach, waste separation at source, and modernising the landfill (Gamaralalage 2012). The government also invited legal experts from Airlangga University to work on the necessary regulations. A member of this team was Tri Rismaharini, then head of Surabaya's Sanitation and Landscaping Department (Dinas Kebersihan dan Pertamanan) (Colombijn 2016). She later became Bambang's successor as mayor, continuing and expanding upon his vision of building a cleaner and greener city.

In short, the early 2000s were a critical juncture both for the development of waste policy and for political reform in Surabaya. The waste crisis of the early 2000s not only coincided with a political crisis, it contributed to it, and ensured that better waste management would be a core goal of the successor political regime that came to power as result of these twin crises. As argued by Mustafa (this volume), the appointment of Bambang also initiated a period of wider political reform in the city, in which progressive city leadership was backed by a broad civil society and media coalition. Crucially, the fact that Bambang came to power as the result of a broad coalition predisposed his government to developing a participatory model of waste management, which involved the community and private actors while also demonstrating government leadership.

Partnership with the community

One distinctive feature of the Surabaya approach to waste management is the emphasis the city places on community participation, especially in managing waste collection services at the neighbourhood level and implementation of the 3R principles, including by encouraging composting by households. The city government, under Mayor Bambang DH, began to develop its community-based approach to waste management in 2002. One part of the new approach involved integrating existing community-based waste collection and transport services with government services. Community-based waste collection, as in most Indonesian cities, was a longstanding feature of Surabaya's waste management system. Under this system, neighbourhood associations (*rukun tetangga*) or citizens' associations (*rukun warga*) in most (though not all) *kampung* organised waste collection from households. They would hire waste collectors, provide waste carts, collect service fees (currently around Rp 15,000–30,000 per household per month), and then transport and dump the waste at the nearest temporary landfill site. Small and medium enterprises, meanwhile, offered waste collection and transportation services from shops, apartments, hotels, shopping malls and similar sites. However, during Bambang's tenure, the city realised these services were collecting only about half of the waste being generated in the city, and mismatches between the schedules of waste carts arriving at temporary landfill sites and government transport from these sites meant waste was piling up at the temporary landfill sites.

Learning from this situation, the city government, with help from ITS, Airlangga University academics and Kitakyushu officials, developed a new solid waste management system that encouraged more neighbourhood associations to run waste collection services and to introduce 3R practices, especially community-level separation into dry and wet waste, and composting of wet waste. In developing this approach, the government built on achievements of earlier eras (including the Kampung Improvement Program, mentioned above) to extend waste collection services to more people, including those living in inner city *kampung* areas. In essence, the government acted to provide general guidance for communities to organise their own waste collection and transport at the household level, including by arranging matching transportation schedules to ensure waste did not build up at temporary landfills. As a result of this approach, there was an increase in the waste collection rate (i.e. the amount of waste collected compared with the amount generated) from around 50 per cent in 2001 (Gamaralalage 2012: 2) to 90 per cent in 2007 (Premakumara et al. 2011: 464).

Another form of community-based waste management encouraged by the city government is waste banks (*bank sampah*). Waste banks aim to attract participation in recycling waste by helping people to access its economic benefits. Specifically, they operate on the principle that enabling people to benefit from the economic potential of waste nurtures their interest in separating recyclable waste at home, and so reduces the amount of waste going to landfill. The first waste bank in Indonesia was established in Yogyakarta as a citizen's initiative in 2006; since 2012, the national government has regulated waste banks as a form of citizen's participation in waste management (under Ministry of Environment Regulation 13/2012 on Guidelines for Implementing Reduce, Reuse and Recycle through Waste Banks). By 2022, there were 296 waste banks and one central waste bank in Surabaya. However, recent studies argue that despite the increasing number of waste banks in the city, their effectiveness in reducing waste to landfill is still low. In 2018, waste banks in South Surabaya reduced the amount of waste going to landfill by around 0.146 per cent (Warmadewanthi and Haqq 2019: 8), while another study shows that waste banks reduced only 0.15–0.33 per cent of the waste generated in Surabaya during 2019–2021 (Jamaludin et al. 2023: 60). Problems such as limited community participation and dependence on buyers of recyclable waste contributed to this outcome. Even though waste banks have not been as effective in reducing waste as initially hoped, other forms of citizen participation in the city have been more effective.

The city government also invested in raising public awareness about its new community-based model. For example, starting in 2005, it held a Surabaya Green and Clean competition among *rukun tetangga*. This is a competition to find the cleanest and greenest *kampung* in the city. The competition covers several categories, including cleanliness of streets and the environment, drainage and sewerage, waste recycling, and greenery (Gervasi 2011). The winner of the competition is announced every May, during the event marking the city's anniversary, with the assessment taking place over the three preceding months. Besides receiving prizes, the winners are featured in the *Jawa Pos* newspaper. Every time this competition was held, the number of participating *rukun tetangga* increased, in part due to community interest in the mass media coverage for the winning community. In short, the government tried to foster a sense of community pride around its waste program, and by doing so it helped to discipline people's behaviour when it came to waste.

The community-based approach that has been central to the government's waste management plan has also involved partnerships with private companies and the mass media. One private company that became deeply engaged in waste management in Surabaya is PT Unilever (a multinational company that produces various goods ranging from bath soap and detergent to food and drinks, which are widely consumed in Indonesia; one of its largest factories in Indonesia is in the Rungkut industrial area in Surabaya). In 2000, as part of its corporate social responsibility activities, PT Unilever established the Unilever Peduli Foundation (UPF), which focuses on promoting the 3Rs program. The company built and funded a composting and recycling facility in Jambangan ward between 2001 and 2004. In addition, UPF developed community-based waste management activities that included raising citizens' awareness of the 3Rs and providing waste carts to communities to improve waste collection. Between 2005 and 2014 the company ran these and similar activities under a formal agreement with the city government. Further, numerous NGOs in the city including Pusdakota (Pusat Pemberdayaan Komunitas Perkotaan, Centre for Urban Community Empowerment), an NGO established by Surabaya University; Walhi Surabaya (Wahana Lingkungan Hidup Indonesia, Indonesian Forum for the Environment); and Komunitas Nol Sampah (Zero Waste Community) work with the government and the community to manage waste. With support from the influential *Jawa Pos* newspaper (the largest newspaper in East Java) and NGO activists, this collaboration replicated the Jambangan model initiated by UPF and extended it to other wards through the Surabaya Green and Clean Program (Chandra and Jatmika 2022; Gilby et al. 2017; Prasetiyo et al. 2019; Tahir et al. 2014).

As part of the Surabaya Green and Clean competition and in collaboration with UPF, the government began to recruit environmental cadres in 2005. These cadres are neighbourhood-level volunteers, mostly women, who are provided with a minor payment to cover their expenses.[3] The government and UPF trained them as campaigners on environmental issues, including waste management. They have played an important role in raising awareness about the importance of waste management at the neighbourhood level, running activities such as disseminating ideas about waste separation in the household and initiating composting in their neighbourhoods. In 2021, there were around 23,000 environmental cadres in Surabaya (Hakim 2021).

---

3 In addition to environmental cadres, the city government also appointed health cadres and *juru pemantau jentik* (mosquito larvae monitors). In 2022, it merged those groups into Kader Surabaya Hebat (Great Surabaya Cadres). The government allocates monthly honorariums (around Rp 400,000 or US$25 in 2022 and 2023) to these cadres and provides them with uniforms.

State-driven waste management

As mentioned above, reform of waste management in Surabaya has involved significant direct government intervention and investment. This has been evident, for example, in the 3Rs program, where the government has not only used environmental cadres to promote recycling and encouraged the development of waste banks at the community level, but also directly established and funded recycling centres or material recovery facilities (MRFs) and composting houses.

The city government began its program of developing MRFs in Jambangan ward in 2005 (with UPF support, as noted above). By 2020 the government had developed 9 MRFs and 25 composting houses across the city (Pemkot Surabaya 2021: II–85). To improve the waste collection rate, it also developed more temporary landfill sites (*tempat pembuangan sementara*), increasing the number from 163 in 2010 to 187 in 2020 (Pemkot Surabaya 2005: II–84, 2021: II–85). The city government built and funded these facilities mainly by drawing on the local budget, with additional funding support from the national Ministry of Environment and Forestry and the Ministry of Public Works and Human Settlements.

The MRFs receive waste from community-organised collectors who live in the neighbourhoods around these facilities. The Jambangan MRF, for example, receives five to seven tonnes of waste per day from neighbourhoods in that ward (Figure 10.1). Each recycling centre is run by a supervisor (who is a city employee) and several workers, who are recruited from the neighbouring area. At these installations, workers turn organic waste into compost and sort inorganic waste into several types, such as plastic, paper and cardboard, which are later sold to waste buyers. The MRFs receive funds from the city government to cover operational expenses, including paying for workers' salaries. Remaining waste residue that cannot be treated further, typically around 40–50 per cent of the rubbish deposited, is collected by the Surabaya city government and transported to landfill.

Meanwhile, to keep the city and other public facilities clean, the Surabaya city government hires thousands of street sweepers, known as the Pasukan Kuning (Yellow Force)—a name that refers to their yellow uniforms. These people sweep Surabaya streets from 4 a.m. to 10 p.m. daily, organised in three shifts. The government first formed the Yellow Force in 1987 under Mayor Poernomo Kasidi (Puspitasari 2016: 379–80). Then, as now, street sweepers are recruited as casual (or honorary) staff and paid local minimal wages (Faizal 2016). This workforce is an essential part of maintaining city cleanliness, especially in central areas of the city. They collect organic waste (mostly fallen leaves and bark) while sweeping

Figure 10.1 Sorting activities at Jambangan material recovery facility

and take it to the composting facility at the nearest recycling centre. The city government uses compost generated to fertilise plants in city parks and gives it out for free to residents who need it. In 2020, there were more than 2,000 Yellow Force personnel, all paid a salary by the city government.

Along with expanding community-based waste collection, the government has also focused on improving the collection of waste from temporary dumping sites and its transportation to the new final landfill site at Benowo (this site is discussed further below). This has involved considerable investment. By 2022, the city was operating 49 waste compactors and 23 arm-roll trucks to collect waste from recycling centres (Pemerintah Kota Surabaya 2022). The government budget for the operational cost of waste transport services alone was around Rp 170 billion (US$10.7 million) in 2022 (Aning Rahmawati, Vice Chairwoman for Komisi C DPRD Kota

Source: Images by the author (August 2022).

Surabaya, personal communication, 22 August 2022). Data in 2020 shows that Surabaya's government budget for waste management was Rp 368 billion (US$25 million) or around 4.5 per cent of Surabaya's total budget. The ratio of the waste management budget to the total regional budget in Surabaya is higher than in other cities such as Jakarta and Bandung (Wisanggeni et al. 2022). This investment indicates a strong political commitment of the Surabaya city government to handling the waste problem.

It will be apparent from the above summary that the successful introduction of the participatory model of waste management involved a high degree of government leadership and investment. In the past few years, the Surabaya government has allocated a significant waste management budget that includes funds for waste collection and transportation, Rp 130 billion per year in tipping fees paid to the company that manages the city's main landfill (discussed below), honorariums for members of the Yellow Force, and the costs of implementing the various cleanliness competitions. Waste revenue received by the government is about Rp 47 billion per year, and includes income from waste levies[4] and land rent paid for the landfill. There is thus a large gap between waste expenses and income. The government makes up this shortfall, reflecting a significant investment of political capital by the city's leadership. For such reasons, the community-based and state-driven waste management approaches are two sides of a coin—both require state or government resources to work well.

Private sector involvement: The waste-to-electricity program

In addition to involving citizens and investing its own resources, the city government also engages with the private sector to deal with the waste problem. As well as pursuing partnerships with private actors, such as PT Unilever and Jawa Pos, in promoting and raising awareness about waste issues, the city government also relies on partnerships with the private sector to operate and manage its landfill at Benowo. Since 2012, the Surabaya government has made a private company its leading partner in managing waste dumping. The origins of this go back to the waste crisis of the early 2000s.

---

4   The waste levy is a charge that residents must pay to the government. The amount is adjusted according to the location of residence and the voltage of the electricity service subscribed to by residents. Billing and payments are made simultaneously with water bills, or, for residents who do not subscribe to government water services, through the subdistrict.

In 2001, before the city's new waste management plan was devised, the government closed the Keputih landfill for good and Benowo began to serve as the city's final dumping site (the Keputih site was later turned into a public garden, Taman Harmoni, Harmony Park). Up to 2011, the city managed Benowo as an open dumping site, whereby waste piled up without treatment. This approach created pollution in surrounding areas, repeating the earlier problems experienced at Keputih. Informal waste actors, waste pickers and intermediate waste buyers could freely enter the landfill and carry out their own waste treatment activities, which basically meant collecting and selling recyclable waste under unpleasant conditions. In effect, thousands of waste pickers at the landfill were informal partners of the city government in treating waste.

In 2008, the waste reform team consisting of government officials and academics proposed an advanced solid waste management solution: converting waste into electricity. But such an investment would be costly. To cover the projected budget shortfall, the team proposed a partnership scheme using the build-operate-transfer model. In this model, a private investor covers both the cost of constructing the electricity plant and the development of the required facilities in the landfill (for example, the leachate control system and office buildings), and is responsible for their operation. For its part, the city government provides the land (i.e. the existing landfill). The private operator pays a land rent to the government, while the government pays waste processing fees (a tipping fee) according to the volume of waste that goes to landfill. The energy produced in the process belongs to, and can be sold by, the private investor. At the end of the contract period the building and facilities are transferred to the government and become public assets (Hermana 2021; Kurniawan and Setyobudi 2013; Kurniawan 2016; Manalu and Ma'ruf 2020).

The Surabaya government secured funding from the national government to pursue this proposal. Procurement started in 2009, but no private companies were initially interested. In 2011, following the election of Tri Rismaharini as mayor, the government opened a second procurement attempt; this time, four companies placed bids. The winner was PT Sumber Organik (PT SO), which proposed using gasification technology at the site to turn waste into electricity. PT SO was established in 2009 and according to its company profile that year was based in Tangerang city (on the outskirts of Jakarta). Its main focus was building construction and general trade. By 2016, its company profile stated that the company was domiciled in Surabaya and now focused mainly on waste management, including turning waste into electricity.[5] At the time of bidding, PT SO's proposal

---

5 Company profile of PT Sumber Organik, obtained from the Ministry of Law and Human Rights in 2022.

charged a higher tipping fee than its competitors, yet it was awarded the contract. The procurement team claimed that PT SO won as gasification technology offered the best deal in terms of waste reduction targets and environmental safety (gasification technology is relatively environmentally friendly as it does not release toxic chemicals, such as dioxin, into the atmosphere, unlike incinerator technology). The company took over management of the Benowo landfill in 2012, began to build its waste-to-electricity facility there in 2013 and started to produce electricity in 2015. Despite many challenges, President Joko Widodo eventually inaugurated it as the first such plant in Indonesia in May 2021.

In the intervening period, the Surabaya government had to overcome several obstacles. One of the most difficult concerned the central government's regulatory regime which, when the project was conceived, did not provide a legal basis for the tipping fee or for the sale of electricity generated by the waste-to-energy plant to the state electricity company, PLN. At the start of the cooperation agreement, there were no national-level technical regulations on the nature and structure of private sector partnerships in waste management, including rules on tipping fees. This restricted the Surabaya government's ability to move as quickly as it initially planned, and required a long process of lobbying, and coordination and consultation with the central government. Only in 2018–2019, after the national government issued Presidential Decree 35/2018 on Accelerating the Construction of Waste Processing Installations into Electrical Energy Based on Environmentally Friendly Technology, as a result of the Surabaya city government's urging, did central regulations allow for waste management models such as the one in Surabaya.

Another major problem was that some local politicians and NGO activists expressed suspicion about the procurement process, given that the winner proposed charging the Surabaya government the highest tipping fee. Moreover, one of PT SO's commissioners was closely related to a prominent local politician, Wisnu Sakti Buana, who sat on the procurement committee and was the chief of the city branch of the Indonesian Democratic Party of Struggle (PDI-P). Some observers expressed concern that the procurement process was part of a political negotiation following the 2010 mayoral election (prior to the procurement, Wisnu Sakti Buana was widely seen as the strongest PDI-P candidate for mayor, but the party instead nominated Tri Rismaharini, giving rise to suspicions that the Benowo contract was a kind of compensation for Wisnu). This suspicion prompted the Surabaya Anti-Corruption Community Alliance (Aliansi Masyarakat Anti Korupsi, AMAK) to report the case to Indonesia's Corruption Eradication Commission (Komisi Pemberantasan Korupsi, KPK). The Surabaya police followed up on this report by summoning members of the procurement team, including academics from ITS, for questioning. Later, they dropped the case, citing insufficient evidence (Antara News 2013; Hermana 2021; kanalsatu.com 2013; Kornus 2016; Mu'in 2013).

Since the beginning of the partnership, however, there was a tug of war between the DPRD and the local executive over budgetary allocations for the landfill, especially regarding the tipping fee. For example, in 2013, DPRD members did not approve an additional budget for the tipping fee (the government had initially proposed Rp 57 billion but during budget revisions later in the year increased this to Rp 63 billion; Mu'in 2013: 90). Some of them stated the approval of this expenditure had only involved the DPRD leadership board (Dewan Pimpinan), where Wisnu Sakti Buana was the chief, but required approval of the entire Surabaya DPRD. Members also criticised the magnitude of the increase of the tipping fee and the fact that it exceeded the rate specified in the contract signed with the city government (Mu'in 2013; Muiz 2013; personal communication with a DPRD member and a journalist in August 2022). At the beginning of the cooperation in 2012, the tipping fee paid by the city government was Rp 119,000 per tonne for a minimum daily waste intake of 1,000 tonnes. By the end of the twentieth year, the tipping fee would be Rp 266,668 per tonne (Kurniawan and Setyobudi 2013). Such criticisms continue to this day.

Overall, there have been widespread suspicions in Surabaya that establishing the plant at the landfill involved elements of rent-seeking and patronage. Though no solid evidence has been produced to support this claim, there were widespread criticisms that procurement and budgeting for the landfill lacked transparency. It should be noted that, even if proven, these allegations are far from unique: informal practices such as corruption, rent-seeking and patronage are not only commonplace in waste management systems, they may, in certain situations, play a significant role in supporting innovative policies to address garbage disposal (Strach et al. 2019). Corruption, for instance, contributed to enhancing cities' capacity to manage waste in the United States between 1890 and 1929 (Strach and Sullivan 2022).

In Indonesia, corruption is normally seen as a major source of poor governance in many sectors, including in waste management. For example, in 2018 in Malang city, 41 out of 45 members of the DPRD as well as bureaucrats and the mayor were involved in a case of so-called *korupsi berjamaah* (collective corruption), wherein the executive bribed legislators to support various policies, one of which was for the expansion of the Supit Urang landfill (Aminudin 2018; Rafie 2018). While observers have seen the Surabaya model of reform as succeeding because of the ability of reforming mayors to reduce corruption and rent-seeking (Mustafa 2017;

see also Mustafa, this volume), waste reform in Surabaya perhaps also shows that successful politicians in Indonesia often have to play a double game, following rules and procedures in some areas while bending them in others in order to achieve their goals (Aspinall and Berenschot 2019: 249). This may be a case of 'positive rent seeking outcomes' (Davidson 2010: 1744) in local development.

Conclusion

In this review of Surabaya's experience of waste management over the past two decades, I have shown that Indonesian cities have the potential to embark on far-reaching programs of governance reform. While problems remain with waste management in Surabaya, the city has made enormous progress. Part of what made reform possible were factors specific to Surabaya's history. In particular, the way a major waste crisis around 2000 contributed to a mass movement to remove the mayor helped embed waste reform in the subsequent political reform. These protests became part of public memory in Surabaya, underlining that waste was an essential issue for the city. However, I have also pointed out that post-2002 city governments were able to draw on legacies of a long history of waste collection and transportation, and community organisation, dating back as far as the colonial period.

Two critical variables contributed to Surabaya's success in reforming waste management. The first was strong and ongoing leadership. The Indonesian public commonly associates waste reform in the city with Tri Rismaharini, mayor of Surabaya from 2010 to 2019. During her term, the city received many national and international awards for cleanliness and environmental quality. She mobilised the bureaucracy and citizens to carry out various city cleanliness and greening programs. Risma's predecessor, Bambang DH, was equally important in initiating reform of waste management, and Eri Cahyadi, Risma's successor, is continuing her approach.

The role of leadership commitment in Surabaya's waste reform affirms previous studies stressing the role of leadership in policy reform at the local level (e.g. Grindle 2007; von Luebke 2007, 2009). Generally speaking, leadership of reform or innovation in the public sector is critical, not only in driving development of new policy ideas but also in removing hurdles blocking new initiatives, whether from political opponents or the existing policy context (Leftwich 2010; Sandford 2002; Scholten 2010; Slimane 2012; Smith 2007). Surabaya's experience demonstrates that committed leaders can seek and propose new initiatives on how to deal with the waste problem, ensure the bureaucracy focuses on the issue, mobilise financial, network and other resources to design and implement reform, encourage public awareness and negotiate with the national government to remove regulatory barriers.

However, my review of Surabaya's experience also shows that we need to broaden our understanding of leadership beyond the formal leadership provided by government. Informal leaders, such as neighbourhood leaders and NGO activists, can also contribute a great deal to waste reform (Azizah et al. 2021; West 2008). They can mobilise and supervise citizens' participation at the grassroots level, including by raising awareness about waste issues and providing motivation for behaviour change (Shaughnessy et al. 2017). In Surabaya, environmental cadres (or, as they are now known, Great Surabaya Cadres) have played an important role in leading change such as the introduction of waste separation and composting activities in the city's neighbourhoods.

This brings us to the second important variable in shaping waste reform outcomes in Surabaya: strong citizen participation and civic activism. In general terms, my analysis of waste reform sits well with the argument made by Mustafa (2017 and his chapter in this volume) that civil society played a central role in determining the result of governance reform in Surabaya, not only by supporting successive reformist mayors, but also by voicing demands for reform and providing proposals for change. As a result, one defining feature of waste reform in Surabaya from the start was an emphasis on community-based waste management. This model requires active participation from ordinary citizens. Waste banks, environmental cadres and those who operate the recycling centres play a critical role in waste management in the city. Community groups have responded enthusiastically to the government's clean and green *kampung* competitions. Numerous NGOs in the city have worked with the government and the community to manage waste. Expert and alumni-based networks, especially from ITS and Airlangga University, have also played a key role in designing and implementing waste reform.

For all the success, there are also limits to what Surabaya has achieved, and important points of qualification to reflect on as other cities look to Surabaya for inspiration. Let me mention three such points. The first is that although waste-to-energy solutions might be increasingly important in Indonesian cities, it should be noted that this policy in Surabaya negatively affected informal waste actors, especially waste pickers and intermediate waste buyers, who had previously played important roles in recycling waste. Although I did not emphasise it in this chapter, these groups were pushed aside from the Benowo landfill; considering that such actors are present in all landfills in Indonesian cities, it will be necessary to consider how their interests can be accommodated in future reform elsewhere. Second, the Surabaya case also shows that informal practices, both negative ones such as rent-seeking and more benign ones such as the connections forged via alumni networks, might play a role in driving innovative policies. Future studies of the politics of waste governance reform will need to take informality seriously. Third, despite the achievements of Surabaya's waste reform, it should be emphasised that the Surabaya city government has been unable to reduce waste generation. Most of the reforms it successfully implemented were targeted at managing waste, not preventing it. If this approach continues, and is followed in other Indonesian cities, ever more resources will be needed to tackle the waste problem. Eventually, Indonesia will need to move beyond waste management and learn how to prevent the creation of waste in such vast quantities.

References

Aminudin, Muhammad. 2018. 'TPA Supit Urang: Pemulung mati hingga korupsi massal DPRD Malang [Supit Urang landfill: Mass corruption in Malang DPRD revealed after death of scavengers]'. *detikNews*, 6 September. https://news.detik.com/berita-jawa-timur/d-4199974/tpa-supit-urang-pemulung-mati-hingga-korupsi-massal-dprd-malang

Antara News. 2013. 'AMAK: Pengelolaan sampah Surabaya berpotensi korupsi berjamaah [Anti-Corruption Community Alliance: Surabaya's waste management has the potential for collective corruption]'. Antara News, 29 September. https://jatim.antaranews.com/berita/118660/amak-pengelolaan-sampah-surabaya-berpotensi-korupsi-berjamaah

Aspinall, Edward and Ward Berenschot. 2019. *Democracy for Sale: Elections, Clientelism, and the State in Indonesia*. Cornell University Press. doi.org/10.7591/9781501732997

Azizah, Nur, Azifah Retno Astrina and Nadlirotul Ulfa. 2021. 'Leadership and city waste policy: A case study of waste management in Depok city, West Java province, 2014–2017'. *PCD Journal* 9(2): 65–82. https://journal.ugm.ac.id/v3/PCD/article/view/3386/1189

BBC News Indonesia. 2023. ' "Api masih terus membara" di TPA Sarimukti, ratusan warga menderita ISPA dan iritasi mata ['Fire still burns' at the Sarimukti landfill, hundreds of residents suffer from ISPA and eye irritation]'. BBC News Indonesia, 27 August. www.bbc.com/indonesia/articles/c2l8vg5wpxno

BPS (Badan Pusat Statistik, Statistics Indonesia). 2018. *Statistik Lingkungan Hidup Indonesia 2018* [Environmental statistics Indonesia 2018]. BPS.

BPS (Badan Pusat Statistik, Statistics Indonesia) Kota Surabaya. 2020. *Kota Surabaya dalam Angka 2020* [Surabaya city in numbers 2020]. BPS Kota Surabaya.

Bunnell, Tim, Michelle Ann Miller, Nicholas A. Phelps and John Taylor. 2013. 'Urban development in a decentralized Indonesia: Two success stories?' *Pacific Affairs* 86(4): 857–76. doi.org/10.5509/2013864857

Chandra, Rizki and Sidik Jatmika. 2022. 'Unilever Surabaya corporate social responsibility (CSR) policy in maintaining environmental sustainability in Surabaya in 2014–2020'. In *Proceedings of the International Conference on Public Organization (ICONPO 2021). Digital Governance and Crisis Management in COVID-19: A Call for Action*. Atlantis Press. www.atlantis-press.com/proceedings/iconpo-21

Christy, Firdhy Esterina. 2020. 'Urbanisasi Indonesia 10 tahun terakhir [Indonesia's urbanisation in the past 10 years]'. *Tempo*, 6 July. https://data.tempo.co/data/805/urbanisasi-indonesia-10-tahun-terakhir

Colombijn, Freek. 2016. '"I am a singer": A conversation with Johan Silas, architect and urban planner in Surabaya, Indonesia'. *Indonesia* 102: 7–30. doi.org/10.5728/indonesia.102.0007

Concord Consulting. 2015. 'No time to waste: Indonesia's garbage problem'. *INA Magazine*, 9 July.

Davidson, Jamie S. 2010. 'How to harness the positive potential of KKN: Explaining variation in the private sector provision of public goods in Indonesia'. *Journal of Development Studies* 46(10): 1729–48. doi.org/10.1080/00220388.2010.492866

Dethier, Jean-Jacques. 2017. 'Trash, cities, and politics: Urban environmental problems in Indonesia'. *Indonesia* (103): 73–90. doi.org/10.5728/indonesia.103.0073

detikJogja. 2023. 'Jogja darurat sampah buntut penutupan TPA Piyungan [Jogja waste emergency in aftermath of Piyungan landfill closure]'. *detikJogja*, 30 July. www.detik.com/jogja/berita/d-6849285/jogja-darurat-sampah-buntut-penutupan-tpa-piyungan

Dick, Howard W. 2002. *Surabaya, City of Work: A Socioeconomic History, 1900–2000*. Ohio University Press.

EBTKE (Direktorat Jenderal Energi Baru, Terbarukan dan Konservasi Energi; Directorate General of New, Renewable Energy and Energy Conservation). 2021. 'Presiden Jokowi resmikan instalasi PSEL pertama Indonesia [President Joko Widodo inaugurates Indonesia's first PSEL installation]'. Ministry of Energy and Mineral Resources, 7 May. https://ebtke.esdm.go.id/post/2021/05/07/2862/presiden.jokowi.resmikan.instalasi.psel.pertama.indonesialangen

Faizal, Achmad. 2016. 'Di Surabaya, pendapatan petugas kebersihan bisa lebih dari Rp 6 juta [In Surabaya, a cleaner's income can be more than Rp 6 million]'. *Kompas.com*, 25 September. https://regional.kompas.com/read/xml/2016/09/25/16065521/di.surabaya.pendapatan.petugas.kebersihan.bisa.lebih.dari.rp.6.juta

Fallahnda, Balqis. 2023. 'Kenapa TPA Piyungan tutup dan apa solusi sampah warga Jogja? [Why is the Piyungan landfill closed and what is the solution for the waste of Jogja residents?]' *tirto.id*, 24 July. https://tirto.id/kenapa-tpa-piyungan-tutup-dan-apa-solusi-sampah-warga-jogja-gNhw

Feliciani, Fitria Aurora. 2023. 'Path leading to urban sustainability: Reflections from solid waste management in Surabaya'. In *Routledge Handbook of Urban Indonesia*, edited by Sonia Roitman and Deden Rukmana, 352–66. Routledge. doi.org/10.4324/9781003318170-30

Finaka, Andrean W. 2020. 'Demografi dan urbanisasi Indonesia 2010–2045 [Indonesia's demographics and urbanisation, 2010–2045]'. Indonesia Baik. https://indonesiabaik.id/infografis/demografi-dan-urbanisasi-indonesia-2010-2045

Gamaralalage, Premakumara Jagath Dickella. 2012. 'Kitakyushu city's international cooperation for organic waste management in Surabaya city, Indonesia and its replication in Asian cities'. Institute for Global Environmental Studies, Kitakyushu. www.iges.or.jp/en/pub/kitakyushu-citys-international-cooperation/bi-enja-zz

Gervasi, Manuela. 2011. 'Surabaya, Indonesia: Green and clean initiative'. Inclusive Cities Observatory. www.uclg-cisdp.org/sites/default/files/Surabaya_2010_en_final.pdf

Gilby, Simon, Matthew Hengesbaugh, Premakumara Gamaralalage, Kazunobu Onogawa, Eddy S. Soedjono and Nurina Fitriani. 2017. 'Planning and implementation of integrated solid waste management strategies at local level: The case of Surabaya city'. IGES Centre Collaborating with UNEP on Environmental Technologies (CCET). https://ccet.jp/publications/planning-and-implementation-integrated-solid-waste-management-strategies-local-level-0

Grindle, Merilee S. 2007. 'Local governments that perform well: Four explanations'. In *Decentralizing Governance: Emerging Concepts and Practices*, edited by G. Shabbir Cheema and Dennis A. Rondinelli, 56–74. Brookings Institution Press. www.jstor.org/stable/10.7864/j.ctt1261v1

Hakim, Abdul. 2021. 'Sekitar 23 ribu kader lingkungan di Surabaya edukasi cara pemanfaatan sampah [Around 23,000 environmental cadres in Surabaya are being educated on how to use waste]'. Antara News, 15 September. https://jatim.antaranews.com/berita/525165/sekitar-23-ribu-kader-lingkungan-di-surabaya-edukasi-cara-pemanfaatan-sampah

Henry. 2023. 'Dana pengelolaan sampah cuma 0,5 persen dari total APBD, KLHK ajak produsen kelola sampah secara mandiri [Waste management funds only 0.5 per cent of local budget, Ministry of Environment and Forestry invites producers to manage waste independently]'. *liputan6.com*, 16 June. www.liputan6.com/lifestyle/read/5320727/dana-pengelolaan-sampah-cuma-05-persen-dari-total-apbd-klhk-ajak-produsen-kelola-sampah-secara-mandiri

Hermana, Joni. 2021. 'PIB 6 | Kerjasama pemerintah dan BU tempat pembuangan akhir Benowo [Collaboration between the government and BU Benowo landfill site]'. ITS Professor Talks, YouTube, 2 June. www.youtube.com/watch?v=fUQ21TFvT1U

Jamaludin, Kemal, Dewie Tri Wijayati and Andre Dwijanto Witjaksono. 2023. 'Effectiveness of waste bank program to reduce solid waste into landfill in Surabaya city'. *International Journal of Multicultural and Multireligious Understanding* 10(4): 48–63. https://ijmmu.com/index.php/ijmmu/article/viewFile/4504/3903

kanalsatu.com. 2013. 'Kejari Perak bidik tipping fee pengelolaan sampah di TPA Benowo [Kejari Perak targets tipping fee for waste management at Benowo landfill]'. kanalsatu.com, 10 November. http://kanalsatu.com/id/post/12402/kejari-perak-bidik-tipping-fee-pengelolaan-sampah-di-tpa-benowo-

Kemenko Bidang Ekonomi [Ministry for Economic Affairs]. 2015. *Kajian Kebijakan dan Strategi Nasional Percepatan Pengelolaan Persampahan* [Study of national policies and strategies to accelerate waste management]. Kementerian Koordinator Bidang Perekonomian Republik Indonesia. www.ekon.go.id/

source/publikasi/Kajian%20Kebijakan%20dan%20Strategi%20Nasional%20 Percepatan%20Pengelolaan%20Persampahan.pdf

Kornus. 2016. 'Laporan LPAI Jatim ke KPK jalan ditempat, AMAK desak KPK usut kerjasama pengelolaan sampah TPA Benowo [East Java LPAI's report to the Corruption Eradication Committee is in, AMAK urges the KPK to investigate cooperation in waste management at Benowo landfill]'. Media Koran Nusantara, 5 November. https://mediakorannusantara.com/laporan-lpai-jatim-ke-kpk-jalan-ditempat-amak-desak-kpk-usut-kerjasama-pengelolaan-sampah-tpa-benowo/

Kurniawan, Faizal and Shintarini Kristine Setyobudi. 2013. 'Klausula tipping fee dalam kontrak kerjasama pemerintah dengan swasta (public-private partnership) pengelolaan persampahan [Tipping fee clause in public-private partnership waste management contract]'. *ADIL: Jurnal Hukum* 4(1): 24–48. doi.org/10.33476/ajl.v4i1.27

Kurniawan, Hendrysan Krisna. 2016. 'Studi deskriptif strategi public private partnership pengelolaan sampah di TPA Benowo Kota Surabaya [Descriptive study of public-private partnership strategies for waste management at Benowo landfill, Surabaya city]'. *Jurnal Kebijakan dan Manajemen Publik* 4(2): 210–19. www.google.com/url?sa=t&rct=j&q=&esrc=s&source=web&cd=&ved=2ahUKEwidm57zv86AAxWLqVYBHVgGBe4QFnoECBgQAQ&url=https%3A%2F%2Fjournal.unair.ac.id%2Fdownload-fullpapers-kmp58b6f8df08full.pdf&usg=AOvVaw1CGZ-1JdNXBtzN7VCes--a&opi=89978449

Leftwich, Adrian. 2010. 'Beyond institutions: Rethinking the role of leaders, elites and coalitions in the institutional formation of developmental states and strategies'. *Forum for Development Studies* 37(1): 93–111. doi.org/10.1080/08039410903558327

Liputan6. 2001. 'Jalan masuk TPA Keputih ditutup warga [Residents close entrance to Keputih landfill]'. *liputan6.com*, 25 October. www.liputan6.com/news/read/22472/jalan-masuk-tpa-keputih-ditutup-warga

Liputan6. 2002. 'Wali Kota Surabaya Sunarto dipecat [Surabaya Mayor Sunarto fired]'. *liputan6.com*, 16 January. www.liputan6.com/news/read/27280/wali-kota-surabaya-sunarto-dipecat

Manalu, Gyovani and Muhammad Farid Ma'ruf. 2020. 'Kerjasama pemerintah Kota Surabaya dan PT Sumber Organik pada program pembangkit listrik berbasis sampah di TPA Benowo Kota Surabaya [Collaboration between Surabaya city government and PT Organic Sources in the waste-based electricity generation program at Benowo landfill, Surabaya city]'. *Publika: Jurnal Ilmu Administrasi Negara* 8(20): 10. https://ejournal.unesa.ac.id/index.php/publika/article/view/33385/29915

Marijan, Kacung. 2008. 'The 1999 decentralization policy, local politics, and local capacity of the port city of Surabaya'. In *Port Cities in Asia and Europe*, edited by Arndt Graf and Chua Beng Huat, 86–104. Routledge. doi.org/10.4324/9780203884515-11

Maulidiya, Pipit. 2019. '8 kali berturut-turut terima Adipura, Kota Surabaya resmi raih penghargaan tertinggi Adipura Kencana [Surabaya city wins Adipura award 8 times in a row]'. *Tribun Jatim*, 14 January. https://jatim.tribunnews.com/2019/01/14/8-kali-berturut-turut-terima-adipura-kota-surabaya-resmi-raih-penghargaan-tertinggi-adipura-kencana

Mu'in, Fathul. 2013. 'Mengurai bau "busuk" penganggaran TPA Benowo Surabaya [Unravelling the 'rotten' smell of Surabaya's Benowo landfill budget]'. In *Menelisik Korupsi Anggaran Publik 2013: Kumpulan Liputan Isu Anggaran* [Examining public budget corruption 2013: Coverage of budget issues], edited by Arfi Bambani. AJI Indonesia.

Muiz, Ahmad Amru. 2013. 'Investor: Pengelolaan sampah TPA Benowo tetap jalan [Investor: Benowo landfill waste management continues]'. Surya.co.id, 2 October. https://surabaya.tribunnews.com/2013/10/02/investor-pengelolaan-sampah-tpa-benowo-tetap-jalan

Mustafa, Mochamad. 2017. 'Democratic decentralisation and good governance: The political economy of procurement reform in decentralised Indonesia'. PhD thesis. University of Adelaide. https://hdl.handle.net/2440/117256

Pemerintah Kota Surabaya. 2022. 'Atasi bau sampah, DLH Surabaya tambah armada truk compactor [To overcome the smell of rubbish, DLH Surabaya has added a fleet of compactor trucks]'. Surabaya City Government, 28 June. www.surabaya.go.id/id/berita/67667/atasi-bau-sampah-dlh-surabaya-tambah-armada-truk-compactor

Pemerintah Kota Surabaya. 2023. 'Surabaya tujuh kali raih penghargaan Adipura Kencana dari KLHK RI, Wali Kota Eri Cahyadi: Ini apresiasi bagi warga! [Surabaya wins Adipura Kencana award seven times from the Indonesian Ministry of Environment and Forestry, Mayor Eri Cahyadi: This is appreciation for residents!]'. Surabaya City Government, 1 March. www.surabaya.go.id/id/berita/72836/surabaya-tujuh-kali-raih-penghargaan-adipura-kencana-dari-klhk-ri-wali-kota-eri-cahyadi-ini-apresiasi-bagi-wargahttps://www.surabaya.go.id/

Pemkot Surabaya. 2005. *Rencana Pembangunan Jangka Panjang Daerah Kota Surabaya 2005–2025* [Surabaya city regional long-term development plan 2005–2025]. Surabaya City Government. https://bappeko.surabaya.go.id/images/File%20Upload/RPJPD-2005-2025.pdf

Pemkot Surabaya. 2021. *Rancangan Akhir Rencana Pembangunan Jangka Menengah Daerah (RPJMD) Kota Surabaya Tahun 2021–2026* [Surabaya city regional medium term development plan, final draft, 2021–2026]. Surabaya City Government.

Prasetiyo, Wibowo Heru, K.R. Kamarudin and J.A. Dewantara. 2019. 'Surabaya green and clean: Protecting urban environment through civic engagement community'. *Journal of Human Behavior in the Social Environment* 29(8): 997–1014. doi.org/10.1080/10911359.2019.1642821

Premakumara, D.G.J., M. Abe and T. Maeda. 2011. 'Reducing municipal waste through promoting integrated sustainable waste management (ISWM) practices in Surabaya city, Indonesia'. *WIT Transactions on Ecology and the Environment* 144: 457–68. doi.org/10.2495/ECO110401

Puspitasari, Dela Eka. 2016. 'Surabaya sebagai kota Adipura pada masa kepemimpinan Poernomo Kasidi pada tahun 1984–1994 [Surabaya as an Adipura city during Poernomo Kasidi's leadership, 1984–1994]'. *Avatara* 4(2). https://ejournal.unesa.ac.id/index.php/avatara/article/view/14768

Rafie, Barratut Taqiyyah. 2018. 'Begini cerita lengkap soal korupsi berjamaah 41 anggota DPRD Malang [Corruption of 41 members of the Malang DPRD]'. kontan.co.id, 7 September. https://nasional.kontan.co.id/news/begini-cerita-lengkap-soal-korupsi-berjamaah-41-anggota-dprd-malang

Razak, Abdul Hamied. 2020. '1.000 ton sampah di Sleman tak terangkut imbas TPA Piyungan tutup [1,000 tons of garbage in Sleman not transported due to closure of Piyungan landfill]'. *Harianjogja.com*, 12 April. https://jogjapolitan.harianjogja.com/read/2020/04/12/512/1036595/1.000-ton-sampah-di-sleman-tak-terangkut-imbas-tpa-piyungan-tutup

Redaksi Asiatoday. 2021. 'Investasi Rp704,4 miliar, PLTSa pertama di Indonesia resmi beroperasi [First PLTSa in Indonesia officially in operation, with investment of Rp 704.4 billion]'. *AsiaToday.id*, 8 May. https://asiatoday.id/read/investasi-rp7044-miliar-pltsa-pertama-di-indonesia-resmi-beroperasi

Sandford, Borins. 2002. 'Leadership and innovation in the public sector'. *Leadership & Organization Development Journal* 23(8): 467–76. doi.org/10.1108/01437730210449357

Scholten, Peter. 2010. 'Leadership in policy innovation: A conceptual map'. *Nature and Culture* 5(1): 31–48. doi.org/10.3167/nc.2010.050103

Shaughnessy, Brooke A., Darren C. Treadway, Jacob W. Breland and Pamela L. Perrewé. 2017. 'Informal leadership status and individual performance: The roles of political skill and political will'. *Journal of Leadership & Organizational Studies* 24(1): 83–94. doi.org/10.1177/1548051816657983

Slimane, Melouki. 2012. 'Role and relationship between leadership and sustainable development to release social, human, and cultural dimension'. *Procedia – Social and Behavioral Sciences* 41: 92–99. doi.org/10.1016/j.sbspro.2012.04.013

Smith, D.J. 2007. 'The politics of innovation: Why innovations need a godfather'. *Technovation* 27(3): 95–104. doi.org/10.1016/j.technovation.2006.05.001

Strach, Patricia, Kathleen Sullivan and Elizabeth Pérez-Chiqués. 2019. 'The garbage problem: Corruption, innovation, and capacity in four American cities, 1890–1940'. *Studies in American Political Development* 33(2): 1–25. doi.org/10.1017/S0898588X19000087

Strach, Patricia and Kathleen S. Sullivan. 2022. *The Politics of Trash: How Governments Used Corruption to Clean Cities, 1890–1929*. Cornell University Press.

Tahir, Akino, Mitsuo Yoshida and Sachihiko Harashina. 2014. 'Analyzing community-based waste management in Surabaya: Factors affecting successful replication'. In *The 25th Conference on Environmental Information Science 2011*, 131–36. www.jstage.jst.go.jp/article/ceispapers/ceis25/0/ceis25_131/_pdf/-char/en

UNDESA (United Nations Department of Economic and Social Affairs). 2011. 'Chair's summary: Second meeting of the Regional 3R Forum in Asia: "3Rs for green economy and sound material-cycle society"'. Background paper No. 17. CSD19/2011/BP17. UNDESA. www.un.org/esa/dsd/resources/res_pdfs/csd-19/BackgroundPaper17KualaLumpur.pdf

von Luebke, Christian. 2007. 'Local leadership in transition: Explaining variation in Indonesian subnational government'. PhD thesis. Australian National University, Canberra. doi.org/10.25911/5d78d9d4509c1

von Luebke, Christian. 2009. 'The political economy of local governance: Findings from an Indonesian field study'. *Bulletin of Indonesian Economic Studies* 45(2): 201–30. doi.org/10.1080/00074910903040310

Warmadewanthi and Millati Haqq. 2019. 'Implementation of waste banks for reduction of solid waste in South Surabaya'. *MATEC Web of Conferences* 276: 06021. doi.org/10.1051/matecconf/201927606021

West, David. 2008. 'Informal public leadership: The case of social movements'. In *Public Leadership: Perspectives and Practices*, edited by Paul 't Hart and John Uhr, 133–44. ANU E Press. doi.org/10.22459/PL.11.2008.11

Wisanggeni, Satrio Pangarso, M. Puteri Rosalina and Albertus Krisna. 2022. 'Anggaran rendah, sampah melimpah [Low budget, abundant garbage]'. *Kompas.id*, 20 May. www.kompas.id/baca/desk/2022/05/19/anggaran-rendah-sampah-melimpahhttps://www.kompas.id/baca/des

11 Traffic congestion in urban Indonesia: What can we learn from the Jakarta metropolitan area?

Muhammad Halley Yudhistira and Andhika Putra Pratama

One of the classic problems that arises as a country urbanises is traffic congestion. As more and more people pack into urban areas, and especially as urban sprawl generates large commuter zones around urban cores, road usage often outstrips capacity. While traffic jams are a familiar problem for people in all of Indonesia's rapidly growing urban areas, they are particularly a challenge for people in the Greater Jakarta metropolitan area, where urban sprawl is most extensive.

The Jakarta metropolitan area is the largest metropolitan area in Indonesia, both in terms of land size and economic magnitude. It consists of an urban agglomeration that stretches over all of one province (Jakarta) and parts of two others (Banten and West Java), and includes Tangerang city, South Tangerang city, Tangerang district, Depok, Bogor city, Bekasi city, Bogor district and Bekasi district, with a total area of about 6,700 km^2 (BPS 2023). It also accounts for approximately 22.6 per cent of the national urban population, around 10 per cent of the national population and 23.6 per cent of national gross domestic product (GDP) (Roberts et al. 2019: 57; Yudhistira, Indriyani et al. 2019). The metropolitan area's per capita regional GDP is almost twice that of Indonesia's per capita GDP (BPS 2023). Over recent years, the demographic and economic weight of the Jakarta metropolitan area has been driven especially by the areas located outside its core. This urban periphery around Jakarta experienced the highest growth in urban population of any type of urban area in Indonesia between 2004 and 2016, with an annual population growth rate of 4.8 per cent per year; in contrast, the Jakarta core grew at only 1.4 per cent per year (Roberts et al. 2019: 63). While Jakarta's core has been relatively stable, urban settlements in Jakarta's periphery grew at 9.1 per cent per year between 2000 and 2014 (ibid.: 64), indicating considerable conversion of agricultural and vacant land into built-up areas.

Growth of this massive urban agglomeration has generated a major problem with road traffic congestion. According to the 2023 edition of the TomTom Traffic Index, Jakarta is the ninth most congested city in Asia.[1] Among Southeast Asian countries, it is second only to Manila, the capital of the Philippines. The statistics were even worse before the pandemic, when in 2019 Jakarta was the sixth most congested city in Asia, the tenth most congested in the world, and second only to Bengaluru among megacities with more than 8 million inhabitants (TomTom Traffic Index 2019). According to the 2022 data, it took an average of 22 minutes and 40 seconds to travel ten kilometres in the city centre of Jakarta, equivalent to an average speed of only 22 kilometres per hour (TomTom Traffic Index 2023).

In this chapter, we discuss urban transport development and policy in Indonesia, focusing on the Jakarta metropolitan area. Drawing on publicly available data and a review of several empirical studies, we review transport infrastructure development and policies and explain transport behaviour in the Greater Jakarta region over the past two decades. We show that lack of investment in transport supply and the rise of motorcycle use are the main drivers of congestion in the Jakarta metropolitan area. We also pick out key lessons and recommend what can be done to improve mobility in the region. We further propose a new institution—a metropolitan authority—that might help policymakers tackle the difficult coordination and planning issues that arise in traffic planning (and other policy areas) in the Jakarta region due to the need to coordinate between the Jakarta provincial government and the eight other districts located adjacent to Jakarta. Though we focus on the Jakarta region as the site of the most extreme traffic congestion in the country, we also acknowledge that traffic congestion is an increasingly serious problem in many parts of urban Indonesia, and will require new policy thinking across the country.

This chapter starts by identifying the root causes of traffic congestion in Indonesia, especially Jakarta, examining both demand and supply problems, and analysing Jakarta's performance compared to other

---

1 www.tomtom.com/traffic-index/ranking, viewed April 2024.

metropolitan areas worldwide. The next section describes government efforts to reduce congestion, focusing on highways, bus services and railways. A third section discusses demand management policies and notes their limitations. We then introduce our proposed solutions to Jakarta's traffic woes, focusing on a proposed Jakarta Metropolitan Authority but also looking at investment options. We conclude by stressing that the goal for Jakarta should not be complete eradication of congestion, but the enabling of greater mobility for Jakarta residents.

Causes of traffic congestion in the Jakarta metropolitan area

Traffic congestion occurs as a result of a demand–supply imbalance in the transportation network (Tang and Hu 2019). Specifically, road congestion occurs when road demand from vehicles exceeds the road capacity in a particular area over a certain period. In Jakarta, congestion is far more severe than in other metropolitan areas in Indonesia. In the Greater Jakarta area, approximately 23 per cent of commuters spend more than 90 minutes commuting one way between home and office, while less than 5 per cent do so in other metropolitan areas like Surabaya, Bandung and Medan (Figure 11.1). In examining the causes of the Jakarta metropolitan area's extreme traffic congestion, we must examine both demand and supply factors.

Figure 11.1 Time spent commuting one way per work day (% of commuters)

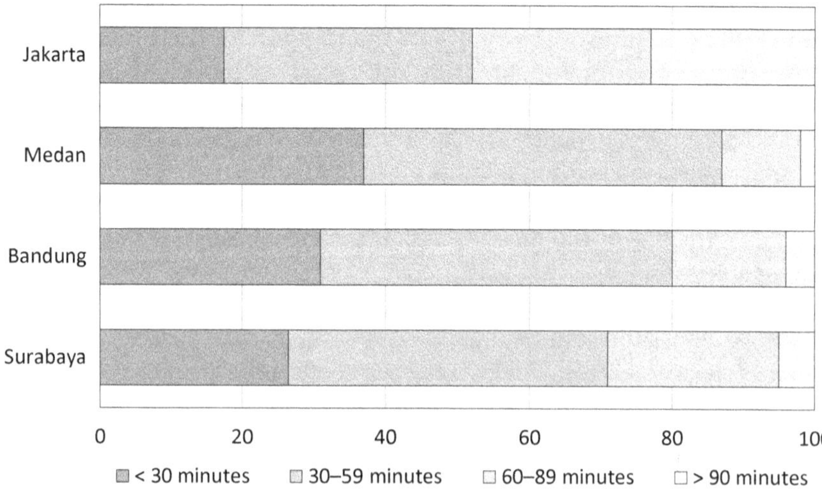

Source: BPS (2019).

Demand side

On the demand side, the rapid growth of the wider Jakarta urban area has resulted from an increase in population and growing average income of individuals working in the city. Both factors place greater demand on the region's roads with the second factor being as important as the first: when individuals have higher wealth they are induced to solve their own mobility problems by buying private motorised vehicles, often starting with motorcycles and later moving on to cars.

In contemporary Indonesia, the cost of owning and using a motorcycle is low due to relatively easy access to credit and the low price of subsidised gasoline, and has further been encouraged by programs of road construction (Hook and Replogle 1996; Savatic 2016). In 2002, 37 per cent of households in the Jakarta metropolitan area owned at least one motorcycle; by 2010 the number had increased significantly to 75.8 per cent (BPS 2010). According to government records, in 2018 over 18 million private cars and motorcycles were registered and by 2022 there were over 21 million registered private vehicles in Jakarta (BPS 2022b). This situation has caused the number of private vehicles, especially motorcycles, to multiply on Indonesia's roads, exacerbating congestion especially within the Greater Jakarta region.

The changing usage patterns of different modes of transport over time is known as 'modal shift'. According to the Japan International Cooperation Agency (JICA 2019), in 2002 only 36.6 per cent of Jakarta metropolitan area inhabitants used private motorised vehicles to commute (14.6 per cent used cars and 22 per cent used motorcycles) (Figure 11.2). But the proportion using motorcycles grew sharply in subsequent years, increasing to 58.7 per cent in 2010 and 75.8 per cent in 2018. Private car use decreased slightly in 2010 but overall remained at similar levels from 2002 to 2018. These numbers are consistent with the Jabodetabek[2] Commuter Survey conducted by the National Statistics Agency (Badan Pusat Statistik, BPS), which found an increase in motorcycle use from 57.5 per cent to 62.7 per cent of commuters surveyed between 2014 and 2019 (BPS 2019).

The BPS Jabodetabek Commuter Survey also covers average commuting time, distance and cost. The data show that average commuting time and distance decreased by 11.6 per cent and 5.2 per cent respectively between 2014 and 2019. Plausible explanations for these decreases might include the rise of motorcycles and of individuals avoiding commuting by renting

---

2 Jabodetabek is an acronym given to Jakarta and the surrounding metropolitan area, including Bogor, Depok, Tangerang and Bekasi.

Figure 11.2 Modal shift of Jakarta metropolitan area commuters, 2002–2018 (%)

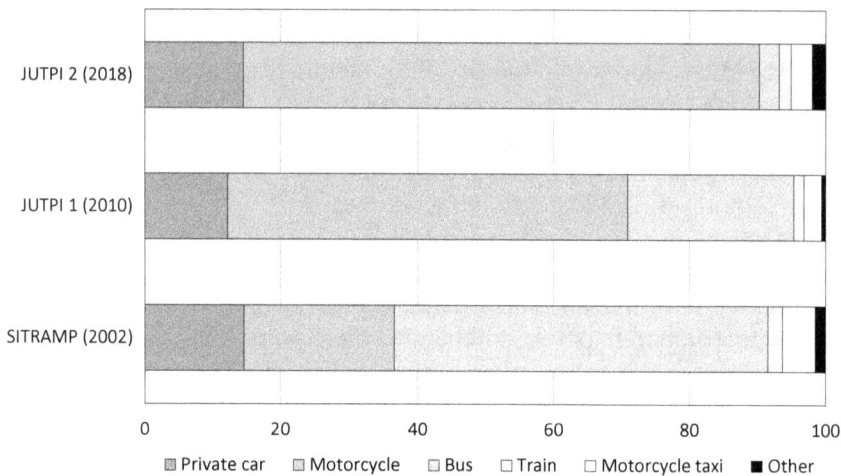

Note: JUTPI = Jabodetabek Urban Transportation Policy Integration Project; Jabodetabek = Jakarta and the surrounding metropolitan area, including Bogor, Depok, Tangerang and Bekasi; SITRAMP = Study on the Integrated Transportation Master Plan for Jabodetabek.
Source: JICA (2019).

small living spaces near their offices for weekdays, while maintaining houses in the suburbs. Conversely, average travel costs rose by 21.6 per cent. Fluctuation of petrol prices is believed to be a major cause (Sofiyandi and Siregar 2020: 4), again pointing to the significant share of private motorised vehicles in the commuter mix.

The increase in the proportion of road users relying on motorcycles as their primary mode of transport has seen a dramatic decline in bus usage. Bus providers in Jakarta are divided into two primary services: TransJakarta and private providers. TransJakarta is a system of public buses using dedicated lanes managed by a local government-owned enterprise. It operated a fleet of more than 4,400 vehicles in 2022, servicing more than 145 million passengers per year. The number of users of the TransJakarta service increased slightly from 2.46 per cent in 2014 to 3.43 per cent of Jakarta metropolitan area commuters in 2019 (BPS 2014, 2019). The steep fall in bus usage over the past two decades—Figure 11.2 shows a fall from 55 per cent of commuters using buses in 2002 to just 2.9 per cent in 2018—is thus driven by a virtual collapse in the use of private bus providers. This collapse no doubt has several causes, including the unreliable frequency of many private services, and the often uncomfortable nature of the buses they provide, but it also reflects the rise of alternatives, notably motorcycles. At the same time, train services still make a relatively modest contribution to transport in Greater Jakarta, around 9.2 per cent of total modal share (BPS 2019).

In the past few years, ride-hailing services have also grown as a share of the commuting market in urban areas, especially in the Jakarta metropolitan area. In Indonesia, ride-hailing services mostly consist of motorcycle services offered by companies such as Gojek and Grab. Based on the 2019 BPS commuting survey, 4.2 per cent of the population use online ride-hailing services for commuting to and from work within the Jakarta metropolitan area (BPS 2019). Ride-hailing now services many of the commuters who formerly used non-TransJakarta buses, especially female commuters, for both safety and comfort reasons (Sofiyandi and Siregar 2020: 6). Online ride-hailing services have a reputation as being safe and fast, especially among female commuters, contributing to their success.

In recent years, some commentators have believed that the rise of ride-hailing services will be an alternative solution to traffic congestion in the Jakarta metropolitan area (Suatmadi et al. 2019). However, another study (Hall et al. 2018) has suggested that their contribution to solving Jakarta's travel problems will be contingent on whether ride-hailing services complement or substitute for public transit. If they move people out of public transport such as TransJakarta buses or trains, they will likely worsen congestion. Even when assuming that they complement public transit, such as by providing a means for commuters to get to bus stops or train stations from their homes, the increased road-use demand generated by these services and the flooding of streets with ride-hailing service drivers looking for fares could ultimately outstrip the benefits of higher ridership in public transit.

Supply side

On the supply side, a major problem is that the Jakarta government was late and slow in expanding its public-owned mass transport infrastructure, so this infrastructure did not keep pace with the population growth of the Greater Jakarta region. One of the main reasons is the simple fact that it requires large investment to build the infrastructure required. At the same time, existing privately owned public transport providers did not have appropriate incentives to improve the quality and frequency of the services they offered. Privately owned public transport such as *angkot* (small vans) and public buses operated without competition, as if they were a natural monopoly on their routes, and without strong quality control. Thus they did not have incentives to improve their less-than-decent services, generating a vicious circle: with low investment, demand decreased, creating further pressure not to invest in better fleets. The result was a lack of transport supply within the greater metropolitan area.

Compared to other large metropolitan areas across the world (Table 11.1), Greater Jakarta has relatively weak public transport infrastructure, despite having a large population of more than 31 million people, pointing towards high levels of ownership of and dependence on private vehicles. In 2021, the Greater Jakarta area had only 418.5 kilometres of heavy rail tracks, 15.7 kilometres of mass rapid transit (MRT) tracks and around 48 kilometres of light rail transit (LRT) tracks (as discussed below, the MRT and LRT networks are relatively recent additions to Jakarta's transport network). These tracks are supported by 80 heavy rail stations, 13 MRT stations and 24 LRT stations. Total track length is comparable to that in the Greater London area, which is about seven times smaller in area than the Jakarta metropolitan area. The low number of stations is also striking: Singapore, which covers a much smaller area and has about half the rail length of Greater Jakarta, has one-and-a-half times the number of railway stations of Jakarta metropolitan area. Public transport daily ridership statistics in Jakarta are also comparatively low. Railway transport in the Jakarta metropolitan area serves a little under 1 million people a day; Singapore, London and New York City have three to six times as many daily public railway users. The Greater Tokyo area reports a massive 41.4 million daily rides. Yet the Jakarta metropolitan area's population is comparable to that of Tokyo, and substantially higher than those of Singapore, London and New York.

These differences are perhaps understandable due to historical differences. Indonesia's railway development was held back during the unstable early years of Indonesia's independence (see Kusno, this volume). By contrast, the Tokyo and London railway systems were mostly built by the 1930s and New York City's elevated railway system was consolidated by the end of the 1800s. In the Jakarta region, railway development proceeded well into the twentieth and even the twenty-first century; there has even been expansion since the 2010s, led by Ignasius Jonan (former chief executive officer of KAI, the state-owned Indonesian Railways corporation 2009–2014 and Minister of Transportation 2014–2016). During this era, new stations such as Raskasbitung, Nambo and Cikarang have finally reached deeper into the suburbs. Even so, the number of stations is still small, making the interval between stations significant and reducing flexibility for passengers.

The picture is more mixed when we compare Jakarta to other developing Southeast Asian megacities. It lags behind Bangkok, though in recent times both Jakarta and Bangkok have opened new MRT lines and plan to build more. However, despite its significantly lower population, ridership rates in Bangkok are much higher than in metropolitan Jakarta, indicating a much greater coverage of major population centres by the

Table 11.1 Metropolitan rail services: Major world cities

Metro area indicators	Jakarta Metropolitan Area	Singapore	Greater Tokyo	New York City	Greater London	Bangkok Metropolitan Region	Metro Manila
Area	11,037 km²	734 km²	13,555 km²	12,000 km²	1,569 km²	7,776 km²	8,099 km²
Population	31 million	5.6 million	32 million	20 million	8.9 million	11 million	28 million
Railway length (kilometres)	418.5 (heavy rail) 15.7 (MRT) 48 (LRT)	216.5 (MRT) 28.8 (LRT)	2,459	1,115	402	169	114
Number of stations	80 (heavy rail) 13 (MRT) 24 (LRT)	134 (MRT) 41 (LRT)	1,510	493	272 (tube) 375 (trains) including: 45 (light railway) 39 (tram) 18 (heavy rail) 113 (overground)	123	82
Ridership (people per day)	1 million	3.6 million	41.4 million	5.5 million	4.5 million	1.18 million	600,000
Ridership as proportion of metro population	3%	64%	129%	28%	51%	11%	2%
Roads length (kilometres)	11,500	3,500	25,000	13,000	14,000	4,700	3,000 (Greater Manila only)

Note: MRT = mass rapid transit, LRT = light rail transit.

Source: ADB (2005), BPS (2022a), Ho (2013), KAI (2021), Ministry of Transport Thailand (2020), New York City MTA (2023), Siridhara (2021), Tokyo Metropolitan Government (2020), Transport for London (2017).

Bangkok MRT network. However, ridership in Jakarta is higher than that in Metro Manila, which is notorious for having an overcrowded and uncomfortable service.

Government efforts to reduce congestion

To manage the pressing issue of congestion in Jakarta, successive governments in Jakarta have tried to increase supply by investing in various forms of transport infrastructure and, to a more limited extent, to control demand. Generally speaking, under Suharto's New Order government, the main focus was on developing private travel and, especially, investing in highways and tollways, which exacerbated problems of urban sprawl. In the post–New Order period, governments have increasingly turned to public transport. We discuss the main policy responses in terms of roads, buses and rail below.

The effort to improve public transport in Jakarta has occurred slowly, and involved multiple governors and multiple central government leaders. For example, in the case of MRT Jakarta, a development plan was first proposed in 1985, but definite action happened only after President Yudhoyono declared it a national strategic project in 2005. From then, the development was continued by Governor Fauzi Bowo (2007–2012) and Joko Widodo (2012–2014). The TransJakarta network was initiated by Governor Sutiyoso in 2001.

Highway networks

A major component of Greater Jakarta's transport system since the Suharto period has been highways and toll roads. Highways continue to expand at a faster rate than public transport. Since 1990, more than 270 km of highways have been built, compared to only 15.7 km of MRT, 48 km of LRT and 40 km of the old Dutch rail line that was reactivated. The evolution of the highway network within the Jakarta metropolitan area started with the opening of the Jagorawi toll road connecting Jakarta and Bogor in 1976. The first intra-city toll road opened in 1985, connecting the Soekarno-Hatta international airport to Jagorawi through North Jakarta, followed by another intra-city toll road through Central Jakarta in 1997. The development of the toll network was then expanded through the outer ring roads of Jakarta and other toll roads radiating outwards to the suburbs. By 2023, there were at least 348 km of toll roads under operation and more than 75 km planned or under construction (Figure 11.3).

There are at least two reasons why highways and toll roads have expanded much more rapidly than public transport. First, governments have long seen constructing toll roads as more financially viable than

Figure 11.3 Jakarta toll road networks

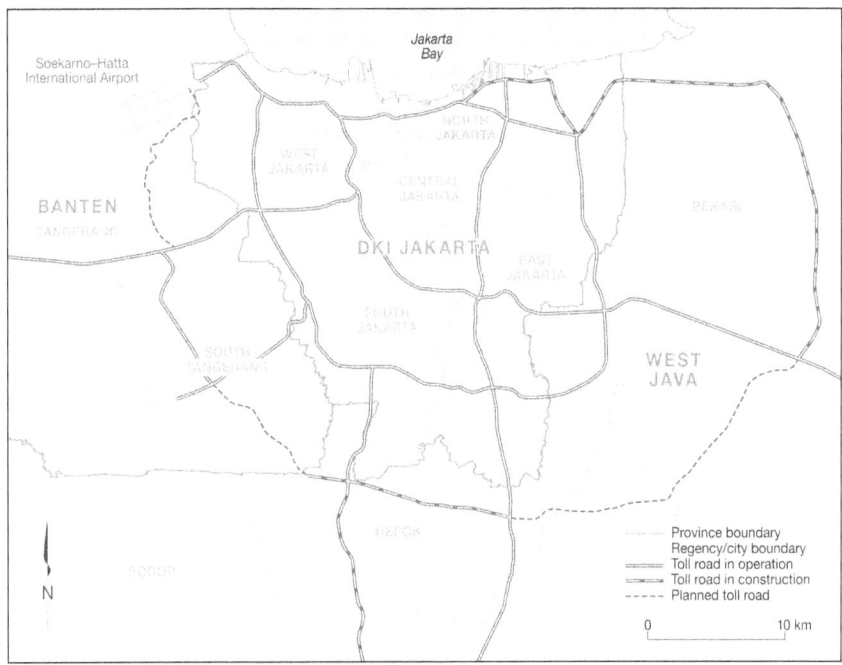

Source: CartoGIS Services, Australian National University.

public transport, because while the former generates clear revenue potential into the future, public transport services are more likely to absorb public subsidies than generate revenues. Second, the rapid development of Indonesia's highway system under Suharto was encouraged by the collusive and nepotistic nature of the political economy at that time. Suharto's family members, particularly his children, and cronies were granted concessions to build many of Jakarta's toll roads, and these became a lucrative source of income for them (Aditjondro 1998; Davidson 2015; Hoffman et al. 2004).

The toll roads connect the city centre of Jakarta with the surrounding municipalities, including Tangerang, South Tangerang, Depok, Bogor and Bekasi. The development of these highways has reduced the opportunity costs of living outside the city centre of Jakarta (see Elyda, this volume), generating transport-led suburbanisation in the surrounding regions (Yudhistira, Indriyani et al. 2019). It is one major factor driving change in urban spatial structure, not only in terms of population growth and patterns of land usage in the suburbs but also suburbanisation of economic activity, as evident from the changes in night light intensity across the Jakarta metropolitan area (Yudhistira, Indriyani et al. 2019; Pratama et al. 2022). In short, highways have fed urban sprawl around Jakarta and hindered more compact development in the region.

It is well known that sprawling development of urban areas can induce adverse impacts. It increases energy consumption (Glaeser and Kahn 2010), reduces productivity (Fallah et al. 2011) and increases the costs of providing public goods and services (Hortas-Rico and Solé-Ollé 2010). Developing policies to reduce urban sprawl and improve mobility within the Jakarta metropolitan area should be an urgent government priority.

Bus services

Jakarta's bus rapid transit (BRT) network, TransJakarta, is the largest BRT network in Southeast Asia. It was initiated in 2001 under Governor Sutiyoso and modelled on the TransMilenio system in Bogota, Colombia (Susilo and Loentan 2019). The construction was not only financially costly (Rp 120–300 billion or US$7.3–18.4 million per lane), but also unpopular since it sacrifices at least one lane on each road used to create a dedicated bus lane, increasing congestion in the other lanes. Since the first lane opened in 2004, there has been a slow and steady development in the service. Today it comprises around 251.2 km and 260 shelters, stations or stops within the Jakarta metropolitan area and serves more than 800,000 passengers per day. TransJakarta operates more than 4,300 buses with a dedicated lane on most of the major roads within Jakarta city. In addition, TransJakarta has arguably improved its services in terms of the quality of bus shelters and vehicles. In 2020, the network further expanded its road transport by introducing JakLingko, a network of paratransit minibuses that travel down smaller roads that TransJakarta is unable to serve.

During its early years TransJakarta exacerbated existing traffic problems. The network was introduced by converting existing mixed-use lanes into busways, reducing road capacity by up to 50 per cent in some corridors. Commuter trips along the expansion corridors took longer after the TransJakarta network was built. Moreover, rapid transit buses were on average as slow as traditional buses that travelled along mixed-traffic lanes, and around 20 per cent slower than motorcycles (Gaduh et al. 2022: 7). As a result, the introduction of the system did not reduce the incentive to own motor vehicles, especially motorcycles which, as we have seen, continued to expand greatly in usage rates (ibid.).

Another problem is that TransJakarta provides services only in Jakarta province, while the other municipalities that make up the wider Jakarta metropolitan area do not operate BRT systems. As a result, the BRT system does not reach deep into the suburbs that surround Jakarta, which is where most people working in Jakarta live. Overall, the TransJakarta network fails to target numerous residential areas, not only those lying beyond Jakarta's provincial borders but also some low-income communities within Jakarta province (Wentzel 2010: 50). In sum, despite offering a large bus network, many things can still be improved to promote the effectiveness of TransJakarta to mobilise people within the Jakarta metropolitan area.

Meanwhile, as noted, ridership in private buses has plummeted over the past decade, due to their operators' inability to improve their services and upgrade their fleets. These buses operate mostly on a 'paratransit' model: while operating along fixed routes they typically lack fixed timetables and travel times. The same pattern predominates in bus and minibus transport in the suburbs surrounding Jakarta, which leads to low public transit ridership in these areas. The rise of ride-hailing services, starting in around 2014, has also put pressure on buses. Ride-hailing services are a substitute for low-range transport modes within cities and have caused many people to shift from public transit in many parts of the world (Hall et al. 2018). In Jakarta, their relatively cheap fares, particularly during the early years of competition among providers, were also a major driver of passengers shifting from public buses and minibuses, as was their faster travel time and reliability—given that these services mostly use motorcycles—even during congestion.

Railways

Four different operators run the urban railway network in the Jakarta metropolitan area. The Commuter Line is the backbone of Jakarta's railway network with 418.5 km of track and more than 80 stations. With a pre-pandemic daily ridership of more than 900,000 passengers, this network connects Jakarta and its surrounding suburbs. The line is operated by KAI Commuter, a subsidiary of the state-owned Indonesian Railways (Kereta Api Indonesia). The network was built on the lines inherited from the Dutch colonial era, and was revitalised in the 2000s in cooperation with the Japan International Cooperation Agency (JICA) and the Tokyo Metropolitan Government. The Commuter Line service has improved greatly during the past two decades. For example, KAI Commuter reactivated the Tanah Abang – Parung Panjang line with almost 35 km of railway (the line had been inactive since early independence), and largely resolved problems of overcrowding and passengers illegally riding without tickets, which had haunted the train operator since at least the late 1990s. If in the past one regularly saw passengers hanging out of the doors, and even riding on the roofs, of Jakarta Commuter Line trains, this image has now largely disappeared.

The second railway network is MRT Jakarta, operated by PT MRT Jakarta, a regional enterprise owned by the Jakarta provincial government. The MRT project was first initiated as part of a national strategic project by President Yudhoyono in 2005, and continued by successive Jakarta governors. It was funded by a loan from the Japanese government through JICA of approximately Rp 13 trillion (US$800 million). The network at present offers an MRT line connecting Lebak Bulus in South Jakarta to the central roundabout at the famous Hotel Indonesia site (Bundaran HI) in the heart of Central Jakarta. It began operating in March 2019. It carries up to 80,000 passengers per day with a total length of 15.7 km and six underground and seven elevated stations. The MRT is being expanded; the current line (phase 1) is part of the North-South line, which will eventually connect Lebak Bulus to Ancol in North Jakarta. The second phase of the North-South Line to Ancol is expected to be completed in 2030. Phase 3 (an East-West line) is envisioned to be 87 km long from Cikarang to Balaraja, and phase 4 (12 km long) will connect the current Fatmawati station in South Jakarta (phase 1) with the LRT Jabodebek[3] line.

There are two separate LRT systems, LRT Jakarta and LRT Jabodebek. LRT Jakarta was initiated in 2015 under Governor Basuki Tjahaja Purnama and cost around Rp 5.3 trillion (US$325 million) from DKI Jakarta's budget. LRT Jakarta began commercial operations in December 2019. It opened with a 5.8 km line connecting six stations from the Velodrome to Pegangsaan Dua connecting North Jakarta and Central Jakarta. The difference between the MRT and the LRT is that the latter uses a light metro system with two cars per train that can carry 270 passengers in total, whereas each MRT train has six carriages that can carry a total of 1,200–1,800 passengers. In 2022, LRT Jakarta was able to carry 1,800 passengers per day. The Jakarta government intends to continue to expand the LRT Jakarta network throughout the city of Jakarta; however, most of the proposed lines are still under feasibility studies.

While LRT Jakarta provides a network within Jakarta province, LRT Jabodebek operates a light rail system that connects Jakarta and two municipalities in the suburban periphery. It was initiated by President Joko Widodo in 2015 with a plan to serve the 2018 Asian Games. The construction deadline was missed and its first two lines only opened in September 2023 with 42.1 km of line and 18 stations connecting Depok, Jakarta and Bekasi. Construction costs were about Rp 33 trillion (US$2 billion); current daily ridership is 56,000 passengers per day.

---

3   Jabodebek is an acronym for Jakarta, Bogor, Depok and Bekasi.

The investment to expand the railway network in the Jakarta metropolitan area has increased in the past decade. However, lines are still scattered and the Commuter Line, MRT, LRT Jakarta and LRT Jabodebek have not yet been fully integrated into a single system. This lack of integration has led to less than optimal daily ridership in rail services, other than the Commuter Line. Improving connectivity will not only improve traffic but also benefit economies of scale of rail service provision in the Jakarta metropolitan area.

Demand management policy

As congestion became an increasing problem, Jakarta's government began to introduce demand management policies in the city centre. Jakarta's then governor, Sutiyoso, introduced the first demand management policies in 2003 (soon after he initiated the TransJakarta busway system), when he created a high-occupancy vehicle policy on several main roads in Jakarta. The policy, also known as 'three-in-one', prohibited vehicles with less than three passengers from using certain roads. In 2016, the three-in-one policy was revoked due to its inefficiency in solving congestion and for its negative side effects, notably the generation of the job of 'jockey'—individuals, often children, who hired themselves out to ride as passengers at entry points into roads where the policy applied.

Revoking the three-in-one policy led to worse traffic, not only on the designated roads, but also throughout the city of Jakarta; delays increased by 69 per cent during peak hours (Hanna et al. 2017). Although Hanna and colleagues pointed out these problems with the ending of the three-in-one policy, they did not argue that the policy had been beneficial: if a vehicle policy such as the 'three-in-one' does not induce a sufficient number of people to carpool or use public transport, it instead directs traffic onto non-designated roads, thus shifting the location of traffic congestion rather than reducing it.

When the three-in-one policy was revoked it was replaced by an 'odds and evens' policy whereby, during specific time spans, only vehicles with odd numbers on their registration plates could use designated roads on days with odd-numbered dates and those with even-numbered plates could do so on days with even numbers. The policy improved road traffic by reducing travel time by 3 per cent on average after a month of its implementation (Yudhistira et al. 2019: 3). The effect was higher during the afternoon peak hour from 5 pm to 7 pm, during which travel time fell by 7–8 per cent.

Transport economics theory characterises congestion as a negative externality (Small and Verhoef 2007). Congestion occurs without internalising congestion costs into travel costs. Therefore, according to this theory, the simplest way to reduce congestion is by putting a price on it. The current demand restriction policy in Jakarta has aimed to increase travel costs by imposing non-monetary charges on travel costs, but has proven to be ineffective.

An alternative would be to introduce a Pigouvian tax (an economics term for a tax on a market activity that generates negative externalities) such as electronic road pricing (ERP) for every time a vehicle passes certain roads or a parking fee every time a person goes to the office in the city. Experience elsewhere shows that ERP can not only improve traffic flow but also provide additional revenue that can be used to expand transport supply (Lehe 2019). This option has been discussed in Jakarta over the past decade, but has not yet been formulated into a specific policy with a clear timeline.

Parking policies have also been used to reduce congestion in developed countries. In contrast, through much of Southeast Asia, including Jakarta, there is much uncertainty and confusion concerning parking policies, which manifests in low compliance with parking restrictions and a great deal of informal parking fee collection (ADB 2011). Local thugs and gangsters (*preman*) control much of the on-street parking in Jakarta, resulting in unsafe conditions for drivers (Nainggolan et al. 2006). Parking policy reform might thus have several positive effects in Jakarta. Using parking fees as instruments should be customised depending on location and demand characteristics. Charging high parking fees would be suitable in the Jakarta city centre and in office complexes, and could reduce the use of private vehicles. Parking in suburbs, particularly next to railway stations and bus shelters, by contrast, should be expanded to facilitate the use of public transport.

Overall, however, such solutions have their limits. Demand management policy affects only designated areas and a small portion of roads around them. Localised effects will not be enough to solve the massive traffic congestion problems that afflict the entire Jakarta metropolitan area. Learning from experience, these policies often affect commuting negatively, with people evading roads where the restrictions are in effect, resulting in worsened congestion in other places. While demand management policy reform is desirable, it should not be seen as offering a comprehensive solution to Jakarta's traffic problems.

Improving institutions and revenues for better urban transportation

Governments in the Jakarta metropolitan area face various institutional problems in dealing with traffic congestion. Two are particularly serious: first, the fact that congestion crosses administrative boundaries and, second, the inadequacy of financing. As a result, most solutions offered so far to Jakarta's traffic woes have been partial and ad hoc in nature. Preparing effective and lasting solutions to the Jakarta region's congestion problems will require serious political will from multiple institutions. Simplifying the institutional set-up within the Jakarta metropolitan area is one approach that may reduce transaction costs and enable the development of more comprehensive transport policies.

Introducing the Jakarta Metropolitan Authority

In megacities, where physical space is limited, it is important to have a large and diverse transport supply that does not rely on a single transport mode. Improving mobility in megacities needs a holistic transportation policy (Li et al. 2022). The Jabodetabek Urban Transportation Policy Integration Project Phase 1 (JUTPI I) 2011—a project funded by JICA— conceived a plan for Jakarta to comprehensively improve its urban mobility, including by developing all its transport systems. However, only 5 per cent of the proposed projects in the railway system development have been implemented so far. This is far below other projects, such as bus transport (27 per cent), traffic control systems (25 per cent) and road network development (53 per cent) (JICA 2019: 3).

In Jakarta, it is evident that the current transport supply is still not sufficiently large or diverse to move people around the metropolitan area in a timely manner. As we have seen, rail-based transport, despite increased investment, is particularly inadequate compared to most other megacities (Table 11.1). Yet rail is one means of transport that can mobilise a lot of people (mass) within a short time (rapid). Moreover, rail transport produces less carbon dioxide emissions than other transport modes (Cresci et al. 2019). Further investment is thus needed to make rail-based transport the backbone of mobility within the Jakarta metropolitan area. However, the cost of building heavy rail systems is much higher than that of bus transit or light rail transit systems (Zhang 2009), which largely explains the lag in Jakarta's rail development. Building a heavy rail network in Jakarta will require major commitment from policymakers and massive financing.

As in other major metropolitan areas, managing urban issues in the Jakarta metropolitan area involves solving problems that cross administrative boundaries. This poses major coordination challenges, given that each transportation project tends to be organised on an ad hoc basis among the various governments (provincial, municipal, national) and agencies involved. Generally speaking, lack of coordination in transport planning can result in inconsistencies in public transportation route design and ticketing systems, access restrictions, lack of connectivity and duplication (OECD 2015). In the Jakarta metropolitan area there is generally poor coordination among service providers, resulting in discontinuity and fragmentation of services—such as those that have seen the BRT largely ending at the administrative boundaries of Jakarta province. The absence of good public transport services reaching into the suburbs beyond Jakarta province, meanwhile, is a disincentive for people to use public transport, largely explaining the high dependence on private vehicles and resulting congestion. Solving traffic congestion in Jakarta will require acknowledging traffic sources in adjacent provinces and districts, and designing systems that work efficiently across administrative boundaries.

Tokyo, New York, London and Singapore have each addressed this challenge by establishing an institution (typically named a metropolitan authority) with the power to rule over urban development (or some aspects of it) in their entire metropolitan areas. The Jakarta metropolitan area lacks such a body. Metropolitan governance structures can improve competitiveness; conversely, governmental fragmentation can make metropolises less productive (OECD 2015). Such structures represent an effort to close the gap between socioeconomic areas and administrative jurisdictions (Brenner 2003; Davoudi 2008), enabling the political representatives in a metropolitan area to coordinate more effectively (Ayuso and Coll 2016).

For example, Tokyo has its own Tokyo Metropolitan Government, which governs over Tokyo's 23 special wards, 26 cities and 5 towns, each of which still has its own local government. Although private (or semi-public) entities provide Japan's, and consequently Tokyo's, railway services, the metropolitan government instructs and monitors these services, as with other urban development policies. For Jakarta, too, we believe a Jakarta Metropolitan Authority should have authority that includes but goes beyond transport policy, to also cover basic urban services, like utilities (water and sanitation), housing policy, land use and tourism. The establishment of such a Jakarta Metropolitan Authority would not replace the current local government structures. We expect it to be similar to the Tokyo Metropolitan Government, but with less responsibility (for instance, not including education or health affairs).

Financing transport infrastructure

Provision of urban transport infrastructure requires not only strong political commitment but also massive financing. Indonesia's national government views the development of urban rail transport in Jakarta as a national strategic project, and has committed to accelerate the construction of urban transport networks, particularly in and around Jakarta. According to the National Railway Development Masterplan (2018), funding the urban rail expansion up to 2030 is expected to cost around Rp 205 trillion (US$13 billion). However, even the national government budget will likely not be able to provide all the capital needed to build Jakarta's urban transport infrastructure. Increasing sources of financing is important to ensure the improvement of transport supply in Jakarta.

Various options are available. An obvious one is to boost fiscal capability by streamlining and restructuring regional taxes and levies to enhance the provincial and district governments' revenue streams (Clifford Chance 2021; Lindfield and Teipelke 2017). Both central and local governments should also optimise the financial relationships between them by restructuring central government allocations to local governments based on their performance at providing public services and by requiring a minimum proportion of capital expenditure at the regional level. These efforts would encourage local governments to improve public services and induce more productive budget spending.

Promoting private sector involvement in urban transport development projects is also essential. The Ministry of Finance has developed four facilities for public-private partnership (PPP) projects in Indonesia (Ministry of Finance 2023), but it should be possible to go further, for example, by using the local government bonds market to provide funds for critical infrastructure projects. Governments should also investigate other financing options, especially related to land value capture. Land value capture aims to capitalise on the increase in the economic value of an area due to successful urban redevelopment—such as connection to a public transport corridor—by collecting increment taxes or betterment charges or by other joint development mechanisms. The Jakarta government has already used one of these mechanisms, charging additional fees on buildings that exceeded standard height limits (through Gubernatorial Regulation 210/2016). It then used the revenue to build the Semanggi Flyover in Central Jakarta. Exploring similar mechanisms centred around urban transport development might help improve Jakarta's transport infrastructure. Establishing a Jakarta Metropolitan Authority might improve government capacity to mobilise revenue to finance urban transport development. For example, such an authority could suggest adjusting property values (which are the base of the property tax) along proposed railway lines.

Conclusion

The roots of the massive traffic congestion experienced in the Jakarta metropolitan area go far back in history and are the consequence of past policy decisions to concentrate investment in the region's roads and highways. While confronting this problem will require massive investment and diversification of Jakarta's transport infrastructure, especially through expansion of its rail network, one issue we have stressed in this chapter is that collaboration among the local authorities that make up the region will be a key to finding solutions. Cross-institutional coordination is necessary to avoid incompatibility across municipality-level and metro-level projects, establish seamless interconnected public transport systems, and to connect housing and transportation projects in ways that improve residents' quality of life. We believe that the government intervention needed to facilitate and monitor this complex collaborative effort would be enhanced by establishing a Jakarta Metropolitan Authority with power to execute metropolitan-level services, including transportation infrastructure and policies. The overarching goal will be to build an inclusive transport system that reaches deep into the urban periphery surrounding Jakarta and supplies the community with the affordable and reliable public transport they need. Doing this will allow residents to free themselves from their dependency on private vehicles, and so unravel traffic congestion.

However, even developing extensive transport supply, including more mass public transport, will not result in zero congestion. Data from the TomTom Traffic Index shows that cities with more than 8 million inhabitants, even those with extensive transport infrastructure, like London, New York and Tokyo, still experience traffic congestion. Therefore, policymakers should rethink their policy objectives, and move away from the unrealistic goal of eliminating congestion and instead think of how to reduce congestion and so improve the mobility of people in the city. The ultimate goal should be to allow people to move in and around the city within a reasonable time frame, not to eliminate congestion altogether.

Understanding the roots of the congestion problem in Jakarta is key not only to improving the current state of mobility in Jakarta but also to start developing better transport management policies for other cities in Indonesia. At the current pace, cities like Surabaya, Bandung and Medan are only a few years away from experiencing similar traffic problems to those of Jakarta. Around the country, residents of urban areas complain of increasing traffic jams, making this an increasingly urgent national problem, negatively affecting the quality of life of large numbers of Indonesian citizens. We should learn from Jakarta while we still have the opportunity to do so.

Acknowledgements

We thank Fitawhidan Nashuha for assistance with data collection, as well as Professor Edward Aspinall and Amalinda Savirani for comments and feedback that greatly improved the manuscript.

References

ADB (Asian Development Bank). 2005. *Bangkok Urban Transport Project*. ADB.
ADB (Asian Development Bank). 2011. *Parking Policy in Asian Cities*. ADB. http://hdl.handle.net/11540/123
Aditjondro, George J. 1998. 'Suharto and sons (and daughters, in-laws and cronies)'. *Washington Post*, 25 January, p. C01.
Ayuso, Anna and Josep Maria Coll. 2016. 'The role of metropolitan areas in the governance of development challenges: Towards the European urban agenda'. Paper presented to the European Metropolitan Authorities Forum, Torino, 12 February. www.cidob.org/en/content/download/63292/1959653/version/6/file/EMA_Policy_paper_ENG.PDF
BPS (Badan Pusat Statistik, Statistics Indonesia). 2010. 'Survei Sosial Ekonomi Nasional (Susenas)'. BPS.
BPS (Badan Pusat Statistik, Statistics Indonesia). 2014. 'Survei Komuter Jabodetabek'. BPS.
BPS (Badan Pusat Statistik, Statistics Indonesia). 2019. 'Survei Komuter Jabodetabek'. BPS.
BPS (Badan Pusat Statistik, Statistics Indonesia). 2022a. 'Jumlah penduduk berdasarkan kabupaten kota [City and district populations]'. BPS.
BPS (Badan Pusat Statistik, Statistics Indonesia). 2022b. 'Perkembangan jumlah kendaraan bermotor menurut jenis [Number of motorised vehicles by type]'. BPS.
BPS (Badan Pusat Statistik, Statistics Indonesia). 2023. 'Luas daerah menurut kabupaten/kota (km^2), 2020–2022 [Area by district/city (km^2), 2020–2022]'. https://jakarta.bps.go.id/indicator/153/38/1/luas-daerah-menurut-kabupaten-kota.html
Brenner, Neil. 2003. 'Metropolitan institutional reform and the rescaling of state space in contemporary Western Europe'. *European Urban and Regional Studies* 10(4): 297–324. doi.org/10.1177/09697764030104002
Clifford Chance. 2021. 'Alternative funding models for future infrastructure projects'. Clifford Chance. www.cliffordchance.com/content/dam/cliffordchance/briefings/2021/01/alternative-funding-models-for-future-infrastructure-projects.pdf
Cresci, Jean Pierre, Kevin Smeets and Laetitia Plisson. 2019. 'Why cities need rail'. *Velocity* (September). www.oliverwyman.com/our-expertise/insights/2019/oct/oliver-wyman-transport-and-logistics-2019/rail-and-logistics-trends/why-cities-need-rail.html
Davidson, Jamie S. 2015. *Indonesia's Changing Political Economy: Governing the Roads*. Cambridge University Press.

Davoudi, Simin. 2008. 'Conceptions of the city-region: A critical review'. *Proceedings of the Institution of Civil Engineers: Urban Design and Planning* 161(2): 51–60. doi.org/10.1680/udap.2008.161.2.51

Fallah, Belal N., Mark D. Partridge and M. Rose Olfert. 2011. 'Urban sprawl and productivity: Evidence from US metropolitan areas'. *Papers in Regional Science* 90(3): 451–72. doi.org/10.1111/j.1435-5957.2010.00330.x

Gaduh, Arya, Tadeja Gračner and Alexander D. Rothenberg. 2022. 'Life in the slow lane: Unintended consequences of public transit in Jakarta'. *Journal of Urban Economics* 128: 103411. doi.org/10.1016/j.jue.2021.103411

Glaeser, Edward L. and Matthew E. Kahn. 2010. 'The greenness of cities: Carbon dioxide emissions and urban development'. *Journal of Urban Economics* 67(3): 404–18. doi.org/10.1016/j.jue.2009.11.006

Hall, Jonathan D., Craig Palsson and Joseph Price. 2018. 'Is Uber a substitute or complement for public transit?' *Journal of Urban Economics* 108: 36–50. doi.org/10.1016/j.jue.2018.09.003

Hanna, Rema, Gabriel Kreindler and Benjamin A. Olken. 2017. *Citywide Effects of High-Occupancy Vehicle Restrictions: Evidence from the Elimination of '3-in-1' in Jakarta*. NBER Working Paper No. 23295. National Bureau of Economic Research. doi.org/10.3386/w23295

Ho, S. 2013. *Mass Rapid Transport System*. Singapore National Library.

Hoffman, Bert, Ella Rodrick-Jones and Kian Wie Thee. 2004. *Indonesia: Rapid Growth, Weak Institutions*. Working Paper No. 30780. World Bank. http://documents.worldbank.org/curated/en/576941468774895009/Indonesia-rapid-growth-weak-institutions

Hook, Walter and Michael Replogle. 1996. 'Motorization and non-motorized transport in Asia: Transport system evolution in China, Japan and Indonesia'. *Land Use Policy* 13(1): 69–84. doi.org/10.1016/0264-8377(95)00025-9

Hortas-Rico, Miriam and Albert Solé-Ollé. 2010. 'Does urban sprawl increase the costs of providing local public services? Evidence from Spanish municipalities'. *Urban Studies* 47(7): 1513–40. doi.org/10.1177/0042098009353620

JICA (Japan International Cooperation Agency). 2019. 'Jabodetabek Urban Transportation Policy Integration Project Phase 2 in the Republic of Indonesia'. JICA and Coordinating Ministry of Economic Affairs.

KAI (Kereta Api Indonesia, Indonesian Railways). 2021. *Annual Report 2020*. KAI.

Lehe, Lewis. 2019. 'Downtown congestion pricing in practice'. *Transportation Research Part C: Emerging Technologies* 100: 200–23. doi.org/10.1016/j.trc.2019.01.020

Li, Zongzhi, Adrian T. Moore and Samuel R. Staley. 2022. *Megacity Mobility: Integrated Urban Transportation Development and Management*. CRC Press.

Lindfield, Michael and Renard Teipelke. 2017. 'Explainer: How to finance urban infrastructure'. C40 Cities Finance Facility. www.c40knowledgehub.org/s/article/Explainer-How-to-finance-urban-infrastructure?language=en_US

Ministry of Finance Indonesia. 2023. 'Dukungan pemerintah [Government support]'. Ministry of Finance, Jakarta. https://kpbu.kemenkeu.go.id/read/1093-1256/pjpk/dukungan-pemerintah

Ministry of Transport Thailand. 2020. *Transport Statistics 2018*. Ministry of Transport, Bangkok.

Nainggolan, Azas Tigor, Mahatma Chrysna and Tubagus Haryo Karbiyanto. 2006. 'Politik perparkiran di Jakarta [Parking politics in Jakarta]'. Forum Warga Kota Jakarta.

New York City MTA (Metropolitan Transportation Authority). 2023. 'Board and committee meetings'. New York City MTA. https://new.mta.info/transparency/board-and-committee-meetings

OECD (Organisation for Economic Co-operation and Development). 2015. *Governing the City*. OECD Publishing. doi.org/10.1787/9789264226500-en

Pratama, Andhika Putra, Muhammad Halley Yudhistira and Eric Koomen. 2022. 'Highway expansion and urban sprawl in the Jakarta metropolitan area'. *Land Use Policy* 112: 105856. doi.org/10.1016/j.landusepol.2021.105856

Roberts, Mark, Frederico Gil Sander and Sailesh Tiwari, eds. 2019. *Time to ACT: Realizing Indonesia's Urban Potential*. World Bank. doi.org/10.1596/978-1-4648-1389-4

Savatic, Filip. 2016. *Fossil Fuel Subsidy Reform: Lessons from the Indonesian Case*. IDDRI.

Siridhara, Siradol. 2021. *Sustainable Urban Transport Index for Bangkok and Impacts of COVID-19 on Mobility*. UNESCAP. https://hdl.handle.net/20.500.12870/3565

Small, Kenneth and Erik T. Verhoef. 2007. *The Economics of Urban Transportation*. Routledge.

Sofiyandi, Yusuf and Atiqah Amanda Siregar. 2020. *Exploring the Changes of Commuting Patterns, Commuting Flows, and Travel-to-Work Behaviour in the Jakarta Metropolitan Area from 2014 to 2019: A Comparative Analysis of Two Cross-Sectional Commuting Surveys*. LPEM-FEB UI Working Paper 54. University of Indonesia.

Suatmadi, Anissa Y., Felix Creutzig and Ilona M. Otto. 2019. 'On-demand motorcycle taxis improve mobility, not sustainability'. *Case Studies on Transport Policy* 7(2): 218–29. doi.org/10.1016/j.cstp.2019.04.005

Susilo, Budi Hartanto and Apriyanto Loentan. 2019. 'Kajian operasional bus rapid transit Trans-Jakarta dan TransMilenio Bogota [Operational study of Trans-Jakarta bus rapid transit and TransMilenio Bogota]'. *Jurnal Teknik Sipil* 4(1): 87–104. doi.org/10.28932/jts.v4i1.1299

Tang, Qing and Xianbiao Hu. 2019. 'Triggering behavior changes with information and incentives: An active traffic and demand management-oriented review'. In *The Evolving Impacts of ICT on Activities and Travel Behavior. Advances in Transport Policy and Planning*, vol. 3, edited by Eran Ben-Elia, 209–50. Academic Press.

Tokyo Metropolitan Government. 2020. *Tokyo Statistical Yearbook 2020*. Tokyo Metropolitan Government.

Transport for London. 2017. *Mayor's Transport Strategy: Supporting Evidence: Outcomes Summary Report*. Mayor of London and Transport for London. [And 'Addendum to the Mayor's Transport Strategy (MTS): Proposal 24.1'.] https://content.tfl.gov.uk/mts-outcomes-summary-report.pdf

Wentzel, Lisa. 2010. 'Urban mobility among lower income communities in Jakarta: A study of the bus rapid transit system'. Masters thesis. School of Architecture and the Built Environment, KTH Royal Institute of Technology, Stockholm.

Yudhistira, Muhammad Halley, Witri Indriyani, Andhika Putra Pratama, Yusuf Sofiyandi and Yusuf Reza Kurniawan. 2019. 'Transportation network and changes in urban structure: Evidence from the Jakarta metropolitan area'. *Research in Transportation Economics* 74: 52–63. doi.org/10.1016/j.retrec.2018.12.003

Yudhistira, Muhammad Halley, Regi Kusumaatmadja and Mochammad Firman Hidayat. 2019. *Does Traffic Management Matter? Evaluating Congestion Effect of Odd-Even Policy in Jakarta*. LPEM-FEB UI Working Paper 29. University of Indonesia. www.lpem.org/wp-content/uploads/2019/01/WP-LPEM_029_MHY_v3.pdf

Zhang, Ming. 2009. 'Bus versus rail: Meta-analysis of cost characteristics, carrying capacities, and land use impacts'. *Transportation Research Record: Journal of the Transportation Research Board* 2110(1): 87–95. doi.org/10.3141/2110-11

12 Contested public spaces in urban Indonesia

Rita Padawangi

In Indonesia's cities, public space is hotly contested. Consider the following two examples. In 2019 the Supreme Court ruled to annul part of a by-law in Jakarta on allowing street vending. The plaintiffs were individuals from the Indonesian Solidarity Party. They argued that street vendors restrict the rights of other citizens, especially pedestrians, to use sidewalks and that they profit commercially from their operations on public space at the expense of pedestrians' and other people's access. The Supreme Court ruled in favour of the plaintiffs and ordered the revocation of chapter 25(1) of Regional Regulation 8/2007 of Jakarta, which authorised the governor of Jakarta to decide that parts of public spaces could be used for street vending. The ruling stripped the governor of some power to govern sidewalks. At the same time, this ruling is an indication of how the Supreme Court views who the 'public' is, at least in the case of sidewalks in Jakarta (Padawangi 2019b). The outcome of the case, which excluded street vendors from using sidewalks for business, was also a manifestation of the Supreme Court's view on what is appropriate use of public space.

The exclusion of street vendors from public spaces in this Supreme Court ruling is similar to the second example: a large project a decade and a half earlier. In 2003, then Jakarta Governor Sutiyoso initiated the redevelopment of Medan Merdeka Park—arguably Indonesia's best-known public park, which surrounds the National Monument (Monumen Nasional) and is lodged amid several of Indonesia's most important government buildings, including the Presidential Palace. Governor Sutiyoso ordered the building of four-metre-high fences around the park, which displaced thousands of street vendors who had long been operating in the area. The project prompted civil society activists to form a 'human chain' around the park to protest. Yet the provincial government continued to build the fences and consequently evicted 3,000 street vendors. Although the project also included more greenery in the park, historian J.J. Rizal called it an expression of 'feudalism', because the limitation of access resembled the exclusivity of parks around *kraton* (sultans' palaces) rather than the original vision of the Medan Merdeka Park as a space open to people from all walks of life (Yuniar 2020).

Cases such as these show that public space can be heavily contested. When one says 'public space', everyone seems to have some idea of what it is. Yet the idea in one person's mind might be quite different to that in the next person's. One person may think of a city square. Another might think about sidewalks. Yet another may think about city parks. Others still may think about shopping malls (though urban scholars might argue about the extent of their publicness, city residents may well consider shopping malls as public spaces: Kusumowidagdo et al. 2016; Schmidt 2012).

Public space seems to be something that each city must have, yet the term covers a broad range of spaces. Indeed, scholars have noted that the term 'public space' can refer to anything from streets, parks, pavements, beaches and city squares to digital spaces of the media, internet and social media (Smith and Low 2006: 2). Such scholars identify public spaces as places where strangers can meet, discuss and shape ideas, conduct social activities and carry out collective actions (Sennett 1977; Simmel 1903; Weber 1921). The diversity of public spaces can thus be traced to the diversity of places of social interaction in the city, with urbanism quintessentially associated with heterogeneity and density (Wirth 1938). Meanwhile, urban theorists often view public spaces as being integral to urban life, both in the form of the built environment physical spaces— as well as the social spaces in which discussions among citizens can take place.

Public spaces in Indonesian cities, as elsewhere, are also governed spaces, with different governing authorities determining allocation of locations and resources for public spaces. Such authorities can also have different rules about who constitutes the 'public' that can access these spaces. As a result, as the examples that open this chapter show, public spaces are also contested spaces: on one hand, the term 'public' carries a sense of accessibility for 'the people', but the authorities determining access to particular public spaces may have varied ideas about which groups the term includes or excludes, raising what Neil Smith and Setha Low (2006: 3) call, with regard to public space, the 'dimensions and extent of its publicness'.

My discussion in this chapter focuses on considering concepts of and contestations over public space in Indonesian cities. I ask: How is public space understood, implemented and practised in Indonesian cities? In particular: Who gets to decide what citizens get to use public space and for what purpose? I address these questions by arguing that, in Indonesia, the social and political actors involved in constructing and governing public spaces determine who gets to decide the inclusion and exclusion. Based on who the actors involved in the making of public spaces are, the following are three kinds of public spaces that we can observe in Indonesia.

The first type is public spaces provided by 'managerial' city leadership. In these spaces, the city government is the main political actor driving the conception, planning and physical construction of the spaces. These public space projects are usually funded by the government budget, and they are usually located on government land. The second type is 'public' spaces provided by private capital. These spaces are planned, designed and built by the private sector. They are built on privately owned land, or on land controlled by the private sector. They become 'public' spaces because they are open to the public, and access can be free of charge. But the private sector entity that owns the space can enforce its own rules of conduct. The spaces can range from what planners call 'privately owned public spaces' that resemble public plazas, to shopping malls that are publicly accessible but in which the private management's rules and opening hours are applied. The third type is community neighbourhood-level public spaces. These public spaces are initiatives of local residents, usually at the neighbourhood level, who wish to have a shared space that caters for public use. These spaces can take the form of neighbourhood alleyways, parks and other locations. Residents usually have their own ways of managing such public spaces, including *gotong royong* (mutual cooperation) for repair and cleaning. Residents who are involved in managing and maintaining these spaces often also impose community rules on what activities are permitted: they govern the do's and don'ts of such spaces.

This chapter is structured by way of a sequential discussion of the three categories above. Nevertheless, it should be stressed at the outset that the above types are not mutually exclusive categories. In reality, many public spaces in the city are mixtures of two or all three types. The mix of these types of public spaces signifies the spectrum of relationships among stakeholders, as well as these stakeholders' ability (or lack of ability) to work together in providing and managing these public spaces. The intention in using the three categories here is thus not to reify them, but to illustrate the interconnectedness among these spaces in the city's everyday life.

City beautification and managerial leadership

Urban governance in Indonesia has changed significantly since *reformasi*. Political decentralisation has given greater autonomy to city governments to make decisions about urban development. As elsewhere in Southeast Asia (Harms 2012), cities in Indonesia have begun to compete to project their images nationally and globally in order to attract investment and visitors by using slogans, visual presentations and local urban projects. Citizens now directly elect city leaders, who thus need to craft appeals that residents will find attractive or important. Many do so by developing policies to improve the visual appearance of the city, improve service delivery and expand city infrastructure. As a result, one of the defining features of the new model of leadership in Indonesian cities has been an emphasis on beautification of the city, and the construction or renovation of such public spaces as parks, sidewalks, waterfront areas, bikeways and the like. In cities such as Jakarta, Bandung and Surabaya, city leaders have invested major political capital—and city budgets—in pursuing such projects.

In this era of decentralisation, one new form of city leadership has seized national and international attention: managerial leadership. Managerial leadership of a city refers to a governance style that emphasises efficient top-down management of a bureaucratic apparatus to ensure effective delivery of public services, such as housing, education and health care. Discussions of managerial city leadership in various development studies publications are largely positive, emphasising how such leadership can ensure delivery of decent public services despite the presence of often subpar bureaucracies (Budd and Sancino 2016). Such leadership also arises in a context in which cities are increasingly important as places of investment for global flows of capital, which increases the stakes of urban governance. As a result, 'urban governance and leadership has become a distinctive political practice, characterised by a techno-managerial, "non-ideological" approach' (Maclean 2017: 127).

This purportedly 'non-ideological' approach to governance, while delivering public services, may conflict with an idealised vision of the city as constituting a society. For example, the need to maintain order in the city to allow for efficient and effective governance might lead city leaders to deploy paramilitary forces that use violence, as observed in the leadership of Rodrigo Duterte of Davao City in the Philippines. However, the same need to provide security might also be fulfilled with popular participation and a collaborative approach, as demonstrated in the city of Medellín, Columbia, under Mayor Sergio Fajardo (Maclean 2017). So, the broad rubric of 'managerial leadership' can thus coexist with many different governance styles.

Chief examples of managerial leadership in Indonesia, seen in terms of the provision of public spaces as one of the public services of the city, include several city mayors who have become very well known in the era of decentralisation. Perhaps the best-known example of a managerial city leader in Indonesia was Joko Widodo of Solo. The rise of Joko Widodo from being a mayor of Solo, a city of under 1 million people, between 2005 and 2012, to becoming governor of Jakarta in 2012 and eventually the country's president in 2014, is an example of how managerial leadership can be used to craft an image of being a capable leader in a way that garners substantial popularity. Stories of Jokowi's ability, when he was mayor of Solo, to relocate street vendors from Banjarsari Park without using violent force, as well as of how he oversaw the consensual relocation of a riverbank community, became highlights of his gubernatorial campaign in Jakarta in 2012. Subsequently, his ability to transform Jakarta's Tanah Abang market by peacefully relocating vendors into the Blok G building in 2013, and his Pluit Reservoir Park project in the same year that involved relocation of poor settlements—reportedly 1,600 families—were part of his presidential campaign in 2014. These demonstrations of ability to deliver public services qualified him as a good managerial leader. Since becoming president, his administration has likewise highlighted his managerial style—obscuring his ideological stance—when framing his success as a national leader, as exemplified by his emphasis on infrastructure development and social assistance programs.

Many of the new breed of managerial urban leaders have emphasised in their election campaigns their success in building architecturally beautiful and neat landscapes. Examples include Ridwan Kamil, the mayor of Bandung from 2013 to 2018, who successfully clinched the West Java gubernatorial election in 2019 by highlighting his record of urban improvement projects in Bandung as mayor. Most of these improvement projects were public spaces, such as Taman Film Pasupati in the Tamansari area and Teras Cikapundung. Taman Film Pasupati is a public park under the Pasupati flyover that features a large screen with a terraced slope covered by synthetic grass. The park is open to the public and since opening has become a popular place for children to play, for youths to hang out, and for visitors to take photos and post them on social media. Located on the Cikapundung riverbank, Teras Cikapundung is a park with neatly landscaped greenery and public access for water sports on the river. As of 2024, both parks are listed on TripAdvisor—an online website that features reviews of places as user-generated content—within the top ten parks to visit in Bandung.

Another example is Tri Rismaharini, affectionately called Bu Risma, who was re-elected as mayor of Surabaya in 2015, in part by highlighting her achievements in revitalising public parks in the city. One of these parks was Taman Bungkul, a popular public park that at one point boasted free wi-fi internet connection. She also involved the United Cities and Local Governments, an international city organisation for local and regional governments, with the City of Surabaya government to sign an agreement with Indonesia's Ministry of Public Works to commit to resource allocation for public space projects (UN-Habitat 2016). In general, her emphasis on city tidiness and green spaces was key to her public appeal. Bu Risma was also known for 'cleaning up' the famous Dolly red-light district in Surabaya in 2014, by removing all the prostitution-related establishments and sex workers (detikJatim 2022).

Managerial city leadership, as demonstrated by Joko Widodo, Ridwan Kamil and Bu Risma, is different from other forms of leadership in Indonesian cities in that it features images of improved public spaces as highlights of mayoral achievement. Images of neat and beautiful government-provided public spaces are appealing in the context of Indonesia, where many cities have long struggled with maintaining public spaces. These mayors' projects resemble one another in that they feature aesthetically pleasing design elements, and they are public, in the sense that they are accessible to citizens. City residents, as political constituents of these mayors, are able to have first-hand experience of these spaces, or to see them visually, either directly or through the media. These projects are thus regularly presented in the media as highlights of these mayors' achievements, and serve as political capital for them when they seek re-election, or when they aim for higher political office.

The popular emphasis on such leaders' success at achieving 'real results' invites a critical reading. A critical reading requires us to question how these leaders make those grand projects and visually beautiful spaces possible, how the financing models they use are structured, the extent to which their projects require compromises with powerful political and economic actors, and the extent to which the projects affect populations located at the margins of society.

While space restrictions make it impossible to investigate all of these issues fully, let us look at one obvious example: these city beautification projects often have negative impacts on marginal residents of the city (see also Padawangi 2019a; Padawangi and Douglass 2015). One such case was the 2015 demolition of Kampung Kolase to make space for Teras Cikapundung Park in Bandung. Mayor Ridwan Kamil ordered the demolition, as the *kampung*[1] was situated on the Cikapundung riverbank.

---

1   A *kampung* in Indonesia refers to a self-built settlement.

Under the law on water resources at the time, there was a mandatory 'setback' of developments on the riverbank to provide space between the water body and buildings. Kampung Kolase was one of many self-built urban settlements throughout Indonesia that predated the law, yet it was subjected to demolition as a result. In place of the *kampung*, Mayor Ridwan Kamil planned to build the park that became Teras Cikapundung. Kampung Kolase residents, approximately 39 families, many of whom had lived there for decades, had to move to Sadang Serang public housing (Prasetyo 2018). In the place of their former *kampung*, the city of Bandung and the Balai Besar Wilayah Sungai Citarum (Citarum River Governance Office) built Teras Cikapundung as a physically appealing park where people can enjoy a stroll along the Cikapundung River.

Another example of a popular public park development that involved forced evictions occurred in 2016 when the Jakarta government under Governor Basuki Tjahaja Purnama—popularly known by his nickname 'Ahok'—evicted residents of Kalijodo, a *kampung* in North Jakarta along the West Flood Canal, to build one of his signature child-friendly public open spaces. At the time, the Jakarta government labelled Kalijodo a red-light prostitution area and said it was occupying land that was supposed to be a 'green corridor' (*jalur hijau*). The government initiated forced evictions of Kalijodo residents, moving them to Marunda and Pulogebang public housing sites, following a fatal vehicle accident in the area, where the driver was found to have been under the influence of alcohol, allegedly due to a visit to a café in Kalijodo. A combination of the military, the police, the municipal police (Satpol PP) and the city's transportation office mobilised 15 backhoes and 5,000 personnel to demolish the settlement (*Tempo.co* 2022). After the demolition, the provincial government turned Kalijodo into a public park covering an area of over 5,000 square metres, with the development paid for by Sinarmas Land, a major property developer, to the tune of Rp 3.6 billion (US$230,000). Kalijodo Park has since become a green space that is accessible to the public, with a portion of it allocated to a skateboarding park and a child-friendly area that features a large playground.

By emphasising their managerial qualities in their election campaigns, city leaders have highlighted their abilities to deliver public services, usually portraying these public space projects in a positive light. In some cases, the story of the processes behind these projects also became a highlight; for example, the public consultations involved in Joko Widodo's revitalisation of Banjarsari Park in Solo were highlighted when he campaigned in Jakarta's gubernatorial election in 2012. But not all these city leaders drew attention to the processes they had used to achieve their grand projects in their political campaigns. For example, Ahok's gubernatorial campaign in 2017 did not highlight the governor's use of forced evictions, such as those in Kalijodo Park; rather, the emphasis was on his ability to 'get things done' and his image as a 'tough leader' who could deliver for the public.

Private capital and public spaces in Indonesia

The contradictions of public space are particularly obvious in Indonesian cities, because as in most cities around the world, space is a commodity that is bought and sold for profit. In other words, spatial distribution in most cities follows the logic of the capitalist economy. In a capitalist economy, cities are sites of capital accumulation: land and space come with price tags and become more expensive as the urban population grows, generating more demand. A capitalist allocation of space means that those who have greater financial resources have more access to space, while those who have fewer resources have less access. This greater access brings not only ability to use or consume the space, but also ability to have a say in decisions about who else can use it and how. Asef Bayat (2012) thus argues that the public space concept will fade when spaces become economic assets, even as they continue to play a role in social and cultural reproduction.

City residents from various walks of life not only access spaces built by the government; they also frequently access spaces built by the private sector, such as shopping malls and housing complexes. The bigger the city, the more likely there are powerful private sector entities with sufficient capital to finance projects that are large enough to cater for public use. Yet the private sector also needs state support to build large spaces that are open for public access. At the very least, state actors often endorse large-scale private developments through regulations, or deregulation. In the 1980s, then president Suharto adopted 'measures of deregulation and debureaucratisation' to induce development projects, including in cities and on their outskirts, paving the way for the state to award 'large tracts of state-held land' to 'well-connected business conglomerates, along with newly created development rights' (Herlambang et al. 2019: 632). At the time, Suharto was already connected to a network of businesspeople and army officers, many part of his own family's business empire, who could take advantage of this deregulation. Suharto's policies induced the real estate boom of the 1980s (Douglass and Jones 2008).

Most of the large private developments took place as large peri-urban housing complexes, but there were, and are, also large-scale commercial projects in cities. Shopping malls started to grow in big cities in Indonesia in the mid-1980s, notably Tunjungan Plaza in the centre of Surabaya, followed by malls in Jakarta and Bandung in the 1990s. Shopping malls in big cities emerged along with the growth of the urban middle class. Members of this class were becoming consumers in and of these spaces. Shopping malls became even more popular as hangout places in Jakarta due to the perceived decline in safety following the May 1998 riots (Kusno 2004, 2013). Compared to the older shopping centres, shopping malls offered a wider range of commercial entities and experiences, from retail shops to food and entertainment facilities, as well as spaces for events that resemble town squares. Different from public spaces that are built and managed by city governments, spaces in malls are usually managed by private companies.[2] These companies determine the regulations on access and use of space within these domains, while the city government's influence is more indirect, and mostly expressed through regulations over land and building control. Although shopping malls also function as 'public' spaces that can bring together city residents from various walks of life, the governance of these spaces is private and private management makes the decisions over who is included and who is excluded.

Private governance of publicly accessible spaces also takes place in housing complexes. The larger these housing complexes, the more likely they feature open spaces for social activities that are targeted mainly at residents but are sometimes also open to the general public. In terms of appearance, these spaces may be similar to those built by the government—and include facilities such as parks and sports complexes— but the management is in the hands of the private sector developer. It is the developers who determine inclusion-exclusion rules and other regulations concerning the use of these spaces, and they typically prioritise their own interests and the profit to be realised from properties they sell and manage, without considering the social impacts. Segregation and exclusivity, for example, may be marketable features of these gated communities, including of the 'public' spaces in the compounds, as Corry Elyda discusses (this volume) with regard to gated communities in South Tangerang. This marketability of exclusivity also partly reflects the middle class's lack of confidence in the government's ability to establish safety in public spaces (Kusno 2004).

Private sector managers of public space generally exclude citizens who are not in line with their commercial interests, either because they do not directly provide sufficient revenues or because, indirectly, they are considered to undermine the image (often of luxury, elegance

---

2   An exception is the case of Sarinah, the oldest shopping mall in Jakarta. Established in 1962, it is managed by a state-owned enterprise.

and exclusivity) that managers seek to generate for their spaces. Street vendors, for example, may be able to negotiate terms to pursue their businesses in public spaces managed by the government, but that room for negotiation in privately governed 'public' spaces will entirely depend on whether the private management sees their presence as beneficial. Thus, street vendors are unable to operate in shopping malls if they are not tenants, and are typically denied entry at the door. Besides producing such immediate exclusions, segregation and exclusivity also have longer-term social impacts as they engender feelings of hierarchy and superiority among the 'new generations of people growing up in middle-class gated communities with their own schools and universities, self-segregated from the urban majority' (Herlambang et al. 2019: 631).

Private ownership and government of spaces such as gated communities, shopping malls and other private developments are not the only roles that private capital can play in the making of 'public' spaces in the city. Private capital can also penetrate public spaces built by city governments, notably through corporate social responsibility programs and other development contributions made by private companies. Kalijodo Park, as mentioned earlier, is not only an example of a public park built over a forcefully evicted settlement; it is also an example of a public space built by the city government with development contributions provided by a private developer (in this case, Sinarmas Land). Another well-known new public park in Jakarta, Tebet Eco Park, was built during the governorship of Anies Baswedan with contributions from Astra Land, a real estate developer that is part of the Astra Group. This park was designed as a 7.3 hectare open green space that features naturalised riverbanks with a wetland flood-retention function, an attractive bridge that connects two sides of the park that were previously separated by a road, and spacious children's play areas. It is advertised as being based on a concept of harmonising ecology, social life, education and recreation. When private developers make financial contributions to support these urban public spaces and to build aesthetically pleasing facilities within them, they boost their public profiles and attract positive media coverage. Different from the gated communities and shopping malls, the governance of these spaces is in the hands of the city government.

Neighbourhood-level public space

Public space in the city comes in various scales. It certainly includes large-scale spaces such as city parks and shopping precincts. But many public spaces come at much smaller scales. In everyday life in cities of Indonesia, citizens most often experience public spaces in their immediate surroundings, in places such as local streets, alleyways and parks. Such locations are also more likely to be subject to contestation over interests and needs than large-scale public spaces run by city administrations, because their governance is within reach of the residents who are using those spaces every day. These residents likely know personally the individuals in charge of such smaller-scale spaces on a daily basis. They likely know who to go to whenever there is a dispute about usage, and such disputes are typically settled by negotiation among neighbours and community members.

In these smaller-scale public spaces, citizens often play the key role in making collective decisions about rules of usage. For example, people often convert streets and alleyways in urban *kampung* to facilitate public events, such as weddings, funerals, festivals, exhibitions, art events and street markets. For example, Kampung Bukit Duri in South Jakarta used to hold an annual event called Pasar Rakyat (the People's Market), in which the main street of the *kampung* was converted into an exhibition ground in which local people and artists they invited could open booths to sell food, arts and crafts. The market also featured music and dance performances by residents and artists.

Typically, it is the people involved in the day-to-day governance of neighbourhoods, notably the leaders of the local *rukun tetangga* (RT, neighbourhood association) and *rukun warga* (RW, citizens' association), who make decisions collectively about using their streets and other public spaces for public purposes. Residents' relationships with these leaders may affect their ability to influence decisions on the usage of neighbourhood-scale public spaces; hence, inclusion-exclusion processes may still occur. Nevertheless, the community leaders who head RTs and RWs are part of the same residential neighbourhoods as their neighbours and are likely to know all the residents in person. Therefore, negotiations about the use and maintenance of public spaces at this scale are relatively accessible to the residents.

Looking at relatively small-scale public spaces in neighbourhoods provides us with insights into community governance. In a long-term observation and community engagement project in Surabaya through the Southeast Asia Neighbourhoods Network, our research team documented changing uses of public spaces over time in Kampung Peneleh, a relatively old self-built settlement in Surabaya. For example, since the research team started ethnography in Kampung Peneleh in 2017, one distinctive finding concerns a ban of motorised vehicles in the alleyways of the *kampung*. It is unclear when exactly the ban started, but for at least a decade motorcyclists have had to turn off their engines and push their vehicles from when they enter the *kampung* to when they reach their own home, and this rule applies to delivery riders as well. The residents made this rule to reduce noise, perceiving a quieter environment to be a collective good in the *kampung*: their alleyways are narrow, making it easy for noise generated by motor vehicles to penetrate their doors and windows.

In fact, alleyways in Kampung Peneleh have multiple uses. For example, their uses change according to the festive seasons. Besides being used for festivities such as weddings and Independence Day celebrations, the alleyways completely transform during the days building up to Idul Adha (the Feast of Sacrifice, a major event in the Islamic calendar), when they fill with sheep and cows as *qurban* animals. On a more regular basis, the alleyways are spaces where children play everything from hide and seek to alleyway football. Children and youths also use the community cemetery as a football field in the afternoons.

The alleyways of Kampung Peneleh are thus an example of how neighbourhood-scale public spaces can accommodate a range of activities pursued by various groups of residents. These activities need not be related to one another; at times, they can contradict each other. When one group uses the space, others may need to make way. Collectively agreed management of various interests is a distinctive feature of public space at this scale. At the neighbourhood level, it is obvious that public space is an expression of collectivism: space needs to be shared, both as a necessity and as a means of enhancing the quality of everyday life. The management of public space in the neighbourhood is a microcosm of politics: negotiations take place among different groups over different uses. Sometimes such negotiations require tolerance of groups whose preferences do not accord with those of others—such as religious events that are not celebrated by members of other religions. Often, minority groups have to make way and do not have the same ability to use space for public purposes as the majority. Collective management of public spaces may well contain local tensions and contradictions. Yet, collective decision-making on the management and use of public spaces, no matter how imperfect, is key to connecting public space and an active citizenry.

In many places in urbanising Indonesia, governance of neighbourhood-scale public spaces involves residents making collective decisions about how such spaces are to be used. An observation of neighbourhood-scale public spaces in Kampung Yoboi in Sentani, Papua, provided me an opportunity to experience the community's colourful walkway, which connects houses in the village, the dock and a nearby sago forest. Residents painted the wooden planks in multiple colours to improve the appearance of their community. Initiated by youths during the COVID-19 pandemic, the community engaged in local fundraising to purchase the paint and *kampung* youths then did the painting. The walkway improvement garnered attention from local and national government, which then provided funding to extend the walkway into the community's sago forest (Yewen and Kurniati 2022). The *kampung* also has a publicly accessible community library, which they call a 'reading house' (*rumah baca*), as a node of communal activities. Currently funded by World Vision, the *rumah baca* began with the initiative of a community member, Hanny Felle, who was campaigning to improve literacy in Kampung Yoboi. Initiatives such as these demonstrate that individuals and households can play a major role in public space provision. Focusing on the neighbourhood scale allows us to observe how active citizens can make, improve and maintain public spaces.

Observing neighbourhood-scale public spaces also allows us to look closely into social governance of space. In such settings, the *who* questions regarding public space—who can access the space, who makes decisions over the space—have generally clear answers: a set of community leaders, who head the governance structure of the neighbourhood, typically decide on access, often in response to requests and needs of community members. Some communities are highly inclusive in how they make rules about use of their public spaces, others are exclusionary, with most falling somewhere in between. In most Indonesian neighbourhoods, community membership is generally determined by residency. Membership in turn typically brings inclusion into decision-making processes, such as the right to elect sub-neighbourhood leaders (RT heads) or to participate in community meetings (*musyawarah*). The broader public beyond the community are included to the extent that they can access and use the public space of the community for everyday activities, but they are generally excluded from making decisions over its use. Walkways and alleyways may be accessible to the broader public beyond members of the specific community, but the broader public do not have direct access to the local community governance structure and cannot make decisions, for example, on whether or not motorcycles are to be allowed.

Many communities make use of their spaces conditional on certain rules. During my observation of community activities in an urbanising village in Ubud, Bali, for example, the community hall (*balai banjar*) was an example of a public space that was open to all residents (but not to outsiders without permission), with the condition that those visiting it had to wear traditional Balinese costume. The hall was a space where community members could hold their public events, such as preparations for traditional ceremonies, community meetings and elections of community leaders.

In sum, most community-level public spaces in Indonesia's *kampung*— such as the *kampung* alleyways, walkways and community halls I have mentioned here—are governed at the neighbourhood level. They are generally also relatively free of top-down intervention by higher levels of government. The community leaders governing these spaces may have to deal with higher levels of government when it comes to working out issues such as land ownership, building permits or criminality. They may have access to funds from higher levels of government for small-scale infrastructure and improvement projects. However, it is residents and their elected leaders who are responsible for the day-to-day governance of these neighbourhood-scale public spaces. Indonesia's system of grassroots urban governance provides many opportunities for citizens to decide collectively on the use of public space at the micro level.

Thinking critically about public space in the city

So far in this chapter, I have proposed a critical assessment of how different kinds of public space are understood and governed in contemporary urban Indonesia. The rapid transformation of Indonesia's urban landscape and the popular appeal of urban beautification projects provide relatively few opportunities for critical reflection on the social costs of urban Indonesia's drive to generate neat, green and beautiful public spaces, or to respond to the widespread trend towards privatisation of public space. Critical voices have certainly emerged; for example, the Jakarta branch of the Legal Aid Institute (Lembaga Bantuan Hukum, LBH) publicly called the forced eviction of Kalijodo settlement a human rights violation. More broadly, LBH Jakarta (2016) noted that river dredging and embankment projects, and promotion of 'public order', were the top two reasons for forced evictions in Jakarta in 2015–2016. Evictees in Jakarta, namely those from Kampung Pulo, Kampung Bukit Duri and Kampung Akuarium, even filed lawsuits against their evictions in 2015 and 2016; one lost the case (Kampung Pulo), one won (Bukit Duri) and another decided to drop the case (Kampung Akuarium) as they eventually were able to negotiate with the Anies Baswedan government that replaced that of Ahok, who had authorised their evictions.

However, Ahok, despite his role in the evictions, enjoyed consistently high approval ratings as governor. A survey by Media Indonesia's Media Research Centre in September 2016 showed that a majority of citizens were satisfied with his leadership: 81 per cent were satisfied with his 'toughness', 78 per cent were satisfied with the cleanliness of the city and 49 per cent were satisfied with the part he played in flood management (Jayabuana 2016). Another survey, by the Saiful Mujani Research Center in October 2016, showed the same pattern of 75 per cent overall satisfaction, with 80 per cent stating satisfaction on cleanliness and a majority satisfied with flood management (Nailufar 2016). This high satisfaction did not translate into Ahok's re-election in 2017; he lost to Anies Baswedan. There were indications that the forced evictions did have a negative impact on Ahok's vote (Savirani and Aspinall 2017), even if it was not the main driver; yet his role in these evictions did not dent his image as a capable leader who was 'not corrupt' and could get things done (*Liputan6* 2020). Such outcomes suggest why managerial-style city leadership and its manifestations in aesthetically pleasing public spaces have become such a widespread pattern in contemporary Indonesia: many members of the public apparently want this style of public service delivery from their city leaders.

In fact, the problem lies not in the beauty and neatness of the new public spaces being created by city governments under the new urban managerialism, but rather in the processes of getting there. When we see 'beautiful' and 'neat' public spaces in cities, it is important to critically assess what it took to create them, whether the people affected by them were accorded citizenship rights, and whether repression and marginalisation were involved. When a visitor sees Kalijodo Park in Jakarta, it is unlikely they will realise that creating the park involved the forced eviction of at least 2,296 people with methods that included intimidation and other human rights violations (LBH Jakarta 2016). When an ordinary visitor goes to Teras Cikapundung in Bandung, likewise, they rarely know that creating it involved the forced eviction of an entire *kampung* community. In these and many cases, creating new 'public' spaces involves marginalisation.

Raising questions about who constitutes the 'public' in Indonesia's public spaces not only requires us to think critically about processes of marginalisation generated by the increasingly hegemonic managerial urban governance, but it also leads us to glimpse alternatives already present in the many small-scale public spaces found through urban and urbanising Indonesia. The forms of collective governance found in *kampung* in Indonesia's towns and cities and in *banjar* in Bali are living examples of how communities can govern public spaces as common resources. At this scale, community leaders often have a very clear idea of the 'public' they are aiming to serve—and of the boundaries that separate members of their own community from outsiders. Community members typically have relatively easy access to decision-makers. Collective governance of public spaces in *kampung* of course generates its own internal messiness, inequalities and tensions. It can give rise to new forms of exclusion, alongside inclusion. Such dynamics are unavoidable, perhaps necessary, features of collaborative social structures. Overall, however, collective governance of public spaces in *kampung* provides insights into what can be achieved through the initiatives of ordinary people.

If neighbourhoods generally have collective processes to manage public spaces, higher levels of governments tend to adopt professional patterns of management that provide little room for citizen engagement. It is also more difficult for people to imagine a clear sense of 'the public' at larger scales, such as at the city level, than in the more intimate communities of the *kampung*. Indonesia's system of population registration of course provides one answer: the 'public' in a city are those who hold an identity card (Kartu Tanda Penduduk, KTP) issued there. But this is also problematic, because cities in Indonesia are highly diverse and they constantly attract migrants and visitors. While urban public spaces in local neighbourhoods such as Kampung Peneleh in Surabaya or Kampung Yoboi in Sentani point to residents' ability to collectively build, maintain and safeguard their own public spaces at relatively intimate scale, the main streets and squares of big cities like Jakarta are answerable to a wider group of citizens, especially in terms of their political function.

For example, what are 'appropriate' uses of a main street in the capital city? Should it be a thoroughfare only for cars and other vehicles to use? Should it be pedestrianised? Should motorcycles be part of the traffic? Should *becak* (three-wheel pedicabs) be allowed? These are questions only with regard to traffic flow, but even such apparently 'pragmatic' questions can raise political issues, such as marginalisation (*becak* have long been banned from Jakarta's streets) and power inequalities, such as those that separate those who can afford automobiles and those who cannot. However, there are more openly political uses that can be even more contested, such as whether main city streets should be open for public protests and political rallies. Indeed, public spaces in the city, especially those that relate to centres of power and are of symbolic importance to many people outside the city, come with a political expectation that they will also serve citizens beyond the city's administrative boundaries. Hence locations like Jalan Thamrin in Jakarta or the Gedung Sate (Governor's Office) in Bandung are places that regularly attract protestors from outside the city who come to express diverse political demands and viewpoints. Such functions are of course essential to the role that cities can play, not only in providing public space but in generating a public sphere.

Conclusion

In this short chapter, I have not been able to elaborate much on how public spaces are used for public protests, or for other overtly political purposes. But I hope to have shown that even apparently mundane and everyday practices of governance of public space in Indonesian cities are themselves inherently political. In particular, they all raise questions of who constitutes the 'public' with the right to use these spaces. The ability to decide on how public spaces are used and managed should be a distinctive role of citizens; the outsourcing of those decisions to large-scale private developers is a dampener of democratisation of public space in Indonesia. We therefore need to adopt an attitude of scepticism when surveying the new physical landscapes of urban Indonesia. As well as expressing amazement at and admiration for the new beautifully manicured parks and green spaces that are emerging in Indonesian cities, we also need to engage in critical questioning when we see such landscapes. We need to examine the power relations that produce them and analyse whose voices were heard and whose voices were ignored in their creation.

More generally, I hope my analysis has shown that nurturing critical spatial perspectives is urgently needed. In the future, we need more discussion of inclusion and exclusion practices in Indonesia's urban governance. We need to challenge patterns of marginalisation and repression that have already become embedded in the capitalist-managerial city. The political aspect that is inherent to the concept of public space means that governance of public space is not only about practical or technical management of matters such as cleanliness and aesthetics. It also needs to encompass an ideological aspect: governance of urban space should be consistent with the ideological bases of the society in which it operates. For example, if upholding human rights and democracy are basic principles that operate at the ideological level to frame managerial city leadership (and the new breed of city leaders certainly claim to be acting in the name of democracy and human rights), then the way public spaces are in practice designed, built and operated should not contradict, let alone sacrifice, those principles.

My analysis suggests that a new vision should be achievable. The examples of neighbourhood-scale public spaces in this chapter provide encouraging evidence that it is possible to infuse new modes of more open governance into the management of public spaces (Public Intellectual Forum 2020). Neighbourhood-scale experiences show that urban Indonesians can construct beautiful, clean and green public spaces while enabling meaningful participation of residents, no matter how imperfect or challenging such processes may be. Indonesian cities need to become places that allow meaningful roles for ordinary citizens to socially construct their public spaces, starting from the neighbourhoods, but also moving up in scale to encompass large-scale urban spaces.

References

Bayat, Asef. 2012. 'Politics in the city-inside-out'. *City & Society* 24(2): 110–28. doi.org/10.1111/j.1548-744X.2012.01071.x

Budd, Leslie and Alessandro Sancino. 2016. 'A framework for city leadership in multilevel governance settings: The comparative contexts of Italy and the UK'. *Regional Studies, Regional Science* 3(1): 129–45. doi.org/10.1080/21681376.2015.1125306

detikJatim. 2022. 'Riwayat penutupan Dolly, sindiran untuk Risma hingga bebas prostitusi [History of Dolly's closure, from a critique of Risma to prostitution cleanup]'. *detikJatim*, 18 June. www.detik.com/jatim/budaya/d-6133606/riwayat-penutupan-dolly-sindiran-untuk-risma-hingga-bebas-prostitusi

Douglass, Mike and G.W. Jones. 2008. 'Mega-urban region dynamics in comparative perspective'. In *Mega-urban Regions in Pacific Asia: Urban Dynamics in a Global Era*, edited by Gavin W. Jones and Mike Douglass, 320–49. NUS Press.

Harms, Erik. 2012. 'Beauty as control in the new Saigon: Eviction, new urban zones, and atomized dissent in a Southeast Asian city'. *American Ethnologist* 39(4): 735–50. doi.org/10.1111/j.1548-1425.2012.01392.x

Herlambang, Suryono, Helga Leitner, Liong Ju Tjung, Eric Sheppard and Dimitar Anguelov. 2019. 'Jakarta's great land transformation: Hybrid neoliberalisation and informality'. *Urban Studies* 56(4): 627–48. doi.org/10.1177/0042098018756556

Jayabuana, Nuriman. 2016. 'Kepercayaan publik modal besar Ahok [Public trust is Ahok's capital]'. *Media Indonesia*, September.

Kusno, Abidin. 2004. 'Whither nationalist urbanism? Public life in Governor Sutiyoso's Jakarta'. *Urban Studies* 41(12): 2377–94. doi.org/10.1080/00420980412331297582

Kusno, Abidin. 2013. *After the New Order: Space, Politics, and Jakarta*. University of Hawai'i Press. doi.org/10.21313/hawaii/9780824837457.001.0001

Kusumowidagdo, Astrid, Agus Sachari and Pribadi Widodo. 2016. 'Visitors' perceptions on the important factors of atrium design in shopping centers: A study of Gandaria City Mall and Ciputra World in Indonesia'. *Frontiers of Architectural Research* 5(1): 52–62. doi.org/10.1016/j.foar.2015.11.003

LBH (Lembaga Bantuan Hukum; Legal Aid Institute) Jakarta. 2016. 'Penggusuran Kalijodo, pemerintah DKI lakukan pelanggaran HAM [Kalijodo eviction, Jakarta government commits human rights violations]'. LBH Jakarta. https://bantuanhukum.or.id/penggusuran-kalijodo-pemerintah-dki-lakukan-pelanggaran-ham

Liputan6. 2020. 'Menko Luhut sebut Ahok mampu bersih-bersih korupsi di Pertamina [Coordinating Minister Luhut says Ahok can clean up corruption at Pertamina]'. *Liputan6*, 25 February. https://www.liputan6.com/bisnis/read/4187524/menko-luhut-sebut-ahok-mampu-bersih-bersih-korupsi-di-pertamina

Maclean, Kate. 2017. 'Disarming charisma? Mayoralty, gender and power in Medellín, Colombia'. *Political Geography* 59: 126–35. doi.org/10.1016/j.polgeo.2017.05.001

Nailufar, Nibras Nada. 2016. 'Survei SMRC: 75 persen warga DKI puas dengan kinerja Ahok [SMRC survey: 75 per cent of Jakarta residents satisfied with Ahok's performance]'. *Kompas.com*, 20 October. https://megapolitan.kompas.com/read/2016/10/20/20290451/survei.smrc.75.persen.warga.dki.puas.dengan.kinerja.ahok

Padawangi, Rita. 2019a. 'Forced evictions, spatial (un)certainties and the making of exemplary centres in Indonesia'. *Asia Pacific Viewpoint* 60(1): 65–79. doi.org/10.1111/apv.12213

Padawangi, Rita. 2019b. 'Pedestrians, vendors: Unite for more, wider sidewalks!' *Jakarta Post*, 16 September.

Padawangi, Rita and Mike Douglass. 2015. 'Water, water everywhere: Toward participatory solutions to chronic urban flooding in Jakarta'. *Pacific Affairs* 88(3): 517–50. doi.org/10.5509/2015883517

Prasetyo, Frans Ari. 2018. 'Berebut lahan (kota) dan kepastian tenurial (Bagian II, Selesai) [Fighting over (city) land and tenurial security (Part II, Complete)]'. ARC Indonesia, 10 October. https://arc.or.id/berebut-lahan-kota-dan-kepastian-tenurial-bagian-ii-selesai

Public Intellectual Forum. 2020. 'Beyond a "new normal": Towards a new paradigm for transforming society'. Draft 0.91. Working Group on Cultural Institutions Development, Directorate of Cultural Workers and Institutions Development, Directorate General of Culture, Ministry of Education and Culture, Indonesia.

Savirani, Amalinda and Edward Aspinall. 2017. 'Adversarial linkages: The urban poor and electoral politics in Jakarta'. *Journal of Current Southeast Asian Affairs* 36(3): 3–34. doi.org/10.1177/186810341703600301

Schmidt, Leonie. 2012. 'Urban Islamic spectacles: Transforming the space of the shopping mall during Ramadan in Indonesia'. *Inter-Asia Cultural Studies* 13(3): 384–407. doi.org/10.1080/14649373.2012.689708

Sennett, Richard. 1977. *The Fall of Public Man*. W.W. Norton & Company.

Simmel, Georg. 1903. *The Metropolis and Mental Life*. Blackwell.

Smith, Neil and Setha Low. 2006. 'Introduction: The imperative of public space'. In *The Politics of Public Space*, edited by Setha Low and Neil Smith, 1–16. Routledge.

Tempo.co. 2022. '6 tahun penggusuran Kalijodo: Rencana Ahok hingga sosok Daeng Aziz' [6 years of Kalijodo eviction: Ahok's plan to Daeng Aziz]. *Tempo.co*, 28 February. https://metro.tempo.co/read/1565422/6-tahun-penggusuran-kalijodo-rencana-ahok-hingga-sosok-daeng-aziz

UN-Habitat. 2016. 'Public space in Surabaya enhances community spirit, preserves heritage'. UN-Habitat, 2 August. https://unhabitat.org/public-space-in-surabaya-enhances-community-spirit-preserves-heritage

Weber, Max. 1921. *The City*. The Free Press.

Wirth, Louis. 1938. 'Urbanism as a way of life'. *American Journal of Sociology* 44(1): 1–24. doi.org/10.1086/217913

Yewen, Roberthus and Pythag Kurniati. 2022. 'Menengok cantiknya Kampung Yoboi, desa wisata di atas Danau Sentani (1) [See the beauty of Yoboi village, a tourist village on Lake Sentani]'. *Kompas.com*, 4 April. https://regional.kompas.com/read/2022/04/04/100532978/menengok-cantiknya-kampung-yoboi-desa-wisata-di-atas-danau-sentani-1?page=all

Yuniar, Resty Woro. 2020. 'Monas dan polemik proyek revitalisasi: "Gubernur Ali Sadikin hingga Anies Baswedan gagal memahami visi Sukarno" [Monas and the revitalisation project polemic: 'Governor Ali Sadikin to Anies Baswedan failed to understand Sukarno's vision']'. BBC News Indonesia, 4 February. www.bbc.com/indonesia/indonesia-51367418

13 Urban security governance in contemporary Jakarta

Ian Wilson

A rapid staccato pop of pistol fire echoed down the long dimly lit corridor. I was at the Senayan shooting range in central Jakarta to meet with senior players in Jakarta's booming private security industry. 'We come here regularly to hone our skills, socialise and to meet and train clients', shouted Pak Brata. Hailing from a military family, he is director of Agung Rahardja Manunggal Yahya, or PT ARMY, a security company specialising in VIP bodyguard services and security for 'national vital objects', or *objek vital nasional*, typically extractive industry facilities. A career security professional, he has done specialist training in Israel and the United States and accompanied clients to Somalia and Iraq. As a senior figure in the nationalist paramilitary organisation Pemuda Pancasila (Pancasila Youth), Brata is also responsible for coordinating its 'core commandos' (*komando inti*, KOTI), who undergo focused physical and ideological training and are tasked with protecting the organisation's leadership. As we attempted to talk over the din, a group of Bank Negara Indonesia (BNI) executives clumsily shot at paper targets under the instruction of another security company director. 'He's just finished providing briefings to BNI and Shangrila Hotel Group on 2024', says Brata. 'An election year means lots of business for us. Companies want contingency plans, like how to get staff to the airport if there's unrest, potential hotspots and risks to company assets.' Noticing my interest in the executives' bespoke gold-plated pistols being diligently cleaned by pistol range staff, he added 'more and more corporate clients are carrying guns nowadays. The more they have, the less safe they feel'.

What does it mean to be secure in twenty-first century Jakarta? While for the city's bank executives it may mean access to a firearm and specialist bodyguard services, for others it can be a matter of securing a place to live free from risk of eviction. Security perceptions and needs depend upon who and where you are in the city. Rather than consisting of fixed properties, security is politically constructed and contested, conceptually and in practice; notions of security and risk are also central to how cities are planned, built, governed, inhabited and imagined (Zeiderman 2016). Terrorism, for example, has strengthened the idea of urban space as a prime site of international violence and insecurity, with cities now included as security referent objects—that is, as the thing that needs to be protected or secured (Beall et al. 2013). Urban security governance reflects and reproduces sociopolitical ordering practices, with those in politically and socially dominant positions often able to dictate how governments and private actors alike conceive and enforce security. It is also shaped by socioeconomic forces and the perceptions and insecurities of residents. This is particularly the case in Global South cities such as Jakarta, which are characterised by dense highly heterogeneous societies and often extreme forms of socioeconomic inequality and spatial segregation. In such cities, people with contrasting if not conflicting interests live, work and operate in close proximity to one another.

The economists Jayadev and Bowles (2006) outlined the concept of 'guard labour' to refer to those employed or otherwise engaged in the protection of private property and the enforcement of claims on resources and maintenance of distributional advantages in a society.[1] They argue growing guard labour workforces are linked to high levels of inequality as states commit a larger fraction of the economy's productive potential to protecting the sociopolitical order that produces inequalities. Guard labour often has a distinctly urban and sociospatial component, with high population density and economic disparity in large cities producing increased physical segregation, heightened control of access to buildings and infrastructure, and often multiple overlapping surveillance and policing regimes of privatised space. The greatest expansion of guard labour economies in recent years has been in low and lower-middle income countries in the Asia-Pacific, driven by rising urbanisation, income inequality, perceptions of insecurity and demand for private in lieu of public security services, as well as by the role played by private security as a desired status symbol for affluent classes (Freedonia 2022).

---

1 Jayadev and Bowles include a wide range of occupations in their definition of guard labour: supervisory labour, private guards, police, judicial and prison employees, and military and civilian employees of departments of defence.

Indonesia has been, in this regard, long ahead of the global trend whereby over half the world's population now live in countries with more private security guards than public police officers (Provost 2017); Indonesia has one of the highest per capita ratios of private security in the world.[2]

Approaching urban security as a contested political domain that shapes and is shaped by socioeconomic relations and interests, this chapter considers urban security governance in contemporary Jakarta by examining two security 'providers' and interrelated sets of security practices: private security companies and social organisations (*organisasi masyarakat*, *ormas*). I argue that processes of urban and socioeconomic change are producing changes in the market for, and governance of, security in Jakarta, giving rise to a recalibration, if not tensions, between two models of security provision. The first, referred to as 'horizontal security', is based in security practices in *kampung*, the poor and low-income neighbourhoods that have historically dominated Jakarta. This form of security provision has been non-technological and largely dominated by informal groups such as *preman* (gangsters), local strongmen and *ormas*, usually acting in coordination with formal security agencies. It was typically oriented towards pursuing modes of social and political control forged during the authoritarian New Order regime (1966–1998). The second, 'vertical security', is a newer, corporatised model that involves professionalisation of security services, their transformation into a market commodity, and the 'fortressing' of upper-middle and high-income residential spaces such as high-rise buildings, business centres and gated communities. This mode increasingly entails the integration of emerging forms of security technology, such as facial recognition and artificial intelligence, and collaboration with transnational security actors. While Jakarta's built environment has become gradually more vertical and marked by more spaces for the exclusive use of a growing upper-middle class, it will be shown that there is not a simple process of one security model displacing another. Rather, both models continue to be closely intertwined and, in some instances, mutually supportive in the reproduction of sociospatial inequality.

This chapter begins with an outline of urban security governance in Jakarta during the New Order, when the regime sought to discipline and

---

2 According to the Indonesian Security Industry Association (Asosiasi Badan Usaha Jasa Pengamanan Indonesia, Abujapi), as of June 2023 there were 5,407 registered security providers in Indonesia with a workforce of approximately 1.6 million. This does not include the large numbers of informal and illicit security providers. This compares with the relatively low per capita number of police personnel at approximately 450,000 in total, or one per 600 citizens.

integrate security threats, such as *preman*, as state-sanctioned security actors. It then examines the post–New Order fragmentation of security governance and the emergence of a dynamic private security market, as well as the regulatory role played by the police. Driven by Jakarta's urban transformation, it is suggested the marketisation of security has favoured high-capital, often transnational, private security providers, which has facilitated a technological turn in security provision. The chapter continues with an analysis of changes in *kampung*-level security and the dynamic and ongoing, albeit often contradictory, role played by *preman* and *ormas*, before concluding with observations on the relationship between horizontal and vertical security regimes.

Protecting from 'the enemy within': Indonesia's urban security model

The New Order regime placed an obsession with order (*ketertiban*) and security (*keamanan*) at the centre of political and ideological discourse. There was a kind of institutionalised regime paranoia, with security officials both positioning the state as the central coordinating security actor and engaging constantly in attempts to calculate the threats to the state emanating from within society (Bubandt 2005). 'Security' was founded through the establishment of the state as the central coordinating security actor with *keamanan* and *ketertiban* becoming ideological and institutional cornerstones of the regime. Security operated as a totalising discourse that tied aspects of daily life together, while at the same time officials were often decidedly obtuse about whose or what's security was being endangered by the threats they identified.

From the late 1970s sustained urbanisation had both demographic and spatial impacts, producing increasingly densely populated informal residential settlements. The regime harboured deep concerns regarding supposed dangers to the state posed by the byproducts of economic inequality: poverty, crime and, in the words of Admiral Sudomo, commander of the Operational Command for the Restoration of Security and Order (Kopkamtib), 'too many people' (van der Kroef 1985: 747). State agencies subjected low-income neighbourhoods to a range of often contradictory interventions, classifications and governmentalities that framed, shaped and constrained political agency and which were designed to ensure social and political passivity while simultaneously being deeply intrusive and disruptive (Wilson 2019). Meanwhile, the low per capita ratio of police produced a shortfall of security provision that gave opportunities to gangs and other protection-offering groups to grow and expand.

By the 1980s, officials began to see the rise of informal security actors as a threat to the legitimacy of the police, with the national chief of police, Awaloedin Djamin, predicting that unless something was done, Indonesia would see organised crime equivalent to the Yakuza in Japan, or the Mafia (Barker 1998). Highly reported instances of violent crime also panicked the middle and upper classes. In Jakarta, the 1980s was the beginning of a period of significant urban transformation. Construction of the first of what would be hundreds of new town developments had begun, catering to an emergent aspirational middle class in a city that been dominated by *kampung* (Herlambang et al. 2019). Oligarchic interests had also begun to consolidate, given that 'the families of powerful officials and military officers ... directly entered the world of business in their own right as owners of capital and as shareholders' (Hadiz and Robison 2013: 47). This convergence of state and capital necessitated a new organisation of urban security.

The police established the Environment Security System (Sistem Keamanan Lingkungan, Siskamling) in the early 1980s as a means of reorganising the local security apparatus. Based upon the territorial system used by the military and in Indonesia's community security traditions, Siskamling comprised networks of security posts manned, depending on location, by either local residents or registered security guards under the direction and monitoring of the police. Known as Pos Kamling, these posts were subject to inventory, classification and inspection. This new system served to reassert state control, at least partially, over security governance by breaking down territory into small, readily observable units, which in turn fragmented the territorial domains of gangs and local rackets.

Siskamling operated as a framework for the integration and disciplining of various security actors. Residents, *preman*, gangs, martial arts groups and commercial security providers, among others, were recruited into two types of security guards. The first type consisted of civil security guards (*pertahanan sipil*, *hansip*) and resident-organised night patrols (*ronda malam*); they were made responsible for neighbourhood security. The second category, security guards (*satuan pengamanan*, *satpam*), had the task of guarding commercial properties, who paid them for their services. Coordinated by a specially created police division known as 'Society Guidance' (Bimbingan Masyarakat, Bimmas), all *hansip* and *satpam* were required to participate in police-run training courses, after which they were issued a licence and a uniform.

By the mid-1990s, the number of *satpam* was already significantly greater than the police (Barker 1998). The Siskamling model generated a vast expansion of security and surveillance throughout urban Indonesia.

Operating as extensions of the police, *satpam* authority was limited to the properties they guarded. Commercial property and business owners were responsible for finding and paying *satpam*. This system had some hiccups, especially because some intended consumers of *satpam* services defaulted to employing informal groups or gangs, due to fear, undersupply of formal *satpam* or cost pressures. As Barker (1998) noted, the initial lack of sufficient numbers of officially recognised *satpam* resulted in a brief partnership between the police and gang-run security businesses. This partnership soon declined due to enforcement of new regulatory measures intended to shut down non–state approved security providers and screen out 'bad apples'. For example, ex-convicts were prohibited from working as *satpam* (a measure still in place today), a move that excluded large gangs, such as Prems, that consisted of networks of ex-convicts.

Security governance via Siskamling also operated as a means to absorb the unemployed or under-employed into the ranks of guard labour, offsetting the risks to *keamanan* and *ketertiban* they might otherwise have posed. The growth of formal guard labour thus pushed organisations and individuals with links to criminality into a more precarious position, as seen in the Petrus (Penembakan Misterius, Mysterious Killings) extrajudicial killings of the 1980s in which security agencies conspicuously targeted ex-cons, petty criminals and recidivists. The formalisation of the sector also brought gangs and protection organisations more firmly under the patronage of state agencies, primarily the military, upon whom the gangs' own security was at least partially dependent (Wilson 2015).

Siskamling resulted in two distinct but interrelated sets of practices that formed the basis of later horizontal and vertical security regimes. One involved institutionalisation of a proto state-private model for security governance of business, commercial assets and property through the sociospatial organisation of the *satpam* system. This model entailed an Indonesian version of what Pow (2013) has called 'defensive urbanism', a security practice that combined the social preferences of growing middle and upper classes, entrenched paranoia of the regime about the urban masses, and the consolidation of state-capital interests, especially over peri-urban land development. A second set of practices was visible in *kampung* and mixed low-income neighbourhoods, where Siskamling combined self-policing by community members with subjection of residents to localised security regimes, often led by local gangsters and strongmen, whose authority was underpinned by relations to state authorities, in particular the military (Wilson 2015). This system of securing low-income zones did not focus on protecting residents and their property from crime or threats of redistribution, as *satpam* were doing in wealthier locales. Rather, its point was the political regulation and control of urban society.

Fragmentation and liberalisation: Post–New Order security governance

The end of the New Order saw fragmentation of security governance across Jakarta. From being integrated within a central state, security and protection activities rapidly became privatised and atomised within the context of more diffuse and ambiguous forms of authority. The violence of 1998 shook the city; now, residents actively sought security, often directly through local community groups, social organisations and vigilantism. New democratic rights and freedoms combined with a resurgence of localism generated vocal and organised demands from residents for security of place in the city and greater access to space and services. There was also a proliferation of new organisations and groups, many of which made aggressive claims to territory—physical, economic, social and moral.

The immediate outcome was an explosion of security actors, and of violent contestations over territory, authority and legitimacy. The early 2000s in Jakarta were something of a wild frontier period, as old security regimes fell or were challenged by new contenders. Lucrative control over parking, for example, in districts such as Tanah Abang and Menteng, resulted in bloody turf wars between rival gangs, *ormas*, civil ordinance police (Satpol PP) and residents (Wilson 2015).

The Police Law of 2002 was an attempt to establish a new decentralised mode of managing this complexity, by recognising a 'limited non-judicial policing role' for police-recognised 'voluntary societal security groups' (Pengamanan Masyarakat Swakarsa, Pam Swakarsa) within a 'territorial sphere' (*lingkungan kuasa tempat*).[3] This change gave state-sanctioned legitimacy, and all the opportunities this opened up, to commercial security providers, and to an array of social, community and political organisations with direct or tangential concerns with security (Dinata 2020). It also amounted to a managed privatisation of security, even if it was not a full neoliberal outsourcing of state competencies, insofar that the creation of a private security market from the early 2000s did little more than formalise the older harnessing by the state of *preman* and *satpam*. It did, however, generate an eventual drive towards professionalisation and a market competition dynamic after the relative turbulence and territorialism of the early 2000s. The new framework also consolidated a lucrative gatekeeper function for the police.

---

3 This move triggered significant concerns from civil society groups, considering that militias and gangs organised by elements of the military, also known as Pam Swakarsa, had played a prominent violent role in 1998 when mobilised by the military against student demonstrators.

To legally operate, security companies now needed to be registered with the police, and all *satpam* were required to undergo at least one of three levels of police-directed training. Defined as members of 'a professional group performing limited non-judicial police functions' and recognised via recruitment by a registered security company, *satpam* were empowered to operate as proxy police within the property of their work environment. In 2006, a national security providers association (Asosiasi Badan Usaha Jasa Pengamanan Indonesia, Abujapi) was established as the sole government-recognised body for commercial security providers. Reflecting the hybrid public-private status of *satpam*, Abujapi has formal relations with the police while also being a member of the Chamber of Business and Commerce (Kamar Dagang dan Industri Indonesia, Kadin). To be formally recognised and registered, private security providers need to affiliate with Abujapi. The 'voluntary societal security groups' outlined in the police law were not limited, however, to security companies; instead, they encompassed everything from customary security actors such as Pecalang in Bali, through to established paramilitary organisations like Pemuda Pancasila and Banser (the affiliate of the mass Islamic organisation Nahdlatul Ulama), to newer social and religious organisations such as Forum Betawi Rempug (Betawi Brotherhood Forum) and Front Pembela Islam (Defenders of Islam Front). Continuing recognition of such groups signalled continuity with longstanding official Indonesian security doctrines recognising the need for societal mobilisation against potential political and ideological threats from within.

Going up: Private security and urban change in Jakarta

Private security is changing cities globally. Its presence is most intense in Global South countries where social inequality is high and public security is fragmented or tenuous, and where changes in the structure of urban development and governance have been rapid (Garmany and Galdeano 2018). Changes in the political economy of security providers in Jakarta over the past two decades are symptomatic of these broad global trends.

As the impacts of the 1997–1998 economic crisis waned in the early 2000s, there was a boom in office buildings, apartments, shopping malls, gated communities and integrated superblocks.[4] All these developments created increasing demands for private security. The relative porousness

---

4 Superblocks are integrated urban developments that include offices, residences, recreational facilities and commercial facilities such as shopping malls within a single large-scale mega-project. Jakarta currently has approximately 30 superblock developments. See Herlambang et al. (2019).

of social relations in Jakarta's *kampung* and mixed neighbourhoods stands in contrast to the fortress-like urbanism of these new developments. At the same time, commercialised and controlled private spaces have increasingly assumed the functions of public spaces, with malls, of which Jakarta has over 180, being used as de facto public gathering places. In the face of problems such as traffic congestion and air pollution, malls and superblocks are places to which many escape for entertainment and relaxation, with security and safety key attractions. Unlike civic spaces, however, these commercial locales are highly undemocratic spaces governed by regulations and security practices imposed by owners and operators.

Segregation in many of the largest cities in the Global South has a strong class component, marked not only by the concentration and isolation of distinct groups of people: the poor in slums, the consuming upper-middle classes in gated spaces (Garrido 2021). Like Manila, Mumbai, Rio de Janeiro and other major Southern cities, contemporary Jakarta has an interspersion of low-income neighbourhoods and affluent enclaves amid urban-majority areas that are neither poor nor solidly middle class. Relations of residents of gated estates and superblock complexes with people from the outside are not completely severed, but are rather reduced to an array of 'functional' interactions with housekeepers, delivery drivers, retail workers and cleaners. There is usually limited non-resident pedestrian traffic. Spatial segregation is less a matter of an absence of social relations than a consolidation of unequal relations between different groups—in ways that are regulated by security practices.

A central selling point to middle- and upper-class consumers of gated and vertical estates in Jakarta is the idea of physical and moral security and detachment/autonomy from the city's infrastructural and social woes. As Gómez (2021) has argued, the apolitical nature and over-securitisation of malls and superblocks is linked to the ambivalence of their users towards the value of the public sphere and their perceptions of public street space as inherently disorderly and insecure. Such attitudes in Indonesia also build upon longstanding security discourses emphasising *ketertiban* as both fundamental to political stability and as a guiding principle of urban management, particularly of the streets. *Satpam* and other private security providers primarily perform a function, not of reducing targeted forms of crime—which have relatively low rates in Jakarta—but as gatekeepers for this social-spatial order via screening, monitoring and regulation of entitlement of entry into private spaces. This gatekeeping role performed by private security in turn functions to consolidate the perception among the inhabitants of these private spaces that they constitute a homogenous community who are in control of their own environment. Security operates as a process for determining inclusion and exclusion, facilitated by the architecture of most estates, superblocks and vertical buildings that operates via a portal gate system with limited, if not single, entry points.

The changing infrastructural face of Jakarta, in particular shifts towards verticality amid the proliferation of high-rise and multistorey buildings and hyper-financialisation of urban space, has generated new kinds of security market demands and opportunities. Integrated security management systems, for example, have become particularly popular in Jakarta's superblocks and commercial districts. Such systems reflect corporate perceptions of security and risk, which extend far beyond conventional concerns with crime or terrorism, to incorporate concerns for pre-employment screening, and information, financial and reputational security. Companies like Secom, for example, offer technology-based security systems that are pitched as enhancing efficiency and productivity and that consolidate 'organisational resilience' by enabling workplace monitoring of staff. Techniques used include AI-powered facial recognition CCTV systems which produce logs of employee data such as attendance, body temperature and workstation use compiled into worksheets to be used by human resource managers (Secom n.d.).

The growing demand for digital surveillance technology and integrated security systems has attracted significant interest from foreign security companies to Indonesia (interview with security practitioner, July 2023). The infrastructure and foreign investment drive of the Joko Widodo administration has accelerated this trend, with industry analysts describing Indonesia as one of the biggest expanding security tech markets (Pao 2018). International security companies operating in Jakarta offer reputational advantages, capital-backing and access to cutting-edge security technology and integrated security systems. Typically, they subcontract local guard labour providers or buy them up and then retrain and rebrand them, to meet the 60:40 foreign ownership requirements for the sector. This influx of foreign firms has caused some disquiet. One Jakarta security company director complained:

> Unlike us, they can circumvent police regulation. We are constantly struggling with cash flow due to delayed contract payments. Foreign companies have more capital, so they can outbid us to secure contracts, then scoop up smaller companies facing collapse. (Interview with Jakarta security company director, July 2023)

One company that has a well-established and extensive presence in Jakarta is G4S, a subsidiary of the United Kingdom–based Securicor group, the world's largest security company. Other major international players in Jakarta include GardaWorld, a Canadian private security firm; the United States–based security and risk management company Global Guardian;

and Secom, Japan's oldest security company, which began operations in Indonesia in 1994.[5] Secom combines 'digital *satpam*'—security personnel fitted with GPS tracking devices that upload movement and GoPro video data—together with integrated technology such as real-time facial recognition, drone surveillance, electronic access control and 24-hour surveillance control centres that are pitched to businesses and households of the rich.[6] Despite the rhetorical commitment of the Jakarta city administration to smart-city security infrastructure, the private security sector's technological push has operated largely outside regulation. It was only in 2016 that Jakarta's governor Basuki Purnama Tjahaja, or Ahok, proposed integrating the patchworks of privately run CCTV and facial recognition infrastructure into a centralised police-managed network, a plan that ended with his departure from office (Salim 2015).

In Jakarta's hyper-competitive private security marketplace, companies place strong emphasis on training and professionalism as a point of differentiation, together with niche specialisation. Personnel executive bodyguard services, for example, have grown in popularity among Jakarta's upper classes, becoming 'the new nanny'. Even so, companies still signal their functional connections to formal authorities, in particular the military, in order to establish their reputations. Serving military commanders are often company advisers or honorary chairpersons, and private security is a staple post-retirement military career path. One company, PT Suksesindo, for example, which offers janitorial services, labour supply, parking systems and security guards, advertises an exclusive vendor relationship with the Agency for Supply of TNI Personnel (Badan Penyalur Tenaga Kerja TNI, Kabalur TNI), a body that provides active, retired or pre-pension TNI personnel to clients 'so that you can concentrate on your core investment and business' (Suksesindo n.d.). Clients and security companies alike particularly desire personnel with military backgrounds in sectors with heightened potential for conflict or need for persuasion, such as land development, manufacturing and banking.

Many larger companies operating in Jakarta engage an array of commercial and informal security actors, determined by need and context. The land developer giant Agung Podomoro, for example, has a mix of in-house security and contracted private security company providers

---

5   Secom's early entry into the Indonesian market, via its subsidiary Secom Bayangkara, was facilitated by the police Brata Bhakti Foundation, which had a 35 per cent share of its operations. For more on the Brata Bhakti Foundation, see Baker (2013).
6   See secom.co.id/services

alongside ongoing relations with several paramilitary and *preman* groups. In managing protest and opposition to Podomoro's commercial interests, the company deploys and coordinates various mixes of these different kinds of security. In 2015, for example, local fishers in Pluit, North Jakarta, demonstrated against the expansion of land reclamation in Jakarta Bay that impacted their livelihoods (Fitriani 2015a, 2015b). The protest was held in front of the Green Bay Pluit superblock, owned by Podomoro, where around several hundred fishers were met by an array of security actors. These included local *preman* already familiar to the fishers, because the *preman* had occupied a small island next to the reclamation site for several weeks in order to prevent the fishers from using it (Pribadi 2015). Members of two paramilitary groups, Laskar Merah Putih and Badan Pembinaan Potensi Keluarga Besar, both with long working relationships with Podomoro, were also present in numbers. Dressed in paramilitary attire, they acted in ways clearly intended to intimidate, some taking photos of demonstrators, others casually taunting them. Cordoning off the street in front of the mall were black uniformed in-house Podomoro *satpam*. Several held banners declaring 'local support' for the reclamation of Jakarta Bay. Meanwhile, several dozen police sat in the background, watching events and only moving to mediate after tempers flared up.

Using intimidation and thuggery in land disputes in Jakarta, while common—particularly in forced evictions—is generally not the preferred approach of corporate clients, who are generally sensitive about negative publicity. This aversion has generated markets for more sophisticated intelligence-based security services. Global Security Service Indonesia (GSSI), for example, provides dispute mediation and investigation services that includes mapping potential local resistance to a client's business interests, usually in relation to land acquisition (interview with GSSI director, July 2023). This intelligence gathering extends to embedding agents within local communities to monitor and identify sentiment. When necessary, according to one security operator, these agents can 'spread false narratives to disrupt and divide sentiment opposed to our client's interests' (interview with security company director, July 2023).

The trend of professionalisation and specialisation within the private security industry in Jakarta has not, however, necessarily translated into improved working conditions for *satpam*. The ambiguous status of *satpam* as 'neither *aparat* [apparatus] nor worker', the historical function played by 'security' in absorbing surplus 'disruptive' populations into guard labour, and the role of *satpam* as an extension of the state in the policing of social protest, come together to obstruct efforts by *satpam* to unionise (GUA Security 2021). The police have strongly opposed unionisation, arguing it threatens the 'limited police role performed by *satpam*' and could lead to situations in which '*satpam* join labour protests rather than protect their clients' assets' (ibid.). *Satpam* labour is inherently precarious, with many *satpam* working on or below minimum wages and on short-term outsourced and contract-based employment (Jurnal Security 2022). It is also costly for individuals to attain professional advancement within the industry by undergoing accredited police or specialist training; even the financial burden of mandatory updated uniforms usually falls on *satpam* themselves.[7] Underpayment of wages, and even non-payment, in the sector is commonplace, with protests and strikes by *satpam* increasing in frequency (Amana 2022). However, trade unions have shown little interest in the sector outside its role as an inhibitor of strike action and labour organising.

Ormas, preman and Jakarta's *kampung*

> Security is envisioned not in the maintenance of tight boundaries and circumscribed information exchange but in the capacity of residents to imagine various circuitries for reaching each other, as well as implicating themselves in each other's economic, and sometimes religious and social lives. (Simone 2013: 252)

The proliferation of private commercial security has been intertwined with Jakarta's urban transformations, such as the segregation of increasingly vertical city space, capital-intensive property developments and subsequent expansion of forms of 'fortress urbanism'. In Jakarta's *kampung* and mixed urban-majority neighbourhoods, security is understood, practised and driven by different uncertainties, perceptions of risks and imperatives. For many residents, securing a livelihood in the city, and a place to live, is the primary focus of everyday life. For such people, security is less a matter of a defensive position, involving gating and screening, than a process of constant negotiation, managing of interests and instrumental seeking of opportunities. For example, informal street vendors will often negotiate, both individually and collectively, with various *preman* and *ormas* in order to identify and secure arrangements that allow them to sustain their livelihoods.

The figure of the *preman* has been ubiquitous throughout Jakarta's history, embodying contradictions concerning security and order (Wilson 2015). During the New Order, *preman* became synonymous with the worst excesses of the regime and the collapsing of public authority into

---

7 Some companies subsidise ongoing *satpam* training, though often it is done on a salary-save basis.

criminality (Ryter 1998; Wilson 2015). In contemporary Jakarta, however, the relationship between *preman* and the neighbourhoods in which they live and operate is complex and contingent, shaped by the altered social relations of post-authoritarian Indonesia. During the New Order, *preman* acquired authority by engaging in intimidation and coercion, and with the backing of the military or police. Such forms of authority are now tempered by an environment in which there are multiple and often competing sources of authority and claim-making, and where at least some degree of community support is necessary for *preman* to operate successfully.

This situation also extends to *ormas*. Organisations such as the ultranationalist paramilitary Pemuda Pancasila performed an important function during the New Order, organising and disciplining otherwise disruptive elements, such as unemployed urban youth and petty gangsters (Wilson 2015). In return for doing so, and for performing other tasks such as harassment of activists and ideological policing of public discourse, Pemuda Pancasila was allowed to pursue its economic interests, including by operating street-level rackets. This and similar arrangements made it attractive for *kampung* residents to affiliate with Pemuda Pancasila and similar groups of local strongmen, as doing so afforded protection from formal security actors, such as the police, and provided important access to economic opportunities.

While continuing to reproduce old-style paramilitarism of this sort, many organisations that have emerged since 1998, such as Forum Betawi Rempug (FBR), combine the territorial authority of *preman* with claim-making expressing the grievances of historically marginal communities, in this instance the Betawi ethnic group indigenous to Jakarta (Wilson 2022). Contemporary *ormas* like FBR occupy a space residing somewhere between community organisation, vigilante group, political party, non-government organisation, employment agency and security guard: they act as a fulcrum and opportunity structure for numerous interests. Operating akin to a franchise with city-wide networks of guard posts, groups like FBR still constitute a significant security presence throughout Jakarta.

The relationships between *preman* or *ormas* and specific neighbourhoods or communities typically change over time. Brutal local regimes, such as that of debt collector John Kei, who was imprisoned in 2012, and again in 2021, for murder, are no longer tolerated by residents and thus tend to be short-lived (Debora and Patnistik 2021). The fragmentation and heterogeneity of actors, and the complexity of local political economy arrangements in post–New Order Jakarta, have given rise to necessity for compromise. Violence is no longer the default strategy of local security regimes. Instead, *preman* increasingly depend for their local authority on their abilities to problem solve by working across boundaries and jurisdictions, negotiating with higher authorities, neighbouring communities or rival groups, or connecting neighbourhoods to networks of opportunity. Skills and capacities in these areas increasingly determine the length and success of *preman* careers.

City government security agencies such as Satpol PP, of course, have their own authority to uphold *ketertiban umum*, under which they manage street economies and urban *kampung* (Wirya et al. 2023). In doing so, they may collaborate with *ormas* and local *preman* but just as often come into open conflict with them, in clashes of competing security orders. Residents of Jakarta's *kampung* and mixed neighbourhoods, for their part, may be subject to predatory behaviour such as extraction of protection fees by *preman* and *ormas*, but in other contexts may benefit from the kinds of patronage these groups distribute and by their ability to mobilise people and resources in defence of shared interests. The 'double-edged sword' of security means, in practice, that *preman* and *ormas* are simultaneously a vehicle for redress and protection for residents as well as contracted third-arm agents of repression acting on behalf of the state, commercial actors or other external interests. *Ormas* often attempt to organise around ideas of territory, claiming authority over particular areas. Doing so takes different forms; some *ormas* try to monopolise an economic sector or patronage network within a specific area (for example, operating a protection racket in a market or bus terminal); others operate as nodes in networks of exchange that span different parts of the city (for example, an ethnic militia sharing job opportunities among its city-wide branches). In mixed urban-majority neighbourhoods, such as Tanah Abang or Tambora, numerous organisations with various territorial stakes engage in ever-changing enmities, alliances and compromises.

Police frequently coordinate with *ormas* during key events, such as elections or labour protests. *Ormas* are potential, and not infrequent, sources of conflict and disorder, and as a result are important partners for the police in security maintenance. During the build up to the 2024 elections, for example, there was considerable coordination between police and *ormas* leaders in Jakarta to ensure that rival political affiliations of *ormas* did not result in conflict, and to harness the social infrastructure of *ormas* to monitor their communities for signs of unrest and to manage potential tension. In some cases, local *ormas* made claims of territorial authority, such as by unilaterally proclaiming a neighbourhood as being committed to supporting a particular candidate or political party.

Despite regulatory frameworks ostensibly governing private security companies, *ormas* are also significant players providing contracted security for factories, businesses and even port facilities. They frequently do so within a local political economy in which local government seeks to coopt the disruptive potential of *ormas* through clientelism. Groups such as FBR, for their part, have tried to capture leadership positions in neighbourhood-level organisations such as *rukun warga* (citizens' associations) and *rukun tetangga* (neighbourhood associations), to secure access to private buyers of security and to facilitate distribution of contracts and resources to their networks.

Although *ormas* and private security companies operate under different rationales and logics of security, they are often intertwined. Many *ormas* operate either registered or informal security companies. Security company directors in Jakarta, for their part, frequently describe their interactions with *ormas* as being time-consuming and expensive. In the words of one director:

> A fundamental difference is that we offer a professional service to paying clients. *Ormas* make claims based on some idea of entitlement or territory and have no skills or professionalism. Often they see us as challengers or interlopers, and so we are forced to manage that accordingly. In some cases, they will stir up locals to oppose our clients, even attack staff or destroy property. It's just a completely different mindset. (Interview with security company director, July 2023)

A security company director who is also a senior figure within Pemuda Pancasila further explained the separate, but interconnected, realms of operation of private security companies and *ormas*:

> If someone wants professional and reliable security services, we provide that via our security company. If they want a mass of people for some political reason or as an intimidatory group, then our *ormas* can potentially help there. (Interview with security company director, July 2023)

Despite the drive towards professionalisation, older logics of the *preman*, in which the sources of insecurity and security are one and the same, still prevail:

> Sometimes clients undervalue our services or significantly underestimate levels of risk to their assets or operations. In some instances, it's helpful to remind them by generating a little bit of chaos. By way of example, as part of operations for corporate clients, like those wanting to set up a new manufacturing business, we map potentially disruptive local elements such as *preman* and *ormas* then seek to coopt and coordinate them, usually through buying off a local boss or official and recruiting some to low-risk, low-skill roles. If our client is being difficult or reluctant to pay we go back to these local lads and say, hey, look, deal's off, nothing to do with us anymore. After the consequences of this start to hit home, often the client will quickly come back begging for our help. (Interview with Jakarta security company director, June 2023)

Conclusion

Urban security governance in contemporary Jakarta consists of uneven patchworks of policing and security provision. The ability and willingness of consumers to pay for security goods and services increasingly determines what actors operate where. The police are perhaps the greatest beneficiaries, operating as paid regulators of the burgeoning private sector and as political gatekeepers of informal and 'community'-based security, alongside continuing in their own formal role.

The changing practice of security governance in Jakarta over the past two decades, such as the increasing role of private transnational actors and security technologies, reflects wider urban transformation and changes in socioeconomic relations. Greater sociospatial segregation of Jakarta's upper-middle classes in hyper-securitised spaces such as superblocks and gated and fenced estates will, if Jakarta follows trends elsewhere, reproduce cultures of anti-democracy, with the experience of the everyday for privileged residents becoming, as a product of fortress urbanism, more detached from and counterposed with the heterogeneity and cacophony of the streets. Meanwhile, increasing use of digital surveillance, and moves towards its city-wide integration via government smart-city frameworks, constitutes a challenge to older patterns of security management, especially the historical political function of security as an absorber of low-skilled labour (itself often framed as a security risk). The COVID-19 pandemic, for example, was devastating for the 'boots on the ground' security industry; Abujapi estimated up to 1,000 registered companies went out of business in Jakarta alone due to a combination of pandemic-related decline in demand together with uptake of CCTV and digital surveillance technology (interview with Abujapi directors, 2023). Reduced demand for *satpam* labour, meanwhile, facilitates the consolidation of high-capital transnational security actors such as G4S, Secom and Titan, a United States–based security firm with a strong presence in Southeast Asia, including Indonesia.

Meanwhile, old patterns of 'horizontal security', found in the complex entanglements of different community, social, government and business actors in Jakarta's *kampung* and mixed urban-majority neighbourhoods, remain deeply intertwined with social and power relations fundamental to everyday struggles to survive and secure a place in the city. In the absence of alternative sources of income and social certainty for lower-class Jakartans, *ormas* and other forms of informal security will likely survive and even continue to grow, not just as sources of (in)security, but as crucial opportunity and brokerage structures for lower-income residents trying to negotiate a place and secure citizenship rights in the city.

Superficially, it appears that vertical security practices are displacing horizontal practices, reflecting Jakarta's rapidly changing skyline. In fact, both remain closely connected, if not intertwined, mechanisms for managing and maintaining sociospatial divisions within the city.

References

Amana, Rizki. 2022. 'Di-PHK sepihak, puluhan satpam Puspiptek gelar aksi demo [Unilaterally laid off, dozens of Puspiptek security guards hold demonstration]'. *WartaKota*, 10 March. https://wartakota.tribunnews.com/2022/03/10/di-phk-sepihak-puluhan-*satpam*-puspiptek-gelar-aksi-demo

Baker, Jacqui. 2013. 'The Parman economy: Post-authoritarian shifts in the off-budget economy of Indonesia's security institutions'. *Indonesia* 96: 123–50. https://hdl.handle.net/1813/54622

Barker, Joshua. 1998. 'State of fear: Controlling the criminal contagion in Suharto's New Order'. *Indonesia* 66: 7–43. doi.org/10.2307/3351446

Beall, Jo, Tom Goodfellow and Dennis Rodgers. 2013. 'Cities and conflict in fragile states in the developing world'. *Urban Studies* 50(15): 3065–83. doi.org/10.1177/0042098013487775

Bubandt, Nils. 2005. 'Vernacular security: The politics of feeling safe in global, national and local worlds'. *Security Dialogue* 36(3): 275–96. www.jstor.org/stable/26298960

Debora, Sonya Teresa and Egidius Patnistik. 2021. 'John Kei divonis 15 tahun penjara [John Kei sentenced to 15 years in prison]'. *Kompas.com*, 20 May. https://megapolitan.kompas.com/read/2021/05/20/16375031/john-kei-divonis-15-tahun-penjara

Dinata, Andhika. 2020. 'Perpol 4/2020, polemik dan kontroversi Pamswakarsa [Political regulation 4/2020, Pamswakarsa polemic and controversy]'. *Gatra.com*, 18 September. www.gatra.com/news-490657-politik-perpol-42020-polemik-dan-kontroversi-pamswakarsa.html

Fitriani, Feni Freycinetia. 2015a. 'Demo tolak reklamasi: Massa nelayan dihadang security pendukung reklamasi [Demonstration against reclamation: Fishermen confronted by security supporting reclamation]'. *Bisnis.com*, 2 December. https://jakarta.bisnis.com/read/20151202/77/497870/demo-tolak-reklamasi-massa-nelayan-dihadang-security-pendukung-reklamasi

Fitriani, Feni Freycinetia. 2015b. 'Nelayan Muara Angke gelar demo tolak reklamasi 17 pulau [Muara Angke fishermen hold demonstration against the reclamation of 17 islands]'. *Bisnis.com*, 2 December. https://jakarta.bisnis.com/read/20151202/77/497860/nelayan-muara-angke-gelar-demo-tolak-reklamasi-17-pulau

Freedonia. 2022. *Global Security Services April 2022*. Freedonia Group. www.freedoniagroup.com/industry-study/global-security-services-4399.htm

Garmany, Jeff and Ana Paula Galdeano. 2018. 'Crime, insecurity and corruption: Considering the growth of urban private security'. *Urban Studies* 55(5): 1111–20. doi.org/10.1177/0042098017732691

Garrido, Marco. 2021. 'Reconceptualizing segregation from the Global South'. *City & Community* 20(1): 24–37. doi.org/10.1111/cico.12504

Gómez, Luis Alfonso Escudero. 2021. 'The reconfiguration of urban public-private spaces in the mall: False security, antidemocratization, and apoliticalization'. *Sustainability* 13: 12447. doi.org/10.3390/su132212447

GUA Security. 2021. 'Terkait aksi buruh nasional, ini himbauan Abujapi untuk BUJP di Indonesia [Re national labor action, Abujapi's appeal to BUJP in Indonesia]'. GUA Security, 6 December. https://gardautama.co.id/terkait-aksi-buruh-nasional-ini-himbauan-abujapi-untuk-bujp-di-indonesia

Hadiz, Vedi R. and Richard Robison. 2013. 'The political economy of oligarchy and the reorganization of power in Indonesia'. *Indonesia* 96(1): 35–57. doi.org/10.5728/indonesia.96.0033

Herlambang, Suryono, Helga Leitner, Liong Ju Tjung, Eric Sheppard and Dimitar Anguelov. 2019. 'Jakarta's great land transformation: Hybrid neoliberalisation and informality'. *Urban Studies* 56(4): 627–48. doi.org/10.1177/0042098018756556

Jayadev, Arjun and Samuel Bowles. 2006. 'Guard labor'. *Journal of Development Economics* 79(2): 328–48. doi.org/10.1016/j.jdeveco.2006.01.009

Jurnal Security. 2022. '*Satpam* protes masalah gaji, ini penjelasan outsourcing mereka bernaung [Security guards protest over salary: This is the explanation of their outsourcing company]'. Jurnal Security, 17 June. https://jurnalsecurity.com/*satpam*-protes-masalah-gaji-ini-penjelasan-outsourcing-mereka-bernaung

Pao, William. 2018. 'What's driving Indonesia security growth?' *Asmag.com*, 29 November. www.asmag.com/showpost/30382.aspx

Pow, Choon-Piew. 2013. 'Consuming private security: Consumer citizenship and defensive urbanism in Singapore'. *Theoretical Criminology* 17(2): 179–96. doi.org/10.1177/1362480612472782

Pribadi, Andy. 2015. 'Proyek reklamasi Pantura dijaga preman bertato [Pantura reclamation project guarded by tattooed thugs]'. *WartaKota*, 23 November. https://wartakota.tribunnews.com/2015/11/23/proyek-reklamasi-pantura-dijaga-preman-bertato

Provost, Claire. 2017. 'The industry of inequality: Why the world is obsessed with private security'. *The Guardian*, 12 May. www.theguardian.com/inequality/2017/may/12/industry-of-inequality-why-world-is-obsessed-with-private-security

Ryter, Loren. 1998. 'Pemuda Pancasila: The last loyalist free men of Suharto's order?' *Indonesia* 66: 44–73. doi.org/10.2307/3351447

Salim, Hanz Jimenez. 2015. 'Ahok gandeng polda metro bangun pusat kontrol CCTV [Ahok collaborates with metro police to build CCTV control centre]'. *Liputan6.com*, 6 August. www.liputan6.com/news/read/2287689/ahok-gandeng-polda-metro-bangun-pusat-kontrol-cctv?page=4

Secom. n.d. 'Facilities monitoring'. Accessed 16 January 2024, https://secom.co.id/services/facilities-monitoring

Simone, AbdouMaliq. 2013. 'Cities of uncertainty: Jakarta, the urban majority, and inventive political technologies'. *Theory, Culture & Society* 30(7–8): 243–63. doi.org/10.1177/0263276413501872

Suksesindo. n.d. 'Jasa pengamanan (Security)'. Accessed 16 January 2024, www.suksesindo.com/berita/layanan/jasa-pengamanan-security

van der Kroef, Justus. 1985. ' "Petrus": Patterns of prophylactic murder in Indonesia'. *Asian Survey* 25(7): 745–59. doi.org/10.2307/2644242

Wilson, Ian Douglas. 2015. *The Politics of Protection Rackets in Post–New Order Indonesia: Coercive Capital, Authority and Street Politics*. Routledge. doi.org/10.4324/9780203799192

Wilson, Ian. 2019. 'Urban poor activism and political agency in post–New Order Jakarta'. In *Activists in Transition: Progressive Politics in Democratic Indonesia*, edited by Thushara Dibley and Michele Ford, 99–116. Cornell University Press. www.jstor.org/stable/10.7591/j.ctvpwhg5w

Wilson, Ian. 2022. 'The political economy of polarization: Militias, street authority and the 2019 elections'. In *The Jokowi-Prabowo Elections 2.0*, edited by Hui Yew-Foong and Made Supriatma, 109–26. ISEAS Publishing. https://bookshop.iseas.edu.sg/publication/7813

Wirya, A., A. Muzaki and N. Puspitasari. 2023. *In the Name of Public Order: An Assessment of the Concept and Implementation of Public Order in Indonesia*. Lembaga Bantuan Hukum Masyarakat, Jakarta.

Zeiderman, Austin. 2016. *Endangered City: The Politics of Security and Risk in Bogotá*. Duke University Press. doi.org/10.2307/j.ctv11g97hx

14 Leading the way: A mayor's perspective on urban leadership in Indonesia

Bima Arya Sugiarto

Since the introduction of direct local elections in Indonesia in 2005, urban issues have garnered increasing scholarly attention. Numerous observers—including some who write in this volume—have suggested that urban leadership has emerged as a pivotal factor alongside urban planning in influencing how a city develops, and how effective a city government is at meeting the aspirations and needs of its residents. In this chapter, I bring my personal perspective on this issue, drawing on my decade of experience as mayor of Bogor city (2014–2024) and as chairperson of the Association of Indonesian Municipal Governments (Asosiasi Pemerintah Kota Seluruh Indonesia, Apeksi) since 2021. I focus on investigating urban leadership dynamics, the obstacles mayors encounter as they go about the tasks of urban governance and planning, and the models of leadership employed. While I draw primarily on my own experiences, I am sure that the perspectives articulated here mirror in many respects the daily experiences of many mayors and regional leaders in Indonesia. At the same time, from my position as Apeksi chairperson, I have observed how mayors in different parts of the country exhibit unique leadership approaches to tackle the myriad challenges faced by their respective cities, so I acknowledge from the start that no other mayor's experience or perspective will exactly resemble mine.

This chapter is organised into five sections. The first section discusses how the campaign process influences leadership effectiveness in each city. The next section addresses the challenges and issues confronted by mayors during their tenure. The third section discusses the leadership strategies they commonly adopt to confront these challenges. The fourth section provides an overview of the future of Indonesian cities within the context of democracy, regional autonomy and decentralisation. I conclude by emphasising my optimism and faith in Indonesia's system of local governance.

Campaign funds and public policies

Local political campaigns play a pivotal role in determining election outcomes and shaping the subsequent decision-making processes of elected officials. Consequently, the issue of campaign funding becomes important. If a mayoral candidate lacks sufficient personal financial resources to fund their own campaign, securing adequate funding sources poses a significant challenge.

Running a campaign in a direct mayoral election is costly, even for candidates who do not engage in 'money politics'. It is an undeniable reality that Indonesian politics demands substantial funding, with financial resources often exerting a determinative influence on election results. How a candidate manages their campaign logistics and funding sources significantly impacts their style and efficacy of leadership once they are elected. Winning a campaign with limited resources is very difficult. However, examining numerous local elections and their outcomes in Indonesia reveals that leading a city becomes considerably more challenging when the winning candidate is entangled with sponsors or donors who have underwritten their campaign. This situation aligns with the old adage that 'there is no such thing as a free lunch', as every offer of campaign support inevitably comes with a cost in terms of the subsequent policies.

A commonly observed pattern in many Indonesian cities involves the donation of campaign funds by businesspersons in exchange for an implicit commitment by the candidate that the donor will be able to secure government projects for them funded by the city budget (*anggaran pengeluaran dan belanja daerah*, APBD), either through competitive bidding or direct appointments (with the latter possible only for emergency and small-scale projects). Established players in the realm of government projects are thus frequent campaign donors. They offer their support to the candidate who is forecast to stand the best chance of winning, or they assist an incumbent in securing a second term as a form of payback for securing past contracts.

This practice opens the door to external interference in determining project allocation and implementation, ultimately undermining the principles of transparency and accountability, and potentially meaning that important projects go to the mayor's political allies rather than to the best-qualified contractors. Another substantial repercussion of such patterns is the erosion of a mayor's autonomy in policymaking: rather than having a free hand to determine the future development of their city, such a mayor comes to office bound with commitments and obligations.

The role of members of a candidate's campaign team or inner circle is often pivotal. These individuals are often important players in local political affairs in their own right, and they can either facilitate or obstruct the interests of business sponsors. Complications frequently arise when members of campaign teams exceed their authority and engage in agreements without the candidate's knowledge, leading to substantial problems either in the campaign period when such deals become exposed, or later on, when the sponsors ask for special treatment.

As such, the foremost challenge for a candidate who wants to govern independently lies in preserving their independence during the campaign period, thereby mitigating the risks of losing autonomy to business interests. In my own case, I recollect a particular instance when several major businesses offered campaign donations, all of which I declined due to the clear indications that vested interests were involved. For example, a tobacco business offered to support the campaign, with it being clear they had an interest in changing Bogor's tobacco control policy.

When I first ran for election in 2013, by the campaign's culmination, campaign expenses had not exceeded Rp 10 billion (then equivalent to about US$870,000), a sum significantly lower than the expenditures of other candidates. I kept campaign costs down by relying primarily on face-to-face meetings with constituents, and by promising fresh ideas about how to change and improve the city. My primary funding sources were derived from family and friends, senior leaders of my own political party, and donors who exhibited no apparent personal interests in the city's budget or development policies.

In sum, the efficacy of a government is often determined from the start: it is profoundly influenced by how the winning candidate managed their relationships with the people and businesses who supported their political campaign. Greater independence during the campaign translates to a broader scope of autonomy when wielding authority. A more independent candidate can implement policies that align with their campaign promises and vision; a candidate who was dependent on donors may have little choice but to spend their term in office repaying their political debts.

Challenges and leadership dilemmas

I won my first election as city mayor in 2013 by a slim margin of 1,755 votes, following a fiercely competitive and negative campaign. Initially, my belief was that this campaign would be the most arduous phase of my political journey. However, the post-election political landscape I encountered—and I believe all newly elected mayors face similar challenges—introduced far more complex and demanding circumstances. It quickly became evident that it was no simple task to translate campaign promises and aspirations into tangible policies. Leading a city takes more than ideas, courage and even formal political power. It takes, above all, a clear understanding of the complex local political map, a strategic sense and an ability to pick priorities. It quickly became apparent to me that my days of being a political observer and commentator were over and I lost my status as a 'media darling'. Now, every utterance I made and every action I took had tangible consequences within the local landscape.

Upon taking office and beginning to run the city government, I experienced a sense that I now had the power and authority to enact the vision and mission I had taken to the voters. Nevertheless, it did not take long for me to realise that the mayor is not the sole significant political player in the city. Many influential figures, including senior local parliament members, high-ranking bureaucrats, law enforcement personnel, activists, media professionals and business leaders, pursue their own interests and each has their own source of political power and leverage. Frequently, these actors collaborated to secure their own stakes and benefits within a system that had evolved into one marked by high levels of collusion and pragmatism.

One of the primary challenges thus revolved around effectively leveraging the city budget for the greater good of the populace. In Bogor city, as in every city around the country, numerous stakeholders exerted influence over the planning and execution of governmental initiatives, with the most influential players often securing procurement contracts funded by the city budget. Businesspersons frequently had insiders within the bureaucracy, and even within the procurement system itself, who could safeguard their interests by ensuring they got their 'share' of projects. One unexpected problem I confronted was interference from law enforcement personnel in city development projects, something my experience as Apeksi chair tells me is a recurring concern for mayors around the country. These law enforcement officials sometimes sought a 'share' in project implementation. For example, they wanted their own favoured companies to secure projects, or they wanted to be paid to provide security for these projects. Failure to meet their demands could lead to the 'criminalisation' of the bureaucracy: this often involved certain local non-government organisations and media personalities exposing an alleged case of wrongdoing in government administration, leading to the opening of a criminal investigation, but with an implicit (and sometimes explicit) message that the problem would be resolved if the law enforcement officials got the rewards they wanted. Despite President Joko Widodo issuing stern warnings in 2016 against these and similar practices by law enforcement agencies, these practices persisted and remained a primary concern for many regional leaders throughout my own period in charge of Apeksi.

I have learned that a fundamental ingredient of political success for mayors who truly want to improve their cities is thus developing a deep understanding of the internal workings of the city bureaucracy. Elected mayors often inherit a local bureaucracy that is dominated by senior bureaucrats who have risen to their positions through non-meritocratic, outdated and unprofessional channels. Like many mayors, I found it a challenge to deal with the bureaucracy's traditional top-down approach to development planning, in which there was very limited scope for public participation. It was disheartening to witness that departmental programs produced through this process often exhibited little alignment with my own vision and plans as mayor. In essence, while mayors came and went, department programs remained relatively static. At the same time, government budget allocations were not consistently efficient or effective, with many allocations directed towards activities that had limited substantive impact on the community but which provided benefits for bureaucratic actors or their associates. For instance, the planting of 50 trees could incur a cost in the tens of million of rupiah, primarily attributable to expenses related to producing T-shirts, setting up tents, and providing food and beverages for guests—expenses that often benefited insiders through kickbacks or similar practices.

Amid this complex and demanding backdrop, the middle class in Bogor was experiencing rapid growth. Bogor city is part of the Greater Jakarta metropolitan area, and many middle-class residents commute to Jakarta for work. These people are potentially part of a constituency for change. Unfortunately, however, they generally lack organisation and are sceptical about or disengaged from local matters. Their involvement in local policies is thus generally limited (see Elyda, this volume, about disengaged voters in South Tangerang).

In mid-2014, a few months after taking office as mayor, as a result of all these challenges, my experience was akin to being that of a solitary figure in the city, burdened with a seemingly impossible mission. I wanted to bring change to the city and improve its amenities for the benefit of the population, but I felt surrounded by self-interested players who wanted only to pursue their own short-term agendas.

Leadership strategy and choices

In the face of these challenges, surrendering was not an option. It became increasingly obvious that I needed to develop effective strategies if I wanted the city bureaucracy to work towards my long-term goals. The foremost consideration was how to break the pernicious cycle of corrupt practices—a cycle that had greatly impeded Bogor's progress and that remains a major problem for many urban areas around the country.

The pivotal element, as I perceived then (and still do), rests on the leader's integrity. Thus, it is important for a leader—in a city, this means the mayor—to publicly proclaim, exemplify and substantiate an unwavering commitment to refraining from personal enrichment and not to accept any gifts that might compromise the integrity and autonomy of policymaking. It is not a select group who take this approach; in my role in Apeksi I have observed numerous mayors who serve as inspiring role models, epitomising high levels of integrity—it is not the case that all Indonesian urban areas are stuck in cycles of money politics and corruption. When a mayor makes a personal commitment to act with integrity, the call goes out to all civil servants, urging them to concentrate on their professional duties rather than simply pleasing the mayor and their bosses, or engaging in corruption or other forms of unprofessional conduct. The primary focus for all civil servants in a city should centre on their defined work responsibilities; it is in turn the responsibility of the highest-ranking leader in every department to set an example in breaking the vicious cycle of corruption.

Traditionally, promotions within the civil service frequently come with the expectation that the person being promoted will provide financial contributions to their superiors, including the mayor, particularly if they work in a strategically significant and well-funded department such as public works, education or health. Furthermore, in most cities it is established practice to collect a monthly 'contribution' from departments that are capable of providing one; these contributions are then managed by individuals the mayor trusts as a kind of informal 'operational fund'. Unfortunately, both patterns of collecting informal payments inhibit mayors from effectively establishing a meritocratic system of rewards and punishments. When bureaucrats are rewarded and punished on the basis of their ability to provide informal funds, rather than on their work performance, then the effectiveness of the city administration is undermined and the ultimate loser is the city itself.

Faced with these complex challenges, only two courses of action are viable: either succeed in enhancing bureaucratic capacity and the bureaucracy's ability to service the population, or face abject failure in delivering on campaign promises.

Bureaucratic reform and public services

The primary avenue for addressing these challenges is bureaucratic reform, with careful planning and management of the city budget the determining factor. Fixing up the city budget is key because, as explained above, the old politics of collusion always involves vested interests accessing the budget, and is facilitated when the budget is managed in a non-transparent manner. The imperative is thus to make the budgetary planning process more inclusive and participatory. During my term as mayor, I advocated active involvement of academic institutions and communities in formulating medium-term regional development plans. The planning process needs to engage stakeholders, as a planning process devoid of community participation and reliant solely on technocratic systems and inputs hampers the alignment of a city's development with the aspirations of its residents. I therefore also ensured that city budget documents were accessible to the public, allowing citizens to gain insight into the allocation and distribution of spending within the city. Under my government, multiple channels were established to facilitate public input, encompassing criticisms, suggestions and aspirations, not only for the planning phase but also for implementation and evaluation.

Bureaucratic reform also means delivering tangible benefits to residents, and making their lives easier. In 2019, the Bogor Public Service Mall (Mal Pelayanan Publik) was officially inaugurated, serving as a benchmark for cities throughout Indonesia. This mall, located in one of the city plazas, is a kind of one-stop shop for a range of city services— citizens can go there for everything from paying taxes and attaining a business licence, to getting a driver's licence or obtaining a passport. Residents can even now complete marriage ceremonies at the mall, with the mayor or deputy mayor potentially serving as witness. In fact, this mall goes beyond establishing a new system for providing services to citizens; it is also dedicated to nurturing a reliable service culture for citizens by making visible to the Bogor public that the city administration is there to serve them, and that they have the right to expect timely and efficient service from the government. The Public Service Mall thus not only enhances the government's accessibility and service provision but also has the objective of ensuring citizen satisfaction with the everyday operation of government.

Along the same lines, and in order to ensure that the city was embraced and cherished by its residents, my government made great efforts to enhance the quality of public facilities, including parks, pedestrian areas, government buildings and urban slums. Revitalising areas previously under the influence of local thugs (known as *preman*) was a particularly challenging task and frequently required negotiations with long-established mass organisations representing these groups in such areas. Concessions and relocation often played a significant role in these negotiations, for example, providing these groups with alternative sources of income or moving them to new locations.

Acknowledging that ambitious goals in bureaucratic reform must be accompanied by an appropriate incentive and reward system, the government I led introduced new mechanisms for rewarding and punishing civil servants. Punishments could include being transferred to less important posts, something that civil servants consider to be very serious. Part of this new system involved increasing the income of civil servants. Currently, the allowances and incentives of civil servants in Bogor city rank among the highest in Indonesia. Increasing allowances and performance incentives also has the benefit of disincentivising corruption and other improper behaviour.

'A city for all': Building community support

Many governments of Indonesian cities, including Bogor, have faced the challenge of making the city inclusive and accessible for all citizens. A particular challenge, especially in the sometimes tense environment of communal politics in the post-Suharto era, is affording equal rights to all residents, including the freedom to practice their faith. Bogor has grappled with the perception of being an intolerant city. In 2014, the Setara Institute—a national non-government organisation that focuses on issues of tolerance and minority rights—labelled Bogor as an intolerant city due to longstanding problems with a church in the city, the Yasmin Church, which could not be constructed or used by its congregation owing to opposition from nearby residents and Islamic groups.

After 15 years and over 100 meetings with various stakeholders, the Yasmin case was ultimately resolved. For many of those involved, the solution devised by the city government was not ideal, as the church had to relocate approximately one kilometre from its original site. Nevertheless, in my view this was the most reasonable and feasible course of action among the available alternatives. This case had to be resolved. I had promised to fix it during my election campaign, but this went beyond a campaign fulfilment; I also wished to reinstate Bogor's reputation as a city for all, where no one is left behind. On numerous occasions, I emphasised that the DNA of Bogor's residents lies in their 'unity in diversity'.

Of course, this approach came with political costs, but there are also political benefits to encouraging a sense of civic culture and community unity. Where local politics is still governed by a pragmatic and transactional culture in which various political actors and interest groups come together in ever-changing deals and coalitions to pursue their interests, a mayor can become vulnerable to shifts in local elite coalitions. A viable and essential alternative involves cultivating robust community support. Since 2010, and especially since taking the helm of Apeksi, I have witnessed a new generation of local leaders recognising the significance of garnering support from various communities, including intellectuals, religious leaders, entrepreneurs and creative groups. Such groups can provide the necessary backing when a mayor wants to improve a city by challenging existing vested interests.

A noteworthy example in Bogor is the existence of Bogor Sahabat or Friends of Bogor. This community group comprises influential figures from diverse backgrounds and serves as an important partner to the city government, providing input and monitoring the implementation of city policies, but also sometimes sharply criticising the city government. The Bogor Sahabat community is especially dedicated to social diversity and environmental protection, and has constructed a potent network within the community, which has backed government initiatives on these issues, while also acting as an independent watchdog. Given that most mayors face fluctuating political party support and have to deal with assorted pragmatic interests seeking benefits from city policies, support from citizens, civil society and the community can be a critical counter-balance. Cities that are more advanced than others frequently owe their progress, in part, to the presence of a robust local civil society (see Mustafa, this volume, for further discussion on this subject).

The challenge is that not all cities boast a strong civil society tradition. Some cities, most notably Surabaya and, to a lesser extent, Malang and Bandung, possess well-established civil societies that have, over the long term, provided support to local government reform initiatives. It must be acknowledged that Bogor lacks a robust civil society tradition. Bogor's historical character is that of a city designed for rest and recreation, where people escape the heat and hassles of Jakarta. In the Dutch colonial era, Bogor was known as 'Buitenzorg', which roughly means 'carefree'. In such circumstances, it takes substantial effort by city leaders to cultivate a network of community engagement and to foster a local culture where residents come to genuinely care about their city and critically assess it.

Building robust citizen support entails more than strengthening connections between the mayor and organisations or communities. It is imperative that the mayor is consistently engaged with citizens, remaining close to them on a day-to-day basis and forging an emotional connection with them. Again, this is part of achieving the kind of public support that will enable a mayor to push through reform, even when it harms vested interests. In my own case, from the beginning of my administration, it became customary for me to engage with the public directly, responding not only to citizen invitations to attend and take part in community events, but also to respond, directly where possible, to their requests for help in improving their daily lives and neighbourhoods.

To this end, under the Tenda Walikota program (the term literally means 'mayor's tent' but was also an abbreviation for *tanya dan dengar*, or 'ask and listen'), I spent many nights with citizens to engage in dialogue and listen to their concerns. Additionally, I ran a regular program whereby I would visit the office of a different urban ward (*kelurahan*) every week and hold a half-day meeting there, allowing me to receive direct input from citizens regarding the performance of ward heads and their personnel, as well as to evaluate the local potential within that ward and subdistrict. In addition, when I made field visits to various parts of the city, I tried to include in the agenda dialogues with key grassroots actors, such as small business owners, cadres from the PKK (Family Welfare and Empowerment Program) and *posyandu* (integrated health services), community service institutions, and *rukun tetangga* (neighbourhood association) and *rukun warga* (citizens' association) members.

In fact, nearly every weekend during my decade as mayor I devoted time to an activity I had never imagined would be part of my mayoral duties: acting as formal witness in citizens' marriages. At times, I knew the bride and groom beforehand, but more often I did not. It was a source of great pride for these citizens to have the mayor act as witness, and it meant they forged an emotional, even familial, connection with the mayor. I know from many of my colleagues that this practice is commonly undertaken by regional leaders in Indonesia and is an effective means to garner robust grassroots social support.

National elite support

To be a successful mayor, especially one who wants to improve their city, it is important not only to build support at the grassroots and among local communities. It is also important to establish networks with national-level political elites. Lacking a good relationship with the provincial governor or with national political leaders is one of the most common, and serious, obstacles a mayor can face when trying to effectively perform their duties. Problems in these relationships can arise for many reasons, but they are often caused by differences in political party affiliation and/or electoral competition. In many cities, I have witnessed how municipal government programs falter and even fail when the mayor and governor do not have a good relationship, either due to personal incompatibility or competing political affiliations, or when the mayor has poor political connections in Jakarta.

Building good relations with higher-level political leaders is important for at least two reasons. First, it can be important for mayors to seek provincial or national financial and regulatory support when they want to pursue big-ticket development items, such as major transportation or infrastructure projects. Second, and even more importantly, mayors often find themselves entangled in legal issues when they lack strong political support networks in Jakarta. Law enforcement agencies are still centrally organised, and therefore ultimately responsible to the national government; when a mayor lacks strong backing in Jakarta, such agencies can target them with the kind of 'criminalisation' discussed above, either in pursuit of their own material interests or as an act of political punishment.

As a result, to ensure the smooth running of a city administration, it is exceedingly important for a mayor to be proficient at engaging in effective communication and lobbying with policy influencers at the national (and provincial) level. In my own case, from the beginning, I worked diligently to initiate, nurture and maintain relationships with party leaders, ministers, the West Java governor and even President Joko Widodo. Mayors can initiate and maintain such connections by participating in routine events in Jakarta or the provincial capital. The frequency of a mayor's presence at a governor's or ministry's events can significantly influence the quality of their relationships with the relevant officials.

Compromise for change

It follows from all of this analysis that when a mayor (or any other leader in regional Indonesia) sets out to pursue their objectives, it is not always feasible to achieve their ideal targets. It is certainly unrealistic to expect leaders to satisfy every expectation of all the diverse interest groups that make up a city, but it is equally impossible to ignore all the important actors and groups who can potentially frustrate or impede a leader's plans. Thus, it is important for mayors to cultivate a sense of realism, and to recognise that the ideal outcome is often simply unattainable. Leaders must be prepared to engage in negotiations and compromises, shifting from Plan A to Plan B or even Plan C when necessary. Decision-making is not always black and white. When the primary goals are unattainable, leaders must exhibit the flexibility to explore alternative routes with more realistic goals.

In my own experience, numerous challenges required me and my team to adjust our targets and strategies when confronted with real-world obstacles. The case of the Yasmin Church is a notable example of an imperfect solution to a difficult problem, achieved through a process of negotiation and adjustment. Such instances of problem solving via compromise were not confined to controversial cases like the Yasmin Church, however, but extended to other agendas, including bureaucratic reform and cooperation with the local parliament (Dewan Perwakilan Rakyat Daerah, DPRD).

However, it is also possible to go too far in pursuit of compromise. During my time in city politics, a dominant trend I have observed is reluctance on the part of city leaders to take risks. They fear that resistance to change will derail their governments. In such scenarios, city leaders prioritise harmony and stability over confronting public or bureaucratic resistance. The typical result is stagnation in city affairs.

In some instances, I myself faced criticism for not meeting public expectations, with some policies deemed less than ideal. Nevertheless, I determined early on that decisions must be made, issues must be resolved and progress must be achieved by selecting from the best available options within the constraints I confronted as mayor. I also tried to prioritise issues with broad public support, and that connected to residents' daily lives. Overall, I believe I was successful in doing this. When assessing government outcomes and measuring success, one valuable yardstick used by most city leaders around Indonesia is public satisfaction, as indicated by credible surveys. In July 2023, a Charta Politika survey reported an 84.5 per cent approval rating for my administration's policies among Bogor residents. The most significant appreciation was extended to government performance in infrastructure, health care and the government's commitment to maintaining unity within diversity.

Of course, I understand that I was not able to fully address all the longstanding challenges that confront city governance in Bogor—and which can be found in most if not all Indonesian cities. For example, corruption and illegal behaviour on the part of some government officials was not completely eliminated. However, I am confident that during my term in office a solid foundation was laid for a more transparent and citizen-oriented governance than had previously been present in Bogor. The next mayor will find it challenging to swiftly alter course and revert to past practices, given the current greater strength of civil society as a guardian against policies and actions that do not align with citizens' expectations. My hope, of course, is that a new mayor will be able to build on the achievements of reform reached under my administration to achieve further incremental improvements.

Democracy, local autonomy and the future of cities

In discussions of local politics in Indonesia, some people express frustration about the persistence of old problems such as corruption and elite dominance. But from my perspective, the system of direct elections and the principle of local autonomy have facilitated the emergence of exceptional pro-reform leaders who have had a very positive impact on regional governance. Local autonomy, in particular, has given rise to a cohort of inspiring leaders who engage in a mutual exchange of knowledge, support one another and share ideas about how to improve local governance. Several exemplary figures, such as Azwar Anas (*bupati* or regent of Banyuwangi, 2010–2021), Ridwan Kamil (mayor of Bandung, 2013–2018, and governor of West Java, 2018–2023) and Tri Rismaharini (mayor of Surabaya, 2010–2020), have provided valuable insights about how to improve local governance. These leaders, and others like them, have been a source of profound inspiration for me personally during my time both as mayor of Bogor and as chairperson of Apeksi.

Presently, it is not difficult for mayors to monitor the political decisions and public policies of our peers. Most mayors actively disseminate their policies to the public through various media outlets. They also generally showcase their achievements on social media platforms. This open exchange of information fosters a culture of learning and innovation among city leaders. Apeksi has also taken the initiative to establish various learning forums for city leaders. These forums help mayors and other senior city officials such as regional secretaries and department heads to share ideas and discuss practical topics varying from public service innovations, development permits, climate change, waste management and the green economy through to empowering micro, small and medium-sized enterprises promoting local products. I have witnessed city leaders deriving inspiration and new ideas from one another, fostered by the principles of direct democracy and local autonomy.

The book *If Mayors Ruled the World* written by Benjamin Barber and published in 2013 holds an almost sacred significance for mayors across the globe. I received a copy of this influential work from the senior economist

Faisal Basri before I became mayor in 2014. Benjamin Barber's perspective asserts that city leaders wield substantial influence and authority and can drive innovation in ways that transcend not only municipal boundaries but also national borders.

However, in the Indonesian context, there is a disconcerting trend of recentralisation. The national government is progressively reasserting its authority, a matter of grave concern for many mayors and *bupati* in the country. This trend is observable, for example, in the enactment in 2020 of the Omnibus Law (Law 11/2020 on Job Creation), which has led to the central government reclaiming numerous powers related to permits and environmental regulation. The central government often cites the standardisation of services as its rationale, and says it is driven by concerns over the suboptimal quality of the bureaucracy in numerous regions. These concerns, so it is claimed, have prompted the central government to reinforce its authority in areas such as permits and investment.

As Apeksi chairperson, I frequently expressed unequivocal criticism of this recentralising trend. The message from Indonesia's local government leaders is clear: local democracy, local autonomy and local wisdom should not be sacrificed for the sake of economic growth and investment. Indeed, it is doubtful that economic growth and investment will improve over the long term if Indonesia once again adopts a centralised system with little scope for local initiative and experimentation. Moreover, the existing system already features a framework for oversight and guidance of regional governments by central ministries, including incentives and rewards for excellence, and works well in practice. The central government demonstrates its appreciation when regional governments achieve exceptional performance in specific domains, by allocating them special funds. Additionally, a city index system, based on scoring and ranking, is already implemented across various facets of governance, including bureaucratic reform, health care, legal matters and diversity, motivating cities to continually improve their systems and policies. Enhancing systems for supervision of regional governments is a far better approach than pursuing recentralisation, which comes with many risks of eroding or even reversing much of the progress Indonesia has made in local government.

Conclusion

My personal experiences as mayor of Bogor, and as the leader of Indonesia's association of mayors, provide me with many reasons to be optimistic about the future of Indonesian cities. To be sure, there continue to be many problems in local government in Indonesia, including in urban areas. Many of these problems are either legacies of bad practices of the past, or they flow from the high-cost nature of Indonesian elections. But there is also plenty of evidence that local government leaders—especially in Indonesia's many vibrant cities—are surmounting these problems. Many of Indonesia's cities have become real sites of innovation and reform, pioneering new forms of government that enable greater public participation and are better at providing citizens with the services and amenities they want and need. While further experimentation is certainly required, I firmly believe that local autonomy and democracy are indispensable prerequisites if Indonesia wishes to continue to make progress in governance, and if it intends to ascend to being one of the world's top five economies by 2045—a goal proclaimed by central government leaders. Local autonomy and democracy serve as a bedrock of the system that has fostered real change in patterns of urban governance, not only enabling citizen participation but also fostering innovation and collaboration within and across cities. This system of democratic local autonomy also fosters responsive and innovative leadership at the national level, by providing a pathway for capable leaders (President Joko Widodo being the most famous example) to move up from the municipality to the national stage. Rather than abandoning a system that has encouraged real progress, we should be aiming to build upon its successes.

Index

A

Adipura Kencana award, 218, 224
agriculture
  households across regions, 63
  land conversion, 64, 245
  proportion of GDP, 1
  Suharto era, 2
Ahok (Basuki Tjahaja Purnama), 11
  approval rating as governor, 280–281
  campaign against, 40
  forced evictions policy, 18, 174–176, 179, 182, 189, 273, 274, 280, 281
  governance reform, 13, 40
  Kalijodo Park, 273–274, 276, 280, 281
  railway system, 256
  security infrastructure/police integration policy, 296
air pollution, 3, 42, 218
  2023 crisis, 4, 223
  cause of deaths, 5
  contributing causes, 4–5, 218
army (TNI), 37, 207–208, 274, 296
  see also military
Asian financial crisis, 39, 83, 157, 293
Association of Indonesian Municipal Governments (Apeksi), 306, 309, 310, 311, 314, 318, 319
authoritarianism, 1, 25, 79, 82, 129, 288

B

Bambang DH
  attempted impeachment, 134
  bureaucracy reform, 14, 133–134, 135, 137, 209
  waste management reform, 219, 225, 226, 235

Bandung
  Cisangkuy River, 202, 203
  Citarum Harum Taskforce, 202–203, 207
  Citarum River, 206
  Citarum River Patrol, 207, 208, 213
  civil society, 213, 314
  corruption/collusion, 211, 212
  disaster risk management, 88
  drainage regulations, 212
  flood defence infrastructure, 198, 202–203, 206, 208–213
  flood management, 198–213
  high-speed train, 3
  industrial companies, 206
  military collusion, 9, 10, 206–208, 213
  political dynasty, 210–211
  public spaces, 271
  traffic congestion, 5, 246, 262
  urban population, 52
  urban renewal, 18, 271
  waste management, 201
Banjarsari Park, 271, 273
Banten, 57, 101, 142–143, 154, 155, 163
  see also South Tangerang
Baswedan, Anies, 14, 175, 179, 276, 280, 281
Bekasi, 51, 244
  light rail, 256
  T-line railway, 28
  toll road connection to Jakarta, 253
  urban population, 52
  waste site, 5
Benowo landfill, 218, 220, 221, 223, 230–233, 236
'Bike to Work' (BtW), 14

Bogor
  APBD Gate scandal, 138
  bureaucracy, 138, 139–140, 141
  bureaucratic corruption, 311, 317
  bureaucratic reform, 312–313, 317
  civil society, 137–141, 146, 313–315, 317–318
  community engagement, 313–315
  demonstrations, 138
  Dewan Perwakilan Rakyat Daerah (DPRD), 138, 140, 143, 317
  governance reform, 137–141
  local tax-levy ratio, 114
  mayor's personal experience, 10–11, 14, 306–320
  media, 137, 139
  T-line railway, 28
  urban population, 52
Bogor Public Service Mall, 312
Bowo, Governor, 252
budget, national
  environment, 222
  housing, 183
  urban transport infrastructure, 261
budgets, local, 98–128
  average per capita revenues, 111, 112
  budget expenditure, 114–128
  budget revenues, 111–114
  central government mandatory spending requirements, 98, 98n–99n, 114, 118, 120–121, 123, 126, 261
  environmental, 222
  General Allocation Grant (DAU), 111, 125
  intergovernmental transfers, 111, 112, 113, 114, 125
  local taxes and levies (PDRD), 112–114, 127
  local tax-levy ratio, 113
  own-source revenue (OSR), 111, 112–113, 125
  proportion of government spending, 99
  spending by classification and district category, 115, 117
  spending by government function and district category, 119
  spending per capita by function and district category, 120
  stakeholder influences, 309–310, 312

  transparency, 312
  waste management, 222, 230–231
  see also finance
bureaucracy
  inefficiency, 27, 129
  quality, 208, 310, 319
  see also collusion; corruption
bureaucratic reform, 319
  Bogor, 312–313, 317
  Surabaya, 131, 134–135
bus services, 248
  bus rapid transport network (BRT), 254–255, 260
  Jaklingo, 254
  private, 248, 249, 255
  share of commuters, 248
  TransJakarta, 248, 249, 254–255

C

Cahyadi, Eri, 219, 235
capital city, new (Ibu Kota Nusantara), 3, 6, 42, 64
case studies, governance reform
  Bogor, 137–141
  South Tangerang, 141–146
  Surabaya, 131–137
Chosiyah, Ratu Atut (Atut), 143, 154–155, 166
Ciputra Group, 156, 157, 204, 205
cities, see kota
civil society
  Bandung, 213, 314
  Bogor, 137–141, 146, 313–315, 317–318
  composition, 130
  drainage regulation enforcement, 199, 200–201, 204–208, 209, 211
  role in governance reforms, 13, 14, 114, 129–147, 199, 209, 213, 219, 225, 236, 314
  South Tangerang, 141–145, 146
  Surabaya, 13–14, 131–137, 146, 209–210, 211–212, 314
climate change, 5, 42, 178, 197, 214
collusion, 9
  bureaucracy, 4, 10, 13, 16, 30, 41, 81, 86, 89, 208, 210
  flood management, 199, 206, 207–208, 209, 213
  military, 9, 10, 206–208, 213
  property developers, 10, 13, 16, 81, 86, 210

Semarang, 210, 212
see also corruption
colonial period, 31–36, 37, 38, 42
  transport network, 255
  urban planning, 79, 86
  waste management, 219, 224, 235
community engagement, 85–86
commuting, 16, 258
  commuter zones, 141, 153–154, 155, 158, 161, 244
  different modes, 155, 252–257
  modal shift, Greater Jakarta, 247–249
  number of commuters, Greater Jakarta, 8, 154
  time spent, 5, 168, 246, 247, 254
  see also bus services; railway systems; roadways
complaint reporting, citizen, 12, 15, 209
corruption, 9, 40, 81, 234, 311, 313, 318
  Bogor, 137, 138, 139, 140, 141, 317
  bureaucracy, 114, 208, 210, 211, 234, 311
  government challenge of, 4, 11, 12, 14, 81, 129, 141, 143, 317
  influencing planning decisions, 10, 28, 92
  strategies to reduce, 134, 136, 138, 139, 140, 141, 210, 313
  business and politics ties, 4, 9, 10, 12, 93
  election campaigns, 9, 11, 307–308
  entrenched, 11, 12, 41, 93, 130, 139
  property developers, 16, 92
  South Tangerang, 13, 141, 143, 144, 145, 154, 155
  Surabaya, 131, 133, 134, 136, 233, 234
  see also collusion; predatory elites
Corruption Eradication Commission (KPK), 144, 210, 211, 233
COVID-19 pandemic, 182, 184, 245, 278
  effect on economic growth, 107, 108, 110
  effect on local district revenues and expenditure, 111, 116, 118, 121, 126
  effect on local districts, 105
  effect on security industry, 302
  impact on poverty reduction, 106
crime, 164, 170, 182, 289, 290, 294, 298–299

D

Davnie, Benyamin, 145, 155, 167
decentralisation, 26, 30, 82, 88, 89
  asymmetric policies, 100, 127
  budgets and revenue, 99, 111
  commencement, 129
  disaster management, 88–89, 127
  effect on access to public services, 99, 103, 107–111
  effect on urban planning, 39–42, 82, 93, 270
  move to recentralisation, 319
  role of civil society in effectiveness, 129–147
  waste management, 90–91, 222
democratisation, 4, 12, 15, 19, 39, 41, 91, 93, 146, 283, 292, 320
  see also civil society
deregulation, 25, 30, 274
Dewan Perwakilan Rakyat Daerah (DPRD), 39, 98n
  Bogor, 138, 140, 143, 317
  Malang City, 234
  South Tangerang, 144, 145
  Surabaya, 133–134, 135–136, 225, 230, 234
Diany, Airin Rachmi (Airin), 143, 144, 145, 155, 166
disasters
  disaster management, 88–89, 214
  disaster vulnerability, 75, 84, 88–89, 197
  see also climate change; flooding
drainage, 131, 134, 144, 197–214
  regulations, 10, 89, 199, 200, 209, 213, 214
  see also flood management; flooding

E

East Java, 12, 35
  urban localities/urbanisation, 61, 161
  see also Surabaya
Eastern Indonesia, 49–50
  agricultural households, 63
  in-migration, 51
  urban localities, 57, 58, 61, 62
  urban localities, distribution, 74
  urban population, 49, 50, 64
ecological issues, 4, 5, 29
  see also environment; flooding

economy
  growth, 15, 83, 107, 109–110
  knowledge-based, 6
  regional growth, 62
  urban, 2, 14
education
  free, 145
  gated communities and *kampung*, 167–168
  local government spending, 12, 111, 118, 120–121, 126
  primary, 127, 145
  private, 121, 156, 168
  quality, 121, 167–168
  school enrolment rate, 107–108
  secondary, 127
  vocational skills training, 182, 185
elections
  2024, 300
  campaign funding, 9, 11, 307–308
  citizen participation, 142, 166, 167, 170
  coalition-building, 130
  ID cards and voting, 165–166
environment
  agencies, 10, 206, 208
  budget, 222
  degradation, 39, 42
  disasters, 88–89
  Jakarta, 39
  regulations, 10, 38–39, 227, 319
  see also air pollution; climate change; ecological issues; flooding; pollution; traffic congestion; waste management, solid; water
Environment Security System (Siskamling), 290–291
environmental cadres (volunteers), 219, 223, 228, 229, 236

F
Family Hope Program (PKH), 183
fertility rates, 46, 49, 51, 52
  rural-urban comparison, 54
finance
  central government resources, 26
  international donors, 30, 39
  local election campaigns, 307–308
  local government expenditure, 114–128
  local government resources, 9, 111–114
  see also budget, national; budgets, local
financial crisis, Asian, 39, 83, 157, 293
flood management, 12, 197–214
  Bandung, 198, 201–203, 206, 208–213
  collusion, 199, 206, 207–208, 209, 213
  drainage regulations, 10, 199, 200–201, 209, 210, 213, 214
  infrastructure, 18, 179, 198, 199, 200–203, 209, 213, 214
  infrastructure expenditure, 202, 203
  local politics, 198, 199, 208, 212, 213, 214
  Semarang, 198, 199, 201–203, 205, 208–210, 212, 213
  Surabaya, 198, 199, 200–205, 208, 209, 212–213
  see also flooding
flooding
  causes, 5–6, 10, 197, 200, 201, 206, 218
  kampung, 178, 179, 180, 204, 205
  number of cases, 201–202, 203
  number of people affected, 202, 203
  prevention, 2, 18, 179, 198, 199, 208, 214
  rainfall, 203, 205
  sea levels, 4, 6, 197
  see also flood management
food markets, subsidised, 182
food security, 64
foreign investment, 81, 270, 295
future outlook, 19, 48, 283, 320

G
garbage, *see* waste management, solid
gated communities, 16–17, 83, 86
  Alam Sutera, 155, 157–158, 162
  Bintaro Jaya, 155, 156, 158–164, 167
  BSD, 155, 157–165, 167
  infrastructure, 4, 83, 159–164
  marketability, 159, 275, 294
  political disengagement, 164–166, 169–170
  price of housing, 156, 158, 159, 166
  proportion of population, 169
  schooling, 167–168
  security provision, 17, 150, 151, 158–159, 160, 163–164

social gap separation from *kampung*, 16, 17, 150, 151, 160, 166–169
see also middle class; South Tangerang
GDP
  historical, 1
  informal economy contribution, 86
  government expenditure on housing, proportion, 177
  Jakarta metropolitan area proportion, 244
  regional gross domestic product (RGDP), 106–107
  urban contribution, 2
Global North, 76, 77, 78, 81, 84, 86, 93
  definition, 76n
Global South, 6, 7, 16, 17, 75, 77, 78, 84, 86, 183, 287, 293, 294
  definition, 76n
Golkar Party, 143, 154, 155
governance challenges, 4–8
governance reform
  Bogor, 137–141
  South Tangerang, 141–146
  strategies to improve, 147
  Surabaya, 131–137
  see also leaders, new generation of reforming; leadership, local
Government Regulation 18/2021 on Management Rights, Land Rights, Vertical Housing and Land Registration, 152–153
Government Regulation 35/2023 on General Provisions on Local Taxes and Local Levies, 113
Gubernatorial Decree 111/2014 on Rusunawa, 182, 186
Gubernatorial Regulation 210/2016 on height limits, 261

H

health care
  attended births, 109–110
  free, 12, 145
  local government spending, 99, 112, 118, 120–121, 122
  national health insurance scheme, 112
  private, 108, 156
health risks, 5, 90
highways, *see* roadways

housing
  apartments/units, 152–153, 156, 157, 158, 176, 180
  balanced housing ratio 1:2:3, 80–81
  government rent assistance, 180, 182
  government-subsidised, 177, 185
  inequality, 16–17, 24, 83–84, 151, 177–178
  policy, 24–25
  prices, 24, 153, 156, 158, 159, 166, 178
  private estates, 16, 36, 83, 155–159, 204, 205, 274
  property price to income ratio, 151–152
  regulations, 158
  Rumah DP Nol Persen (Zero Down Payment), 185
  shortages, 16, 87–88, 152, 176–177
  small-scale complexes, 158–159, 164
  social/public, 7, 16, 17, 18, 24, 25, 33, 36–37, 152, 181, 174–191, 273
  South Tangerang, 154–170
  substandard, 87, 176
  see also gated communities; *kampung*; rental social housing
human development index, 15, 105, 111, 125, 154
human rights, 283
  violations, 280, 281

I

Ibu Kota Nusantara, *see* capital city, new
Ichsan, Pilar Sagar, 145, 155, 167
ID cards, 165, 190
independence, Indonesia's, 1, 4, 78, 82, 250, 278
Indonesia Corruption Watch, 143
Indonesia Disaster Information Database (DIBI), 201
Indonesian Democratic Party of Struggle (PDI-P), 133, 135, 233
industrial sector, 58
  automobiles, 29
  employment, 6, 12
  extractive industries, 62
  rural industrialisation, 63–64
inequality, 3
  housing, 16–17, 24, 151, 177–178
  income, 83–84, 106, 287
  infrastructure, 159–160

inter-regional, 127
security/sociospatial, 287, 288, 291, 302, 303
urban, 4, 15–18, 41, 86, 282, 287, 293
informal sector/informality, 9, 75
bureaucracy, 10, 86, 89, 311
description/definition, 86
economy, 86, 88, 91, 178
employment, 6, 17, 27, 36–37, 54, 70, 86, 88, 178, 184–185
housing, 2, 3, 17–18, 33, 86, 89, 131, 178, 188, 289
land market, 37, 42, 89
military fundraising, 206, 207
politics, 93, 212, 220
role of poverty in urban planning, 82–86
rule (indirect rule), 34–36
security arrangements, 36, 39, 288, 290, 291, 296, 298, 301, 302
waste management, 90, 232, 234, 236, 237
see also collusion
infrastructure, 3, 11, 28, 224
first world financial donors, 30
flood prevention, 10, 18, 200–203, 208
inequality, 159–160
local government spending, 121, 123, 124
private provision, 17, 80, 83, 151, 159–162
tourism sector, 62, 63
transport, 8, 61, 79, 252–257
see also railway systems; roadways
Instagram, 14
Integrated Urban Infrastructure Development Program (IUIDP), 29–31
international comparisons, urbanisation, 47
international donor groups, 30, 39, 142
investment
global, 58, 270, 295
private, 79, 126

J

Jabodetabek commuter survey, 247–248
Jabodetabek Urban Transportation Policy Integration Project Phase 1 (JUTPI I) 2011, 259
Jabotabek, 28–29
Jakarta
bus services, 254–255
development, 27, 28–29, 38–39
highway networks, 252–254
housing, 151–154, 177–178
kampung policy, 179–180
land prices, 152
minimum wages, 153
number of workers, 151
Outer Ring Road, 29
PDRD potential, 114
periphery/outskirts, 16, 51, 65n, 29, 150–170, 244–245
population, 3, 8, 52, 151, 244, 250
property price to income ratio, 151
railways, 255–257
sea wall, 6
security provision, 17
sinking city, 6
Special Capital Region of Jakarta, 98n, 102, 104
traffic congestion, 3, 5, 8, 29, 244–262
urban road system, 29
urbanisation, 37, 38
Jakarta metropolitan area, 5, 137, 244–262, 310
population, 244, 250
size, 244
see also Jakarta
Jakarta Metropolitan Authority, proposed, 245, 259–260, 262
Jakarta province
bus rapid transport network (BRT), 254–255, 260
environment budget allocation, 222
rail network, 256
Japan
Japan International Cooperation Agency (JICA), 255, 256
Surabaya/Kitakyushu sister city, 90, 225, 226
Java
periodic inundation, 6, 198
rural politics, 35

urban growth, 8
see also East Java; Java-Bali region; West Java
Java-Bali region
　agricultural households, 63
　distribution of urban localities, 71
　local government spending, 121, 123
　population data by new district classification, 102–104
　urban localities, 57, 58, 61
　urban population, 49, 50, 57, 61, 64, 66
Jawa Pos group, 132, 135, 220, 231
Jawa Pos newspaper, 227, 228
Jaya Real Property, 156
Jaya Realty, 159, 161

K

kabupaten (rural districts), 7–8, 15, 51–52
　budgets, 98–128
　distinction from *kota*, 100
　new classification criteria, 101–103
　number, 98
　see also rural areas
Kalijawi, 91, 93
Kalijodo Park, 273–274, 276, 280, 281
Kalimantan
　agricultural households, 63
　in-migration, 51
　new capital city, proposed, 3, 6, 42, 64
　population data, 104
　urban localities, 57, 58, 61, 62
　urban localities, distribution, 72
　urbanisation, 61, 64
Kamil, Ridwan, 11, 13, 18, 271, 318
　kampung evictions, 272–273
kampung, 6–7, 17, 84, 178–180
　alleyways, 277–278
　colonial era, 31–36
　definition, 272n
　disaster-prone areas, 89
　effect of municipal development, 33–34
　eviction compensation, 186–187, 188
　evictions/forced relocations, 17–18, 36, 37, 84, 174–175, 179–180, 272–273, 274, 281
　flooding, 204, 205

　land certificates (BPN), lack, 178, 179, 180
　land market financialisation, 41
　livelihoods of dwellers, 7, 17, 18, 89, 90, 176, 184–185
　number of autonomous, 98
　public space management, 18, 276–280, 281, 282
　security, 17, 18, 291, 298–301, 302–303
　self-evictions, 41–42
　South Tangerang, 158, 160, 161, 164, 166
　tenure insecurity, 7, 32, 84, 86, 89, 178, 179, 180, 188
　upgrading, 179
Kampung Improvement Program, 7, 37, 132, 179, 224, 226
Kasidi, Poernomo, 219, 224, 229
kota (cities)
　budgets, 98–128
　distinction from *kabupaten*, 98, 100
　housing shortage, 177
　number, 98
　reclassification criteria, 101–103
　urban population growth, 51, 52
　see also subjects beginning with urban
Kotaku program, 85, 91

L

land
　changes in use due to urbanisation, 62, 63–64
　kampung, 36–37, 41–42, 178, 179, 180
　'land mafia', 16, 81, 210
　prices, 89, 152, 177
　subsidence, 4, 6
　use policy, 16, 28, 29, 39, 80–81
Law 5/1974, 38
Law 24/1992 on Spatial Planning, 79
Law 20/2003 on National Education System, 121
Law 24/2007 on Disaster Management, 88
Law 26/2007 on Spatial Planning Law, 80
Law 18/2008 on Solid Waste Management, 220n, 222
Law 36/2009 on Health, 121
Law 11/2020 on Job Creation, 319

Law 1/2022 on Central-Subnational Government Fiscal Relations – 'Fiscal Balance Law', 111, 116, 123, 125
Law 17/2023 on Health, 121
leaders, new generation of reforming, 2, 10–14, 18, 133–137, 138, 219, 225, 235, 271–272, 314, 318
leadership, local
 ability to compromise, 14, 316–319
 autonomy and integrity, 307–308, 311
 Bogor mayor experience, 306–320
 bureaucratic reform, 312–313
 dilemmas, 309–311
 election campaign influence, 307–308
 informal, 235–236, 277, 279–280, 281
 managerial, 13, 269, 270–274, 281
 national-level relationship, 315–316
 role in governance reform, 2–3, 11–12, 13, 18, 114, 133–141, 146, 147, 218, 219, 231, 235–236, 271–272, 283, 318, 320
life expectancy, see mortality rates

M

market liberalisation, 28, 152
Medan
 population, 8, 52
 traffic congestion, 5, 246, 262
Medan Merdeka Park, 267–268
media, 132–133, 137, 139, 142, 144, 227, 272, 276, 309, 310, 318
 Jawa Pos group, 132, 135, 220, 231
 Jawa Pos newspaper, 227, 228
 Suara Surabaya, 133, 135, 209
middle class
 consumption, 79, 83
 growth, 15, 75, 83, 150, 275, 310
 housing, 16–17, 36, 83, 84, 86, 142, 150–170, 276, 290, 294, 302
 political (dis)engagement, 14, 17, 142, 147, 150, 160, 164–166, 169–170, 310
 proportion of population, 83
 see also gated communities; South Tangerang
migration
 out-migration, 50–1
 rural-urban, 6, 7, 46, 52, 54–55

military
 collusion, 9, 10, 206–208, 213
 flood management law enforcement, 202–203
 informal fundraising, 206–207
 paramilitary, 270, 286, 293, 297, 299
 regional head appointments, 37
 role in private security industry, 290, 291, 296
mining, 12, 62, 207
Ministry of Environment Regulation 13/2012 on Guidelines for Implementing Reduce, Reuse and Recycle through Waste Banks, 227
Ministry of Public Works Regulation 12/2014 on the Drainage System in Indonesia, 200
money politics, 9, 307, 311
 see also collusion; corruption
mortality rates, 51, 52
 deaths caused by air pollution, 5
 rural-urban comparison, 54

N

National Affordable Housing Program (NAHP), 87–88
National Agency for Disaster Management (BNPB), 201
National Development Planning Agency (Bappenas), 79, 80
National Land Agency, 29, 30, 39, 178
National Medium Term Development Plan (RPJMN), 87
National Program for Community Empowerment (PNPM), 85, 91
National Tourism Strategic Areas, 62
New Order period
 authoritarianism, 1, 18, 25, 79, 82, 129, 288
 corporatism, 30, 39
 fall of regime, 39, 129, 133, 154
 kampung, 7, 37
 political actors, 137–138, 142, 154, 224
 political control structure, 37, 38
 predatory elites, 129, 130, 132
 private capital, 24, 26, 31, 252
 railways, 252
 rural-urban migration, 6, 54, 64
 security, 288, 289, 299

urban planning, 16, 38, 79–80, 81, 85, 157, 224
urban security, 289–291
see also Suharto, President
non-government organisations (NGOs), 132, 135, 142, 144, 175, 210, 213, 219, 224, 228, 310

O

OECD (Organisation for Economic Co-operation and Development), 100
Omnibus Law, 80, 319
ormas (social organisations), 35, 288, 289, 292, 299–302

P

Partai Amanat Nasional Mandate Party (PAN), 139
Partai Demokrasi Indonesia-Perjuangan (PDI-P), 133, 135
planning regulations, 28, 79, 81, 84
circumventing, 29, 86, 89
planning system, 78–82, 84, 91–93
see also urban planning
police force, 35–36, 37, 139, 164, 202, 233–234, 273, 289, 299
civil ordinance police, 292
coordination with *ormas*, 300
Environment Security System (Siskamling), 290–291
informal relationships, 9, 291, 300, 302
modernisation, 35–36
number of personnel, 290, 291
opposition to unionisation of *satpam*, 297–298
per capita ratio private v public personnel, 288, 289
police-directed training, 293, 298
security industry, 293, 296
Police Law 2002, 292–293
political dynasties
Bandung, 201–211
South Tangerang, 13, 17, 131, 142–145, 151, 154–155, 166, 170
politics
and business relationships, 4, 9, 10, 79, 82, 214
indirect rule, 32, 34–36, 37

predatory elites, 13, 129, 130, 132, 135–136, 137, 146, 210
see also leaders, new generation of reforming; leadership, local
pollution
groundwater, 5, 224
regulations, 207
rivers, 5, 10, 175, 180, 202, 203, 205–208
see also air pollution
poor population, 15–16, 17, 18, 41
community engagement, 85–86, 91, 92–93
housing, 7, 10, 14, 17, 18, 36–37, 41–42, 82, 84, 177
livelihoods, 6, 17, 89, 90, 91, 184–185, 297, 298
political participation, 33, 39, 41, 82
proportion of total population, 84
vulnerability to disasters, 84, 89, 198
see also kampung; poverty
population
analysis of rural/urban villages/wards, 101–102
greater Jakarta region, 3
growth rate, 48, 50
Jakarta, 177
total, 1
see also kampung; poor population; urban population
poverty, 16, 75, 84–86, 88, 177, 183
rate by district category, 106
see also poor population
predatory elites
Bandung, 213
Bogor, 37, 146
local, 13, 41, 129, 130, 132, 135, 136, 137, 146, 147, 300
South Tangerang, 13, 131, 141–145, 146
Surabaya, 132, 135–136, 137, 146, 210, 212
preman (gangsters/thugs), 34, 144, 258, 313
changing role, 299–300
informal security provision, 36, 288, 290, 292, 297, 298–301
Presidential Decree 35/2018 on Accelerating the Construction of Waste Processing Installations into Electrical Energy Based on Environmentally Friendly Technology, 233

Presidential Regulation 3/2016 on Acceleration of the Implementation of National Strategic Projects, 62
Presidential Regulation 15/2018 on Citarum River Revitalisation, 203
private sector
　education, 121, 156, 157, 168
　health 108, 121
　housing, 16, 18, 24, 33, 36, 79, 80, 83, 86, 151, 152, 155–159, 165, 169, 170, 205
　politico-business connections, 27, 79, 214
　public-private partnerships (PPPs), 29–31, 39, 80, 261
　public spaces development, 269, 274–276, 283
　security provision, 17, 37, 158–159, 163–164, 286–303
　services provision, 17, 83, 120, 127, 157, 160–161, 162, 164, 165, 170, 200
　transport, 248, 249, 255, 261
　urban planning role, 10, 75, 77, 78, 79–80
　waste management, 10, 91, 131, 220, 224, 225, 227
　waste-to-electricity program, 231–235
　see also gated communities; property developers
private security providers, 286, 289, 293, 296, 301, 302
　international, 295–296
　see also security provision
privatisation, 25, 26, 28, 30, 31
　public space, 280
　security industry, 292
　see also private sector
Program Keluarga Harapan (PKH, Family Hope Program), 183
property developers, 27, 29, 36, 42, 152, 157, 183, 201
　collusion, 10, 13, 16, 81, 86, 210
　corruption, 16, 92
　informal relations with politicians/ bureaucracy, 10, 16, 39, 79–80, 81, 82
　large-scale, 177
　Location Permits, 39
　small-scale, 151, 155, 158–159
　South Tangerang, 159–160
PT Alam Sutera, 157
PT IPU, 210
PT Pembangunan Jaya, 156
PT Sumber Organik, 220
PT Telekom, 220
PT Unilever, 220, 228, 231
public-private partnerships (PPPs), 29–31, 39, 80, 261
public spaces, 12, 18, 39, 80, 267–283
　community neighbourhood, 269, 276–280, 281–282
　diversity, 268
　government managed, 269, 270–274
　interiorisation, 37
　marginalisation, 272–273, 281, 282, 283
　parks, 267–268, 271–274, 276, 281
　privately controlled, 269, 274–276
　shopping malls, 37, 83, 151, 156, 157, 268, 269, 274–275, 276, 293, 294
　small-scale, 276–280, 281–282

R

railway systems, 3, 8, 28
　advantages, 259
　capacity, Greater Jakarta, 250, 255
　Commuter Line, 255, 257
　development, 250, 256
　high-speed train, 3
　international comparisons, 250–252
　LRT Jabodebek, 250, 256, 257
　LRT Jakarta, 250, 252, 256, 257
　MRT Jakarta, 252, 256, 257
　number of stations, Greater Jakarta, 250
　number of users, Greater Jakarta, 250, 255, 256
　share of commuters, 248–249
　South Tangerang, 155, 158
　train stations, 161–162
　see also commuting
rakyat (common people), 27, 31, 33, 41
　governed through intermediaries, 31, 32, 34–36, 37
　see also kampung
Real Estate Indonesia, 36
recycling, 14, 90, 91, 92, 218, 219, 221, 228–230, 232, 236
　3Rs approach (reduce, reuse, recycle), 222, 225, 226, 228, 229

reformasi era, 2, 25, 78, 80, 91–92
  early period, 133, 137
  new predatory elites, 132
  waste management reform, 224
Regional Regulation 8/2007 of Jakarta on use of public space, 267
Regulation 11/2008 on Guidelines for Housing and Settlement Compatibility, 158–159
rental social housing (*rusunawa*), 174–191
  distribution in Jakarta, 181
  effect on *kampung* evictees, 174, 184, 189–190
  eligibility, 180–181
  lack of community, 189
  purpose, 175, 180–181
  rental arrears, 184, 186, 188
  similarity to refugee experience, 187–188
  temporary nature, 176, 183, 187–189
rice production, 2, 64
ride-hailing services, 249, 255
riots (1998), 132, 275, 292
Rismaharini, Tri (Risma)
  attempted impeachment, 135–136, 209
  budgetary reforms, 136
  bureaucratic reforms, 135, 136
  citizen complaint line, 209
  civil society support, 135, 137, 209
  leadership, reforming, 11, 12, 235, 318
  procurement reforms, 136
  public spaces, 271–272
  waste management reform, 219, 225, 232, 233, 235
riverbank settlements/housing, 7, 131, 132, 180, 271, 272–273
  see also flooding; *kampung*
roadways, 28–29
  gated communities, 161–162
  highway networks, 252–254
  Jakarta Outer Ring Road, 29
  Jakarta toll roads, 61, 155, 157, 158, 252–253
  Jakarta urban road system, 29
  Java toll roads, 61
  mixed use lanes, 254
  quality, 161
  South Tangerang, 154, 155, 157, 158, 161–162
  Sumatra toll roads, 62
  toll road developers, 28–29, 253
  see also commuting; transport
rural areas, 1–2
  industrialisation, 63–64
  national identity, 1
  population, 1, 82
  population age structure, 51, 52–54
  reclassification to urban, 7, 46, 48, 55–58, 64–65
  see also kabupaten (rural districts)
rural-urban classification indicators, 55–56
  need to update, 65
rusunawa, *see* rental social housing

S

sanitation, 5, 85, 121, 224
  access by district, 109, 110
  kampung, 178
  Surabaya, 131, 218, 224
Secom, 295, 296
Securicor, 295
security governance, 286–303
  Police Law 2002, 292–293
security provision
  corporate clients, 297
  gatekeeping role, 17, 292, 294, 298, 302
  horizontal security, 288, 291, 302–303
  industry working conditions, 297–298
  informal, 9, 36, 288n, 290, 291, 296, 301
  kampung, 17, 288, 289, 291, 298–301, 302–303
  number of providers, 288n
  ormas, 288, 289, 292, 298–301, 302
  preman, 36, 288, 290, 292, 297, 298–301
  private, 17, 36, 37, 286–298
  professionalisation, 288, 292, 296, 297, 301
  satpam/guard labour, 287–288, 290–291, 294, 297–298
  Siskamling model, 290–291
  technology use, 288, 289, 295–296, 302
  vertical security, 288, 291, 303

Semarang
  civil society, 213
  collusion, 210, 212
  Dau River, 205
  decentralisation, 40
  drainage regulations, 201, 205–206, 210, 212
  flood management, 198, 199, 201–203, 205, 208–210, 212–213
  flood prevention infrastructure, 198, 201–202, 206, 209
  sinking city, 6
  urban population, 52
sewerage systems, *see* sanitation
shopping malls, 37, 83, 151, 156, 157, 268, 269, 274–275, 276, 293, 294
Sinar Mas Group, 157
Sinarmas Land, 159, 161, 162, 273, 276
Sochib, Chasan, 142–143, 154–155
social media, 14, 140, 160, 169, 268, 271, 318
South Tangerang, 150, 154–170
  civil society, 141–142, 143, 144, 145, 146
  corruption, 13, 154, 155
  crime, 164, 170
  Dewan Perwakilan Rakyat Daerah (DPRD), 144, 145
  election 2020, mayoral, 166, 167
  governance reform, 141–146
  human development index, 154
  infrastructure, 159–164
  in-migration, 165
  kampung, 158, 160, 161, 162, 164, 166, 169
  local revenue, 154, 160
  local tax-levy ratio, 114
  media, 142, 144
  number of private housing complexes, 155, 158
  political dynasties, 13, 17, 131, 142–145, 151, 154–155, 166, 170
  population, 154
  price of housing, 151–152, 153, 156, 158, 159, 166
  private housing estates, 155–159
  property developers, 159–160
  roadways, 154, 155, 157, 158, 161–162
  schools, 168
  security provision, 163–164
  small housing complexes, 158–159, 164
  spending on personnel, 116, 125
  trains/railway systems, 154, 158, 161
  urban population, 52
  water provision, 162–163
  see also Banten; gated communities
Southern Planning, 75–93
  background and description, 76–78
spatial planning, 10, 28, 32, 39, 79, 80
street sweepers, 229–230
street vendors, 2, 10, 131, 134, 144, 162, 276, 298
  Banjarsari Park, 271
  Medan Merdeka Park, 267–268
  Supreme Court ruling 2019, 267
  Tanah Abang market, 271
Suara Surabaya, 133, 135, 209
Sugiarto, Bima Arya (Bima), 14, 138–141, 146, 306–320
Suharto, President
  capitalism, 24, 26, 27, 37, 252, 253, 274
  cronyism, 27, 79, 253, 274
  open economy, 83
  protests against, 132
  public transport, 252
  repression, 40, 41
  rural support base, 1–2
  toll roads, 253
  urban planning, 10, 38–39, 78, 79–80
  urban 'growth coalition', 10, 16, 24–25, 27, 28, 31, 39
  see also New Order period
Sukarno, President, 1, 24, 78
Sulawesi
  agricultural households, 63
  urban localities, 57, 58, 61, 62, 73
  urban population, 49, 50
  urbanisation, 61
Sumatra
  agricultural households, 63
  population data by new district classification, 104
  urban localities, 57, 58, 61, 70
  urban population, 49, 50
  urbanisation, 61
Sumoprawiryo, Sunarto, 133, 134, 225
superblocks, 293, 294, 295
Surabaya
  bureaucracy, 133–134, 136, 210
  City Supervisory Agency, 134
  civil society, 13–14, 131–137, 146, 209–210, 211–212, 314

Dewan Perwakilan Rakyat Daerah (DPRD), 133–134, 135–136, 225, 230, 234
drainage regulations, 199–201, 204–205, 210
early development, 33
economy, 223
elections, mayoral, 133–134
flood defence infrastructure, 201–202, 208
flood management, 12, 131, 198, 199, 200–205, 208, 209, 212–213
Flood Taskforce, 204–205, 208
governance reform, 131–137
Government Resource Management System (GRMS), 136
land size, 223
local tax-levy ratio, 114
mass demonstrations, 132
media, 132, 135
police, 233–234
political reform, 225, 235
population, 12, 52, 223
predatory elites, 135–136, 137, 146, 210
procurement, 12, 134, 136
public spaces, 272
radio stations, 133, 135, 209
traffic congestion, 5, 131, 246, 262
urbanisation, 61
waste crisis, 224, 225
waste management, solid, 8, 90, 91, 131, 132, 201, 218–237
see also Benowo landfill
Surabaya Clean and Green competition, 227, 228
Surabaya Mayor Regulation 14/2016, 201
Sutiyoso, Governor, 252, 254, 257, 267

T

Tangerang, 51
  T-line railway, 28
  urban population, 52
  see also South Tangerang
Tangerang Mayoral Regulation 37/2019 on the Drinking Water Provision System Master Plan for 2019–2039, 162

taxes and taxation
  billboard, 134, 135
  compliance, 134
  land and property, 178, 261
  local, 112, 113–114, 127, 154, 261
  municipal, 33
  online payment system, 139, 140
  Pigouvian, 258
  see also budgets, local; finance
Teras Cikapundung Park, 272–273
terrorism, 287
Tirta Kerta Raharja (TKR), 162
toll roads, *see* roadways
tourism, 62, 63
  'slum tourism', 92
trade unions, 297–298
traffic congestion, 3, 5, 8, 29, 42
  cars, 29, 158, 247
  causes, 246–252
  demand management policy, 257–258
  electronic road pricing, 258
  institutional problems, 259, 260
  international comparisons, 245, 260
  Jakarta metropolitan area, 5, 244–262
  motorcycles, 245, 247, 248, 249, 254
  odds and evens policy, 257
  parking policies, 258
  public transport use, 248–249, 250
  South Tangerang, 161
  Surabaya, 5, 131, 246, 262
  three-in-one policy, 257
  see also commuting; transport
trains, *see* railway systems
TransJakarta, 248, 252, 254–255, 257, 260
transport
  private vehicles, 158, 245, 247, 248
  public, number of users, 250
  ride-hailing services, 249, 255
  see also bus services; railway systems; roadways
transport infrastructure, 8, 249–257, 259
  financing, 256, 257, 259, 261
  international comparisons, 250, 260
tsunami, Indian Ocean, 88

U

United Nations Sustainable Development Goals, 87
United States, 65, 78, 234
urban districts, comparisons
  attended births, 108–109
  classification criteria and district types, 102
  development outcomes, 105–107
  new classification framework, 100–103, 104
  OECD criteria, 100–101
  per capita RGDP, 106–107, 125
  population proportions, 102, 103
  poverty rates, 106
  public service outcomes, 107–111
  sanitation access, 109, 110
  school enrolments, 107–108
  spending patterns, 114–128
  water access, 109, 110
  see also budgets, local; urban localities
urban localities
  distribution across regions, 58, 70–74
  map 2010, 59
  map 2020, 60
  by region, 57
  see also urban districts, comparisons
urban planning, 11, 24–25, 75–93
  community participation, 75–76, 78–79, 81–82, 85–86, 91, 92, 312
  IUIDP, 29–31
  local government role, 79, 80
  role of poverty, 82–86
  undermining, 9, 16, 198
  see also planning regulations; planning system
Urban Poor Consortium, 14
Urban Poor People's Network, 175
urban population
  age structure, 51, 54
  cities and districts over one million, 51–52
  cities and metropolitan areas, 62–63
  distribution, 49–50
  district classification, 102–103
  growth, 48, 49, 54, 221
  growth due to district reclassification, 57–58, 64–65
  Jakarta, 8, 52, 244
  Jakarta outskirts, 16, 29, 65n, 150–170, 244–245
  proportion of whole population, 1, 48–52, 75, 82, 221
  and rural proportions by age, 51, 53
  and rural proportions by gender, 53
  world, urban proportion, 46, 47
urban spillover, 62, 63
urbanisation
  definition, 46
  main drivers, 6, 7, 10, 46–47, 48, 52–55, 64–65, 84, 198, 253–254
  role in economic development, 47
  trends, 7–8, 47, 50, 61, 66, 75, 98, 177, 287, 289
  see also urban districts, comparisons; urban population

V

Village Law 6/2014, 98n–99n, 114
volunteers, 212, 219, 228
vulnerable citizens, 17, 84, 89, 132, 177, 178
  see also poor population

W

Wardana, Tubagus Chaeri (Wawan), 143–144, 155
waste crises, 222–223, 225, 231, 235
waste management, solid
  amount of waste, 5, 90, 221, 223
  community participation, 90, 91, 218, 219–220, 223, 225, 226–228, 236
  corruption, 234–235
  environmental cadres, 219, 223, 228, 229, 236
  government budget, 222, 230–231
  Green and Clean competition, 227, 228
  industrial waste disposal, 201, 203, 206, 207
  informal waste collection, 90, 91, 232, 236
  investment, 230–231
  material recovery facilities (MRF), 219, 220, 229, 230
  media participation, 227, 228
  partnerships with private sector, 220, 227, 231–235

reduce, reuse, recycle (3Rs), 222, 225, 226, 228, 229
regulations, 233
role of national government, 222
scavenging, 90, 91, 232, 236
self-management, 224
state-driven, 220–221, 229–231
street sweepers, 229–230
Surabaya, 8, 90, 91, 131, 132, 201, 218–237
temporary dumping sites, 221, 230
tipping fees, 220, 231, 232–234
waste banks, 12, 218, 223, 227
waste levies, 231
waste-to-energy, 8, 12, 218, 220, 221, 231–235, 236
see also Benowo landfill; recycling
waste prevention, 237
water, 162–163
  access by district, 109, 110
  aquifer recharge zone, 29
  clean potable, 5, 6, 85, 131
  groundwater, 5, 6, 162, 163, 198, 224
  piped water, 5, 6, 109, 162, 163, 165
  quality, 162, 163, 208
  Tirta Kerta Raharja (TKR), 162
  treatment plants, 162, 201, 206
watershed areas
  Citarum, 203, 206, 211
  development, 10
  protection, 28
  see also flood management; flooding
West Java, 28, 31n
  urban localities, 57, 61
  see also Bogor
Widodo, Joko (Jokowi)
  disaster risk management, 89
  flood mitigation, 179
  health care, 12
  housing policy, 7, 18, 87–88, 174, 179, 186–187
  Jakarta governor, 2, 3, 40, 271
  political reforms, 11
  poor settlements, relocation, 271
  presidency, 3, 4, 87, 218, 220, 233, 256, 271, 310, 320
  push for 'mental revolution', 40–41
  railway network, 252, 256
  street vendor relocation, 271
  Surakarta (Solo) mayor, 2, 12, 40, 271
  waste-to-electricity plant, 218, 220

World Bank
  promotion of decentralisation, 26
  promotion of financialisation of *kampung* land market, 41
  promotion of privatisation, 24, 31

Y

Yudhoyono, President, 252, 256

INDONESIA UPDATE SERIES

1989
Indonesia Assessment 1988 (Regional Development)
Edited by Hal Hill and Jamie Mackie

1990
Indonesia Assessment 1990 (Ownership)
Edited by Hal Hill and Terry Hull

1991
Indonesia Assessment 1991 (Education)
Edited by Hal Hill

1992
Indonesia Assessment 1992: Political Perspectives on the 1990s
Edited by Harold A. Crouch and Hal Hill

1993
Indonesia Assessment 1993: Labour: Sharing in the Benefits of Growth?
Edited by Chris Manning and Joan Hardjono

1994
Indonesia Assessment 1994: Finance as a Key Sector in Indonesia's Development
Edited by Ross McLeod

1996
Indonesia Assessment 1995: Development in Eastern Indonesia
Edited by Colin Barlow and Joan Hardjono

1997
Indonesia Assessment: Population and Human Resources
Edited by Gavin W. Jones and Terence H. Hull

1998
Indonesia's Technological Challenge
Edited by Hal Hill and Thee Kian Wie

1999
Post-Soeharto Indonesia: Renewal or Chaos?
Edited by Geoff Forrester

2000
Indonesia in Transition: Social Aspects of Reformasi and Crisis
Edited by Chris Manning and Peter van Diermen

2001
Indonesia Today: Challenges of History
Edited by Grayson J. Lloyd and Shannon L. Smith

2002
Women in Indonesia: Gender, Equity and Development
Edited by Kathryn Robinson and Sharon Bessell

2003
Local Power and Politics in Indonesia: Decentralisation and Democratisation
Edited by Edward Aspinall and Greg Fealy

2004
Business in Indonesia: New Challenges, Old Problems
Edited by M. Chatib Basri and Pierre van der Eng

2005
The Politics and Economics of Indonesia's Natural Resources
Edited by Budy P. Resosudarmo

2006
Different Societies, Shared Futures: Australia, Indonesia and the Region
Edited by John Monfries

2007
Indonesia: Democracy and the Promise of Good Governance
Edited by Ross H. McLeod and Andrew MacIntyre

2008
Expressing Islam: Religious Life and Politics in Indonesia
Edited by Greg Fealy and Sally White

2009
Indonesia beyond the Water's Edge: Managing an Archipelagic State
Edited by Robert Cribb and Michele Ford

2010
Problems of Democratisation in Indonesia: Elections, Institutions and Society
Edited by Edward Aspinall and Marcus Mietzner

2011
Employment, Living Standards and Poverty in Contemporary Indonesia
Edited by Chris Manning and Sudarno Sumarto

2012
Indonesia Rising: The Repositioning of Asia's Third Giant
Edited by Anthony Reid

2013
Education in Indonesia
Edited by Daniel Suryadarma and Gavin W. Jones

2014
Regional Dynamics in a Decentralized Indonesia
Edited by Hal Hill

2015
The Yudhoyono Presidency: Indonesia's Decade of Stability and Stagnation
Edited by Edward Aspinall, Marcus Mietzner and Dirk Tomsa

2016
Land and Development in Indonesia: Searching for the People's Sovereignty
Edited by John F. McCarthy and Kathryn Robinson

2017
Digital Indonesia: Connectivity and Divergence
Edited by Edwin Jurriëns and Ross Tapsell

2018
Indonesia in the New World: Globalisation, Nationalism and Sovereignty
Edited by Arianto A. Patunru, Mari Pangestu and M. Chatib Basri

2019
Contentious Belonging: The Place of Minorities in Indonesia
Edited by Greg Fealy and Ronit Ricci

2020
Democracy in Indonesia: From Stagnation to Regression?
Edited by Thomas Power and Eve Warburton

2022
In Sickness and in Health: Diagnosing Indonesia
Edited by Firman Witoelar and Ariane Utomo

2023
Gender Equality and Diversity in Indonesia: Identifying Progress and Challenges
Edited by Angie Bexley, Sarah Xue Dong and Diahhadi Setyonaluri

2024
Governing Urban Indonesia
Edited by Edward Aspinall and Amalinda Savirani

www.ingramcontent.com/pod-product-compliance
Lightning Source LLC
Chambersburg PA
CBHW072120290426
44111CB00012B/1719